Body, Identity and Interaction: Interpreting Nonverbal Communication

Allan Canfield, Ph.D.

Copley Custom Textbooks
An imprint of XanEdu Custom Publishing
300 North Zeeb Road
Ann Arbor, MI 48106
800-218-5971

Please visit our Web site at www.xanedu.com/copley

Table of Contents

CHAPTER 4

PSYCHOLOGICAL INFLUENCES ON NONVERBAL COMMUNICATION

CHAPTER 5

GENDERED INFLUENCES ON NONVERBAL COMMUNICATION, MAKING SENSE OF GENDER

CHAPTER 6

ETHNICITY AND NONVERBAL COMMUNICATION, MAKING SENSE OF ETHNICITY

CHAPTER 7

AGING AND NONVERBAL COMMUNICATION, MAKING SENSE OF THE AGING PROCESS

CHAPTER 8

TECHNOLOGICAL INFLUENCES ON NONVERBAL COMMUNICATION MAKING SENSE OF COMMUNICATIVE TECHNOLOGIES

CHAPTER 9

SYMBOLIC INTERACTION AND NONVERBAL COMMUNICATION
MAKING SENSE OF SYMBOLIC INTERACTION

CHAPTER 10

Preface

Humans live within the reality of their bodies; eating, sleeping, playing and working. They move about in space and time affected by the weather and the environment. Their five senses provide them with information about the social and physical worlds they inhabit. Their central nervous system makes them sneeze or scratch when they itch. Indeed, the biological body seems to determine much of what humans do. Females give birth when the body is ready; the body grows, ages and dies. Daily activities seem to be timed by biological clocks.

The emotions are enmeshed in nearly every social interaction, whether it is a goodbye wave of the hand or a complex set of interactions, as in sports activities or orchestral performances. At festive activities, like football games, humans share their emotions with others, ritualistically and contagiously, cheering on their team, shouting at the other team, moving in unison in a great wave of collective body motion. People feel happy at weddings; they feel sad at funerals. They display their emotions, which tells others how they feel.

The body is not a mere corpus; it is laden with semantic meanings produced by the owners. Bodies, involved in nearly all activities, do not act by themselves. They are not self-willed. Humans think about their bodies and about their social and physical worlds. They symbolize the body, creating meanings, identifying it, labeling it, using it. They perceive themselves to be fat or skinny, male or female, black, white or old. They perceive, think and act. Humans are people watchers, never tiring of watching themselves or others. After arriving home from work or school, where they have spent the day in interaction with others, they may watch television or a movie that depicting even more human interaction. Humans in the modern world are enmeshed deeply in mediated social worlds that influence the ways they think and act.

Humans possess a symbolizing, sensemaking ability. Having a mind as well as a body, humans perceive their bodies and create a sense of self and identity, the body being a part of that identity. Humans adapt to social circumstances; they present themselves to others in self-promoting schemes. They learn to manage themselves in a complex social world, trying to act in accordance with the perceived expectations of the situation. Very skillful people are adept at monitoring themselves and others as they successfully manage their relationships.

Indeed, it seems that people act and perform dramaturgically as though they had a script, a role, a stage and an audience. They groom themselves, dress appropriately, and act out their lines so that others will get the intended message. Although some actors fumble their lines, in general they seem to be good performers or self-agents. Often, they act in routine, unthinking ways, but even the routine is a learned achievement.

Observers pick up on the actions of others, whether the actors are simply gesturing or enacting a complex, contingent series of action events. action communicates meaning to the observer. The nonverbal act becomes a communicative act.

The spoken word accompanies most nonverbal action displays. People talk to others; but they also talk to themselves in inner conversations with the self. They listen to the words of others, words that are full of symbols and expressions that can fire up the imagination. Human language is framed on a nonverbal lexicon. After taking a walk, a person may say, "I took a step." Words express what people already know in their minds. Words may take the place of actions; actions may take the place of words. In face-to-face situations, humans "talk" to others using both body and words. The body "speaks". What it is saying is a matter of interpretation.

People usually know the meaning of specific spoken words, but when they speak with their bodies, they often miss the details, "catching" the meaning of body action in a kind of *gestalt*, or blurry fashion. Spoken words may be used precisely but they may omit the emotional *semantics* of body language. No words are needed to see disappointment in a face. How many words would be needed to describe that disappointment? As people age they create a knowledge base, a body lexicon, syntax or corporeal semantics, that helps them interpret body actions. They learn spoken language; they also learn body language, bodily communication.

There is a recognizable sameness in most human behaviors. Otherwise it would be impossible for humans to interact intersubjectively. Yet, individuals have body "signatures" that distinguish them. In addition, human communicative behavior is influenced by gender, ethnicity or aging. Communicative media, such as television and the internet, saturate modern societies, influencing behavior.

The proliferation of popular books and magazines distorts how body communication is perceived. Stereotypes are commonly used in print and television media. Human behavior, of course, is more complex than slogans and clichés suggest. This book focuses on the complex, often hidden, processes that influence human nonverbal behavior. By understanding these influences humans can increase their understanding of nonverbal communication. People can learn to be skillful actors and observors of nonverbal presentations.

Scholarly Matters

The study of nonverbal communication continues to grow across the spectrum of research in many fields of study. Good textbooks and research studies are available to the scholar and the student. Courses about nonverbal behavior and communication are found in modern curricula. From its ungainly start, the field of nonverbal communication is now fully grown. There is, of course, far more in the available literature than any book can present.

There is no pretense in this book that the sum of knowledge about nonverbal communication is revealed or explained, nor is there a finely detailed account of how scholars have created that knowledge. Theories and approaches abound but the author believes that a symbolic interactionist approach is particularly useful to both scholars and students.

The symbolic interactionist (SI) aproach, rooted in early pragmatic thought in America, is rich in history and research. It provides an integrated way to help the researcher and the student understand nonverbal communication. By melding together research from several interdisciplinary sources, the symbolic interactionist can interpret meanings of the body, of identity and intersubjectivity. See chapters nine and ten for a discussion of symbolic interactionism.

The body is always on stage, whether the owner is aware of what the body is "saying" or not. It is inherently, inseparably, intersubjectively and interactively involved in nearly all social circumstances. People perceive; they think and act; they observe and make sense; and then, they start all over again in new mind-body-interaction episodes, all of which have communicative potential. Perhaps it is better to describe this process as behavioral communication. The body is not a mere corpus of flesh; it is a dynamic constellation of symbolic meanings, deeply enmeshed in human activities.

Text Structure

There are four parts in this text. Each successive chapter builds on the previous chapter. Concepts from Part I are used in Part II. Although some topics are used in different chapters, they are presented in terms of the special processes described in that chapter.

Chapter One is introductory; as a survey, it presents the topics to be considered in the remainder of the book and introduces the reader to Symbolic Interactionism.

Chapters Two, Three and Four are devoted to cultural, sociological and psychological aspects of nonverbal communication. These processes are woven into the remaining chapters in the book.

Part II offers analyses of master themes that are imbedded in everyday life and how they influence human nonverbal behavior. Chapters Five, Six, Seven and Eight are devoted to the master themes of gender, ethnicity, aging and the media. Every personal or collective act is in some way infused with one or more of these themes. Concepts from Part I are used in these chapters.

The Symbolic Interactionist approach to nonverbal communication provides a particularly illuminating perspective; it fills a niche in the literature. In chapters Nine and Ten in Part III, the Symbolic Interactionist approach is discussed, delving into its history and conceptual underpinnings and focusing on issues and applications. The human body and will were subjects of interest to George Herbert Mead, an early scholar who influenced the growth of what was to become Symbolic Interactionism. Many distinguished contemporary researchers extend the Symbolic Interactionist approach using multiple methodologies, or *triangulation*, to enhance their research.

People present themselves to others in interaction. By improving awareness processes, people can become skillful body communicators. Practical exercises are presented in Chapter Ten for the reader's use for that purpose.

Part IV contains References, a Glossary and an Index (print version). Appropriate notes are included at the end of each chapter in the text as are questions for thought and discussion and suggestions for additional reading. The book is designed for people who are taking a first course in nonverbal communication. It can be used as either a main text or as a complementary book.

The author prefers to alternate the use of he and she or her and him to avoid awkwardness. By using the word American, he is referring to the United States; he is fully aware that people from countries above and below the United States are Americans, too. The author uses Black American, Chinese American, Native American and Cuban American as names in his discussions although there are alternative designations he might have used. The intent is to be respectfully inclusive.

Acknowledgements and Dedications

There are two people who have influenced me to write this book. I am deeply thankful for the friendship and encouragement of Charles Petrie, former faculty member at the State University of New York at Buffalo, now deceased. His friendship and mentoring sustained me over a period of years, starting with my doctoral work and progressing through my teaching and research at the State University of New York at Buffalo. He knew how to bring out the best in his students. I owe much of my inspiration in writing this book to him. I remember the very careful way that he treated facts and theories and their interpretations. He was a keen observer of human behavior.

In very supportive, insightful and practical ways, my wife Nancy has inspired me, always encouraging me as I worked on this project. She supported me as I spent hours and hours with the materials or punched away on the word processor. She knew when and how to tell me that I should clarify this or that, to make a muddled thought more clear. She reminded me that I was writing not only to professional academics but also to students who have had little or no exposure to the field. She stood in for the future reader. I am very thankful to her for her thoughtful support and help. I dedicate the book to her.

I wish to thank the former students in my nonverbal communication classes, whether they were older adults, Black Americans, Hispanic Americans, Native Americans, Chinese Americans or other Americans. Their influences have found their way into this book. In addition, I dedicate the book to my daughters, Jennifer and Jill, now mature and thriving on their own. Their lives will be made more rich and satisfying by engaging themselves even more deeply in a lifelong understanding of others and their nonverbal communication. Finally, I wish to thank Ms. Jena Howard who so carefully proofread my manuscript. Her meticulous scrutiny has helped me improve the book. Of course, I am totally responsible for errors, omissions and other mistakes that may be found.

Chapter 1
Making Sense of Nonverbal Communication

Chapter Overview

This chapter is an overview of the contents of the book. It is designed to show the reader the breadth and nature of the nonverbal topics addressed. Each topic will appear in some way in the remaining chapters treated from the topical perspective of the chapter. Should the reader wish to study the Symbolic Interactionist orientation before reading this chapter, she or he should read Chapter Nine first. It provides an integrated perspective from which to study nonverbal communication.

Although there are misconceptions about the nature of nonverbal communication (Soucie, 1979), there being many popular, sometimes distorted beliefs, it is clear that humans share the meanings of their daily lives intersubjectively through verbal and nonverbal communication. Most daily conversations are conducted face-to-face, the body playing a supporting role in communication. In many circumstances, people use emblems or gestures that can stand alone. Most of the time, however, humans communicate with one another by combining spoken language with body "language". Verbal and nonverbal communication are linked together synchronously (Birdwhistell, 1970, 1975), forming a complete presentation to the partipant or observer. This verbal and nonverbal interface must exist for humans to communicate fully. It is the body, however, that conveys most of the emotional semantics in communicative interactions (Mehrabian, 1981). The potential of human communication is realized only when body messages and spoken messages work together synchronously and harmoniously. Dysfunction and confusion result when the spoken word is contradicted by body messages.

In face-to-face situations, the entire body is presented to the observer. In mediated situations, however, the body is masked. For example, when using e-mail, people substitute for emotions that are normally displayed in face-to-face situations by creating *emoticons* (Herring, 1996). Emotional and paralinguistic cues are artificially produced by e-mail users. It is only in face-to-face communication that the full communicative reportoire can be expressed. In face-to-face situations, people reveal emotions and rhetorical sensitivity as they construct joint, intersubjective nonverbal messages. They can create healthy relationships or they can create dysfunctional relationships.

Nonverbal skills and competencies, of course, are learned. Some pathologies exist, such as autism or schizophrenia, which appear to be neuro-chemically induced; other body related diseases, such as anexoria or body dysmorphic disease appear to be the result of distorted perceptions. Pathologies, such as these, are displayed in particular ways, as in a frozen smile, a reptilian stare, or a very thin body. Normally, however, individuals learn how to use and display their bodies just as they learned how to use spoken and written language, yet a number of scholars indicate that spoken language and nonverbal behavior are processed in different ways in the brain (LeDoux, 1996).

People create a milieau and live within it; both the built and the natural environment are part of the context that influences human behavior. Artifacts, such as buildings, clothes and communicative technologies are created by humans; these artifacts influence their behaviors in turn. The social environment includes dyadic, group and public situations, such as ceremonies and rituals in which humans engage themselves. The built environment includes houses and public structures. Cultural thoughtways influence how buildings are structured. For example, Frank Lloyd Wright, a prominent American architect, designed homes that fit into the environment; the Navajo designed the hogan, a round-shaped building that grew out of their values, beliefs and practices.

This chapter is designed to give the reader an overview of the conceptual material that will be included and used in the remainder of the book. The reader will be introduced to the Symbolic Interactionist (hereafter referred to as SI) approach, an integrative way of studying and applying nonverbal communication.

Aspects of Nonverbal Communication

Research

The reader is aware that there are many ways to study nonverbal communication. For example, Affiliative Conflict Theory, The Expectancy-Norm Model, The Arousal-Labelling Model, The Arousal-Valence Model, The Discrepancy-Arousal Model and The Sequential-Functional Model are recent ways that researchers have investigated nonverbal communication with arousal being the central concern. (Andersen & Andersen,1984; Andersen, 1999). These recent models, just a few selected to illustrate the point, provide unique viewpoints and research models. These important models usually focus on narrow topics. The SI perspective, more aptly described as an approach, rather than a model or theory, is broad and it can include findings from other models without losing its integrity, although researchers from the SI background, tend to use qualitative, ethnographically research methods. (Denzin, 1971;Longmore,1998; Prus, 1996; Ritzer, 1990) (see Chapters Nine and Ten). SI is compatible with a number of other approaches. Of course, the story of human communication is long and complex (Schramm, 1988) and researchers have approached the topic of human communication in multiple ways.

The Symbolic Interactionist Perspective

The Symbolic Interactionist perspective puts emphasis upon human action, or agentry, and upon intersubjectivity and interpretation. People try to make sense of the nonverbal behavior of others and of themselves attaching meaning to the behaviors. Humans frame (Goffman, 1974) their worlds drawing upon their own personal experiences, their personal identity and life scripts. People respond to factual situations, to symbolic worlds found in literature, film, TV and books (Searle, 1995); they create meanings from what they observe others doing, in what they see themselves doing. They perceive, think, create lines of action, interact and then reflect upon the meaning of social events. The SI approach provides a way of looking at the naturally occuring world of human behavior.

Framing Meaningful Acts

All human beings create action sequences. They go to school; they drive a car; they read books; they go to movies, sing, play sports and so on. These action sequences have symbolic value, recognized as forms of doing. Sequences of action are made up of singular acts; for example, people know how to drive cars, but they learned, mastering one simple act, then another. In this process, drivers create schemes; they know the procedural rules, the techniques and so on. Given sufficient practice, they drive almost nonconsciously.

Sequences of acts are usually planned in inner conversations with the self (Vallacher & Wegner, 1985). When performed often, they become routine, requiring little pre-thinking. They are symbolic activities. Drivers invest meaning in what they are doing and derive meaning from doing it. They can tell others what it means to get a driver's license; they can share their joy in being able to take a trip. Whether the action is a simple handshake or a complex display of elaborate rituals, actions such as driving a car, human acts always carry a symbolic mantle, either from the actor's view or from the observer's view. In this sense, the study of nonverbal communication is communication about human actions. The meanings of human actions are shared intersubjectively, forming the basis of community (Blumer, 1969).

Symbolic interactionists suggest that the "actor" is always in the process of doing or thinking about doing; humans are influenced by others in interaction, in groups, institutions, society and culture. Society is not "out there"; rather humans engage interactively to produce society, engaging in self-talk, or conversations with themselves, to interpret behaviors. People take up multiple roles; indeed, they have many versions of themselves, not simply one, which are observed by themselves and others. People continually evaluate, negotiate, and produce "reality"(Charon, 1995; Fine, 1990).

Nonverbal action is usually associated with verbal activity, although it can stand alone. It is dynamic and creative, but it may be patterned and somewhat predictable. Individuals may plan and create lines of action; on the other hand, they may act and react spontaneously. Although people are *agentive* on their own behalf, they are also interpreters of the actions of others. In short, they are performers and they are audience members (Goffman, 1967; Leary, 1996). The human body is always present in social, interactive situations. In mediated situations, as discussed in chapter eight, when people are on the telephone, for example, only the voice is heard; yet it sends nonverbal paralinguistic messages (Pittam, 1994). When e-mail is used, humans construct self images as they relate to others who cannot see them.

Obviously, the human body is a physical entity, but it is the symbolic meaning that humans attach to the body that is important (Benthrall & Polhemus, 1975). For example, when people wish to make their bodies beautiful or handsome, they work on the images that their culture or society presents to them. People share cultural meanings associated with beauty which vary from culture to culture (Buss, 1989, Jankowiak, 1992). In the United States, the media portray the images of beauty in ways that are endlessly clear to the viewer, whether the observer accepts the images or not. In short, the participant in social interaction must decide what to do with the "stuff" of society, to try to make sense of it.

The Body and Identity

The sense of a body self, or *body identity* is inevitably connected to a sense of the social self. The body of course is ever present, always communicating, intended or not. Humans inevitably must construct or create meanings for their bodies, by taking account of the meanings that are imbedded in society and culture. People are able to make quite accurate statements about themselves, about their own bodies, although they may at times deceive themselves. Statements about the self and the body are designed to fit the circumstances (Leary, 1996). For example, people create fictitious selves on the internet, describing themselves in ways that they hope may appeal to others.

In this text, the author focuses on how people make sense of nonverbal communication. People perceive themselves and others symbolically, labeling their own bodies and the bodies of others. People hold conversations with themselves, about themselves, about others and about events. In short, there is a symbolic, cognitive activity involved in the presentation of self and in the interpretation of the nonverbal behaviors of others. In this text, this process is referred to as *sensemaking,* a word that is designed to suggest the often hidden symbolic activity that accompanies nonverbal communication.

Towards a Definition of Nonverbal Communication

There are scores of definitions and assumptions that researchers and scholars use to define nonverbal communication (1). One such definition says that nonverbal communication is comprised of all of the messages other than words that people use in interaction (Hecht & DeVito, 1990), a useful general approach, but it appears to fail to account for how people use words paralinguistically or how people create meaning in their interactions. To some extent, each definition reflects the training and tradition of the scholar involved. In everyday life, humans create meanings by drawing upon implicit assumptions rooted in their personal life experiences; in professional research, on the other hand, scholars make their assumptions explicit so that they are testable and useful. There are several elements involved in human nonverbal communication. Cultural, social and psychological factors enter into nonverbal communication in complex ways, as do gender, ethnicity, age and technology. The milieu, or social contexts, influence human nonverbal communication because these themes are deeply embedded in the contexts of everyday life. Each of these themes contain hidden codes. Space, time and the physical environment influence human nonverbal communication as well. These themes, or background factors, inevitably influence behavior because people take account of the social contexts in which they act. Meaningful lines of action are best created when people are aware of the dynamics of the social context in which they find themselves. Nonverbal communication is deeply influenced by these dynamic elements.

Humans are *socialized* into their worlds but, in becoming socialized, they take part in their own creative unfolding, not being passive; the baby gradually learns to use her body in appropriate ways. As humans go through life to a gerontological or even a centenarian age, they learn to construct new ways of thinking and doing, to modify their own identities, to alter the ways that they use the body. Humans enact strategies of behavior that will help them adapt and survive in a complex social world.

Framing A Definition of Nonverbal Communication

Nonverbal communication is a dynamic process that engages the mind, body and society as intersubjective entities. Humans create symbolic meanings for--and attach them to--the behaviors of self and others. They are influenced by the contexts of action and by master themes in society. In inner conversations with the self, or self-talk, humans propose and enact lines of action to fulfill the perceived demands of the situation, or the expectations of others. In this dramaturgy of behavior, humans learn to modify their nonverbal behaviors to meet the demands of new situations. Human identity, achieved in interaction, is poignantly expressed in self-presentations.

Behavior and Communication

Distinctions between behavior and communication are often made by scholars who study nonverbal communication. For example, it is suggested that spoken words represent something symbolically, but nonverbal communication is not representative of anything else. It stands for itself (Hecht & DeVito, 1990). For reasons dealt with more thoroughly in chapter ten, this text uses the terms behavior and nonverbal communication in similar ways. The better expression would be behavioral communication, the result of blending the concepts of behavior and communication. Except when people are talking within themselves, in self-talk, they are performing acts of meaning in interaction with others. People cannot not communicate! (Watzlawick, Beavin & Jackson, 1967).

The interpretation of self behaviors and the interpretation of others' behaviors is essentially a subjective, symbolic process; that is, to interpret behaviors, whether it is of the self or of others, requires one to think in meaning terms, essentially linguistic in nature. That nonverbal behaviors may arise in different areas of the brain than does spoken language (Andersen, 1999) is not the issue. The end result is that people create meanings in interaction. Even when people perform acts that are not meant to convey meaning to others, observers take note of the behavior and interpret it as they see fit regardless of the inner workings of neuronal processes. In short, people are always "on stage" being observed by others, unless, of course, they are simply ignored or dismissed. The communication-behavior nexus is firm and unavoidable; to focus only upon intentional nonverbal communication without stressing the "accidental" side is to miss what is going on in the theater of action. Humans act intersubjectively, sharing meaningful behaviors with fellow humans. Humans are inveterate actors and observers.

Differences Between Verbal and Nonverbal Communication

A number of scholars have delineated the differences between verbal and nonverbal communication, some suggesting that they are principally localized in different areas of the brain, the verbal in the left hemisphere and the nonverbal in the right hemisphere; that the verbal is primarily culturally based while the nonverbal is primarily biologically based; and that the verbal is digital while the nonverbal is analogic.(2) Further, they are processed differently in the brain, the verbal being processed discretely while the nonverbal is processed as a gestalt (Andersen, 1999). Continued research refines the knowledge about human nonverbal communication. For example, it is suggested that spoken language is predicated on a kind of nonverbal corporeal semantics (Armstrong, Stokoe & Wilcox,1995; Armstrong, 1999;Gilroy, 1996; Ruthrof, 2000) and that the intimate nature of bodily processes are inseparable from verbal processes. It is clear that some aspects of nonverbal behavior are lodged within the individual, unseen, while others are on display publicly. In self-talk, people make sense of events and they make plans or form intended lines of action. These acts of meaning (Bruner, 1990), public and private, are part of the same sensemaking process.

It is omnipresent. All face-to-face interaction has a nonverbal component. It is useful in diverse ways . That is, humans use nonverbal means to persuade or control others, to clarify or embellish verbal expressions, or even to mislead others. It can be used to substitute for verbal expression, as in the use of emblems.

It is emotionally expressive. That is, people from all cultures smile, cry, caress or repress their emotions through body or facial action. Many emotional expressions seem to be at least minimally shared and displayed universally.

It exhibits both phylogenetic and ontogenetic primacy. That is, in the development of human communication, nonverbal behavior predated the development of verbal communication; individuals, upon birth, rely first upon nonverbal means to express themselves.

It has interaction primacy; even before a sentence is uttered, observors take note of body behaviors, trying to make sense of actors' behaviors.

It seems to be trustable. That is, people assume that nonverbal actions do not lie. People tend to believe a nonverbal message when a verbal message contradicts it. (Burgoon, Buller, Woodall, 1995)

Nonverbal communication can accent, complement, contradict, regulate, repeat and substitute for verbal communication.(Richmond & McCroskey, 1992)

It is the thesis of this text, following an SI approach, that the verbal and nonverbal sides of human communication are meaningful events, subjectively interpreted by individuals. To interpret the spoken word one may draw primarily upon the aural system; to interpret a nonverbal act one may draw primarily upon the visual system.

The important thing, emphasized in this book, is that the individual doing the interpreting is making sense of the behaviors of others, resulting in nonverbal communication.

The Complexity of Nonverbal Communication

People seem to use their bodies almost effortlessly, almost routinely without thinking. But, of course, the effortlessness is due to their experience. Everyday routines are the result of learning and achievement (Schegloff, 1986). Once learned, some body behaviors are displayed in the same way again and again without the necessity of personal attention or awareness. Indeed, it would appear that many behaviors are *mindlessly* enacted (Burgoon & Langer, 1995; Langer, 1989). Research reveals that a complex web of factors influence an individual's behavior. Why are some persons very skilled and competent nonverbally while others are awkward, even incompetent?(Hargie, 1986). The ability to manage and present oneself varies considerably in the general population due to a variety of hidden influences.

The complexity of human nonverbal communication may be illustrated by referring to research dealing with the physical face and the eyes, the face being the primary expresser of emotions, having features that seem to have minimum universality. (Ekman, Oster, 1979). The face displays primary emotions in unique ways. The study of *oculesics*, the pupils of the human eye, shows that they respond variously to different circumstances. The pupil either closes or widens under fearful or friendly conditions (Hess, 1975).

Eye movement is a key part of facial behavior, directing others' attention or showing surprise or happiness and other emotional displays. Eye gaze and gaze aversion help observers to know what the actor is up to. It is commonly believed that when people avoid looking one another in the eye that they are not trustworthy, or that they are lying. Are the eyes the window to the soul? Probably not. Cultural display rules influence how people use their faces and eyes. Black and Asian American children, for example, are taught not to look at an adult directly in the eye. Does this mean that they were lying? Stereotypes must be sorted out. The eyes are invariably involved in facial displays.

The face seems to emit emotionally contagious expressions (Hatfield, Cacioppo, and Rapson, 1994); for example, a smiling face may prompt a spontaneous response in another person. Facial expressions show approval, encourage friendship or deceive others (Ekman & Friesen, 1972, 1975; Ekman and Oster, 1979). Unfortunately most humans are not terribly good at detecting deception (Burgoon, Buller, Woodall, 1996; Ekman & Friesen, 1969).

The *leakage hypothesis* (Ekman, 1969)) suggests that, in some Freudian way, the human body leaks information even when actors are not aware of it(3). Perceptive, trained observers can sometimes unmask these hidden meanings. There appears to be a public interest in unmasking the personae of others, ferreting out nonverbal leakage. For example, professionals claim to be able to pick jurists by observing their nonverbal behaviors searching out those leaks of information that might indicate whether the potential juror is qualified to serve on the jury. Probably most people are interested in knowing the hidden secrets of others (Fast, 1970). In short, people try to make sense of how others use their eyes and their faces in interaction. The entire body, not just the eyes or face is involved in nonverbal communication.

Nonconscious and Habituated Behavior

Nonconscious communication refers to the fact that humans act nonverbally without paying attention to themselves. People are not always aware of themselves. The word unconscious, used instead by some writers, may refer to persons who literally are not awake, as is said about the boxer who is knocked out. The use of the word nonconscious refers to the fact that people can be awake but unobserving or unaware of what is going on about them. Of course, human action may operate below the perceptual or sensory threshold. For example, research shows that the the face buzzes with activity hidden just below the visual *threshold* (Birdwhistell, 1970).

As a practical matter, any reader will struggle in answering the following questions: How many facial wrinkles do you have? Does your face have a built-in smile or frown? Is one side of your face different from the other side? Is your facial skin color different from the skin color of your arms or legs? Are the pupils of your eyes normally wide or very small? Under what conditions do they change? Some observers will know the answers to these simple questions. Others will not due to inattentiveness, being unaware.

If it were necessary for humans to keep track of their breathing, the way they walk, or how they swing their arms, they would do little else in life. Habituated behavior enables people to get through the day without unnecessary attention to what they are doing. Dressing for the day, walking to school, having coffee and so on, tasks that may be simple or complex, can be performed without special attention. On the other hand, because they are habituated in their daily behaviors, they may lose sight of the fact that all human behavior is potentially full of rich meaning, as this book suggests. Erving Goffman, a prominent figure in the history of Symbolic Interactionism, unmasked everyday behaviors, finding meaning where others failed to look (Goffman, 1967).

Accidental and Intentional Nonverbal Communication

Unlike most other *primates*, humans plan to do things and then they bring them about. That is, they clothe themselves to keep warm or cool, but, depending on their outlook, they may also dress to show themselves off. In daily discourse, humans use their bodies to make a point, to emphasize or illustrate what they are saying. People can point a finger in an emblematic gesture and convey a definite meaning, no words required. In short, they send intentional messages. Humans use strategies (Berger, 1997); they play games (Berne, 1964); they try to influence others using their bodies. When working jointly with others in common tasks, such as in playing in an orchestra, humans use their bodies in very specific skilled ways; otherwise, they cannot play the part. Humans perform meaningful and intentional acts in the presence of others.

But nonverbal presentations may be judged by others in ways that were not intended by the actor; unintended messages may be received and interpreted by observors. In these instances communication is accidental. In short, humans are always on stage whether they choose to be or not. People "shine" and give off signals and cues that they did not intend to send (Goffman, 1967).

Signs, Symbols, Codes and Display Rules

Social semiotics is a science of language, both verbal and nonverbal. Semioticians make distinctions between signs, symbols, codes and *display rules* (4). Although there are differences in approaches to signs, for the purposes of this book, a sign is denotative and specific. It points to something, as smoke may indicate a fire. A reddened face may indicate that the owner is embarrassed or weary from body exertion. The interpretation is usually framed in context. That is, when a young lady's face is reddened from physical exertion, one knows that she is not embarrassed. The context furnishes the clues to the meaning of her reddened face.

Signs and their usage vary from culture to culture. They are *polysemic*; that is, different persons may interpret them differently, there being many possible meanings. Signs, of course, occur in contexts which aid in their interpretation (Hodge & Kress, 1988; Kim, 1996). Symbols tend to be more complex kinds of signs. Humans create symbols arbitrarily to represent things, people or events. Symbols may be non-specific but meaningful. For example, it is said that wine symbolizes romance, health and the good life. Similarly, a wedding ring symbolizes one's commitment to another; it symbolizes durable value and beauty. Symbols may exist in a master form, as in the Mona Lisa or the Statue of Liberty but their symbolic value lies in their interpretation by the observor, who has a frame of reference. In short, master symbols are *embedded* deeply in a culture or society (Duncan, 1968). Individuals born into that society must learn to make sense of the symbols. Humans construct society (Berger & Luckmann, 1963) and cultural elements; in turn, they must learn how to manage in a cultural milieu that is loaded with symbols. As part of symbolic interactionism, humans learn about cultural symbols, they use symbolic language and they symbolize the human body (Vlahos, 1979). They make sense of things; they create meanings. For example, the word mother may convey comfort, caring and attentiveness; the word father may convey strength, goal mastery and so on. To the abused child, the words mother and father may mean something very frightful. Interpretation, therefore, depends on contexts.

Codes refer to broader categories than do signs or symbols. They are not fixed entities; rather, they are modified over time, in keeping with social change. Deeply buried within a given society are underlying codes that inform humans how they should behave. For example, underlying codes indicate that people should shake hands or issue other forms of pleasant greetings when they first meet. Codes exist even though they may not be written down; humans learn about codes through indirect socialization, as they become aware of social expectations. Behaviors, habits and beliefs are shaped around these underlying codes or display rules.

Emblematic and Gestural Communication

Emblems are body acts that require no verbal accompaniment to be understood. Hand signals, such as waving goodbye, the V for victory sign, the high five signalling victory--all are examples of emblems. Nonverbal emblems may be sufficiently stable to categorize and label them. Scholars have constructed emblem dictionaries illustrating emblematic usage around the world (Morris, 1994). Not all people know the meanings of emblems just as they may not know the meanings of some words. An emblematic sign in one culture may mean something quite different in another, as in the use of the zero shape made by the fingers, which in American culture refers to one thing but in some European societies means something else, perhaps embarrassingly so. (Axtell, 1991). Meaning "OK" in English it may be a "bad" expression in other cultures, something that is not OK. Thus an emblem may be a *taboo* expression. Pantomime is a special form of emblematic communication; few, if any, words are needed to convey what the pantomimist wants to convey.

Artifacts, Ceremonies and Rituals

Artifacts are used in human nonverbal communication, often in the background. The word objectics is sometimes used to refer to artifacts. A boat, a watch or perfumes are artifactual in that they tell observers something about their users. Artifacts are not simply lifeless physical objects; contrarily, people invest meaning in them. They are semantic indicators. Thus, a watch, purchased to tell time, may also convey the status or social standing of the owner to the observer. Artifacts may reveal to others the values of their owners. Archaeologists are specially trained to read artifacts, to show how they represented cultures from the past.

Ritualistic and ceremonial behaviors are usually collective events. Customs and holidays are celebrated by social gatherings, special foods, games and other activities (Alexander, 1988; Deegan, 1989; Turner, 1986). They reflect cultural values and folkways and they exist separately from the individual who takes part in them. Rituals are often associated with religious activities, although much everyday behavior can be ritualized. Rituals are social events, usually jointly performed, that are nonverbal in nature. Going to church, attending synagogue, going to the football game and so on can become ritualized, yet deeply imbued with meaning. They are recognizable, patterned activities that exist in all cultures in different forms.

Ceremonies, similar to rituals, are usually public events that are jointly produced. The wedding ceremony, the funeral, rites of passage, births and so on are ceremonialized according to social custom. For the individuals involved, they take on meaning according to the experiences, life construals and frames of references of the individuals involved. Ceremonies, rituals and artifactual usage occur in all societies, conveying deeply held meanings with which the individual must come to terms. Ceremonial events may be quite structured although they may be altered from one generation to another; they may convey joy, bonding or togetherness, or enact or depict myths, depending on their function in society. Ceremonies involve life and death and all that falls in-between. They can act as rites of passage (Turner, 1967).

The Human Sensorium and Related Phenomena

The Senses

Some texts about nonverbal communication include sections dealing with the sixth sense (Leathers, 1978). However, there has been considerable debate by researchers over whether humans can and do communicate by using the sixth sense. The field of study, called *parapsychology*, has inspired research from both sides, from the skeptics(Blackmore, 1990) to the believers (Tart,1989), the so-called goats and sheep. People who claim to have extrasensorial abilities are fairly numerous in popular American culture. In other cultures, similar powers may be invested in a shaman or a witch doctor (Castaneda, 1969), as in the Navajo culture discussed in this book. Although there is good reason to discuss the sixth sense, given its place in the popular mind and in the minds of some scholars, there is far less clarity about parapsychological research than there is about the five senses; which, when taken together are referred to as the human sensorium, the five basic senses which all primates have.

Ethologists, those who study animal behaviors, usually from an *evolutionary* perspective, point out the sensate differences that are found among various species. Dogs, for example, have a well developed sense of smell; owls have well developed hearing and visual abilities; and monkeys and chimpanzees have well developed tactile abilities. All creatures have a *neurological system*; they are sentient, capable of sensing things in their environment. Evolutionists and ethologists emphasize that this differential development of the senses is due to the need for each species to adapt to complex environmental circumstances in order to survive. Thus, animals who hunt at night need good vision, for example (Wilson, 1992).

Unlike most other primates, humans, who sit atop the primate evolutionary ladder, can knowingly improve the use of their senses. They can employ tools, develop their sensitivities, train the body, build muscles and so on, all of which seems to enable humans to take part in their own evolution. As an everyday example, the ordinary human may not be able to discern between the fine nuances and bouquets found in various wines, but the enologist, trained to do so, can detect and distinguish thousands of odors and tastes associated with wine. Indeed, chemists have created an elaborate vocabulary detailing very fine nuances of smells and tastes that is useful to specialists (Cain, 1990). Although some lower order animals seem to create tools and make plans (Eibl-Eibestadt, 1975), it is not clear how much cognitive ability primates share with humans, although recent evidence suggests that chimps and humans are not far apart genetically. Chimps have learned emblematic vocabularies (Sagan, 1977).

Smell and taste are referred to as chemical senses. That is, they are very closely associated with each other and in close proximity to the brain, serving rudimentary functions. They are referred to as *olfactory* and *gustatory* processes. As in the case of tactility, or touch, they come into play mostly when they are in immediate contact with foods or other items. The chemical senses change as humans age; they are affected by hormonal changes in women who are menstruating or giving birth. Smell and taste perform important basal functions, such as enhancing as food odors. A recent internationally based smell study, performed by National Geographic (Gilbert & Wysocki, 1987) revealed key differences between males and females on a smelling index and how culture influences perceptions of odors and taste. In short, there are cultural overlays resting on top of the physical function of smelling. Another line of inquiry suggests that humans have individualized olfactory signatures. Pheromones, active in lower order animals in the sexual act, may be active in humans, influencing the mating, courtship ritual. Scientific research needs to validate the possibility. Perfume makers would like to know the answer to the question! They have put a perfume on the market called Pheromone.

Oculesics, mentioned above, is a field of study that refers to the use of the eyes and eye movement, including to some extent, perceptual processes (Webbink, 1986). From early studies focusing on what happens when a cat sees a mouse--the iris opens automatically-- (Hess, 1975) to recent research about the color of they eyes, eye attraction and gaze behavior, research about the eyes indicates that the eyes have directive features; that is, humans can influence others merely by the way they use their eyes. When a speaker suddenly looks to the side of the room, her observors may look there as well. Humans can encourage affiliation or they can discourage contact, merely by how they use their eyes. There are cultural, gender and ethnic differences among humans influencing how they use their eyes and in how that use is interpreted by observers. Staring is a common nonverbal activity found among lower order animals.

Aurality refers to the ability of humans to hear, an ability that varies highly among cultures. It also is age-related. The young enjoy loud music; the old enjoy softer music. Hearing can be improve with training. For example, a recent study showed that conductors could hear orchestral sounds that others in the orchestra could not detect (New York Times, Feb 1, 2001). However, the human hearing mechanism does not permit them to hear as well as many lower order animals. In some lower order animals, the use of echolocation mechanisms help them as they hunt, mate or move about in the physical environment.

Tactility, or *haptics*, refers to one's ability to touch and feel, the skin being the largest sensitive organ in the human body. Touching has been associated with gentling and bonding in both humans and other primates (Montagu, 1971) and to attitudes about body accessibility (Jourard, 1966; Jones, 1994)) and self-confidence (Jones, & Brown, 1996). The human skin is sufficiently sensitive that individuals can discern writing patterns performed on their backs, out of sight. The ability to touch, or grasp, differs among lower and higher order species; for example, it is clear that a hippopotamus cannot grasp a tree limb as a simian can. In the case of humans, the use of the fingers, thumbs and hands occurs within the field of vision, greatly enhancing human tactile abilities. Touching, holding, pushing, grasping, shaping, or throwing come easily to human beings. Humans take these activities and possibilities for granted. Most lower order animals can not perform these tasks.

Display rules suggest that how people touch one another conveys important and specific meanings. The question has been asked whether there is a right touch. (Jones, 1994). There are power touches, professional touches, intimacy touches and so on, each having social codes attached. Laws protect citizens from inappropriate touch, as in rape or beatings. In short, touching must be acceptable and appropriate. At one extreme lies touch aversion; that is, some people fear the touch of others, based on their negative experiences. At the other extreme, there is supportive touch. It is said that some cultures promote touch starvation; that is, the natives seem to be starved for affection, which they may not get in interpersonal situations (Jourard, 1966).

In sum, research about the five senses and how they interact in the daily lives of human beings is increasing. Research is showing how these sensory mechanisms, sometimes referred to as nonverbal channels, work together, how they are used in gendered ways, how they vary between cultures and ethnic groups and so on. It is obvious that humans need to know little about these mechanisms even though they rely on them for information. Research suggests that in the Western world especially, the eyes take primacy,(McLuhan, 1964; Ong, 1982) not surprising in an age of television and film; nor is it surprising that engineers have created machines that hear, speak, listen, and send odors.

Framing the "Sixth" Sense

Returning to the topic of the sixth sense. Is there a sixth sense? Do people know things other than through use of the corporal senses? Considerable research has been conducted on human subjects, in an attempt to determine whether telepathy, aura reading, precognition, clairvoyance, remote viewing, the moving of objects by kinetic energy and other phenomena are legitimate aspects of human experience; if so, how are they to be interpreted? The field of parapsychology has serious scholars researching and working on the many issues involved. Again, many scholars dismiss entirely the claims of parapsychologists.

One major issue is whether results of experiments can be replicated; another major issue deals with the nature of the experimentation itself. Subjects, who are thought to have some telepathic ability, often called psychics or sensitives--terms that are often used pejoratively--complain that laboratory situations restrict their performances. For example, Ganzfeld experiments require the subject to be deprived sensorily by placing blinders over the eyes while the eyes are kept open. White noise is used as a mask throughout the experiment. The subject is asked to receive a message telepathically from the sender outside the cage while these sensory impediments are in place. This bizarre experimental method seems to be faulty on the face of it because subjects claim that it interferes with their psychic senses. How can one access the alpha state when machines impede and interfere? Could a psychic, or any subject, relax under these laboratory conditions?

A third issue seems to be centered on the effect of belief. If one is a believer, perhaps she or he is more likely to claim that unusual experiences are psychic experiences. Research about psychic phenomena, the world of parapsychology, seems to be interesting to most people ; yet, the sixth sense does not seem to be established clearly enough to give it the sixth sense label. This is not to say that people who experience psychic phenomena are to be disregarded. Indeed, future research may reveal much more than is presently known. Perhaps new research paradigms will yield better results; the models used until now seem to fail.

Physical Attributes and Kinesics

Somatypes

Humans are fond of watching one another (Morris, 1985); the body, of course, is gendered (Holland & Adkins, 1996). Women and men present themselves to others, whether their body action is confined to the eyes, the entire head, the trunk of the body or the entire body. Body behaviors have been given considerable attention in the research literature, as has somatyping, the idea that body shape and size are correlated with certain kinds of behaviors. Endomorphic, mesomorphic or ectomorphic shapes have been described. (Sheldon, 1959). In early research it was believed that ectomorphs, the tall, thin people, had delicate personalities; medium sized people, the mesomorphs, were generally outgoing or athletic. The endomorphs, very heavy people, were thought to be languorous and slow.

Correlation is not causation, although it is often interpreted as causational. Biological structure may influence attitudes, but it does not predetermine attitudes; attitudes are created by the owner of the body, who in turn is influenced by her or his society. The importance of perceptions and stereotypes associated with body size and shape cannot be overstated, especially in Western countries, where body ideals are promoted by the media, a powerful force in Western societies. Everyone knows, generally speaking, what Miss America should look like, even though the criteria for winning it changes over time. Never should she be too heavy or too short!

Body Language

Body communication has been studied under the general name of kinesics. People often associate the idea of bodily communication (Argyle, 1983) exclusively with the use of gestures, but the field of study is now much broader. A body lexicon used to describe body behavior was created in early research including words like kines, morphs, kinemorphic constructions and other words, created to enhance the study of nonverbal behavior (Birdwhistell, 1970). A kine is the smallest unit of body expression, such as a facial movement; a morph may express the movement by two or more head motions; and, a kinemorphic construction may refer to the movement of the entire upper torso----all in synchrony with the verbal stream. Using this body language system, researchers have attempted to show how the verbal and the nonverbal streams work together in synchrony. Dancing, for example, reveals the integration of the body (Farnell, 1995) and how it manifests action signs.

Paralanguage

Semioticians focus on the ways that spoken language is tied into human behavior (Leeds-Hurwitz, 1993) and they are able to differentiate between male and female language use (Mulac, Ludell, & Bradac, 1986). Within spoken language there are paralinguistic features. Paralinguistic studies focus on how humans use language, rather than with what they actually say. Emotional elements are expressed in everyday conversation; gender and social class markers are found there. For example, older people, males and females and members of various ethnic groups, use different voice pitch, loudness or range of tonality, compared to one another. Females typically have a higher vocal range than do males (Buck, 1982) as is commonly observed. This difference, of course, is not absolute. To a large extent, it is a learned difference.

The word *genderlect* has been used to the distinctive ways that males and females express themselves, as learned through socialization. Not only do males and females differ in the patterning of vocal sounds, but they tend to use different sentence phrasing, different conversational styles and different conversational floor patterns, including different conversational turn-taking styles (Pittam,1994). Animated vocalization has been associated with extroverted personalities, while interrupted speech patterns have been associated with mental and emotional disturbance (Mahl, 1987). Attempts have been made to associate psychological and personality traits with vocal patterns and various paralinguistic styles (Argyle, 1983). As one can hear that the vocal patterns, or voice set, of older people, are very different from the vocal patterns of young children.

People from Latin America may differ substantially in their vocal patterns, or their voice set, compared to Whites or Blacks in North America. Cubans and Native Americans may differ substantially between groups. These are learned and practiced ethnic differences. Japanese "manage the floor" in conversations differently from Americans.

Environmental Influences

Proxemics

It is obvious that humans move about in space; less obvious, is that their ways of moving about vary considerably, based on the ways they have been socialized (Sommers, 1969, 1974). Smaller in body, females need less space generally speaking than do males. The ways that the British, the Japanese, the Arabs and others from other areas of the world use space differ, sometimes substantially. Americans tend to feel crowded when people enter their personal space closer than three feet, the desired norm. Arabs, on the other hand, feel quite normal when they are close to one another in dyads or groups.

It has been said that the ways humans use space is governed by a hidden language(Hall, 1966, 1973); hidden codes exist, guiding people, although they are not aware of them. Humans become aware of the norms of space when that space has been violated. Spatial zones of interaction have been devised, varying by cultures. For example, intimate distance, personal distance, social distance and public distances vary considerably. (Hall, 1966, 1973). The concept of zero proxemics implies that there is no space between bodies, a condition, which, in most instances, makes humans feel uncomfortable. In loving situations, of course, one expects to be touching, body to body. A mother who does not touch her child is said to be cold and reserved. On the other hand, in other situations, space violations occur, as in rape, physical abuse and other demeaning activities. In general, extreme body closeness is shunned from culture to culture but there is considerable variation between cultures.(Altman, 1975)

The concept of territoriality, a concept borrowed from the ethological study of animals (Ardrey, 1966), suggests strongly that humans, like other species, share normative expectations about how their space is claimed. Humans mark their spaces, perhaps by putting a purse on the table to define their space in their absence, or by putting fences between them and their neighbors. Lower order species, by contrast, mark their territory by urination or body rubbing. When students enter classrooms, they tend to choose their seats in accordance with their perception of comfort, barring other reasons, as sociometrists have shown. The use of space varies enormously from situation to situation, from culture to culture; nevertheless, humans follow hidden display rules and context codes as they determine how they will use space.

Chronemics

Chronemics is the study of the human invention and use of time. In some societies, it is clear that humans are almost cultish about time; they follow a cult of the clock. Researchers suggest that humans have built- in physiological, psychological and social clocks (Bruneau, 1979; Gonzales & Zimbardo, 1990) and that there are biological rhythms which vary according to age and sex. For example, some people work best in the morning while others work best at night, like sparrows and owls.

Time, of course, is a human conception. It does not have fixed dimensions. Early Native Americans relied upon seasonal changes for their sense of time, as do many members of traditional cultures in various parts of the globe. Today, some modern Navajo members may live away from the Reservation working in an industry that is governed by the hourly clock, returning at night to the Reservation, where different meanings for time are used.

The sense of time is related even to emotional and body health. Seasonal Affective Disorder (SAD), a form of depression, has been reported to be associated with the dark months of winter (USAToday, Jan 3, 1999). Speed in walking, talking and behaving vary highly between and among regions of the United States based on the underlying hidden codes for the region.

Some cultures are past-oriented; others are present or future-oriented. It is said that American youth tend to be future-oriented while older citizens tend to be past oriented. These generalizations appear to have some validity; but, of course, humans are free to change the way they think and behave.

Other Background Influences on Nonverbal Communication

The environment influences nonverbal communication. Colors in the background are thought to influence moods and behaviors. For example, the soft color of green is often painted onto library walls furnishing a quiet, restful context. Bright red would seem to destroy the study mood. Unfortunately, the study of color and its influence on human behavior is only beginning to receive solid research attention. Anecdotal and popular notions seem to be pervasive. Yet, from a practical view, it seems that humans choose colors in clothing, in their houses, or for their cars because they like them or feel comfortable with them. Not just any color will work for them.

Humans don warm clothing in the winter and shed it in the summer. Clearly, humans create behaviors that are influenced by background variables. The physical environment, like the social environment, is a powerful influence on human behaviors, although the research is not substantial.

Humans create architectural environments which reflect cultural values. As mentioned, the famous Frank Lloyd Wright designed houses to blend into the landscape, creating a prairie style. His houses were designed to let the outdoors in, by using large windows, subdued lighting, skylights and overhangs. Earthy colors were used to blend the buildings into the landscape. This great American architect influenced generations of later architects. He built his houses to fit into the environment, as no prior architect had done, showing Americans how to live more meaningfully within the environmental context.

On a less appealing side, American architecture, referring especially to public buildings, has been referred to as "hard architecture" (Sommer, 1974), meaning that it conforms little to comfortable human use, being designed for the faceless public person. Railroads, prisons, banks and other buildings are said to be hard, rather than soft, and to restrict rather than to open. Modern architecture and ergonomic development attempt to build better structures, more accommodating to the comfort of the users.

Architectural variations throughout the world reflect the values of their builders. The buildings of slash and burn cultures are necessarily temporary; the open courtyards of the Spanish built structures, found in South America and Spain, reflect the need for space, using courtyards. The tribal Navajo member had a sense of place and space that used open pastoral scenes, that incorporated traditional views of the four major directions, that oriented the natives to natural phenomena, such as the sun and the moon. Architectural structures and patterns arise from symbolic meaning of space, time and place found in each culture.

Sources of Knowledge About Nonverbal Communication

Ethology, Biology and Evolution

Darwin, the father of evolution, was interested in how humans emerged and how they expressed themselves (Darwin, 1869 (1967). In recent years, ethologists still follow that interest. Biologists have solved the genetic code, the Book of Life; it now appears that humans are much closer to other species, such as chimps, in genetic make-up than has been previously assumed. The Great Chain of Being, a theoretical-religious view, placed all species, including humans, on an ordered hierarchy in order of importance, a species high on the ladder being more important than one lower down. This belief system is now eroded. It is now known that the common mouse and the chimpanzee share many of the genes that are found in humans and that some genes may have arisen from bacteria, hardly conceivable to early scholars.

It was once believed that male white men were higher on the Great Chain of Being than were women, Blacks and other people of color. It is now understood that there is very little physical difference between these groups; there is nothing to justify the superiority of one color or gender over the others. The study of genetics has given the ethologists new understandings about the inter-relationships of species, especially of higher primates (Agassiz, 1850; Gould, 1981; Wilson, 1992).

Self awareness and self validation seem to be characteristics that humans share, perhaps with chimpanzees, although this is not clear. It is, however, widely debated. The ability to take the role of the other, an important concept in SI, is part of the awareness of self that sentient creatures, such as humans, have evolved. Human aggression seems to be shared among most species whether they are higher order primates or not. For example, the concept of white supremacy, discussed in Chapter Six, was behind White aggression against colored people, the Blacks, the Chinese and Native Americans. Whites in the past often referred to darker skinned people as colored.

Ethologists are evolutionists who study both humans and lower order animals. Human ethologists are interested in universal behaviors such as infant attachment, emotion, dominance, nonverbal behavior and ritual. Comparative study of animal behaviors furnishes a means to put human behavior in context. For example, research on chimpanzee behavior in which the major stars have been Lucy, Washoe and Koko, suggests that humans and chimps are not terribly far apart in their evolutionary development, although there are important key differences. The claim is made that chimps can acquire substantial nonverbal vocabularies when they are raised among trainers. It has been shown that chimps can use tools to do work or to reach food (Eibl-Eibestadt, 1975) and that, by watching their elders, young chimps can learn to do what their parents do. Chimps, parrots and other animals appear to learn things, somewhat like young human children.

Animal communication, as a field of study, is now taught in universities. Parrots are shown to have remarkable "thinking" ability; some songbirds, like finches, can learn new songs, thriving in a song-rich background. A debate rages about whether higher order creatures truly think, as do humans, or whether their behavior is basically instinctive with some modifications. Some evidence shows that dolphins and chimps can recognize themselves in a mirror, presumably a first step in self-awareness. Unfortunately, the issues are confused by the persistent, almost unavoidable, anthropomorphizing of findings, in which scientists interpret animal behavior using human models and assumptions. Human beings are able to be the objects of their own thoughts, unlike most or all other animals. The implication of this ability is that humans can create a sense of self and identity. They can talk about themselves and others and construct meaningful relationships. They can make sense of their social worlds.

Sociobiologists and physical anthropologists are interested in how behavior arises. Is it tied into genetic codes? Is it learned? How does it vary by context? Are animals socialized? Which animals seem to think? How do humans differ from higher order primates? The general field called ethology is yielding important information which can be used to compare human and primate behaviors. Perhaps it is safe to say that there is a balance between nature and nurture that furnishes most of human physical and social growth.

Linguistics and Anthropology

Although the study of linguistics and anthropology have changed considerably in the past few years, spawning many subfields of inquiry, such as sociolinguistics or bio-anthropology, they were studied together for decades. Linguists, like anthropologists, know that the use of language is a key to human studies, as is the study of nonverbal communication. Early theorists assumed that language expressed unconsciously patterned social processes (Sapir, 1928) and that culture and language are one and the same. This linguistic relativity hypothesis was challenged in more recent times (Chomsky, 1980). More recently, issues have been raised about the universality of human nonverbal communication (Eibl-Eibestadt, 1979). The concept of minimum universality has been promoted relative to the display of emotions.

Anthopologists refer to acculturation and assimilation, two ways by which culture gets into human heads. Humans acquire their values, symbols, beliefs, customs, technologies and habits through these twin processes. Human nonverbal ways of behaving are deeply influenced by cultural processes. Anthropologists are interested in ceremonial behaviors, in rites of passage and in how gender, ethnicity and aging are construed in various cultures.

Early anthropologists, perhaps quite unlike modern ones, often used the case study method to study villagers, often in remote places (Kluckhohn, 1965). By studying one or two villagers, it was believed that one could understand the general make-up of the entire village because the subject had assimilated the knowledge, expected behaviors and cultural ways of the villagers at large. The subjects were the carriers of culture, influenced by the acculturation process.

Anthropologists studied chronemics, the time orientation of cultures, ritualistic behaviors and ceremonies and the folkways of a given culture, referring to folk cultures. The general point to be made is that anthropologists know that the cultural background of the inhabitant of a given culture deeply influences the nonverbal behavior of that person and the ways in which humans tend to interpret life. The lifeworld of each inhabitant is created by the person, but the influences on that creative expression are powerful. A person living in a highly tooled and technologically oriented culture may not know how to survive in the jungles of the Amazon, as the local natives do. Their fund of tacit technological knowledge is not useful in a very different pre-technological culture. Tribal natives from the Amazon basin would not know how to survive in New York City.

Sociology and Social Psychology

The concept of socialization is well known to most readers. Starting from birth, perhaps even before, in its daily exposure to human society, the newborn becomes a fully functioning being. The individual is not determined by society to be anything in particular; rather, the individual must learn to make sense of what he experiences in everyday life. The colors blue and pink in American society are associated with the birth of boys and girls and, throughout life, as humans pass through the various stages of growth, from youth through the gerontological age, humans semantically tag themselves and are tagged by other members of society. They are genderized, ethnicized and aged in this construal process (Weigert, 1986, 1997). Ethnicity, gender and age are concepts that are created and applied to groups and individuals. Constructed too narrowly, they serve to isolate their members; constructed too loosely, they fail to serve the members well. The main focus of this book is upon identity adaptiveness or the ability of humans to engage positively with others who are different from themselves. How people think influences what they do.

Standpoint theory (Wood, 1995) suggests that humans are heavily influenced by their birthplace in society. The wealthy have very different expectations for their offspring than do people who live in the ghetto. They learn different ways of behaving. Social codes and the expectations of social class become imbedded in hman thinking. Social class, power and influence, ethnicity, gender and the theme of aging deeply affect how humans communicate nonverbally. These master themes, or variables, are deeply imbedded in daily life. They are revealed in the clothes that people wear, in their characteristic patterns of social conduct and in their expectations. In short, each individual must learn to make sense of the social milieau, to take account of the stuff of society, responding to it, interpreting it, and acting out roles.

Communication

Human identity is rooted in the interpretation and perception of the self, a psychological activity. In interaction with others and in conversations with the self, humans create their identities. They learn that there is an I and a Me in the self and that both are observable in human action. The I is active; the Me is responsive, both being key parts of the sense of self and identity (Mead, 1925,1934). Self concepts, identity and the construal of the meanings of human behavior is the work of psychologists, communicologists and others.

The concept of face (Goffman, 1959; Ting-Toomey, 1994) is closely allied with the concept of identity. Not to be confused with the physical face, it is symbolic. Humans present themselves to others symbolically, using their bodies and their words. People learn how to save face or to promote a confident face. They learn to ingratiate themselves with others (Jones, 1964, 1990). The face gets construed and scripted. People learn to avoid embarrassment and to create positive impressions in the minds of others, who act as audiences.

Psychologists reveal that humans use action language (Vallacher and Wegner, 1985), creating plans for action, both simple and omplex, to accomplish goals. They look back on their activities and make sense of them, building upon them, acting coordinatively with others in joint activities. They evaluate their own success or failure as they interact with others. A complex action may involve days, months or weeks of planned activity, such as those involved in courtships; or, they may be very simple, such as the brushing of the teeth in the morning. Each activity is meaningful to the participant.

A variety of communication models are used in the study of the general field of Communication and, more specifically, in the subfield called Nonverbal Communication. Each model, or approach, has advantages or disadvantages. For example, a sender-message-receiver model is popular in Communication, a linear view. This approach has been widely used in quantitative studies. The symbolic interactionist approach, has a number of advantages not shared by the SMR model, including the view that humans are creative, taking part in an interactive setting in special ways, not necessarily predictable.

Nonverbal communication is not a linear process. It is a contingent process; humans build one action upon another, reflecting upon what they have done in preparation for the next episode. They negotiate and modify their actions as needed.

Key Themes in Nonverbal Communication Research

Gender

Human, gendered identity is constructed and achieved; it is created in a long-term process, influenced by complex, often poorly understood elements in society (Wood, 1994). It is implied sometimes that identity, personality and character are fixed, unchanging concepts; contrarily, they are dynamic, yet fairly enduring clusters of focused concepts. Socialized from birth, humans choose, often unwittingly, how they will define themselves. Even though they are born with explicit sexual characteristics, they will genderize their identities.

Many scholars who hold an essentialist view of sex tend to show how males and females differ categorically; however, they fail to take into account that humans can and do define and redefine themselves as they choose, changing the ways they act in different circumstances (Carol Tavris, 1992). In saying this, it is not meant to imply that the creation of identity is a thoroughly rational process in which all of the elements are clearly known or depicted. Indeed, quite the opposite is often the case. Humans are often confused as they try to come to terms with self identification, especially in a society heavily saturated by the media (Gergen, 1991).

There are biological differences that clearly influence gendered behavior; men do not give birth or have menstrual periods, although it is claimed by some researchers that men have their own pronounced biological shifts. Women in general have smaller bodies than do men. Even this comparative smallness is amenable to alteration. Women can and do become physically powerful. The concept of gender is a powerful, modern concept influencing nonverbal communication(Kotthoff and Wodak, 1997). (See Chapter Five for a thorough discussion of genderized nonverbal communication).

Ethnicity

Race and ethnicity are powerful themes in Western society; indeed, they are universal themes, meaning different things in different cultures. It is no accident that some cultures place people on the social class ladder based on their color alone. Like gender, concepts about race and color are learned. People are born into a colored world but they create the meanings of the world for themselves. Humans construe the meaning of skin color. In relatively simple and static societies, people know where they stand socially, based on skin color; in complex, change-oriented societies, people may move about in society and create new meanings about ethnicity, race or skin color.

Unfortunately, in the United States, a country that espouses an egalitarian ethos, where all people are to be treated equally, entire populations of colored persons have been--in many cases still are--treated as strangers by the dominant and prevailing white class, based almost entirely on the color of skin, although other factors come into play. This stranger-making process is complex and it varies according to the groups being studied.

In this book, four ethnic groups are discussed; each has different historical origins and experiences with early mainstream White Americans. Native Americans, or the Navajo, Black Americans and Chinese Americans are studied along the lines of how they achieved their identity in a white world. Identity is the key nonverbal concept and in the case of each of the above, the stuff of history has forced them to deal with their place in a white society. The presence of Cuban Americans in the United States arises from a very different social motif; usually, they have been treated as friends who fled a hostile home country to find a sense of place in the United States.

Broad themes emerge in this struggle for inclusion. How can a society move from a stranger-making process to a friendship- making process, ignoring differences and building on similarities? This is the modern struggle in a society that is becoming colored more and more, according to the Census 2000 report. (Chapter six focuses on the unique influences on the identities of people of color in the United States)

Age

The study of aging, as opposed to the idea of *ageism*, is about changes in the ways that humans symbolize themselves over a the lifetime. Although biological and genetic factors are influences on the aging processes, they do not determine aging in an absolute sense. Biology influences but does not determine how people age. Stage theorists emphasize the ways that humans are influenced at various stages in their lives. Stages are not fixed and individuals vary greatly among themselves in the ways that they age. Successful aging, a concept that is emerging in modern research, is described in positive ways (Baltes & Willis, 1982; Baltes & Baltes, 1990).

Some aspects of aging do not seem to be under human control, such as the loss of acuity in vision, or the ability to see the color blue. Yet, with technological changes and new medical techniques, the shift from the deficit concepts associated with aging have changed to positive concepts about aging. Present day models of the aging process reveal that aging need not be deleterious! The new paradigms emphasize the role of the aging person, as an active, dynamic person, acting on his or her own behalf to sustain a successful life style. (Chapter Seven deals with aging and nonverbal communication).

Technology and Mediation

People in highly developed technical societies live in environments that are highly saturated by the media. Television in particular deeply influences members of these societies. Technological change is profoundly altering the social landscape of advanced countries (Adoni & Mane, 1984).

Framing the New Media Environment

It appears that print and broadcast media are merging; that there is media abundance, rather than media scarcity. It is now possible to tailor media content to specific, targeted audiences. Interactive media is taking the place of one-way media.

The Information Superhighway is controlled in the main by large corporations or businesses, who use it for their own purposes. At the same time, individuals can construct their own websites.

The internet appears to provide unlimited channels to communicate; it can be used to build communities, to create commerce and for a variety of activities that tend to blur the lines between providers and consumers(Severin & Tankard, 1997).

Mediation in modern societies is a powerful influence on nonverbal communication. The inventor of the internet referred to his invention as a world brain, indicating that the internet functions almost like a neurological net spanning the globe. Other technologies, such as the telephone, e-mail, television, movies and modern satellites have become so common in daily life that they form an embedded social web of which people are largely unconscious (Herring, 1996). National boundaries are changed and traditional cultures are influenced, adapting to new technologies. The new technologies are producing new, symbolic boundaries, new networked, global communities.

Oral culture retains nonverbal, face-to-face situations, employing the full range of the human sensorium; but, as sophisticated communicative technologies emerge, the face-to-face character of oral culture disappears (Ong, 1982). In short, the technological context influences nonverbal communication, both in assumption and practice.

The computer and television have most dramatically altered the social landscape, with more than half of American households owning computers and more than ninety percent having television sets, many owning more than one. Embedded now in the social landscape, television and the computer have dramatically altered how humans perceive things and how they make sense of their worlds. Human nonverbal communication is dramatically affected. (See Chapter Eight for a more complete discussion of this topic).

Related Topics

Research Perspectives

Chapters Nine and Ten deal with the SI research perspective, with issues and problems that arise from that perspective. Although the SI perspective is used in this text, it is broad enough to include research from many disciplines, as noted above. Much of the research cited here is, in fact, taken from research that has been incorporated from other research models. There is, however, a distinctive and large body of research to be found within the SI perspective, an approach that contains many different points of view.

Self Assessment and Nonverbal Skills

Although this book is designed primarily to provide a way to integrate the study of nonverbal communication, it may be useful to people who wish to enhance their skills. People are not born with skills; they must learn how to become skillful, to become good performers on the various social stages they occupy. They are found at various stages of this growth process.

Chapter Ten is devoted to an analysis of problems that interfere with the development of skill. It contains self-assessment tools to help learners become more proficient and insightful about human nonverbal communication. In addition, at the end of each chapter in the book, readers will find questions designed to promote thought and discussion.

Summary

In this chapter, the author has delineated the major aspects of the field of study called nonverbal communication. These aspects, or concepts, will be woven into the following chapters where they best fit. They are offered here to provide a broad overview of the field for the reader, setting up the following chapters. Clearly, context, gender, age and ethnicity deeply influence human nonverbal communication; in turn, they they are influenced by nonverbal communication. It is an interactive process. Human identity is forged from these interactive behaviors.

Modern technologies embed themselves in societies and alter human behaviors, often dramatically. By providing a flexible and dynamic system, symbolic interactionism is an effective interpretive tool, useful to practitioner and scholar alike.

People can create skills to better understand nonverbal behaviors. By using the self-assessment tools in chapter ten, readers can enhance their understandings and become more aware of their place in interactive settings. In Chapter Two, an analysis of the influence of cultural processes on nonverbal communication takes center stage.

Questions for Thought and Discussion

1.   It is clear that humans are not always aware of their own nonverbal behaviors let alone the behavior of others. Why do you think this is the case?

2.   Do you think that most people from other cultures think and behave in ways that are very similar to the ways that you think and behave? How do display rules influence your behavior, for example?

3.   How closely do you think that human beings are related to other animals, such as chimpanzees, in nonverbal behavior? Do you think that it degrades humans to put them into similar categories?

4.   People have body signatures by which they are identified. How valid do you think this assumption is? What nonverbal behaviors distinguishes one of your friends from another?

5.   To what extent do you plan to do things to influence others or to fulfill the expectations of others. How do you put on your best face?

6.   What does your body mean to you, or symbolize to you? What characterizes your metaphorical body, or your symbolic face?

Notes

1.   Although the roots of symbolic interactionism were in early American pragmatic philosophy, modern SI enjoys a special status in sociology, social psychology, communication studies and the humanities. Readers should see Chapter Nine especially where the scholarly history is discussed. A good summary of SI is found in Symbolic Interactionism, Joel M. Charon, Prentice-Hall, 1995.

2.   Scholars differ about the relationship between verbal and nonverbal communication. A good discussion of the topic is found in Nonverbal Communication: Forms and Functions, by Peter A. Andersen, Mayfield Publishing Company, 1999, pp. 15-18. The approach used in his text is functionalist which means that it focuses on how nonverbal communication is used. This text, on the other hand, assumes that both verbal and nonverbal communication require the use of similar perceptual and interpretive processes regardless of their apparent differences. Hearing is associated with the spoken word; vision is associated with nonverbal communication; both, however, are symbolic processes, the subject of this book.

3.   The idea that people unconsciously display body behaviors that reveal their emotional condition is linked to Freudian pschotherapy. The leakage hypothesis, however, has been linked most recently to the study of deception. Ekman and Friesen, two scholars interested in the leakage cues found in deceptive behavior, gave early formulation to the theories behind it. Leakage hierarchies, or how the various body channels release deceptive cues in different ways has been studied by Burgoon and others. See Nonverbal Communication: The Unspoken Dialogue, second edition, McGraw Hill, 1996, pp 331-333 for an excellent discussion of the leakage hypothesis.

4.   Semiotics, or semiosis, refers to how meaning is created by humans and affixed to people, objects, signs, symbols, events and so on, which do not in themselves contain meaning. See Horst Ruthrof (2000) in The Body In Language. New York, especially Chapters One and Two. He delineates how spoken language is dependent on nonverbal behaviors. Various nonverbal elments such as olfactory, gustatory, tactile, proxemic, kinetic, thermal, aural, gravitational, visual and others underly the spoken language.

Suggested Readings

Charon, J. M. (1995). *Symbolic Interactionism: An Interpretation, an Integration.* Englewood Cliffs, NJ: Prentice-Hall, Inc.

DeVito, J. A., & Hecht, M. L. (1990). *The Nonverbal Communication Reader.* Prospect Heights, IL: Waveland Press, Inc.

Vlahos, O. (1979). *Body, the Ultimate Symbol: Meanings of the Human Body Through Time and Place.* New York: J. B. Lippincott

Wood, J. T. (1992). *Spinning the Symbolic Web: Human Communication and Symbolic Interaction.* Norwood, NJ: Ablex Publishing Corporation.

Chapter 2
Cultural Influences on Nonverbal Communication
Making Sense of Cultural Processes

Chapter Overview

Anthropologists have watched and studied people for generations, their research methods varying over time. It is clear to them that people are deeply immersed, enmeshed in the culture in which they are raised. Whether anthropologists look for uniformity or dissimilarity among people, they know that humans are deeply influenced by cultures.

Culture is a cognitively symboled system, meaning that cultural interaction is based on a system of symbols and signs which the natives of that culture share. There are cultural "logics", every culture having a unique sense of semiosis (Merrell, 1998). Humans are born into culture, they maintain it and pass it on to their children. Their lifeworlds are formed though the joint production of meaning (Fortas, 1995). Humans interact symbolically, one with the other, acting out their lives in cultural spheres, such as the kinship group, clan or tribe. Knowledge, norms and symbols are passed from older generation to younger generation along with modes of work and play. Nonverbal behaviors are passed on as well.

Acculturation, or the processes involved in the acquiring of culture, influence human perceptions, which in turn, influence nonverbal behaviors and their interpretation. This is because culture consists of shared cognitive representations(Romney, Boyd, Moore, Batchelder and Brazill, 1996). in the minds of individuals, resulting from a common history, a common language and a common value system.

Cultures have permeable boundaries; they are not fixed. Variability in cultural patterning is obvious as are the contrasts between cultures. Being raised in China is very different from being raised in the United States, say, in St. Louis. The differences in linguistic habits, in customs and beliefs and in the daily patterns of life are clear to those who have spent time in both places. Yet, despite the differences, people living in both cultures are sufficiently similar, so that they share commonly in the tasks of living, growing and dying.

Modern technology is rapidly changing traditional cultures, as will be discussed in chapter eight. Television, film and digital culture, originally confined to Western countries, are now universally dispersed. Indeed, countries as different, one from the other, as Japan and the Netherlands belong to a new technology-based culture, a Northern belt, crossing the traditional boundaries of nation and cultures. As the popular saying implies, humans seem to be constructing a "global village" (Mcluhan, 1964). Could the multimedia explosion be leading to a "global mind" as well? Telematic networks are abolishing time and space which bear upon human identity.

Traditional cultures still exist and they provide contrasting examples of nonverbal communication. The major purpose of this chapter is to show the reader how deeply culture imbeds itself in human behavior. Genetics and bio-physical processes influence human behavior, but the emphasis in this chapter is upon the cultural aspects of behavior. In nonverbal communication, nature meets culture (Segerstrale & Molnar, 1997).

Symbolic interactionism provides a way to view and understand human nonverbal communication. It is a dynamic, creative process that focuses on the symbolic meaning of human interaction. Humans construct meaning in their lives; they enact lines of nonverbal action and performance, as they try to adjust to and influence the people and events in their everyday lives. Not only do humans act in small groups they also engage in unique cultural and ceremonial practices with large numbers of people (Turner,1986).

Readers need to be cautioned that not all members of a given culture think or think or act alike. Within any broad culture, there are ethnic groups whose ways of life separate them out from the mainline culture. Individuals, too, vary in the ways that they present themselves. The word culture is employed as a broad brush, lumping sometimes isolated groups together without giving explicit attention to the thought processes of each individual. (Barth, 1969).

The Many Meanings of Culture

Scholars in the humanities and in the social sciences have shared mutual interests in culture over a period of several years; the boundaries between them appear to be disappearing (Becker & McCall, 1990). The way that culture is defined is often the result of the orientation of the individual researcher.

Multiple Interpretations of Culture

The word culture has many meanings(1). Popular culture, for example, deals with expressive forms which are spread widely throughout a society, often associated with mass communications. People decide what book to read, what film to watch or what social event to attend. High culture, or hoch kultur, on the other hand, is a term that is used to refer to a special or preferred set of social activities enjoyed by the few. For example, in the United States people who love opera are usually interested in other fine arts as well.

The perception is that classical music, museum art and archaeological activities are enjoyed by well educated and monied people. Popular culture, on the other hand, is usually associated with mass communication, film, radio, books and television. Despite these perceptual differences, given the powerful role of the mass media, the classical lively arts seem to be blending with popular culture forming a new cultural hybrid.

By typing the word culture into a search engine on the internet, one may find more than fifty definitions and examples of culture, ranging from cyberculture to teenager culture. These uses of the word are specialized, applying to unique groups, associated with specialized activities. A broader interpretion of culture is used in this text referring to all of the activities that comprise a person's life, including values, beliefs, habits, thoughtways, customs, technology, art, language, religion and ways of making a living (Kluckhonhn, 1965). The word enculturation suggests that a person who is raised in a specific culture will exhibit the norms of that culture. In short, people are bathed in culture, completely immersed in it.

As mentioned, the idea of culture may be unique to humans. Nevertheless, ethologists who study primate behavior including gorillas and chimps, the closest associates of humans on the evolutionary ladder, point to genetic and social similarities between higher primates and human beings. For example, chimp genes may be useful in the prediction of disease patterns in humans, their genetic patterns being very similar to those of human beings. Research shows that chimps can use sign languages and even teach their offspring how to do the same. Perhaps chimps have a culture (Sagan, 1977); chimps can use Ameslan and Yerkish, two nonverbal languages, to "talk" to humans and to one another. Whether chimps or other species have a culture or not is an interesting scientific puzzle; the meaning of the word culture is confined to its application to human beings in this book, although, at various points, ethological research is used for illustrative purposes.

Enculturation Processes: Assimilation and Accommodation

Cultures may be impressed on people both formally and informally. For example, the Zuni of new Mexico have a formal culture that puts pressure on its members, which they cannot disregard if they are to remain members. Most Americans, on the other hand, are generally informal about their culture, except where serious tradition plays a strong role, emphasizing what is right and correct to do, as in fundamentalist religions.

Following SI thinking, humans take account of cultural ways, trying to make sense of them, drawing upon them to give meaning to their lives. Tribal members who wear little but a loin cloth have made sense of the stuff of their culture and adapted accordingly.

Framing Cultural Myths

Myths are forms of spiritual metaphor which help members of cultures organize rituals, celebrations and other human activities. There is a thematic quality to myths, such as stories about creation, heroic accounts, human quests, destructive floods and astronomical figures. Myths define cultures; they may be used to compare cultures (Campbell, 1964).

All cultures have myths that are passed on from generation to generation. The bee hunters, located in remote areas of India, for example, believe that the bee trees are benevolent females. This myth is passed on from parent to child; unfortunately, the tribe is diminishing in size as members die off. Eventually, the myth associated with the tree will disappear (Valli, 1998).

It has been argued that Eastern myths differ from Western myths in the ways that they allude to ultimate reality. In Eastern religions, myths are guides to the beyond. In the West, myths are often associated with icons, figurines or other representations, in the present. In the West, the Creator is involved in His creation (Campbell, 1964).

Myths, of course, provide cultural meaning to the lives of everyday persons. Myths suggest that everyday life is natural or meant to be the way it is. But, analysis of cultural behavior reveals that culture is the product of human action heavily influenced by environmental factors, such as the presence of modern technologies. For example, past-oriented cultures have a degree of permanence that technologically oriented cultures do not have which gives rise to the belief that things are meant to be the way they are.

By comparison, one can actually observe changes taking place in technologically developed countries; the sense of permanency is lost. Grandparents in the United States tell their grandchildren about important changes over the span of their lifetime, from the rumble seat to the picture tube and the internet. Indeed, the speed of change is itself increasing. Communicative technologies are changing society in remarkable ways. The speed of change is faster in highly technical societies than it is in past-oriented, oral societies. For this reason, technologically advanced societies tend to be present or future oriented while societies that have relatively undeveloped technologies tend to be past-oriented. The achievement of identity is complicated in complex, modern societies. The routes to achievement become blurred.

The Creation of Values

Values are embedded in all cultures; as a child becomes enculturated, values are centered in the individual personality and reflected in behaviors (Ball-Rokeach, Rokeach & Grube, 1984). For example, if a society values openness and emotional expressiveness, individuals will reflect those values behaviorally in interaction with others (Gudykunst, 1997).

Values are guides to actions. The cultural background influences the individual; the individual's personal agentry and presentation of self reflect the expectations of others. If, for example, a culture permits the open display of emotions, its members will tend to freely display their emotions.

The Shaping of Worldviews

A worldview, or *weltanschauung*, is shared by members of a culture. Beliefs and ways of thinking become embedded in human thought through the processes of assimilation and accommodation, each a part of the enculturation process. When people assimilate the culture they explore it proactively, adapting it to their needs. When people accommodate themselves to the culture, they adapt or accept, with little modification, the elements of culture and allow them to shape their thinking (Sarbaugh, 1979). Both verbal and nonverbal communicative behaviors reflect these processes. For example, the child raised in a Bedouin society, as a member of a wandering desert tribe, will learn to eat only with the right hand, following the ways of the elders in his tribe. Chinese in traditional China eat with chopsticks.

Cultural Dimensions

Cultures and the societies within them have been described in different ways by different scholars. For example, cultures are said to be high-context or low-context (Hall, 1966) referring to how people in those cultures communicate. Members of high culture context tend to rely less on the written word, many of the meanings of their lives being hidden and unexpressed. Their cultural codes are more implicit than explicit, known by the individual but not expressed directly.

Traditional Japan is a high context society while the United States is a low context society. It is said about visitors to Japan, that although they may have mastered the language, they can not become fully saturated in Japanese culture because they were not born into it. They will always be outsiders.

Cultures vary along an individualism-collectivism dimension, meaning that members in a highly individualist society, for example, will display individualistic behaviors, as in the United States. A Confucian saying applying to Chinese society, a collectivistic society, warns "If a nail sticks up, hammer it down." The ideas behind rugged individualism, demonstrated in the Western expansion movements in early America, do not apply to the Chinese.

Other dimensions that scholars emphasize include the uncertainty-avoidance continuum, the masculinity-feminity continuum, and the power-distance continuum (Gudykunst, 1997). The word continuum implies that there is a range along which cultures vary, each culture being positioned at some point along that range. For example, people in highly male dominated societies, or patriarchies, as in parts of Latin America, may demonstrate a machismo attitude. The Cuban society, discussed in this book, reflects a system of machismo. Matriarchal societies, or those that reflect the emphasis upon the primacy of females, are found in parts of Africa and in past cultures where female goddesses were exhibited and worshipped. Power orientations are different, comparatively, in male and female oriented cultures.

The rugged individualistic tradition, so much a part of early American society, placed men above women in social affairs. Historically, the concept of rugged individualism applied mostly to males, a fact that influences gendered behaviors even in the modern world. The frontier spirit, the rough life, the male drive for gold in the mid-1800's emphasized male primacy, as part of rugged individualism. Levi jeans were built for the wear and tear of the male lifestyle. Today, of course, in a more relaxed society, females wear jeans; the male domination, so characteristic of earlier times, although not completely eroded, has been muted or moderated.

It may be tempting to oversimplify the characterization of cultures along the lines of one dimension or the other. In reality, the themes mentioned above are simplified ways of looking at the dynamics of any society or culture. Cultures are complex. Individual members display diverse behaviors. It is only by sustained, intimate exposure, by the immersion of oneself in a culture, that one can really understand that culture and appreciate the complexity and diversity of cultural life.

Culture as Communication

Culture is created by repeated communicative behaviors and processes, learned from the past by one generation, passed on to the next. Both verbal and nonverbal communication form the base of culture. (Latane, Mar. 09, 1996). Following the SI model described fully in chapter nine, humans create (2)culture by conferring meaning upon interactive events, both verbal and nonverbal. Humans develop a sense of the self, a cultural identity, that includes perceptions of the body and daily experiences. As social beings, humans engage in collective activities. The body becomes specially symbolized in every culture depending on cultural traditions(Vlahos, 1979). For example, in a popular vein in the United States, it is not uncommon to hear the human body described using a continuum from one to ten. The perfect body is a 10, hardly a universal concept.

Cultures vary comparatively, but there are rough resemblances of behavior in societies that share the same general culture. For example, the spoken language is a defining feature of all cultures; highly diversified, there are more than 2500 languages spoken, of which 82 are used by 96 percent of the population of the earth, most of which are unwritten (Mowlana, 1996). Nonverbal communication is highly varied, as well. The spoken language acts as a cultural lens, shaping and influencing human perceptions, while nonverbal communication is the action component. The two, acting together, reflect cultural norms.

Cultural Influences on Nonverbal Communication

The Hierarchy of Races in Early Anthopology

Anthropologists and others are often influenced by evolutionary theory, which has changed enormously in the past few decades. For example, it is now common for evolutionists to deal with gene mutations and chromosomal rearrangements to explain changes in species (Wilson, 1992). In earlier times, Darwinism was associated with eugenics, which suggested that some humans were superior to others; methods such as phrenology were designed to demonstrate the superiority of one race over the other. Although the belief that a particular race may be superior to another has not completely disappeared, it has far less currency in modern evolutionary thought. The study of eugenics has a murky past.

Very early anthropological studies were conducted from a Western, European point of view. The research reflected the values of white male Europeans and Americans. This Western value orientation may be reflected in the concept of a hierarchy of races, a scheme based on the uses of the human body. This view suggested that the eye-man occupied the top of the hierarchy, characterized by Westerners; the ear-man came next, characterized by Asians; then followed the nose-man, represented by Native Americans, followed by the tongue-man, as found among the Australian aborigines. Finally, at the bottom of the hierarchy was the skin-man, as found among Africans (Gould, 1981). Doubtless, this scheme is errant and without merit; as mentioned, it reflected the values of early Western anthropologists. All senses, of course, are present in all cultures, although members of various cultures may appear to value one sense over another.

Symbolizing the Human Body

Humans create meaning by using symbols to represent everyday life. Objects, events, humans, indeed all things, are symbolized by humans in the sensemaking process (Strecker, 1988). As mentioned, the human body is presented in multiple ways in various cultures, ranging from colored bodies, as in the painted black bodies of ancient Mayans who associated black with evil and the underworld or the Blue Men who live among the Tuareg of the Sahara, so named for the color of dye that rubs onto the skin from their clothing.

The use of facial masks is an historic art form in China. Long hair was a symbol of manly strength, as in the Samson and Delilah story. The body is used even to convey class consciousness, as in the early Indian caste system where the human head represented the highest classes and the feet represented the outcastes. Goddesses and gods in early Greek and Roman times bore male and female images. In America, of course, the body is adorned, painted and colored to make one beautiful. In short, the body is the ultimate symbol (Vlahos, 1979).

Rituals associated with birth and death and all that is in between depict the body in various ways. The practices associated with birth and death vary highly between cultures as do rites of passage, such as firewalking. Common in various parts of the world, firewalking is used as a test of mind and spirit over matter. Painful flagellations, ear punctures or other forms of body infliction, are used in rites of passage to enable young males and females to pass into adulthood (Houseman, 1998;Turner,1967). Culture, ritual, place and pain are wound together in the practice of flagellation.

Both human and animal bodies are displayed in tourist places, as in postcards and other advertisements, and in zoos throughout the world as a form of staged tourism (Desmond, 1999). Public displays of corporeality reveal identity, gender, ethnicity and culture. Not only do people watch people but they are fascinated by the behaviors of other species, especially the behavior of animals like pandas (Allen, April, 2001)and chimps. In some countries where primates originate, they are often accorded mystical bonds with humans; in other countries, people are sometimes annoyed at the evolutionary association of humans with primates (Preuschoft, 2000). Yet, it seems that the more other species seem to mimic human behavior, as in zoos, the more popular they are.

Influences on Identity

Self and identity are associated concepts. Humans are uniquely able to take themselves as the object of their own thoughts (Mead, 1934). The ability to reflect on the self has deep implications for human behavior. For example, personal identity is often equated with ethnicity, which may be a concept applied to an individual or to a group. In extreme circumstances, discussed in Chapter Six, it may even become a euphemism for racism; that is, to be ethnic is some societies may mean that the ethnic member is socially ostracized by the group in power.

Identity may be conceived of as an unchanging fixed entity; however, it is a fluid concept. In this chapter, the reference is to the fact that individuals share the same history, origin or cultural heritage, even though their experiences may differ. For example, one might say he is an American, from the American culture; yet, he would have to define it further, perhaps by indicating that he is a child of Swedish immigrants who migrated to Minnesota. In short, the meaning of identity is a loose construction, somewhat mythicised (Abou, Spring, 1997). One's self identity is acculturated, which means that one acquires identity nonconsciously, not quite knowing how it happened. One gains a general semantic memory without having a specific episodic memory(Tulving, 1973). Identity is achieved but one may not be aware of the events and processes associated with the achievement. The concept of identity will be especially important in Chapters Five, Six, and Seven, where gender, ethnicity and age are discussed.

The Cultural Production of Face

It has been said that nonverbal communication is where nature meets culture. Biological and social aspects of behavior are brought together in nonverbal communication. An important concept is that of "face". The concept of face is symbolic and it involves how individuals think of thmselves. It refers not only to the physical face, but to the symbolic aspects of self-presentation. The symbolic face is part and parcel of identity. Psycho-socio-cultural processes are imbedded in the concept of face.

To have face is to have self-respect (Ting-Toomey, 1994). In Chinese culture, for example, mien-tzu refers to both a psychological and a social meaning of face, one that is conferred upon a deserving individual. In China, people are concerned most with their place in the scheme of things, their interconnectedness, following Confucian ideals. Thus the sense of self, of face, in China is very different from that found in the United States where a strong sense of personal independence is fostered (Stipek, 1998).

In Japan, the word kao may refer to the personal body, to personal psychology ot to social behavior. In short, the concept of face implies self-presentation. Because cultures have different display rules for self-presentation, misunderstandings can arise when persons are not informed about the norms of the culture they are visiting. For example, gift giving is an important activity in both North Amerian and Asian cultures. An American might open a gift immediately but the Chinese person would be embarrassed or affronted, feeling a loss of face, were she required to open the gift immediately.

The physical face of course is part of human anatomy. Considerable research has been conducted dealing with the face and how it expresses emotions, referring to the facial primacy hypothesis (Ekman, Friesen, Ellsworth, 1972). Everyday sense tells us that when people frown, grimace or smile they mean something by it. Exactly what they mean is not always clear. People may mask their feelings with a smile; they may play act with a frown; they may grimace but not be in pain. The frozen smile of many Native Americans or various Asian groups is worn in public, masking the inner thought-world and feelings of the individual. In brief, the information in body kinetics is open to interpretation. People may interpret human gestures stereotypically or they may interpret them polysemically. A smile can mean different things to different people.

Cultural Influences on the Senses

There may be a tendency for people to think of the senses as physiological mechanisms only, but the use of the senses, like the use of the face, is influenced by cultural meaning (Classen, 1997). Cultural values are expressed though the senses. Sensory symbolism refers to a social process. Were the readers of this book to travel to countries with contrasting historical and cultural backgrounds, they would note differences among cultures in the ways that they emphasize the senses-- seeing, hearing, smelling, tasting or touching. For example, in oral cultures where there is little print or television influence there is less emphasis upon the specific use of the eyes relative to the other senses than is found in the United States where "the educated eye", so to speak, is emphasized.

Odors and smells vary radically from country to country illustrating the cultural habits and values of the country involved. Tactility and proximal closeness are valued differently by different countries and cultures. The English do not touch one another in public, nearly as much as do the Puerto Ricans, for example. People experience the world through their senses, but their senses are heavily influenced by cultural norms (Classen, 1997).

People even dream about sensate things. In experiments, thirty-three percent of men and forty percent of women in the United States could recall having senses of taste or smell in their dreams. Auditory scenes occurred in approximately 53 percent of all dreams reported. Smell and taste sensations were reported in only 1% of the dreams (Zadra, Nielsen, Donderi, 1998).

It has been said that Americans hide and repress body odors, covering their bodies with perfumes. There is a blandness and sameness in American culture when it comes to body odors, according to this point of view. One ethnic group may claim that members of another group are identifiable by their body odors, as though individual members had body odor signatures.

National Geographic (Wysocki, 1987) reported the results of an international survey measuring smelling behaviors of men and women. The findings include the interesting results that females can smell better than can males and that some personal memories are based on smell. Subjects reported that they had experienced anosmia, or the loss of smell; of six categories of smell, 35 percent of the males and 29 percent of females were odor blind to androstenone (sweat) and galaxolide (musk). The study included the finding that smelling ability may be inherited. It may be inherited but it is overlaid by cultural factors. For example, people from various parts of the world difffered in their abilities to smell the six items. The smell scientist speculated that exposure to an element affects smelling abilities; therefore, different cultures, differentially exposed to smells, have different meanings and usages for smell.

The human ability to smell is not keen, at least when compared to the abilities of many lower order animals, such as dogs. Ethologists and animal communicologists show that nocturnal monkeys have a better sense of smell than do diurnal, or day monkeys Many animals, of course, use smells to mark their territories. This marking ability is less obvious in humans, although it seems to occur. People may be identified by the perfume odors that they wear, which is a matter of choice. Not a matter of choice are the body odors that are emitted from the skin; pheromone research may reveal how the human body emits barely detectable odors. Perhaps the role of human pheromones will become clear as research continues. The New York Times reported on September 28, 2000 that a human pheromone link may have been found by researchers at Rockefeller and Yale Universities. Meanwhile, advertisements proclaim the virtues of this or that perfume product.

Olfaction apparently works differently from the other senses. The olfactic bulb feeds directly into the most primitive part of the brain where it affects emotions, cognition and sexual response. Some evolutionists believe that the sense of smell was stronger in early evolutionary times than it is now, making it somewhat of an imperfect relic. Certainly arachmologists, or people who study human smelling behavior, and perfume makers are keenly interested in smell (Arachmologists, Nov 10, 1997).

For example, touching behavior has been studied quite thoroughly. In the United States, touching activity varies by gender, by place in society and by empowerment. A touching orientation is more commonly associated witih females than it is with males (Dolin, Booth-Butterfield, 1993). Social touch has been related to social competence by some researchers (Jones, 1994). Interestingly, it has been said that Americans suffer from tactile deprivation noted, especially, in the situation in which a mother, herself deprived of a healthy attachment style during early childhood, fails to bond with her child through gentle touch (Bowlby, 1969; Jones & Brown, 1996). The power of gentling and bonding has been amply demonstrated not only in human studies but in studies or lower order primates. Grooming, licking and nudging are intimate ways to help lower order animals raise their offspring (Eibl-Eibestadt, 1975). Healthy human attachment and growth depend on the caring touch as well. Indeed, childhood psychotherapists speak of attachment disorders that afflict young children who have not been cared for in loving, tactile ways.

Cultural Influences on the Emotions

The study of the emotions has received considerable attention because they invariably accompany both verbal and nonverbal expression. The spoken language reveals emotional affect (Besnier, 1990). The primacy of the face in showing emotions has been noted. Research suggests that emotional expressions as shown by the face have minimum universality; that is, various cultures share in common some features of emotional expression (Russell & Fernandez-Dols, 1997) although they may interpret emotional expressions variously. For example, a smile is used by members of all cultures; however, the meaning of the smile is interpreted by taking account of the display rules in that culture. A smile may be used to mask hidden feelings and people can create a facial display without having a corresponding emotion. Indeed, it has been suggested that females in many cultures tend to exhibit a politeness bias, using a smile to do so. The argument about the universality of both language and emotions has continued over the past few years.

Six emotions, known in all cultures, have been studied fairly intensively. They are surprise, fear, disgust, anger, happiness and sadness. Sometimes the emotion labeled interest is added, resulting in the acronym SADFISH (Ekman, 1975). When surprise is shown in these studies, the brows are raised, the eyelids are opened wide and the white of the eye shows more than it does when the eyes are in a resting position. Facial blending, or the interaction of the eyes with the rest of the face is common, resulting in perceived anger or disgust, for example. Attempts have been made to see if members of different cultures perceive the displayed emotions in the same way. It appears, however, that there is minimal universality. That is, members of different cultures will view the emotions in different ways due to enculturation. Some emotions are easier to interpret than are others. Studies reveal that subjects are better at detecting happiness than they are at detecting disgust, for example. Perhaps they are better at displaying certain emotions as well.

Framing Emotions

Researchers have shown how emotional signals are used adaptively and when they are formed in a child's life (Morris, 1992). For example, distress signals are displayed at birth, the baby emerging into a booming, buzzing world of confusion. The social smile is displayed between 8 and 10 months of age; joy is shown by the age of 5-7 months. In short, childhood growth is patterned.(Bruner, 1990) These behaviors may vary from culture to culture. Emotions are revealed in culture-specific ways. Again, it must be emphasized that humans slowly and gradually learn how to take account of the social influences found in their cultures; they make sense of those influences and develop lines of action accordingly. They learn how to present themselves appropriately in a variety of contexts.

Cultural Influences on Body Language, Posture and Gesture

The human body mediates all reflection and action upon the world (Lock, 1993) and it has often been the subject of topics dealing with reproduction, the emotions, human sexuality and shamanism. It is assumed that culture provides the necessary labels for biological and behavioral acts (Ellen, 1984). Cultural symbols for the body vary from culture to culture. The human body has been somatyped in various ways.

Action theorists explain that there is a mind-body connection; actions are tied into antecedent thoughts. Mind, self and interacton are inherently bound together. People often make careful plans and then follow them after which they are able to explain what they have done (Vallacher & Wegner, 1985). Following the SI approach, humans make sense of what they are doing. Their lines of action are often carefully crafted, even though, at times, humans seem to be on automatic pilot, doing even complicated things, apparently without thinking or planning. Researchers refer to body actions as kinesics.

The term kinesics is often translated as body language, body idiom or gesture language (Key, 1980), each suggesting the intimately connected nature of gestures and kinesics. Posture is the key element in kinesics. Gestures are usually localized involving only the face, the upper torso or the hands and fingers. Emblems, unlike much kinesic behavior, can stand alone, without verbal accompaniment. The shaking of hands, a ritual in many cultures, may be done without words being spoken; yet people know what it means. Cultural patterns are revealed in greeting rituals varying considerably from country to country. The Russian bear hug, the Eskimo nose rub, the arm grasp and the handshake are greeting patterns that are assumed to be the norm in each culture in which they are used. It is important to note that people are not required to know the origin of their greeting habits in order to use them efficiently and effectively. People present themselves to others using simple handshakes, gestures or gazes.

Body presentational practices vary widely between cultures. For example, women in the United States are taught to keep their legs together, unless they are wearing jeans, while men cross their legs. Inheriting the Judeo-Christian tradition, young Americans learn the place of modesty, although they may choose to ignore the underlying assumptions. Traditional Asian cultures require women to walk behind men. In India, women whose husbands died, were expected to be burned on the same funeral pyre with their dead husbands. This extreme practice, called suttee in India, is now disallowed, but it revealed the values and practices associated with some classes in India.

Hidden cultural display rules are obviously powerful; members must make sense of these display rules and incorporate them or risk being shunned or even banned in some circumstances. Indeed, shunning, or the banning of members for failing to fulfill the expectations of the social group of which they are members, is not an uncommon practice, even in the United States. Marrying an English, a reference to people outside their faith, is forbidden among conservative Amish groups. By marrying outside the faith and practices of the Amish, a person risks losing Amish identity. As mentioned, some cultural groups impress upon their members very clearly what is expected of them. Other groups are loosely knit, permitting a variety of behavioral patterns.

Twenty key gestures, including actions such as the fingertip kiss, the head toss and the thumps up gestures, were analyzed in 25 different countries, within 40 different contexts, involving 15 different languages. Showing pictographs, researchers asked the 1200 research subjects what each pictograph meant to them (Morris, 1994). The results showed that natives in neighboring countries often shared similar interpretations of the gestures while more remote natives varied in their interpretations. Distance was a key factor. The authors concluded that prejudice and religious beliefs, incorporated in language, influenced the gestural meanings. For example, where it is forbidden to display explicit sexual gestures, it may also be forbidden to display a simple finger kiss. The display rules in various cultures signal what is appropriate and what is taboo. A very large array of nonverbal gestures have been categorized and sorted out; the result is that a dictionary of emblems is available to the researcher or reader (Morris, 1994).

Body language complements verbal language in a synchronous manner (Bull, 1987). When humans speak vocally, their bodies "speak" nonvocally. As a topic shifts, the body may shift; even the vocal pattern changes at the end of a sentence. Eye use is correlated with the flow of speech as well. A person may look away or down, when she ends a sentence. In short, the senses and the body parts work together in human interaction, blending in a reportoire of bodily action. The eyes, however, have primacy in interaction.

Although people learn how to use their eyes in interaction, learning it from their parents and peers, even congenitally blind speakers use their eyes despite their lack of visual models (Iverson, Goldin-Meadow, 1998). Further, it has been shown that babies born blind smile just as do their sighted peers. In fact, they apparently use body gestures structured like sentences and words. Therefore, a nature-nurture controversy exists, as to the sociobiological origin of gestures. Continued research will ferret out the relationships between what comes "naturally" and what is learned.

Meanwhile, it seems clear that context affects the use of gestures. Symbolic interactionism emphasizes the creative nature of human communication; humans must take into account the social influences of context, but they act on their own behalf, creatively. For example, it is considered inappropriate for young Japanese children to look their elders directly in the eyes. Contrarily, in the United States, it is believed that a person is lying if she or he does not look the adult in the eyes! The stereotypical perception of the shifty-eyed person is that she or he is lying, trying to deceive. It is sometimes said that the eyes are the window to the soul in this context. What might this mean?

Culture and Collective Nonverbal Communication

Cultural Symbols

Symbols are cultural products (Strecker, 1988). They are short-cuts to meaning. Created by humans, they take on a life of their own, existently independently of individuals. Symbols represent cultural beliefs, customs and practices. They exist "out there", enduring over time. Human language is symbolic; the human body is symbolized. Even human tools become symbolic; the hammer is associated with the carpenter; books are associated with people in academia, and so on. Symbols are carriers of coded information (Szanto, 1991, Aug) providing meaning to the individuals who use them. The computer is a tool that provides and organizes information; it also symbolizes a level of understanding to its users.

Symbols may be iconic and they may signal things. Elvis Presley, is to many, an American icon. The Statue of Liberty is a symbol of hope to many; it is visually iconic, sending meaningful signals to people who immigrate to the United States. Symbols are indicators of the aspirations, belief systems and neuroses of the cultures that generate them (Page, 1992). Thus, the cross has come to signify Christian cultures; the Swastika, once an honored symbol in India, became a hideous symbol used by Hitler. All cultures have symbols, such as flags, to help identify and unite the members of that society. In short, people respond to symbols, as a form of signal response. Humans create symbols and they become part of cultural transmission. Many of them are master symbols; that is, they enjoy special status among people. For example, the cat became a powerful symbol in early Egypt after it rid the granaries of mice and rats. The cat was gradually elevated to mythical, symbolic status.

Modern symbols are exported in the diffusion of innovation (Rogers & Shoemaker, 1971) process. The logos of modern, powerful companies are exported around the globe, influencing various cultures. People may think of Nestles or Hersheys when they think about chocolate, the association having been made so clear by those chocolate companies. People who live outside that influence, of course, do not recognize the symbols. Inhabitants of the deep forests of New Guinea know less about Western symbols that do the French, for example. Their vocabulary does not include names for symbols with which they are unfamiliar. Yet, some symbols are known throughout the world. The author bought a Coca-Cola from a small boy at the top of a pyramid in the heart of the Guatemalan jungle. Vegetarian hamburgers are sold by MacDonald's in India.

Iconography is a field of study devoted to the study of visual symbols. An icon is a symbolic image. They exist in all cultures, some sacred, and others secular. The minnarets of the Muslim faith are recognized throughout the Muslim world, as are the veils worn by women. Words, too, can be iconic. For example, Superman comics contained the words "zow" and "kerplat" to indicate the physical prowess of Superman. Computer literate people know what an emoticon is but the young man driving the Amish horse-drawn carriage may know little about them. Context, once again, is important in human communication. It is suggested that members of highly developed technological societies are in the midst of an icon revolution, given the fast pace of change.

Symbols, Beliefs and Behaviors

Symbols need not be physical objects or icons. Activities, relationships, events, gestures and ritualistic activities are symbolic, too (Turner, 1986). People make symbolic sense of these activities. Symbols and their uses change over time. One point of view suggests that dominant American symbols once associated with religion or faith, both considered vertical dimensions, are now replaced by symbols that are rooted in a mass culture. The stock market, for example, is conceived from this point of view as a bottomline activity. The God(s) of the rural farmer are not those of the modern businessman, the assumption goes. The plow, not a product of mass culture, has given over to the computer and television, both mass products.

In pre-technical oral societies the NBC peacock is not known, but the symbols and rites of the shaman and the spiritual diviners may be. The churinga is a symbol known in primal and oral cultures, but not known to most Westerners. The Artic Eskimo, whose traditional culture is rapidly dissipating, believed in a mythical goddess, half human and half fish, called Sedna or Takanaluk, who lived in a cave under the sea, where she kept the animals of the sea and gave them to the Eskimo who followed the proper rituals (Hinnells, 1997). The Plains Indians used the tipi, referred to as teepees by outsiders, which was conical in shape, representing cosmological ideas; its structure represented the native's world or universe. Fire within the tipi represented the Great Mysterious and the smoke going through the hole in the top of the tipi represented liberation. The Navajo tribe, which borrowed and used the tipi, have similar traditions, although their structures are more likely to be round-shaped hogans.

Symbols may be dominant or instrumental, depending on their use in rituals or ceremonies. For example, traditionally, the wearing of the Japanese kimono is an expression of transcendent cultural values and the way they are worn is instrumental. Young Japanese girls are taught to move so that the lines of the kimono are kept straight; only the proper amount of flesh is shown to the public. Further, young Japanese ladies must not step up to another level within a home withour taking their shoes off. They should cover their mouth when they laugh and control their emotions.

Paralanguage

Language use expresses more than the spoken message; there is an intimate connection between body expression and language development. For example, the human voice has acoustic properties, such as speed of talking, pitch or intensity, which condition the message stream and affect how a message is interpreted. An excited voice conveys different information to the listener than does a languorous voice. People determine, often stereotypically, the character or personalities of others based on their vocal patterns (Mahl, 1987). Voices are thought to be sexy, masculine, feminine, weak or strong, based almost exclusively on how they sound to the listener (Pittam, 1994). The trained voice of the opera singer is very different from the voice of the throat singer of a remote tribe, their training being based on very different cultural assumptions.

Researchers indicate that a voice in Western societies conveys masculinity when it resonates strongly; a mellow, more warm voice conveys femininity. Some research suggests that humans have vocal signatures. Indeed, people recognize one another by the vocal patterns being displayed. They know who is on the other end of the telephone without seeing them.

Cultural regions vary paralinguistically. It is shown, for example, that Mediterranean people and people from Latin American countries are more likely to be demonstrative and to use more emotion laden speech than are people from English cultures. These are tendencies. Problems arise, of course, when people create stereotypes of others from cultures different from their own. In another vein, the concept of floor management is associated with paralinguistic behavior. People hold and maintain the floor when they interact with others. For example, it has been shown that members of Japanese culture tend to talk simultaneously but that their nonverbal behavior is rhythmic and coordinated . They use back-channeling effectively, letting the other party know that they are listening. Backchanneling can take the form of uh huh or of silent attention. Holding the floor too long or making huge gestures while speaking is considerate impolite to the Japanese (Hayashi, 1996).

Because of cultural differences, Japanese and Americans, each unfamiliar with the others' display rules may feel a sense of arhythmicity. Studies show that American males, for example, use more floor space than do females and they tend to be more aggressive in their behaviors, in contrast to the Japanese. Thus, the Japanese and the Americans may use different rules and assumptions about turn-taking, turn yielding and turn requesting, each critical pieces of floor management (Hayashi, 1996). Even using the eyes to signal the end of a turn may vary between cultures.

In Arab countries, loudness may be suggestive of strength and sincerity and softness may suggest weakness and deviousness (Hall, 1966). Members of black communities use pauses differently than do members of white cultures. A faster speed of talking is associated with Latin cultures compared to people in the United States.

The concept of voice-set is important (Pittam, 1994). Two people, perhaps an older person and a younger person, may utter the same phrase, with the same emphasis, but differences will be shown by their set of voice, a fundamental part of their physiological and social development. Age, gender and ethnicity and even the influence of technologies are shown paralinguistically in human behaviors. The role of silence, not well investigated cross-culturally, is keen; by saying and doing nothing, humans influence one another, as in the silent stare of the mother who is disciplining her child. Silence plays an important role in nonverbal communication.

Rituals and Ceremonies

Nonverbal communication involves both individual and collective behaviors. Performative acts, resulting in theatre, ceremony; ritual and spectacle are forms of nonverbal communication that remind people of their culture, their past, present or future, and provide means of identity (Beeman, 1993; Turner, 1986). Ritual performances in Bali or New Guinea, such as Trance and Dance, may seem bizarre to Americans, but they reveal the power of meaningful ritual to the people involved. The kabuki, in Japan, a shrine-based folk dance and drama, and the Native-American rain dance are familiar to people through movies and television, but most Americans never see in person the more mysterious rituals of people who live in oral cultures.

Rituals are communal activities bonding people together. Just as individual nonverbal communication is often intentional, collective nonverbal communication is intentional although participants may not fully understand the symbolic meanings behind the activity. Most people are familiar with the ritualistic and ceremonial activities found in marriage, courtship and sports activities, but they may fail to see or understand the deeper meaning of these performances, even though they take part in them.

Except in very primal and past-oriented societies, rituals and ceremonies change, especially when Western technology permeates cultures. In societies marked by change, new rituals and ceremonies are invented or old ones are modified. In contrast, oral societies are slow to change; for example, the Yanesha tribes in Amazonia write history into the landscape, using topographs to convey ritual meaning to members of the tribe. The Yanesha are preliterate but their use of topographic writing successfully transmits cultural history and symbols to new members of the culture (Santos-Granero, 1998). Contrast that ritualism with the modern phenomenon called the Rave, where some young Americans ritualistically take part in large musical gatherings, sometimes involving drug use.

Framing Initiation Rituals

In Australia, among the Aranda, male rite initiation includes being tossed in the air and hit with sticks. the young person may be circumcised and the head opened, scarred by having a name carved on the forehead. They may even be smoked and dried out over fires, as part of the initiation rite into manhood (Houseman, 1998). These rituals are used to bind the past and the present together in specific nonverbal ritualistic and collective acts.

In the United States and other countries, hazing can take the form of painful encounter. Outlawed by the military and by many universities and colleges, hazing pain might be psychological or physical. As part of the teenage culture, it may be a way to embarrass a new member of a club, such as making him walk with a can on his head, or, it may be an act of force, requiring the recruit to get drunk by drinking exorbitantly.

Wedding customs contain aspects of ritual and ceremony together, varying widely throughout the world. For example, in times of slavery in the United States, African men and women were not allowed to marry, but a couple could publicly declare their mutual love by jumping over a broomstick to the accompaniment of drums.

Ritualistic, ceremonial collective nonverbal communication exists in all cultures defined by underlying cultural codes, histories and beliefs. They occur in war and in religion; they are part of the daily lives of the members of each culture, binding them to the culture. Such activities may be passed on from generation to generation by story-tellers, shamans, priests and others. In technologically advanced cultures, they are passed along by the media, including libraries. Each generation passes along to the next that which has been received. It traditional societies, the older person passes on knowledge to the young; in modern societies, the young may teach the older person, as is often the situation with the use of computers.

Background Factors and Nonverbal Communication

The General Environment

While it is true that many preliterate natives or citizens live in cultural environments that have few, if any, modern technologies, most people live in environments that have been influenced by the use of modern technology. The lives of preliterate tribes in the Amazon jungle are very different from the lives of people who live in Hong Kong, Tokyo, Berlin or New York City. All aspects of their existence are different, from food gathering to burial ceremonies.

The general environment deeply influences human behaviors, referring to both the natural world and the social world, interacting together. The reliance upon plants, roots, snakes, bugs and various worms and grubs for food is not uncommon in rural societies where modern, packaged foods do not exist. An example from the Northern latitudes where Eskimos ate whale and seal blubber, used the fur from polar bears and produced burnable supplies of oil from their fat is another contrasting example of the influence of the general environment upon human behavior. In modern Western societies, the influence of the general environment is just as keen, although it may not be so easily discerned. One of the influences is noted in how humans perceive time.

Chronemics: Culture and Time

Time, like space, is a hidden dimension affecting nonverbal communication. Western cultures are said to be clock-bound, having a standard meaning for time, a mechanical ideal (Bruneau, 1977; Gonzales & Zimbardo, 1990). Members are clock-bound. For example, people in management positions in the United States often take courses in time management. Vacations, on the other hand, are designed to help people forget the clock. Views of time are shaped by perceptions that are rooted in cultural and social codes. Cultures that focus on the present use objective, linear time. Time in the United States, is a powerful influence on daily behavior (Deegan,1989).

Scholars suggest that there are many forms of time. For example, there are biological, perceptual, conceptual, psychological and social concepts of time(Bruneau, 1977). Time may be monochronic or polychronic (Hall, 1973) indicating that some societies have a uniform and singular meaning of time while others have multiple meanings. Following this reasoning, people in the United States have a monochronic view of time. Western time begins in Greenwich, England.

By contrast, the Navajo tribe marked time by following the seasons. Watches were not useful in traditional Navajo culture, although that is changing. It is not uncommon for Native Americans, especially those who belong to the Longhouse tradition, to ignore the time of the Christianized White man, who is bound to the clock. Native American children who attend schools in the White world may arrive late following their own time schedule. This behavior, of course, is not designed to disturb teachers or principals. Rather, it reflects how time is conceived in the Longhouse tradition, as on the Iriquois reservation in up-state New York. The author taught Indian children who either came from the Christian or the Longhouse side of the reservation, their values differing accordingly.

On a personal level, people know one another by their use of time. Some arrive at functions typically late or early. Some, as mentioned, seem to function best at night while others go to bed and rise early, like owls or sparrows. Humans have built-in and learned needs that affect how they behave in time. Married partners may be affected badly when one needs only two hours of sleep and the other needs ten! Personal time zones, or individualized ways of viewing time, have been outlined by researchers (Gonzalez & Zimbardo, 1990).

Lower order animal behavior has been studied showing how different species react to time changes. Both diurnal and seasonal changes are expressed in their behaviors, from feeding patterns to denning. Clearly, time and its correlates affect nonverbal communication. Even the aging process is cast in chronology. Time speaks! What it is saying must be interpreted.

Proxemics: Culture and Space

With few exceptions, animals defend their territory. Although animals may allow other kinds of species into their territory, they are not likely to permit animals of its own species into that protected territory, especially during rutting or mating season, as in the case of deer. This territorial imperative operates differently in different species. For example, bears and moose range widely, but a chipmunk might stay in a relatively small area for a lifetime.

It is not clear that humans use territories in the same way, although human use of space appears, in some ways, to be an extension of the principle (Ardrey, 1966). Humans create national boundaries and they keep enemies out of their territory. Humans put fences between themselves and their neighbors. In short, humans have a sense of home, of place, of situation to which they attach meanings and emotions. Those places may be marked by language usage, by urban buildings or rural fields, by status in community, or by some other means. Humans create and respond to places, such as sacred places, the south versus the north, features in the environment and so on (Gallagher, 1993).

Culture influences how humans use space. What is crowding to an American does not appear to be so to a Chinese person, migrating to America, who may choose, perhaps from necessity, to live in very crowded conditions, several persons to a room. Apparently they endure the crowded conditions out of economic need but their cultural norms influence them as well. The Chinese are more communal than are Americans (Takaki, 1993). Chinese, especially those raised under Confucianism, are taught about we-ness as opposed to I-ness. Thus, a Chinese person in this example can tolerate smaller spaces than can an American (NPR, Mar 23, 1997).

The Navajo sense of place, their spiritual homelands, is associated with the New Mexico and Arizona border. Cubans, who emigrated to the United States, under forced exile, established Little Havana in Miami, as a home away from home, although they settled in many other places as well. The Chinese who came to the United States to work in the gold mines and railroad construction gradually moved into enclaves, such as Chinatown in the Bowery region of New York City. Black Americans, of course, have established homelands throughout the United States. People create a cultural sense of place. Their children are born into it and identify with it. Proxemics is a word that refers to space. Humans need their space just as lower order animals need their territories. In many ways, the rugged individualism of American life was expressed by the wide open West. "Go West young man" was a phrase that captured the ear of many young men and families. Their place was to be found in open spaces.

Cultures have been described as generally non-contact or contact (Hall, 1973); that is, some cultures emphasize the need for considerable personal space and others need less. Zero proxemics is a term used to express very close contact between humans. It is said that Latin Americans and Mediterraneans are basically contact cultures while many Western soceietes, including Britain, reflect a non-contact orientation. Even intimate eye-contact may be shunned in non-contact countries. Accidental touching in elevators is uncomfortable to many people who are 'civilly inattentive'(Goffman, 1967) in the situation.

Framing Proxemics

Cultures have been lumped together by whether they were contact or non-contact cultures. Findings suggest that Greek and Italians in dyads use touch more than do English, French or Dutch people in dyads. Scots and Irish, apparently, use an intermediate amount of touch. People older than 40 years of age, in dyads, appear to use less touch than do people of younger ages. Although females appear to touch more than do males, the circumstances of their touching affect their behaviors. In short, cultural codes influence people to act along permissible lines of touching.

Sociometric research reveals that touching codes vary widely from culture to culture. Distance between males and females is required in many Muslim countries but in other contact cultures public displays of handholding are permitted. Professional people, such as doctors, exhibit professional touch, a type of touch that is not permitted in other situations (Jones, 1994). Space violation occurs when people invade the space of others without being invited.

Differences in the use of space by members of different cultures may lead to exaggerated or stereotyped perceptions. Many Latin Americans might consider North Americans to be cold and distant while many North Americans might say that Latin Americans like to breathe down your neck. Such stereotypes of course can lead to considerable confusion for travelers. Germans, it is thought, place a high value on orderliness and neatness, everything being in its appropriate place. Japanese, on the other hand, do not think of space as being empty, as an American might; interestingly, until recently, they did not name their streets. indeed, they did not have names for their streets in the age of rickshaws. Corners were special places for them (Leathers, 1978). In studying the spatial behaviors of members of various cultures, it is important to realize that not all members think or behave in the same ways.

Researchers have created a lexicon for space including such terms as primary, secondary, public, interactional and body territories to describe the patterned ways that humans use space (Altman, 1975). Body space is the space that a body takes up; primary space is personal, private space; secondary space may be a bar or church; home territory is under the exclusive control of certain groups, such as clubs; and interactional territory allows unfettered interaction movement.

The architecture of various cultures reflects the unwritten codes that influence the building of the structures. The Spanish plaza is found in cities in Hispanic countries; open spaces mark the Navajo culture. Migrating tribes in Africa build temporary homes for shelter, intended to last but a short time, perhaps a season. Space has symbolic meaning in each culture; its use reflects underlying values. Prisons are designed to restrict the use of space by inmates, as a form of punishment. Goffman referred to prisons as total institutions, places that controlled all aspects of a person's life. The use of space is an important aspect of nonverbal communication.

Symbolic interactionism is an approach that reveals how people live their lives and how they enact strategies for living. Humans try to make sense of the givens of their culture and to enact lines of action that make sense to them, whether they are engaging in dyadic or ceremonial interaction. People accept the stuff of culture; they also modify it. Either way, cultural influences on human behavior are profound.

The Geo-techno Dimension

As will be discussed in chapter eight, modern technologies are altering the landscape of human behavior, not only in highly developed modern states but around the globe. Technological diffusion is reshaping many cultures; as traditional and past oriented societies gain access to modern communicative technologies their social practices are altered. Communicative tools mediate human societies, transforming them.

One of the key changes wrought by global technologies, such as the internet, satellites, film and television and the emerging widespread use of the cell phone, is in the concept of geo-techno space. (3) No longer bound by national or regional boundaries, humans can be in touch with others instantly. Although the great digital divide discussed in chapter nine still exists, the communication landscape of the future will profoundly influence how humans act and interact in terms of time and place (Lebow, 1995, McLuhan, 1964;Mowlana, 1996).

Cyberplace, cyberspace, cyberreality are neologisms that reflect the changes that are occurring. It is true that many highly controlled societies, such as the Iraqi and the Chinese or other theocratic countries and groups, such as the Taliban in Afghanistan, do not permit their citizens to interact with others on the internet, nor do they want their people to get their information from the Americans or from some other European media. It is also true that some highly remote tribes and societies do not have access to modern communicative technologies. Nevertheless, the great technological diaspora is reshaping many cultures around the globe. Nonverbal behaviors and practices are reshaped accordingly.

Summary

Through the enculturation process, human beings learn to identify themselves and to behave in accordance with cultural display rules. culture. Cultures vary one from the other along dimensional lines, such as the matriarchal or patriarchal orientation or the past-future orientation. Humans learn about master symbols, customs and rituals in their cultures and employ them in meaningful ways. Symbols are deeply immersed in the thoughtways of any culture. Not only are they deeply influenced by the many symbols of their cultures, humans are also deeply influenced environmental factors, such as how time and space are defined and used. The diffusion of technology has led to the emergence of a new geo-techno dimension and it is beginning to affect all cultures around the globe. Time, space, place are altered by modern communicative technologies. In chapter three, important social processes that influence human nonverbal communication will be discussed.

Questions for Thought and Discussion

1.   Cultures contain hidden codes that influence the way that the members of that culture act. Can you think of nonverbal communicative behaviors that illustrate this process?

2.   Master symbols are deeply imbedded in every culture. What master symbols come to mind when you think of American culture? What master symbols come to mind when you think of the Chinese culture? What do the symbols mean to you?

3.   Colors have come to mean different things to people in different cultures. What colors do you associate with European royalty? With the American medical profession? With the legal profession? How are colors used in public buildings?

4.   One of the features of any culture is its music. Discuss how you think that people from different backgrounds use music. For example, aged people tend to use music differently from young people. Blacks and Hispanics tend to show different preferences for music. Can you describe those preferences and suggest how the music reflects the identity of each person? Are there gender preferences as well?

5.   As discussed in this chapter, the human body is symbolized differently in different cultures. What are some of the ways that the body is symbolized in American life? What are stereotypes that humans sometimes use to describe body? Think of the role of gender, ethnicity, and age, as you try to answer the question.

Notes

1.   The word culture, according to Edward T. Hall, in The Silent Language, Doubleday & Company, 1973, was first defined in print by E.B. Tylor in 1871; the definition, however, was broad, needing refinement if good research was to be done. A.L. Kroeber and Clyde Kluckhohn, two prominent anthropologists, emphasized empathy as a necessary ingredient for a productive study of humans. The units of analysis, so necessary to good science, however, were lacking in their time. Hall emphasized that culture is exhibited "out-of-awarness"; that is, humans may not able to notice how they are influenced by culture.

2.   Hall used a tripartite model of culture (informal, formal and technical) to give structure to their study and created a theory of culture, or infra-culture that rested on an evolutionary, biological base and that included a primary message system, including interaction, association, subsistence, bisexuality, territoriality, temporality, learning, play, defense and exploitation. See especially chapters two and three. Other anthropological systems of thought have been developed as well, as used in the text.

3.   The emphasis upon the creativity of individuals is a key aspect of the SI approach. Unlike many other research approaches to human behavior, SI focuses on the living worlds of the subjects and on the meanings that subjects create in their interactions. It is a type of sociology of everyday life. By removing themselves from the participants' lived world, researchers who use only a laboratory approach to study human behavior lose the insights of the subjects. See chapter nine, the methods section especially.

4.   It is tempting to say that technology, culture, social processes and so on do things to individuals or influence them. Actually, nonliving objects and processes do not do anything. Rather, individuals who confront

the stuff of society create the meanings. Things do not have meanings within themselves; only humans create meanings. The word is not the thing, as semanticists assure readers.

Suggested Readings

Becker, H. S., & McCall, M. M. (Eds.) (1990). *Symbolic Interactionism and Cultural Studies.* Chicago: University of Chicago Press.

Desmond, J. C. (1999). *Staging Tourism: Bodies on Display from Waikiki to Sea World.* Chicago: University of Chicago Press.

Hall, E. T. (1973). *The Silent Language.* Garden City, NY: Anchor/Doubleday.

Samovar, L. A., & Porter, R. E. (1988). *Intercultural Communication: A Reader.* Belmont, CA: Wadsworth Publishing Company.

Strecker, I (1988). *The Social Practice of Symbolization: An Anthropological Analysis.* New York: Athlone Press.

Chapter 3
Social Influences on Nonverbal Communication
Making Sense of Social Processes

Chapter Overview

In this chapter, some of the topics addressed in chapter one are revisited here, discussed from a sociological perspective. They are themes that wend their way through the the book. Anthropologists, sociologists and psychologists may address the same themes, but they research them in different ways.

Human society is created by humans; in turn, it influences human behavior dramatically and thoroughly. Over time, the interactive behaviors of humans build up a dynamic collectivity, a society. Individuals born into that society may think that the society is fixed, unchanging and enduring because they do not realize that humans create, maintain and modify it. Parents and grandparents, raised under different circumstances than their offspring, behaved quite differently from them. Social change is fast-paced in modern technological societies. When structural changes occur in societies, they influence how people live and behave.

Humans are situated within their society (Carbaugh, 1996; Ellis, 1999); that is, they enact behaviors that make sense to them in terms of where they were born or grew up. Born poor, they enact behaviors that are very different from those who are born to wealth. As noted in the previous chapter, people create a sense of place, a home located somewhere in society, from which they operate and live out their lives. These places change as people move about in society.

Institutions, such as the family, peer groups, schools, religious groups and the media influence human nonverbal communication. Humans act, based on social perceptions that are rooted in their experiences. People try to act appropriately following social expectations. The clothes that people wear, their accents, the foods they eat, and their social behaviors are linked to their situation in society. Background factors, such as age, gender, ethnicity and technology influence human behaviors profoundly. The concept of identity, discussed in general, cultural terms in the previous chapter, is discussed more precisely in this chapter, as sense of self created through the influence of socialization processes (Abrams & Hogg, 1990; Giddens, 1991;Grodin & Lindlof, 1996, Weigert, 1986).

Societies are about collectivities and collective behaviors. Yet, it is about how the individual identifies herself or himself within it that is important. Humans go through life altering their perceptions as they experience new situations. This chapter points to the key factors in society that influence human nonverbal communication. The SI approach is used throughout; it was in the study of society that the main concepts behind the SI approach were developed. Although scholars within the SI approach differ among themselves about how to study society, there is a general coherence overall. Readers will find these differences and similarities described in chapter nine.

A point should be made concerning the differences between a culture and a society. There are no sharp differences but there is a matter of emphasis. Speaking generally, anthropologists have traditionally focused on broad features of a milieau, such as religion, technology, kinship systems, beliefs, languages and thoughtways. Their work was often performed in oral pre-literate societies. Sociologists have tended to focus on human identity achieved through socialization processes. Their emphasis is upon the nature of human groups, institutions, social inequality and the use of power by social elites (Stryker, 1980, 1981). Their studies focus on topics, ranging from the individual in society to the structural elements of a society.

Social Interaction and the Construction of Meaning

Sensemaking or the 'logic in use'

Humans vary considerably in the ways that they conceive of themselves, in the ways they act, and in the ways that they interpret the behavior of others. Yet, they share intersubjectively in behaviors that are common in their society; otherwise it would not be possible to take part in social networks. The everyday reasoning and construal of the meaning of things is sometimes referred to as a logic-in-use. Although the SI approach is broadly compatible with a variety of other approaches, such as social cognition theory and other interactionist approaches, the basis of SI is the subjective experience referred to in this book as sensemaking, an interpretive process. Humans strive to make sense of their social worlds; they internalize the meanings that are generated from interaction with others; they make sense of the actions of others; they create lines of action to respond to the perceived demands of a situation. They engage in joint interactions with others. Throughout this process, humans symbolize the self, others and events through perceptual processes (Mead, 1934;Cooley, 1970; Jones, 1990). People label the objects of their social world, reflecting their perceptions. By naming things, people frame and interpret them. Human behavior becomes patterned and recognized. Indeed, there is a sociology of the emotions, different patterns of emotional display characterizing various groups in American life (MacKinnon, 1994). People try to manage their feelings, which, over a period of time reflect patterned ways of dealing with them.

Human relationships are created. For example, partners in a dyadic relationship define their relationship as a kind of symbolic baby. The relationship is something they created together, existing separately from each of the parties. People identify relationships based on their meanings. A special boyfriend treats his special girlfriend differently from the ways that he treats his friends. They respond mutually in terms that they have created, drawing upon their tacit knowledge of expected romantic behavior. It may not be obvious, but each party in a relationship has an implicit set of rules, a definitional frame for that relationship. People sort out what kind of relationship they have with others, which influences how they will behave.

Framing Interaction Ritual

Erving Goffman, a dramaturgist who influenced the growth and development of symbolic interactionist theory, studied the ritualistic nature of human interactions focusing on daily life. He unmasked everyday behavior. He stressed that people have reasons to behave; they performed 'face-work' in their relations with others, exhibiting deference and demeanor. He believed that people try to avoid embarrassment, to meet the perceived expectations of others and the perceived demands of the situation.

Humans may isolate themselves from interaction, developing behavioral and mental symptoms that separate them from others. People may simply withdraw from others, taking the risks involved. Not all people have an 'interaction consciousness' that tells them when an interaction is going well. They can lose "other-consciousness" by being distracted, the result being an unfocused interaction. (Goffman, 1967) Goffman developed the dramaturgical metaphor in his analysis of human behavior. Humans were on stage, acting in front of an audience, following scripted lines.

Human behavior is both creative and adaptive but it is their definition of the situation that influences how people will behave. Sociologists who study everyday 'natural' behaviors from an SI perspective (Denzin, 1971; Weigert, 1997) attempt to make relevant that which is often obscure. They analyze everyday life, unmasking it, following a logic of implicature, uncovering the deeper meanings to be found in ordinary human events. That which seems to be routine or unimportant to many people may be a rich source of information for the insightful sociologist or analyst.

Revisiting Symbolization

As mentioned, symbols are created by humans; yet, they may take on a life of their own, used again and again over long periods of time by different members of a society. They are intersubjective, interpretive tools although they may not convey exactly the same meaning to each individual. (Duncan, 1968; Stevens, 1998). People are practical semioticians; they symbolically construct the self (Hewitt, 1999); they symbolically construct community (Cohen, 1989). It is because humans are fairly predictable about their use of symbols that society has an integrity. For example, the national elections for the president of the United States are predictable because demographers know about the symbolic patterns of the voters, the patterned semantics of being Republican or Democrat.

Framing the Importance of Symbols

Humans act in a social world that has been constructed symbolically. Without shared symbolic representations, humans could not interact successfully. That is, all humans create individual meanings for the objects in their world, such as cars, the stock market, schools, families and so on but it is in the intersubjective aspects, the shared aspects of this symbolization, that human interaction is possible. Symbols, by themselves, do not have meaning; the meaning is attached to the symbol by the individual. New symbols are created to represent new says of thinking about everyday matters. Language, of course, is inherently symbolic. Long ago, Burke (1945) described language as symbolic action. Humans symbolize all activities in their lives. They create and share meanings. they engage in an interpretive, sensemaking process.

Recently, the Zia Indians in the Southwestern United States, have taken steps to have their sun symbol removed from use by non-native commercial advertisers. The sun symbol is sacred to the Zia but it has been used as a commercial logo by various companies. In short, the Zia native Americans believe that their sun symbol is desecrated when it is used commercially (Auther, 1999, Sept. 4).

The Situated Self, Standpoint Theory, Contexts and Codes

Most people in the United States are not born into affluent situations where access to money may be taken for granted. Most people, born into a work-a-day world, need a job to make ends meet. People are situated economically in society. In like manner, they are situated politically, religiously, by gender and ethnicity and by age. Money and influence go hand in hand. Ethnicity, gender and age are embedded in networks of power, or the lack of it.

Power is unequally distributed in the United States, as it is in all countries. The powerful members in society tend to yield their influence on governing boards of major corporations, including the media. They are situated in very different locations in society than is the everyday person. It is this situationism that influences how people think and act (Carbaugh, 1996). The very wealthy members of society can make choices that are not available to the poor members as in the choices of automobiles, the clubs one joins, the travel that one enjoys and so on. In short, people enact behaviors in keeping with their standpoint in society.

A good illustration is to be found in the history of women and minorities in the United States. They have had less access to power than men have had. In recent years, many women have tried to make up the power difference by collectively creating political and economic organizations that will enable them to present a united front. Women present themselves in accordance with their interpretations of the social situation (Deegan, 1991; Gilligan, 1982, 1988). Similarly, members of ethnic groups enact communicative behaviors that arise from their situation in society. Their unique social history means that they construe life differently from mainstream Whites. The contexts and social codes influencing the ways they think are different from those of mainline white groups.

For example, Cuban Americans in Little Havana in Miami, have a highly politicized Cuban background. They consider themselves to be political exiles from a hostile Cuba. Many of them were forced out of Cuba or voluntarily fled the country. Their political and economic views and how they make sense of their social worlds, arise from a history that is very different from that of most Americans who were born and raised under calm conditions. Their identity is highly politicized. The Chinese, the Navajo, Blacks and Cubans have had unique historical experiences that influence how they think and act, as discussed in chapter seven. Their self-identities have been constructed based on their experiences. Their social behaviors arise from their standpoint in society.

The Influence of Place

As mentioned in the previous chapter, people create a sense of place reflecting their situation in society. They have a hometown, a college that they attended, favorite experiences that they remember and the comforts of knowing where they belong. In a broader sense, the concept of place refers to the geography of being. That is, people will claim national heritage, meaning that they associate themselves with a country, which, in turn is part of a geographic hemisphere. To be American is to be proud of a heritage that is unique in the world. Or, they may be proud of the fact that they were raised in the deep south or some other part of the United States.

The gist of the concept of place is that people create meanings for the places where they have grown up and they are deeply influenced by their sense of place (Gallagher, 1993). Humans are affected by night and day, by temperatures of regions, by urban-rural backgrounds and other factors, all of which are associated with the concept of place. Place, of course, varies greatly for different people, some of whom are mobile, while others are fixed in a geographical area. Some people are cosmopolitan in outlook; others tend to be insular. Thus, for example, one's sense of place may be associated with a small town in Alabama, not far from a large urban setting, which in turn is associated with a southern region where identifiable ways of behaving occur. Context is imbedded in context, each with identifiable social markings.

Agentive and Enactment Processes

Human Agentry and Role-Taking

Humans act agentively and dramaturgically. That is, they act on their own behalf as though they were performers on a stage. Just as vocalized language rests on a symbolic labeling process, nonverbal communication rests on a symbolizing process. People think about what they will say to an audience in a speech class; they also think about how they will dress or appear in front of that audience. Thus, verbal and nonverbal activities rest on a common interpretive process. (1)

The Chicago School of SI emphasizes agentive role-taking behavior. For example, a student takes notes in class, studies and takes tests; as part of social life, the student may join a fraternity or sorority or sing or dance in a performance. The teacher, on the other hand, probably will do none of the above although, as a student she probably did the same things. Perceiving her role to be professional and authoritative, the teacher provides expert knowledge to the student, separating her out from the students. Faculty members may or may not mix with students, depending on how they construct their relationships with students. In short, students and faculty engage in very different nonverbal role-taking behaviors reflecting their self perceptions and their perceptions of the role they will play in the educational system. Role-taking is a key aspect of SI . The ability to take the role of the other person in interaction is what builds social patterns, groups and institutions.

Framing Society

In the final analysis, any society is built up by the joint interactions of people. Society is really the result of ongoing human interaction. It is constructed by humans; it is maintained by humans; it is changed by humans. Humans engage in joint interactions for a variety of reasons. Perhaps they compromise in one situation; perhaps they pursue goals in another; perhaps they stand aside as others interact, and merely watch. But, social patterns, small and large, stable and dynamic, form society. It is through persisting daily interaction that society is built up (Blumer, 1969).

Roles are not fixed and invariant. They are general and dynamic. Students or faculty members can choose how they will perform the roles, giving it the shape that they prefer. Some faculty members lecture; others engage interactively with students in the classroom. The main point is the faculty member acts as her own agent in the role performance. Roles may be continuous and ongoing or they may be short-lived and terminal.

All people engage in multiple role activities, as students, as parents, as workers, as friends and so on. Humans carry with them the experiences of the past which influence how they interpret and discharge their roles. The demands of the situation are interpreted differently by each individual. For example, one may perceive the role of parenting as a protective one, setting about to protect the child from harm; another may perceive the role as a nurturing one, tending to assist the child in the tasks of childhood. The point, once again, is that the perception of the role to be performed governs how that role will be performed; the baggage, positive or negative, brought from the experiences of the past influence how roles are discharged.

People take into account the many social influences that affect their behaviors in role playing. For example, most students are aware that they should not appear in class naked. Most parents know that they should not beat their children. In short, the underlying social codes, usually not written down, inform people about appropriate role playing behavior. People catch on to the rules. Appearing in class naked will get attention; it may also lead to a sense of embarrassment. The perception of appropriateness is part of the sensemaking process. People model and imitate the performances of others in role-taking behavior.

Dramaturgy

The ways that humans enact or act out their lives both verbally and nonverbally has been called dramaturgical, a metaphor used by Erving Goffman. He observed that people act as though they were on a stage, the stage of life, and as though there were an audience observing them. Humans interact with others, acting out behaviors, and they receive appraisals, good or bad, from their observors or fellow participants in the interaction. Humans attempt to influence others by their nonverbal behaviors. For example, the phrase "She was dressed to kill" is a dramaturgical notion understood by most people. The actor may deliberately "dress to kill" to affect or influence others in a particular way, or she may simply have been ignorant of the social expectations of others. As Goffman pointed out, embarrassment usually results from being ignorant about social expectations.

The important point is that humans often plan to present themselves in specific ways to accomplish specific goals or tasks. They can feign friendship; they may smile to hide deceit; they can smile to attract others; they can smile to impress others (Jones, 1964; Leary, 1996). They can "dress to kill". The body "shines" or gives off cues to others; people can choose to direct their presentations in specific ways. People engage in impression management, in self presentation. On occasion, humans act in Machiavellian ways, performing acts to gain an advantage, regardless of the effect on the other parties.

Games and Strategies

The patterned nature of social behavior seems to be game-like when observed from a third-party perspective. For example, the romantic relationship discussed above would appear to be guided by hidden rules and expectations, not unlike the rules of games, such as chess. From a transactional perspective, different from, but not incompatible with SI, a psychiatrist analyzed human behaviors in game terms, suggesting that humans play games in marriages, in sexual relationships, in parties, and in other situations. From this perspective, people put on a game-face and enact roles based on that identity. For example, the female may play the role of a mother and the male may play the child, defining the relationship as a mother-child game, even though two adults are playing the game. There are good games and there are bad games. (Berne, 1964).

Games were important to Mead, the founder of what is now Symbolic Interactionism. Mead believed that childhood games were microcosms of later adult life. (Mead, 1934, 1938). That is, he believed that the play of the child contained within it an early understanding of life's rules, expectations and so on.

In the playing of games, children create social relationships which may or may not be healthy (Lutfiyya, 1987; Maccoby, 1998). For example, it has been suggested in the media that bully behavior on the part of male adolescents may be traceable to the ways that children played games in early childhood. This is probably a common view at a time when adolescent male bullying seems to be on the rise. Games, of course, have boundaries and rules; people develop skills in playing them whether the result is positive or negative. Some people engage skillfully in interaction with others; others act awkwardly, perhaps suffering embarrassment. People engage in joint activities, in interaction rituals, in ceremonies and in episodic events, seemingly playing the social games of life.

Socialization Processes

Early Childhood Activities: Imitation, Modeling, Role-taking and Interaction

It is safe to say that all nonverbal communication or behavior is learned through the processes of socialization. Children are directly and indirectly socialized. Few topics have occupied the attention of sociologists as much as the study of socialization processes. People get their values, beliefs, attitudes, behaviors and expectations from early socialization experiences. True, people will modify and re-interpret their experiences as they age, but the basic patterns are rooted in socialization. How much human behavior is influenced by pre-birth conditions is not clear. For example, it may be that the emotions of a preborn child are influenced by the emotional condition of the mother. An anxious mother may unwittingly pass her anxieties to her unborn child, just as an alcoholic mother may inflict biological harm on the child. Research about these influences is recent and results are unclear. What is clear is that the socialization process is active immediately after birth. The American way of birth is distinctive compared to birthing in earlier societies.

Framing Birthing Patterns

"A survey of birth postures in tribal and ancient societies reveals that squatting, not lying, is the natural delivery position for our species. Even the ancient Egyptian hieroglyphic for birth shows a squatting woman with a baby's head emerging from below her body. The same is true in ancient Babylon, Greece, and in the pre-Colombian peoples of Central America. In ancient Rome, they made use of special birth chairs. These chairs had cut-away seats that permitted the baby to emerge downward while the mother clung on to handles fixed to the front of the chair arms. These devices remained popular in Europe for centuries and were still in use in some regions right up to the beginning of the twentieth century" (Morris,1992, p 11). Apparently this type of birth is easier for women. There is still pain but the process is faster and easier than what modern hospitals do.

Biology certainly plays a key role in human behavior. Sociobiologists vary in their interpretation of how much the biology and chemistry of the body influences the behavior of the child. The nature-nurture controversy continues. It is argued that any trait that enables humans to survive, to find water, air, food and shelter is likely to influence human behavior substantially (Wilson, 1992). Precisely how the nature-nurture interaction works is not known.

Although children are born with predisposing "biological hardware", they are not 'hardwired' as are most lower order animals. In short, they can create their own sense about the body. Most lower order animals, excepting perhaps chimps and dolphins, do not appear to be able to make sense of themselves; although this, too, is debated. In their situation, biology appears to determine their behaviors. In humans, however, biology is not totally determinative of behavior. People learn to behave. Learning is achieved through socialization processes. Children catch on to the meaning of things, of events in their lives. They model and imitate their parents, siblings, peers and heroes. Joint social interactions form the foundation for the growth of the child.

Clearly, the human body is a physical organism, having an obdurate character. As mentioned, however, people overlay the body with meaning, symbolizing it. Yet the body appears to grow and change along fairly predictable lines, almost without regard to how humans think about their bodies. However, at each physical growth stage there are companionate social stages (Erikson, 1980, 1985). For example, the verbal part of the child's communicative reportoire emerges only after the nonverbal part has emerged. Infants learn to control muscles from the top of the body downward; first learning to use their heads, mouth and eyes, then sitting up and finally standing and walking (Haslett & Samter, 1997). Neonates are sensitive to loudness, to the tone of the human voice from early on. In short, early socialization may loaded on the side of the physical body.

People gradually learn about their bodies; they affix meaning to the bodies as they are influenced by various socialization processes. They create body identities. Those who follow Freud's psychoanalytic thinking, might argue that much, pehaps most, nonverbal communication is influenced by unconscious processes; others might argue that underlying, hidden mechanisms, such as the emotions, influence human behavior. But, in the final analysis, it is clear that humans make at least a sketchy sense of their own behaviors and the behaviors of others through the gradual processes of socialization.

Through imitation and modeling, a child may learn to act like his father, a girl like her mother. Cetainly modeling and imitative learning is not linear; rather, it is complex, usually indirect. By seeking out peers later in their lives, children reinforce who it is they think they are. Their self-identity is formative and telogenetic. Throughout their lives, though the various stages of life, individuals attempt to validate who they are, trying to come to terms with their identity.

Framing the Growth of Children

Research over the past 30 years shows that, starting as a newly born baby, a human has a strong orientation to others, to their voices, and even to their smells (Messer, 1994.) At four months, a child can stick out its tongue in response to the mother and at about 15 months the child can imitate facial expressions of the mother and open its hands in response to adults. Even the facial gestures of the child are influenced by mimicry; happiness, sadness and surprise can be imitated by the young child. It has been noted that even sightless children smile, suggesting perhaps that this activity is innate; however, in sighted life, mimicry plays an influential part.

Modeling involves paying attention to key persons; children see their parental behaviors as examples to be followed. Later, of course, the child will enact her or his own stylized way of communicating nonverbally; yet, the early influences will still be there. Walking, eating, speaking and other important life enhancing activities are given an early push through the modeling process, essentially an interactive process (Wywicka, 1996).

Although children act creatively, they are influenced to act in patterned ways, too. Young teenagers, for example, learn how to preen and dress for special occasions, following the lead of their peers. The stuff that becomes internalized is heavily influenced by modeling. Schools, television, play and other processual, ongoing activities serve to influence the child. The child learns to express nonverbal behaviors by taking account of the social exhibits of others. Gradually, the child creates personal schematic lines of action that work successfully in interactive situations.

Play

Children learn to play early in life. It has been said that play is work to the child. Whether it is playing with their food, pretending that a doll is real, or engaging in sport, as mentioned, a child's play is a microcosm of what is to come. In play, children learn to sort themselves out in a form of gender segregation (Maccoby, 1998). A budding style of play emerges for each gender. The young girls learns not to be too aggressive; young boys learn to be somewhat aggressive or agonistic. Children learn to take the role of the other in play, seeing that role in the actions of others. They make friends (Rubin, 1965, 1980) that deeply influence their behaviors.

Joint Attention and Interaction

As in primate and other animal behaviors, the newborn is gentled, touched, and cared about so that it can form a trusting bond with its mother (Bowlby, 1969;Montagu, 1971). The baby does its part by responding with coos and cries, interacting jointly and intersubjectively with its mother. Although other creatures, such as goslings, form a bond with the object nearest to it at birth, a human child forms an attachment that is more mentative and less hard-wired. Fondling and gentling by the animal mother is demonstrated in nearly all mammalian, four legged and higher order animals (Eibl-Eibestadt, 1975, 1979). It also characterizes human, mother-child relationships. Gentling and bonding by touching and cooing form attachments at a critical and fragile stage of development for the child. The early attachment styles of newborns are affected directly by the presence or absence of this mutual bonding process, (Jones & Brown, 1996); as mentioned, young children who lack a gentle and caring mother, who may suffer from physical and emotional abuse, may develop dysfunctional attachment styles.

It is in this early process of mutual bonding between mother and child that the child begins to sense the importance of its body and of itself. The mother, father and key others begin the socialization process that will lead to identity for the child. In short, the self is not a given; rather, it is forged by learning activities, constructed in interaction with others. Mutuality and intersubjectivity are part of the sharing process. The child learns about meanings, about itself and its importance, about appropriate behaviors and so on. Later, the child is able to label, or symbolize, the world because of its early experiences (Bruner, 1990; Moore & Dunham, 1995). At a later time, adults remember their childhood experiences, especially the touching behaviors of their parents, whether good or bad (Jones & Brown, 1996) and they tend to treat their own children as they have been treated.

Self and Body Image

As mentioned, humans are members of the animal kingdom; but, unlike other primates and lower order animals, humans are consciously aware of themselves, taking themselves as objects of their own thought. As a human, a person can say, "I am Johnnie" or "I am Suzie" and have specific ideas in mind about what the name means. Humans construct their identities, achieving a sense of self, which, although it is flexible, contains fairly enduring characteristics. The body, of course, is a critically important part of human identity.

Framing the Self and Identity

Following Mead and others who developed his ideas further, the self is created in interaction with others. People treat themselves as objects and talk about themselves with some certainty. Although the concepts of self and identity have many different interpretations, varying considerably between and among scholars, in this text, a symbolic interactionist view is taken. Identity and self, essentially the same concepts, arise in social interaction; they are involved in all human interactions and performances. "As we communicate toward self we are able to see ourselves in the situation, to recognize who we are in relation to others and vice versa, as well as to evaluate our own action in the situation. We are able to judge ourselves and to establish an identity" (Charon, 1995, p 86).

Although very early on both genders attach themselves to parents, gender segregation gradually occurs and children gradually become relatively independent. It is said that the colors pink and blue, used at birth to distinguish males and females, sets the tone for later gender development (Gilligan, 1982). Through the various stages of life, nonverbal behaviors become genderized (Wood, 1992,1994). Part of the accepted "Me", the object part of the self, is the image of the somatic self that the child gradually learns.

In this book, cultural, social and psychological views of the self are presented. Self, self-concept, identity, self-construal and other terms are used to describe the meaning of the body; they are used nearly interchangeably, although it may be argued by various scholars that critical distinctions should be made for the purposes of research. SI scholars maintain that the self and self-identity are constructed by individuals who take account of the perceptions of themselves by others, internalizing that thinking and incorporating it into a cluster of thoughts, mulling it about in various circumstances, refining it, adding to it, altering it over time. The achievement of identity, of a sense of self, is a dynamic process (Hewitt, 1999; Weigert, 1986).

Although the concept of identity seems to connote an integrity that is played out over a lifetime, some research suggests that the formation of identity may be negatively influenced by a society that is heavily mediated, especially by television (Gergen, 1991). From this view, the influence of television and other modern media, including the internet, appear to confuse and fracture identity to be discussed in Chapter Eight. Born with a body, the individual must learn how to make sense of the body and the self; it is more difficult in modern times, some scholars assert.

Thus, through interactions with others, the child learns the meaning of her or his own body. Through praise and criticism, parents reinforce how their children see their own bodies. Saying to the child, "Oh, you are beautiful" is very different from saying "Why don't you dress up more?" implying that the child is less than attractive. Thus children learn about their bodies gradually. If a child learns that his genitalia are dirty, he may become overconcerned about them. Body images, body concepts, body schemes, body attitudes, and body experiences are phrases used to suggest the symbolic nature of the body. (Fisher, 1986). The young lady, seeing herself as too fat, believes that others see her as too fat, and acts accordingly. She engages in a type of self-fulfilling prophecy. She attempts to avoid embarrassment, sensing that her body does not measure up in a society that "worships" thinness. Severely under duress, she may become anorexic.

Social themes influence body perception as well. A very religious person might say that the body is the temple of God, or built in the image of Christ. The Amish downplay the role of the body, dressing it simply without adornment. In more secular ways, a child might learn that black is beautiful or that being thin and tall is the desired body shape. Young black males may learn how to saunter or swagger as a sign of their identity. Clearly, the "looking glass self" is a powerful metaphor (Cooley, 1970). People look into society as they would look in a mirror and find symbols of identification.

Stages in Life

Humans go through relatively patterned growth periods, labeled by a number of scholars in varying ways. Clearly, human nonverbal communication changes as humans mature, although behaviors from earlier stages persist. Humans can and do change the way they think about the events in their life. Thus, the gerontological age, for example, is viewed as problematic by some people while it is viewed as an opportunity for further growth by others. People can continue to learn new ways of communicating nonverbally. See Chapter Seven for a discussion of the aging process and how it influences nonverbal behaviors.

The stages of life seem to be fairly predictable in American life and a variety of stage-type theories exist. Although stages are not truly fixed, they are somewhat predictably patterned so that children move from early childhood into pubescence and then into adolescence in varying but fairly routine ways, predicated on physiological development, body changes and so forth. The social and physical growth of the child are intertwined . For example, the child is not able to lift a fork to its lips until its motor skills are developed. A child begins to understand what eating means when its linguistic and cognitive skills are developed. From eating with its hands, the child gradually emerges into full-blown maturity, able to perform complex nonverbal tasks, such as hosting a dinner party or eating in a fashionable restaurant without embarrassing herself. The child learns how to act through a complex interactive set of activities with her parents (Conte & Castellofranch, 1995). Stage theories are complex, some very popular and well researched; others very hypothetical. A recent approach to the aging process suggest that tie-signs, which are remembrances of experiences, become more and more important to people as they age, as discussed in the Chapter Seven. In every situation, at whatever stage, humans try to interpret and make sense of their status; in many cases, rites-de-passage mark a stage, such as coming out parties, or retirement parties.

Parents watch their children grow from the neonatal stage, through adolescence to older age. Although parents have gone through various life stages, they may be unnerved by the behaviors of young teens, whose lifestyles may be radically different from their parents. Later, the parents will be grandparents, which calls for a very different set of expectations and behaviors. All people pass through life's stages; at each stage, the individual must make sense of the social world, coming to terms with her or his identity. Their social behaviors, their interactions with others are displayed accordingly.

Nonverbal Competence and the Presentation of Self

Recent research emphasizes the agentive role of humans, starting with children, who learn to act on their own behalf. Children are not "developed" so much as they create ways of seeing the world and ways of acting. They enact themselves, becoming quickly attuned to their circumstances (Hutchby &-Moran, 1998). Children become competent at nonverbal tasks as practical achievements, from playing ball, to later courtship activities. Parents, not usually trained experts in the raising of children, use a folk-type model to guide them (Valsiner,1997). Children learn from a type of teleogenetic process deriving meaning from small action events. For example, when a child is praised for the way she or he handles a fork or spoon, the child is likely to continue to use it in skilled ways. Eating such a thing as a boiled egg, pealing it and then consuming it can be a complex event for a young child. The child must work the mind, eye, hand and mouth together to perform what later will be a simple, routine task. Children learn to present themselves based on what they have learned. They learn to dress, finding out what dress codes are all about. They learn when to smile and when to frown. They create a reportoire of skilled competencies in a presentational style. Their gestures are used to create impressions and to influence people and their general body language becomes part of their communicative package. Studies of feral children reveal how important human socialization is to the child. "Wild" children are stunted in physical, emotional, intellectual and social growth; they cannot symbolize human events appropriately.

Action Theory(2) and Networking

When humans engage in action, they usually know something about why they are doing it and what the likely outcomes will be (Vallacher & Wegner, 1985). The tasks they perform may be very simple or very complex. A simple task might include putting on the right shoes; a complex task might include walking in those shoes to make a sale as a professional staff member of a major commercial company. In each case, people attach meaning to what they are doing, symbolically. Even friendships are formed symbolically; the dyadic relationship is built upon shared activities, perceived symbolically as part of the relationship (Conville & Rogers,1998). The ability to manage relationships competently, to be accepted and to do appropriate things to maintain the relationship is the foundation of effective networking. One learns to play roles and enact lines of action, which are recognized by others and incorporated in the relationship.

One learns how to dress, how to behave appropriately and how to make a good impression on others. One learns to play roles, some of them continuous. For example, being a parent is a continuous activity; frying an egg is discontinous. Playing the part of a mommy or daddy as a child becomes a precursor to the later performance of parenting. These early enactments teach the child how to behave socially, making networking possible.

Interaction and networking form the crucible of identity formation. Interaction and networking with others is foundational to society as well, without which society could not exist. Patterns of association vary by gender, by age and by ethnicity. Modern communicative technologies offer new ways for people to network with one another, whether in work or play. Networking is profoundly influenced by the internet, providing new ways for humans to interact, as discussed in chapter eight.

Peer Groups, Work and Institutional Influences

It is in peer groups that boys and girls learn to identify themselves. Each person is deeply influenced by the members of groups. Young people know what is "in" and what is "out" and in the teenage years, they are careful to follow the acceptable patterns, for fear that they may become stigmatized or even ostracised from the group. Members of the group may find reason to label and ostracize a person, keeping him or her out of the group because they do not appear to fit the social paradigm.

Members of peer groups create labels for various kinds of behaviors, which become identifying keys associated with each member. For example, one member may be the brain or egghead; another may be "Miss Popularity". The references are to the style of behaviors that each person exhibits. The power of peer groups to influence how members feel and think is enormous, as it is in the workplace.

Framing Group Influences

Small and large groups are network structures, the structures created by humans in interaction. Research suggests that the communicative design of the group influences how people relate to one another. For example, when people sit in a simple circle design, equality is promoted among the members of the group; a wheel design with spokes tends to promote the leader who sits in the central position, through whom most messages must go; the Y pattern usually includes a leader at the bottom end of the Y; the chain style of group activity limits conversations except with the person on either side, or on the left or right side, depending on which end the member is sitting; the all-channel group pattern permits all people to talk to all others equally. Morale is promoted more in the all channel group than it is in the wheel or Y pattern (DeVito,1997).

Performing effectively in the workplace requires skilled nonverbal behavior. Indeed, it is in the workplace where humans present themselves with some expertise. An engineer, for example, follows lines of conduct associated with his or her discipline, as does the medical doctor. In short, the socialization process does not end at early adulthood; it continues throughout life. The manager of people in the workplace must possess a leadership reportoire. Leaders, of course, are not born; they construct themselves. Not only must the manager have the ability to lead, or manage, but she or he must appear to lead. The boss's office is usually bigger than those of her support staff. The office usually reflects power and influence, in both direct and subtle ways. For example, the leader's desk may be considerably larger than the desks of the support staff and the office may be furnished with other symbols of the leader's social status. These obvious differences are important to the maintenence of power; yet, the manager must earn the image of being a leader by doing little things to shape an image, such as displaying personal plaques and awards on the wall behind her and taking part in only limited ways in the understaff's activities, distancing herself from them. Bosses and understaff members must learn appropriate roles and behaviors to communicate successfully. Indeed, they must plan to be effective (Berger, 1997). Managers and other professional people must nurture their image to conform to professional expectations.

Monadic, Dyadic and Group Activities

In face-to-face dyadic situations, people usually present themselves in the full view of the other participant. In this situation, verbal and nonverbal interactions are easily observed and when the dyadic relationships is balanced, fair play takes place. In imbalanced dyads, however, one person may try to take advantage of another. For example, the young and the old are particularly persuasible; they are easy to influence, sometimes negatively (Larson, 1983). The more powerful person in the dyad combines nonverbal acts with verbal acts, she or he can persuade the weaker party to do things. The dynamics of groups are influenced by group size.

Framing a 'Law' of Numbers

Is there a law of numbers at work in groups? Dyads, for example, consist of two persons where interactions are very different from the three person group, which is very different from much larger groupings. In a dyad one party may play a game of one-ups-manship, trying to better the other person in the dyad. In a three party group, two people can gang up against one in a coalition, which cannot be done in a dyad. In larger groups, people can create subgroups, which influence how behaviors are managed. Subgroupings can develop in 12 member groups but they cannot form in dyads. In a monad where there is but one person, the individual can hold conversations only with the self. The size of the group influences how people will behave.

Joint interactions are the glue of society. Their continuous flow make up the structures of the wider society, which, when formed, influence the individual. Thus, it is a circular process. The wider society is formed by the micro-enactments of small groups, which, in turn, influence the individual. As mentioned; even romantic relationships, which appear to be free-floating to the individuals involved, are deeply influenced by underlying social codes; lovers in American society follow fairly scripted behaviors as they enact their relationship, their symbolic baby, as it were (Duck, 1992; Knapp & Vangelisti, 1992).

Group dynamics pressure members to conform. As mentioned, nonverbal behaviors may become stigmatized or shunned if they do not conform. Many youth groups, for example, shunned by mainline society, form negative images, continuing as identity groups. Skinheads, religious cults, gangs and other types of groups create identities to make a statement to the wider society. Interestingly, these groups, appearing to be nonconformist, often require strict conformity from their members. Further, their relationship to the wider society is somewhat predictable. Riding a motorcycle with black jacket, long dirty hair and dark glasses is almost a guaranteed way to be arrested in many places in the United States.

Familial Influences

The family is an example of a small group which, as in the spoked wheel example, can be highly structured and authoritarian, or it may be flexible, as in the all-channel example. Varieties of family styles exist and the communication patterns vary by type of family (Arliss, 1993). Size of the family influences relational patterns as well. Modern families may have dinner in front of the television set thereby limiting their conversations. This is but one example of the mediating influence of television, as discussed in chapter eight. Families are small communities constructed symbolically, Family members create meanings that they share intersubjectively, binding them together, some loosely, others tightly.

Families are co-constructed by the members; it is heavily influenced by the wider community as well. In recent America, the diverse forms of the family seem to be increasing. for example, there are: first-marriage families; single-parent families; stepfamilies; cohabiting couple families; geographically separated families; extended families; and, binuclear families in which two nuclear families share their lives with one another. The situation in which women breed children by artificial insemination or in which two people of the same sex marry and adopt children is emerging. In short, American families have new forms (Arliss, 1993). The family, of course, is influenced by social, religious, political and economic processes in American society. For example, elderly people, formerly attached to their family through a kinship ethos are now more likely to live by themselves or in homes for the elderly than they are to live in the extended family.

The family, of course, is the main influence on the behavior of the child. Face-to-face interactions, deeply formed feelings, rules and expectations, and other influences are designed to help the child become an adult in an appropriate way. Yet, the family is itself undergoing major changes in American society and in other technologically developed countries. Traditional family dinner patterns are giving way to discursive patterns of behavior. The laissez faire family seems to be an emergent form in contemporary American society. The patterns of interaction found in traditional families are far different from those found in laissez faire families. Many families in the United States are fractured, resulting in new and different pressures on the family members.

Framing the American Family

A recent University of Chicago survey says that only one in four American families is considered to be traditional, down 45 percent from the early 1970's. Single earner families, where parents are married and together, are now the exception. The survey found that:

56 percent of adults in 1998 were married compared to 75 percent in 1972.

51 percent children in 1998 lived in a household with both parents; in 1972, 73 percent did so.

in 1998, 18.2 percent of children lived with single parents; in 1972 that figure was 4.7 percent.

Making the changing family work is a difficult task in American life. (CNN Online, Nov 24, 1999).

Sex and No Wedding

It appears that romance and marriage are out but casual sex and low-commitment relationships are in among young Americans, a Rutgers University study suggested. They are concerned with "Sex Without Strings. Relationships Without Rings" Apparently young people:

favor living together as a try-out for marriage

believe sex is fun when no strings are attached

fear divorce

see marriage as an economic liability

one half of females see unwed motherhood as an acceptable alternative. In short, the marriage script for young Americans seems to have been torn up(CNN Online, June 06, 2000).

Americans have torn up the script for the nuclear family, directly and indirectly affecting the lives of the children. In place of the relatively stable family where there are two parents and their children, modern America now has large numbers of single parent families, of second marriage familes and the stepchild status that comes with it, of co-habiting but unmarried families, geographically separated families and communal families, although the latter are fewer in number.

Given the rapid changes in society and the consequent changes in the family in the United States, the processes of identification for children, who are often "stepchildrenized" ,may be disrupted and dysfunctionality may be unwittingly promoted. Children must define themselves in the light of new situational and structural influences, as families dissolve, divorce, or separate. For example, parents with small children who divorce go through stages of dissolution in which "grave dressing" acts influence children, whose loyalties to one parent or the other are shaken (Arliss, 1993). Regrettably, the grief of parents in divorce affects how their children perceive the family. Infants, of course, form emotional bonds of attachment. When these are disrupted, children may become anxious, ambivalent or avoidant, carrying these emotional feelings into future situations and relationships (Bowlby, J. 1969; Weber & Harvey, 1994).

The Creation of Relationships

Humans create relationships. They maintain them symbolically, as noted in the frame below.

Framing Relationships

To maintain relationships, humans go through daily rituals. Partner interaction becomes somewhat routinized on a daily basis. Couples may shop on Mondays, go out to dinner on Fridays, visit friends on Saturdays and so on. They may create special events or special holiday practices, such as family reunions, Christmas festivities, or birthday celebrations on a regular basis, as a couple. Couples create places for privacy, such as the bedroom, and places for public interaction, such as the family room. They also create rules of engagement, scripts for undertaking situations of disagreement, for interacting with each other's friends, and so on (Wood, 1995).

Romantic relationships embody distinct notions, different from other relationships. The behaviors that earmark romance are lodged in the sense of romance that Americans share. The old fashioned idea of a knight on a white horse who rescues a forlorn damsel no longer applies; however, romance embodies notions about sharing that other dyads do not share. The level of intimacy that characterizes romantic relationships is itself governed by implicit rules of touching, which are governed by the experiences of the couples. Conservative, religious people may decide that sexual consummation is to be withheld until the couple is joined in marriage; other, less conservative young people, may plunge into the sexual act on the first night. The rules of the dyadic relationship must be defined. However they decide to act, as mentioned, they create a symbolic "baby", the relationship. Underlying, often hidden, codes of conduct influence all relationships. People may agree or disagree about how these codes are to be interpreted, but they must admit their presence and their influence on human behaviors. Male-female relationships will be discussed in more detail in Chapter Five.

Interaction Routines and Public Activities

Face-to-Face Interaction

The presentation of self and the concept of face and script have been dealt with in a previous chapter. It is important to reinforce the ideas behind the concept of face, noting that the concept plays a part in all human behaviors. Because the presentation of self is often conceived of as basically dyadic or small group experience, a way of displaying personal identity to others, it is easy to overlook the fact that it is involved as well in routinized patterns of behavior and in public activities.

Routinized Behaviors

As people age, they return again and again to behaviors that have been used successfully before. Lines of action that have served well in the past continue to be used. One does not have to learn how to shake hands after learning it the first time, although one may have to learn about greeting habits in other cultures when traveling between cultures. When nonverbal activities become routinized, they can be performed with little attention required. People may brush their teeth or brush their hair but be thinking about many other things, perhaps planning the day. As mentioned, humans tend to ignore the fact that routines are achieved. Yet routinization is foundational to the creation of society.

Framing Routine Performances

Clearly, humans conduct their activities using simple gestures and complex lines of action. Because they are so common, people tend to overlook their value to society. People drive on the right side of the road in the United States; to do otherwise would be to undermine the road rules. Not only do people avoid accidents by using a shared road code, but they obey the established laws, which themselves have been socially constructed. Further, the driving venture is part of an interaction ritual that is known to most people in the United States. Driving a car successfully is but one ritualized activity, an example of the multitudes of rituals that form the basis of society. Everyday rituals and routines are full of meaning (Goffman, 1967; Schegloff, 1986).

Contingent Behavior

During the day, especially in novel situations, people both give and respond to others, following a contingent pattern; that is, they do something in response to what others have done, or in response to what they think others will do. People take turns enacting behaviors. A smile may create a smile in the other party. If the boss dresses in a suit and tie, the employee responds in kind. In short, people act contingently, dynamically in response to the behavioral enactments of others. In routinized behavior, however, this creative contingent element may be missing. The behavior is relatively fixed and repetitive with no need to change it. Mindful attention is not needed, as it is in novel situations.

Public Displays

Throughout the stages of life, people engage in public displays and ritualizations, whether they are religious, associated with work and play, or secular. Marriage, graduation ceremonies, worship services, concerts and other collective activities contain formulations of appropriate public behaviors. They contain collective scripts for people to follow. Highly symbolic, they reach into the psyche deeply to influence thought and behavior. Marriages may be performed underwater or from a dive out of an airplane, illustrating how times change; yet, there is a symbolic constancy associated with each ceremony. Indeed, a large part of human lives are played out in public ceremonies, themselves value laden, imbued with beliefs and expected behaviors and outcomes.

The Influence of Master Themes: Gender, Ethnicity, Age and Technology.

Micro, Meso and Macro Processes

Until recently, SI scholars have differed in the past about how they view these processes. Some researchers have focused on the macro aspect of social processes(Stryker, 1980, 1981) while others focused on the micro aspects (Goffman, 1969). At present, there seems to be an attempt to blend the different approaches(Couch, 1997).

Micro processes refer to daily interactive experiences in dyadic or small group situations. Meso processes refer to interactions in larger settings, such as work and school activities, where many people interact. Macro processes refer to those public, society-wide processes that are ongoing, forming the essential character of a society. For example, power is distributed thoughout American society, but it is distributed unevenly. The master themes listed above are macro themes. Macro themes and processes are dynamic, not fixed, although they are somewhat stable. They pervade society at every level, from monadic, dyadic, to group and institutional levels and to national levels. They creep into daily behaviors. Indeed, every society must contend with these master themes.

Even when people engage in self conversations they wittingly or unwittingly take account of these themes. For example, females think differently about events than do males (Gilligan, 1982;Gilligan, Ward, Taylor & Bardige, 1988); members of ethnic groups think about ethnicity differently than do white males. The media, of course, display sex and gender themes continuously, as do the film and print media; even the internet is used to promote sexual themes. Communicative technologies clearly influence members of society, framing the master themes.

There are a number of master themes that influence human behavior, not discussed in this text. For example the role of bureaucracy and capitalism as they influence human lives are not discussed. (Deegan, 1989). Humans are caught up in powerful social matrices that influence nonverbal communication.

Ethnic Behaviors

People may think of Black Americans when they use the word ethnicity. However, Whites are ethnic, too. Described as a subculture, or better as a co-culture, Black American culture contains codes of conduct that are distinct, rooted in their history. Native Americans, Cubans and Chinese are three other ethnic groups, discussed in this book; they play important roles in American society, although their roles have changed significantly over time. Members of these groups tend to construe life differently from mainline white members of society. Ethnicity is symbolically constructed; it is a dynamic concept. Ethnicity is lived. Unfortunately, social barriers are created when artificial boundaries are erected between ethnic groups (Lamont, Fournier & Gans, 1993; Lee, 1997). Economic disadvantage frequently serves to mark boundaries between ethnic groups.

In this book, in Chapter Seven, the author uses the experiences of the Navajo, the Cubans, the Blacks and the Chinese as examples of ethnic identities. Historically, except for the Cubans who immigrated to the United States in recent years, Blacks, Chinese and Navajo members were treated as strangers in a strange land. Unfortunately, the present is influenced by the past. The construal of ethnic identity in the modern bicultural or multicultural American world often carries the problems of the past into the present. Fortunately, a new awareness, an interethnic identity seems to be emerging in modern America, although there are destructive elements remaining.

The demography of the United States is changing dramatically. The 2000 census shows that Hispanics and Blacks each now represent about 13 percent of the population of the United States. To the extent that access to political, economic and educational institutions is denied them, problems are created by those who hold power. As discussed in chapter six, inter-ethnic adaptability and the creation of behaviors that reduce conflict among groups is necessary in a country that considers itself to be egalitarian.

Genderized Behaviors

Gender is a macro-theme that pervades every human relationship, influencing nonverbal communication. From birth, parents apply their tacit, folk-knowledge to the raising of their children. Socialization processes deeply influence gendered identities as indicated by the creation of gendered groups, such as NOW. The distribution of power equally among men and women is a point of contention, a main concern of feminine political groups because they have been denied access to the political and economic power that men have enjoyed. (Howard & Hollander, 1996;Orbe, 1998). Historically, women's voices have been muted. Clearly, the "man-thing" has held sway. For example, until recently, women were not given access to the major professions, a fact which is changing rapidly. Many women influenced the study of sociology prior to the present emphasis upon feminism. People such as Jane Addams, Beatrice Webb, Simone de Beauvoir, Hannah Arendt and others made deep inroads into a profession that was influenced primarily by men (Deegan, 1991). The numbers of women entering law schools, perhaps the mainline profession that influences social policy, is expected to equal the numbers of males in the enrollment year 2001. Gender will be discussed in detail in chapter five.

The Aging Behaviors

There is a substantial difference between the concepts of ageism and aging. Ageism, in American life, has come to mean something quite stereotypical. The aged may be seen as outdated, dependent members of society. They are often represented as people whose cognitive functions may be imparied, whose ability to use their body is impaired, and their ability to perform complex tasks greatly reduced.

However, recent approaches emphasize the concept of successful aging (Baltes & Baltes, 1990), an active, engagment process that can help extend life, enabling people to live more successful lives in older age. The upper limits of aging that result in death are being changed by new medicines, technologies and genetic research, sometimes referred to in the popular mind as the Methuselah factor. As humans age, they can actually improve on some nonverbal.performances.

Changes in the composition of American society reflect that not only is the United States becoming multi-ethnic, it is also aging steadily. The fastest growing segment of American society is the group of people above age 85. Research is beginning to focus on the lives of older people in a country that has historically placed emphasis upon youth. See Chapter Seven.

Technological Mediation

Mediation refers to how modern communicative technologies influence the thoughts and behaviors of humans. Television, the computer and the internet, satellites, film and other media deeply influence human behaviors. Communicative tools, or media, are created by humans; although they act as extensions of the self, they are much larger than the individual, influencing the entire society. Speed, imaging, and usability characterize these media. Indeed, a new social and geographic landscape is being forged by modern communicative technologies. Virtual reality, a phrase hardly used two decades ago, indicates that reality can be simulated by the computer. The power of the media to influence human life is pervasive. Another phrase, the Cyborg phenomenon, discussed over the past few years in highly imaginative ways, appears to have become a reality. Mind, body and machine interact in novel ways, directly influencing human behavior. The role of media and media ecology are discussed in Chapter Eight.

Related Aspects of Social Influence

Social Class, Social Power and Influence

Already mentioned, humans are situated in society, often indicated by economic and educational indices. The general principle is that the more income and education one has the more likely she or he is to be able to exercise power and influence. Sociologists study class behavior based not only on income, but on education, religions, and other forms of association (Persell, 1987).

It is generally believed that all individuals have equal rights and equal opportunities in the American democracy; the egalitarian ethos is a powerful incentive to accomplish the American Dream. However, those who exercise power are inclined to be white Americans who through achievement or inherited wealth and position wield power over the lives of others, not always directly, but in hidden ways. Most people know about the Horatio Alger rags to riches phenomenon, but that phenomenon is less likely to apply to females and ethnic Americans because of hidden, institutional factors that impede their progress. The aged in American society are often said to be past their prime in a country in which younger people hold positions of power.

The benefits of wealth and power are revealed in the ways people dress, in what they own, in their club memberships, and, in general their total life styles. Perhaps it is the choice of a Jaguar over a Chevrolet, of a world tour over a visit to Bermuda, and so on. Power and its uses are enacted; that is, power does not just sit there in society, as may have been suggested by people like Machiavelli or Marx; it is created interactively, intersubjectively, by people (Prus & Scott,1999). In short, standpoint, or situation in society, broadly and specifically influence nonverbal communication but it is in the enactment of behaviors, in response to these influences, that power is created. Going to college at Harvard or Yale can help put the "silver spoon" in one's mouth. Most other members of society must contend with money problems on a day to day basis. They do not engage in such high profile activities.

Regional Influences

Food use is but one behavior that is influenced by region. Dress, speech, beliefs and other behaviors, are influenced as well. Indeed, buying habits, use of language, education levels, attitudes, beliefs and all nonverbal activities are somewhat influenced by the social dynamics associated with a geographic place. As discussed above, the concept of place contains rich overtones of meaning. The sense of identity is rooted in the sense of geographical place, in a familiar milieu. People tend to network and interact with other people who share broadly their outlooks and aspirations. There are people, of course, who spend considerable time trying to escape stereotypes associated with regions.

Regions, as places, influence nonverbal communication extensively. For example, it is known that southerners may speak with a drawl, more slowly than New York City residents usually speak. People from Buffalo, N.Y., are known to walk faster than do people from the Southwest. Auto purchases vary by region of the country. Fords are preferred over Chevrolets in different parts of the United States. Foods that are eaten vary considerably from place to place. Chitlins, rice and grits, by and large, are Southern foods. Where Blacks predominate in the south, one expects to find soul food; on the Navajo reservation in New Mexico and Arizona, one expects to find mutton and corn related foods; in Chinatown, one expects an amalgam of American and Chinese foods. Cubans in Miami's Little Havana are fond of black beans, plantains pork and chicken. In short, patterned eating behaviors are associated with various regions of the United States, as they are throughout the world. Regional behaviors may be very distinctive. Indeed, foodways in general are influenced by social function. For example, in Mexico, panes de meertos, or the bread of the dead is eaten at funerals; Muslims will not eat before sundown during Ramadan; Italian's put almonds in a child's coffin. Food use varies by place and by function (Brown & Mussell, 1984).

The SI approach suggests that human behavior is not determined; rather, the individual chooses to do what she or he wants to do. Thus, one may reject regional foods altogether and create a different approach to eating. Unless a person is in a highly controlled environment, such as the military, a monastery or a prison, she or he is free to decide what to eat or wear or how to act. Restrictive environments, or total institutions, prescribe what will be eaten but, in everyday life, individuals make decisions about what they will do. Foodways may serve as markers of identity.

Specialized Milieaus and Manifest Codes

Everyday, individuals are called upon to perform, to act as agents, to play various roles and to engage in joint interactions with others. Slowly and gradually, people learn how to act so as not to embarrass themselves, to behave according to hidden social codes. Underlying social codes influence human behavior; however, the codes are forgiving in that they permit a variety of adaptive modes of behavior. The hidden rules are not usually directly impressed on people. They are often caught rather than taught, as the saying goes. They are not obviously manifested and certainly, in an open society, they are not written in stone. Signs may say something like, "Do not litter" or "Watch your step", but most underlying rules and codes are not explicitly stated. (3)

However, there are settings in American society where codes are made fairly explicit. An inmate in a prison, a total institution, has very little freedom to make choices about the activities in his life. Inmates know at all times what the institution requires them to do. The rules are explicit. When the inmate eats, where he goes, and what he does are all controlled by prison officials. Social codes are impressed upon the inmate. In most circumstances, however, one finds a relatively fluid situation in which the expectations, prescriptions and proscriptions of behavior are open and lax.

A middle range of prescription is found in medical and legal settings where codes of behavior are clearly expressed. Judges, for example, do not wear colorful costumes, nor do doctors wear street clothes. In short, these professional settings have manifest codes understood by people who work in the setting. In other settings, of course, such as in some religious schools, one is in a clothes-controlled environment and everyone, male or female, wears the same colors and schemes. The uniform hides the backgrounds of the individuals so that both rich and poor dress the same. In brief, the examples used reveal the power of the social milieau to influence the display of nonverbal behaviors. In more relaxed settings, the individual is free to choose what to wear. Every discriminating individual takes account of the prevailing manifest codes in order to perform appropriately (Berger, 1997). Indeed, whether in a controlled or free setting, one's level of nonverbal skill depends on how she or he picks up on the demands of the situation.

Summary

Humans create their sense of self and identity in interaction with others and in conversations with the self. Born into what appears to be a fixed society, the individual learns how to take account of the influences on her or his behavior, accomplished through socialization, influencing the individual from birth to older age. Families, peers, and institutions influence human behavior. Humans are situated in society, inhabiting a space or place, which is part of their identities. Gender, ethnicity, age, technology are influences on nonverbal communication, just as are social class, power, and the dynamics of place and region.

Symbolic interaction, arising essentially from philosophy and sociology contains the dramaturgical assumption that humans are actors, self agents and performers in everyday life, their audience consisting of partipants in interactions. In the next chapter, psychological processes that influence nonverbal communication will be considered.

Questions for Thought and Discussion

1.   In your relationships with other people, how much are you aware of your own nonverbal behavior? To answer the question, think of your personal relationships and of your more formal relationships in work or other situations.

2.   To what extent do you think that humans play games in their daily relationships? In other words, do you observe people designing or creating strategies to influence others? Do you think that you play games in social interaction?

3.   What does it mean that humans play multiple roles in daily life? What roles do you think you play in a period of a day or a week? How did you learn these roles?

4.   Discuss the major influences on your sense of self or identity. How do you think your situation, your sense of place in society, has influenced your behaviors?

5.   How apparent are the stages of life to you and what kinds of expectations do you think are associated with them? For example, if you were to describe your present 'stage' in life, how would you describe it in general terms? What conditions influence how you communicate nonverbally?

Notes

1.   It is the thesis of this book that the process that is used to interpret the meaning of nonverbal behaviors is the same process that is used to interpret verbal, or spoken behaviors. Indeed, the spoken language is an overlay of nonverbal behaviors. See The Body in Language by Horst Ruthrof (2000), New York: Cassell. The author discusses the relationship of the spoken language to corporeal semantics; language acts as a parasite on nonverbal activities. See also Peter Gilroy's book(1996), Meaning Without Words: Philosophy and Nonverbal Communication. Brookfield, MA: Avebury. He stresses the mediation of language and non-language through human experience.

2.   The history of interactionism and its present meanings, uses, methodologies and interpretations are discussed by Gary Alan Fine, Symbolic Interactionism in the Post-Blumerian Age, in Frontiers of Social Theory: The New Syntheses, George Ritzer, Editor, Columbia University Press, 1990. Although the main tenets of interactionism, or symbolic interactionism, may provoke creative discussion and lively differences of opinion by scholars, it enjoys a long, productive history, still continuing. Its main tenets are three, as espoused by Blumer: People act on things based on the meanings they have for them; meanings arise from social interactions; meanings are modified in an interpretive process. See pages 117-157 for a full discussion. A structuralist view of symbolic interaction is presented in Stryker, S (1981) Symbolic interactionism: A social structural version. Addison-Wesley Publishing Company.

3.   Total institutions, such as prisons, the military and various religions, such as religious fundamentalism as found in Islam and Christianity prescribe, even direct, individuals in their daily lives. This is a form of direct impression on the members of these organizations. As mentioned, inmates in prisons are told what to wear, when to bathe, when to exercise and eat and when to sleep. Every behavior is controlled. Other groups, less controlling, do not direct their members to behave in any particular way, permitting widely varying behaviors that are not sanctioned in any way. Erving Goffman discussed controlled behaviors in Total Institutions and in Asylums. The movie, One Flew Over the Cuckoo's Nest was influenced by Goffman's work.

Suggested Readings

Arliss, L. P. (1993). Contemporary Family Communication: Messages and Meanings. New York: St. Martin's Press.

Deegan, M. J. (1989). American Ritual Dramas: Social Rules and Cultural Meanings. Westport, CT: Greenwood Press.

Gallagher, W. (1994). The Power of Place: How Our Surroundings Shape Our Thoughts, Emotions and Actions. New York: Harper Perennial.

Goffman, E. (1967). Interaction Ritual: Essays on Face-to-Face Behavior. Garden City, NY: Anchor/Doubleday.

Prus, M. S. (1999). Beyond the Power Mystique: Power as Intersubjective Accomplishment. Albany, NY: SUNY Press.

Wood, J. T. (1995). Relational Communication: Continuity and Change in Personal Relationships. New York: Wadsworth Publishing Company.

Weigert, A. (1986). Society and Identity: Toward a Sociological Psychology. Cambridge, England: Cambridge University Press.

Chapter 4
Psychological Influences on Nonverbal Communication
Making Sense of Psychological Processes

Chapter Overview

As in the chapters dealing with cultural and social influences on nonverbal communication, topics from chapter one will be discussed here from a psychological perspective. Psychologists have studied human behavior from a variety of perspectives, orientations and approaches, ranging from biological, cognitive and neuropsychological approaches to social psychological and clinical approaches. Today, transpersonal and quantum psychology have emerged, along with various post-modern perspectives. Recently, it has been suggested that psychological study should be based on corporality and corporeal processes (Harre, 1991). Nonverbal communication of course is about corporeality, or the body, and the ways humans perceive and use it.

Human behavior is influenced deeply and profoundly by psycho-genetic factors. The nature-nurture argument continues unresolved although it is clear that body and mind together produce nonverbal communicative behavior. Humans perform "acts of meaning" (Bruner,1990). The child at birth is dependent upon others; later, as the child matures, she builds up social skills and is able to perform nonverbal tasks with competence. As mentioned, it takes time for a child to learn simple tasks like sitting up and eating with a fork and spoon. Later, as a young adult the person will use complex self management skills, managing self impressions, presenting the self competently.

Although SI was developed and shaped in Sociology, it is highly influential in Social Psychology as well (Jones, 1964, 1990; Leary, 1996; Howard & Hollander, 1996). As in other chapters, it is this approach that is taken. Some of the topics discussed in previous chapters are presented from a psychological perspective. Important psycho-biological aspects of behavior are added as well.

Ethological and Biological Influences

Theories of Consciousness

That humans are conscious is not questioned; what consciousness is presents quite another question. "I think, therefore I am" is a famous saying implying that consciousness is evidenced by thought processes which are now understood to be neuro-chemically produced, but in early Egyptian times, the heart was thought to be the center of reasoning. Today, multiple theories of the mind abound. (1)

Framing Theories of the Mind

Multiple theories: One hypothesis suggests that consciousness arises from a combination of memory and attention; a Darwinist view suggests that neural mechanisms compete to provide an accurate model of the world, a theory of the mind; a quantum consciousness approach suggests that the mind is a product of interactions taking place at the subatomic level of reality; an antimaterialist approach suggests that the mind cannot be explained by resorting to materialist explanations; The Haldane hypothesis says that evolution has placed limits on what the mind can do. Rats, for example, cannot think about relativity (Davis, 1997).

Symbolic interactionists relate mind, self and society together interactively; they do not reduce the concept of mind to the level of organisms or neurons. There is an old African saying that declares, "If you can talk, you can sing; if you can walk, you can dance". But the ability to dance is not a material thing; rather, it is cultural and learned. One cannot reduce the dancer to a set of neurons. One cannot talk meaningfully about dancing when it is reduced to a specific area of the brain, as though the activity were simply neuro-chemical.

In Meadian thought, the mind directed and influenced human behavior in social interaction, producing a sense of self.

Ethology and Behavior

Evolutionary psychologists and ethologists assert that human nonverbal communication is shared by other species, especially by higher order primates. (Eibl-Eibestadt, 1975; E.O Wilson, 1992). Even very abusive acts, such as rape, have been cast in evolutionary terms in an attempt to explain why humans rape (NY Times Online, March 14, 2000). Other forms of physical aggression, such as war or street gang fights, have been studied by evolutionary psychologists in an effort to minimize their destructive effects. Perhaps new studies of the genetic make-up of humans and other species will lead to an understanding of aggression or to why males seem to engage in bully behavior more than do females.

Primates and other animals signal with their eyes, they bare their teeth, they play, use tools; parrots even appear to talk like humans (Potter, March 3, 2000). Researchers suggest that the hair that is raised on the back of a dog under fear conditions is somehow related to the goose-pimples that appear on humans when they are scared. In short, there appears to be an evolutionary path that species, along with humans, seem to be trodding (LeDoux,1996). Chimps, for example, have been trained to use a large number of nonverbal phrases or words and cues that appear to be closely akin to the behaviors of humans. Indeed, the Genome Research institute (NHGRI) in Bethesda, Maryland, has shown that the DNA of chimpanees is 98.5 percent identical to the DNA of humans. This naturally leads to the assumption that the differences between chimps and humans is one of degree rather than kind.

Claims have been made that chimps can recognize human speech patterns, but can they think, too? Not if one uses the "hardwired" concept, which refers to the neuronal behaviors of lower order animals; the implication is that animals act without thinking. It is generally believed that lower order animals do not have mentative abilities, but there is a dispute about whether chimps can think like humans do. Humans think about their bodies, about behaviors, interpreting them, symbolizing them. Apparently, chimps, like dolphins, can recognize themselves in a mirror, which suggests that they may have a sense of self, of self-awareness.

All primates have five senses but they are developed differently from those of humans, adapted for specialized purposes or environments. Obviously, humans do not use their hands and arms to swing from a tree as chimps do; the human hand is similar to a chimp's hand but sufficiently different to permit humans to grasp and use tools in sophisticated ways. Many ethologists maintain that human behavior is not far removed from chimp behavior, although there are substantial differences. There are a number of associated issues, not the least of which is the issue of human uniqueness, brought up by people who prefer to think that human behavior should not be ethologically associated with the behavior of lesser animals.

Autonomic Activities

Pupil size and breathing are two activities that are activated autonomously; the autonomic nervous system (ANS)controls the behavior. Both of these body functions may be influenced by context, but essentially they are unwilled actions. The iris changes in size under different lighted conditions and under different emotional situations as early research on cats and animals revealed (Hess, 1975). For example, people attach meaning to pupil size. It is recorded that belladonna was used by early Egyptians to make their pupils enlarge; larger were pupils considered more beautiful than small pupils (Richmond & McCroskey, 1992). Even today, women highlight their eyes for the same reasons. People use body semantics in everyday life; they attach meaning to body actions.

Breathing becomes labored when people are ill or when they exert themselves physically, perhaps by running fast. Although sponge divers and others have learned to increase the time that they can hold their breath, from the moment of birth, when as neonates they gasped for breath, breathing was essentially out of their control. There are limiting thresholds. Even though such body activities are not completely under their control, people attach meanings to them. For example, when people sneeze, they may hear someone say, "Bless you!" in signal response. When people itch or scratch, others may wonder if they need a bath. But itching and scratching are essentially adaptive mechanisms. Adaptors, designed to protect the body, are feedback mechanisms. Tics and spasms are biological phenomena but they are given symbolic meaning by observers. In short, physical behaviors are social behaviors as well. They nonverbally communicate something to the observer.

Neuronal, Sensory, Perceptual and Emotional Processes.

The Brain

With the use of modern imaging machines, such as scanning devices, researchers are beginning to focus on how the brain controls and affects human behavioral activities. PET technology, or positron emission technology, permits researchers to track the flow of blood in the brain; this is important because blood moves to the area of the brain that is associated with the performance of tasks, such as speaking. It is suggested that various activities are localized in the brain while others tend to be spread throughout the brain. Humans enact their lives socially, but they do so heavily influenced by biological-neuronal processes. All human activity, from self talk to action, to perceiving, seeing and remembering, to smelling, touching and the use of the senses are centered in some way in the human brain, in the way it processes information.

Laterilization of the brain, or hemispheric specialization, is gender and sex related; that is, females and males use the brain in differently patterned ways. Recent research suggests that this specialization is not rigid or strictly divided, it is a matter of emphasis. (LeDoux, 1996). Although there is some localization, it now appears that many parts of the brain fire up to accomplish various tasks, although women tend to use the right side of the brain more than do men.

Framing Specialization in the Brain

Approximately 96 percent of the American public is right handed, meaning that language is lateralized to the left; curiously, left-handers, on the other hand, are lateralized to the right for the production of language in only about 15 percent of all cases (Zaidel,1994). Language appears to involve the use of many parts of the brain even though it is basically left-sided. Visual processes, too, seem to be spread across many brain areas; the right hemisphere appears to house perception.

Interestingly, brain size does not appear to be correlated with intelligence(Gould, 45) nor does the brain feel pain, a fact which allows researchers to investigate a living brain. Researchers have investigated pleasure and control centers by touching them and observing finger, facial and other body movements. In a book titled, "Conversations with Neal's Brain", the writer, a reporter, remained awake during an operation on his brain and carried on conversations with the operating doctor, telling him about the sensations that were created when the doctor touched various parts of his brain.

Clearly, the brain influences nonverbal behavior in the thought-act process. Altzheimers disease, epilepsy, Parkinsons's disease and other physical maladies interrupt and impede neuronal processes, illustrating the intimate connection between the functioning of the brain and human behavior. How humans interpret the meaning of behavior, however, is a symbolizing process.

In England, a university professor, head of the Cybernetics Department at the University of Reading, a futurist, has wired himself, implanting a computer chip into his nervous system, hoping to discover whether the brain can pick up sonar signals (CNN, Dec 7, 2000). The attachment of machinery to body functions, including the brain, is becoming more common in modern societies. The belief is that scientists can understand the brain better and maybe even improve how it works by connecting machines to the body. A contemporary imaginative metaphor refers to these efforts as the Cyborg Factor.

Psychology, Biology and The Senses

The senses were discussed in Chapter Two showing how cultural beliefs influence the ways that natives in the culture view the senses. In this chapter, the five senses are discussed from a bio-psychological perspective. Each of the five senses--taste and smell acting as chemical senses and touch acting as a contact sense-- is located in a specific controlling area of the brain. Smell, for example, is controlled at the base of the frontal lobe, closely tied into the brain. People use figurative language that reveals how they think about the senses. People may say that something "smells like a dead rat"or that something "tastes rotten" or that "you can't touch him with a 10 foot pole". In short, humans symbolize all bodily activities, think about them and incorporate their thoughts in language. In fact, human languages contain many references to sensate activities. Below, the five senses are outlined showing their importance and how they relate one to the other. The research involving each sense is variously developed, more interest being shown about the visual sense, for example, than about the smelling sense.

Oculesics. In Western cultures, as mentioned, vision, or sight, dominates the sensual world, touch being not far behind. The ability to see is a result of highly complex neural functions. If the retina is blemished, for example, or if neural connections from the eye to the brain are impaired, as may happen more to the aged in society than to younger people, the 20/20 standard is not met. Perception is associated with seeing. For example, it may be that two people seeing the same color may not label it the same way because they do not construe it in the same way.

People who have synesthesia, a disease in which the victim confuses colors, numbers, days, and activities, as part of their visual production process, are not able to use their brain in a normal way. The neuro-chemical network is imbalanced. Various parts of the brain intrude on one another, forcing colors onto objects that are not normally colored. In short, the meaning of an object is not located in the object, but in the brain and in the symbolic world of the perceiver. Humans see things selectively; that is, the focus of their attention is usually directed to something that is salient or important to them. In interaction, people may focus mostly on the eyes or the mouth. Selective attention enables people to focus, to disregard that which they think is irrelevant. The downside is, of course, that they may miss important actions or events by focusing narrowly on a specific target.

The physiological mechanism through which humans see, of course, is the eye, which is symbolized in various ways. As mentioned, it is said that the eyes are the windows to the soul or that people have a third eye, which discerns spiritual entities. In popular writings, shamans are said to see through their navels (Castaneda, 1969).

Meteorologists use the "eye on the sky" and people "eye-ball" this or that and "big brother is watching us". He doesn't "see what I mean". The CBS network uses the eye as an icon of identification. All of the above examples show how physical processes become social-perceptual processes. Human language is closely tied to body behaviors. Indeed the spoken language can be related back to nonverbal behaviors either directly or indirectly.

Haptics. Touch and tactility have been studied by ethologists and researchers concerned about human behavior. The skin, which is the largest organ of the human body, is variously sensitive. That is, the skin on the elbow is not nearly as sensitive as the skin of the underarm. Using a kind of "dermal vocabulary", one can even discern what is being written on his back.

Tactility, or touch, is coded; that is, humans create rules of conduct for touching. Touch codes vary among the young and the old, between the genders, and by situation. For example, in the United States, males are not supposed to touch females above the knee or near the breasts, even though the female may be wearing a skimpy bikini, her body visible to the eye. On the other hand, lovers touch intimately, following romantic ideals. Babies are touched all over their bodies by their parents. Older people may be touch deprived, especially when they have lost their companion or live in homes for the aged. Touch codes are gendered. It is suggested that males and females differ in how they use comforting strategies through touch. In general, women are more likely to touch in order to comfort others than are men (Dolin & Booth-Butterfield, 1993).

Thus, humans take into account the social rules that influence how they touch. Different contexts allow different behaviors. For example, a medical doctor is permitted to touch her patients professionally, whether they are men or women, as part of their medical codes (Jones, 1994). As mentioned in chapter two touch codes vary considerably from one culture to another.

Aurality. The ability to hear varies considerably between species and across the human age span. Lower order animals may have well-developed hearing abilities, as do many creatures of prey. In humans, hearing is aided by the receipt of information from the other senses. There is generalization across some senses (Green, Hulse, & Mowsfield, 1999). Indeed, in many human actions, the reportoire of senses is involved, each sense coordinated with the other. For example, when people hear something, they orient their bodies toward it, to visualize it. The senses, taken together as a sensorium, enable people to locate themselves. A sound in the night may arouse the emotions or strike fear in their minds and people go searching for the source or meaning of the sound.

To compensate for the lack of hearing, hearing-impaired people may "hear" others by lip-reading, a skill that most people do not acquire. Popular myth says that Native Americans could put their ear to the ground to hear what the white man could not hear. As with the other senses, people have hearing thresholds, or levels, below or beyond which most humans cannot hear. This range of frequencies may be constricted as people age.

Olfaction. Smelling ability varies considerably from culture to culture as it does among animal species. Perhaps it is the least examined sensory mechanism. It cannot be mediated by thought, unlike the other senses. The ability to smell is elemental. The olfactory bulb at the top of the nose feeds directly into the limbic system, which is the most primitive part of the brain, where the emotions, cognition and sexual response are initiated. Therefore, odors can evoke powerful emotions. The anthropologist E.T. Hall suggested that Americans are culturally underdeveloped regarding the sense of smell, resulting in olfactory blandness and sameness (Horvitz, 1997). Despite this belief, or perhaps because of it, arachmologists are enjoying a new status in American life, testing odors to see if they stimulate romance or to determine what appeals to the consumer public. Aromachology, the study of smells, is a term claimed to be coined by researchers at the Olfactory Research Fund.

Whatever the status of research, in the everyday world, people associate fragrances with colors, knowing how a red rose smells, even attaching romantic thoughts to the colors and odors. People associate thoughts with odors; memories are associated with smells. Smells, visual images, tactility, sounds, tastes and emotions work together to produce memories. There is generalization across sensory modes. The smell of grandmother's kitchen brings warm feelings. Smell memories, experiences in life that are associated with smells or odors, are triggered and brought to consciousness when similar smells are encountered in the present.

As another illustration, it was said that the the country doctor was able to detect diseases, or miasma, by their smell and appearance, experience playing a role (Montagu, 1971). Whatever the truth of this example, other claims are made that the sense of smell is involved in mate selection and that pheromones, arising from glands in the armpits, let an interested person know about the individual's health and sexual desirability. Further, arachmotherapists claim that one can improve her mood merely by smelling certain essences. For example, it is claimed that peppermint and vanilla reduce anxiety. For now, these claims are without evidentiary foundation. It is known, however, that gender and age affect the ability to smell.

Researchers have attempted to classify smells into a scale, much like a musician classifies notes on a scale or painters select colors from the color spectrum. Some research suggests that there are nine basic odors that may be combined in many ways (National Geographic, 1987). Enologists and winetasters are able to detect fine nuances between and among varieties of wines, something that the average drinker may not be able to do. It appears that the ability to smell can be improved with training.

Gustatory Processes. In order to taste things, people must touch them with their tongues, although tastes can be triggered by memories. One can almost taste something by thinking about it. The tongue is able to distinguish very coarse textures from very fine ones and very sweet ones from very sour ones. Young children pucker their lips when something tastes sour, indicating that this sense may be somewhat hardwired. Yet, people acquire tastes and taste preferences, one person preferring what another dislikes. The ability to distinguish tastes is affected by cycles in the female body and by aging factors; different tastes are preferred as one goes through life stages or experiences significant body changes. In the production of foods, the chef knows that special customers prefer their foods salty or spicy, but that others want them to be bland. What people prefer depends greatly on how they have symbolized various tastes and on the foodways with which they were familiar in their youth. It is probably the case that many northerners have never tasted vinegar pie, a southern treat, nor have they tasted hot, green chili peppers associated with the southwest. In short, tastes are associated with experiences, often regionally based, as the study of foodways shows.

Important to this section about the senses is the fact that people are furnished with knowledge by the senses, which they use to help them evaluate how they feel and think about things, in the construction of meaning. The senses do not operate independently; rather, they are coordinated around specific tasks. They work together in nearly every situation. The more that the senses are coordinated, the more knowledge the individual can derive and use.

The Emotions

The study of the emotions was jump started by Charles Darwin, who believed that they served evolutionary, adaptive functions. Their study has attracted a large amount of research (Andersen & Guerrrero, 1998; Goleman, 1995; Izard, 1977, 1990). The SADFISH emotions, referring to seven types of emotions discussed in Chapter Two, have been studied by a number of scholars, some of whom believe that these emotions are universal and innate (Ekman & Friesen, 1972). But, it is not clear how emotions were developed even though it would appear that each emotion may have been developed for adaptive reasons (LeDoux, 1996). The experience of fear, for example, may serve as an evolutionary warning signal that danger is afoot.

Framing Fear

Fear seems to be pervasive in human affairs. Humans express fear when they must deal with symbolically labeled fear items, such as snakes, tigers, airplane crashes, blood, horror movies, and so on. They become alarmed, scared, frightened, anguished, panicked, unnerved, and defensive, to name a few responses that characterize fear.

Action often precedes thinking when people are startled by something, such as the very loud noise that disturbs the sleep. People respond reflexively. A frightened person may be temporarily unable to speak, the protective response system taking over. Terrified people may lash out, scratch, bite, hit or kill. Fear, it appears, is expressed in similar ways across the animal kingdom; in this sense, the fear response plays an important role in evolution, resulting in an almost programmed response. Too much fear, of course, is a problem for humans, often requiring psychoanalysis (LeDoux, 1996).

It is not clear where the emotions are centered in the brain; they may occupy different areas of the brain. Emotions, apparently, are associated with a modular network in the brain, connected in the frontal cortex region, but how they "fire up" is not clear. Is there an underlying neural mechanism that controls the various emotions? The fact that children who were born sightless may smile, even though they do not see what they are smiling about, suggests that there may be something emotionally innate causing the display. On the other hand, people learn through experience to display their emotions. One usually does not laugh at a funeral, nor does one usually cry when she is happy.

Important research continues to focus on how the emotions function (Andersen & Guerrero, 1998). It is interesting that people may feel something but not display the feeling in any discernible way. It is clear, too, that people can force a smile and create a feeling of happiness. One can imagine a happy moment and then feel a sense of happiness. People smile when they feel good about something; on the other hand, the act of smiling can produce good feelings, an interesting twist. A smiling face is associated with good feelings.

Framing Display Rules

To understand one another, humans must be able to understand emotional displays, which vary from culture to culture, between genders and ethnic groups and even by age. Five display rules have been used to analyze nonverbal behaviors. They are:

repetition. The body can be used to say yes or no in keeping with spoken words, by shaking the head for example;

substitution. The body can speak emblematically without words;

complementing. The body can be used to reinforce what is said;

contradiction. The body can be used to oppose verbal statements;

emphasis. Nonverbal gestures can be used to make a point in a verbal discussion (adapted from Ekman & Friesen, 1969.

Some researchers believe that there are emotional tonics, or pre-existing states, that when aroused, produce emotional displays (Andersen & Guerrero, 1998).

As discussed previously, a body of research suggests that people leak emotional information even though they may not want to. People can mask various emotions, but they may also give themselves away. For example, when deliberately lying, humans may unwittingly give off signals, perhaps by exhibiting nervousness, or by producing an obviously feigned smile. (Buller & Burgoon, 1998). It would seem that emotional display rules must be circumvented if a person is to deceive others successfully. Researchers want to know to what extent one can mask feelings and to what extent observers can detect the masking. Some evidence suggests that observers can distinguish emotions at little better than the chance level and it appears that spontaneous emotions may be more difficult to detect than prolonged emotions. Other research suggests that positive emotions of joy and happiness may be more distinguishable than negative ones, such as sadness and disgust (Ekman & Friesen, 1975).

Whatever the emotion, it is clear that emotional behavior is learned in context through socialization; children learn what is appropriate and what is not (Buck, 1982, 1984). Indeed, the concept of emotional literacy or EQ, like the concept of the intelligence quotient (IQ) is promoted by a number of scholars and people who are interested in emotional health.(Goleman, 1995), The assumption is that people can learn about emotions-- how to feel them, display and control them. For example, people who display angry outbursts inappropriately or people who are "locked in" emotionally can change these negative emotional displays which were learned during their early socialization.

An individual's emotions are influenced by the context. For example, crowd behavior is emotionally contagious behavior, influencing individuals within the crowd. The emotional contagion thesis suggests that humans pick up on the feelings of others and act just like them, sharing emotional behaviors; collective emotion is the result. The emotions may be spontaneous, but they arise from the context. When people watch musical performances they share in a context that permits the display of emotions. Emotions are shared by members of a marching band, by students who march for a cause, by people who attend a concert. The meaning of the event influences how emotions will be displayed. There is a relationship between the meaning of the event and how emotions are displayed.

This thought-emotion relationship has received recent scholarly attention. Scholars, focusing on the relationship between cognition and the emotions, suggest that much thinking, perhaps most, is accompanied by emotion. Thoughts are connected to feelings. Thoughts usually are centered on experiences, which have an emotional flavor. In other words, the college professor may talk about a topic in a dispassionate way; yet, when pressed to talk about the topic, he may reveal an emotional attachment to the ideas in the topic. When people say they have a favorite topic or a good idea, they may be saying that they are emotionally, positively oriented to the idea. Yet, people can and do control their emotions, framing them in accordance with cultural display rules. "Men don't cry" or "don't be a sissy" are statements that young male Americans have heard, indicating that they should be stoic and strong. Perhaps these teachings have led many young males to be out of touch with their own emotions. Of course, people must learn to manage their emotions through affect control; otherwise, they will not act appropriately toward others. (MacKinnon, 1994). For example, professional therapists, have learned about emotion and its relationship to emotional and mental health; they are able to control their emotions as they relate to clients in therapy. They co-construct therapeutic reality, displaying and controlling their emotions for the purposes of analysis and therapy.

In summary, there is an intimate connection between the emotions and body action. Emotions are expressed through body actions, or body channels, such as the eyes, the hands or the voice, as in yells and shouts (Planalp, 1999). People may involuntarily sweat, urinate, vomit or blush, expressing uncontrolled emotions, which are not intended by the actor to communicate anything in particular. Yet, when observed by others, they are given meaning, whether the actor likes it or not. This type of accidental communication is common. People see happiness in a walk, in the way that the arms swing and in the speed of walking. Depressed people tend to gesture less and to hold their heads down more than do nondepressed people (Segrin, 1998). Certainly emotional expressions vary by circumstances. When one is sick or deeply fatigued, perhaps it is easier to show depression, even sadness, but when one is feeling healthy, perhaps it is easier to show the sparkling smile.

Symbolic interactionists focus on the symbolic nature of body action and upon the idea that there may be multiple interpretations of any given action by an actor. Human behavior may be interpreted polysemically or monosemically. People may walk slowly for a variety of reasons, not merely because they are depressed; the seasoned observor knows that any particular interpretation may miss the mark.

Chronobiology

Recent medical research is focused on how time and biology interact. The topic centers on built-in biological and psychological clocks, in a field called chronobiology. The evidence, just emerging, suggests that digestion, respiration and hormone production fluctuate over the course of a day, a week, or even a year, mostly because people respond to dark and light, to sleep and temperature and to other background conditions. (Snyderman, Jan 24, 2001). Scholars, of course, have studied chronobiology under several different themes.

Framing A Chronobiological Growth Pattern

Humans change in patterned ways over the period of time from birth to death. A basic model of physical development that applies to Americans suggests the following:

The prenatal stage: The basic body structure forms (pre-birth).

Infancy: The senses of the child are fully engaged (to age 3).

Early childhood: The motor skills develop (3-6 years).

Middle childhood: Physical growth slows; cognitive gains (6-12 years).

Adolescence: Physical changes are profound; reproductive maturity occurs (12-20).

Young adulthood: Health peaks; cognition is more complex (20-40).

Middle Age: problem solving ability is high; menopause (40-65 years).

Late adulthood: Slowed reaction time; coping with losses (65 yrs, older) (Papalia, Olds, & Feldman, & Feldman, 1998).

This physiological model of growth, above, shows how time interacts with human growth, how people grow physically, cognitively and socially over a period of years. Modern research suggests that there are diurnal changes in the body as well, influencing behaviors throughout the day. People have suggested that they are "day" or "night" people; perhaps recent research will review the dynamics of diurnal change, whether male or female.

Psychological and Symbolic Processes

The Perceptual-Attribution Process

Humans become aware of themselves and their social world through perceptual processes. They make sense of things through a perceptual lens. Perceptions yield knowledge, although it is not always accurate. People label one another and attach labels to themselves based on their perceptions. Individual experiences influence how the self and social acts are viewed; the construal of the self, for example, is largely dependent upon how parents and others have influenced the child.

Psychologists know that human perceptions are biased, that they involve stereotyping, that they parcel out reality according to the limitations of experience and that they tend to focus on what is considered important by the person. For example, some White Americans perceive Black Americans people as threatening so they reduce their contacts with them. Native Americans, the Navajo in this case, do not celebrate Columbus Day, having a very negative association with the white man's arrival. In short, humans selectively attend to matters that are salient; perceptions may be shared widely, such that regions of a country may have a regional flavor.

Perceptions are based on sensory mechanisms; pain, pleasure, and other emotions arise from sensory experiences (Baron, 1996). People learn to adapt and use information that is provided by the senses. For example, children learn that unheated bath water feels cold and expect it when they take the next bath. In short, perceptual baggage, learned from the past, is brought to the present. When humans attribute meaning to an act, event or to themselves and others, they affix semantic markers, or labels, to the the phenomena. For example, one child may attribute meanness to the parent who is spanking or scolding another child, identifying with the pain being inflicted on the child.

The attribution process, of course, is involved in nearly every daily activity; unfortunately, it may result in stereotypical thinking. Lacking further information, in a first impression, one may conclude something about the other that does not bear out over time. First impressions may not be lasting impressions. People who hastily attribute demeaning qualities to another person are using early closure, not being open to the receipt of new, accurate information. The attribution process is a way of finding causes in other people's behavior. People attribute wealth to doctors; sometimes they attribute chicanery to lawyers. Women may say that he is doing the "man thing"; men may say that she is acting "just like a woman". In short, the attribution process, although it is necessary part of the symbolizing process, may be selective, distorted and based on little information.

When people with anexoria describe themselves as being fat or overweight, when in fact they are very thin, they have distorted the image of their bodies. Not realizing that being fat is a cultural perception, they become slaves to a concept, one that can be changed. For example, it has been shown that Black American women tend to obsess over their weight far less than do White American women (Angier, Nov 7, 2000) and that media images contribute to anexoria according to the British Medical Association (CNN, May 30, 2000). In short, perception and attributions may be distorted.

In another example of distorted perceptions and attributions, it has been reported that shyness is the third most common mental disorder in the United States. Shy people, of course, are not inclined to seek help, due to their self-image. Unfortunately, they may have labeled themselves as weird or socially misfit. Dr. Mark Olfson of Columbia University reports that from the onset of the shyness disorder, on average, it is thirteen years before shy people seek professional help (CNN, Jan 16, 2000). One purpose of this book is to show readers how the symbolizing process works, expecting that this knowledge will help them create meanings that rest on solid foundations, through careful analysis.

Consciousness, Nonconsciousness and Dreams

Since the development of early psychoanlaytic theory under Freud, Jung and others, the unconscious was thought to be a repository of information about the meaning of things that happen in life. Freud thought that the patient gave off unconscious signals, by moving the foot or by walking the fingers. His patients were not aware of these signals. In other words, the body spoke its own language; the discerning psychotherapist's job was to know meanings that were hidden from the patient, bringing them to light as a form of ventilation therapy.

People may say they feel fine but their body may be tightened up in "knots", indicating that they are out of touch with their bodies. Just how the unconscious, or subconscious mind influences everyday behavior is not entirely clear. Certainly body chemistry combined with life experiences will go a long way to help explain these relationships. It is not only the schizophrenic (Birdwhistell, 1970) who may be out of touch with his or her body; humans, in general, may be out of touch with their own body and related social processes. Self-awareness is a variously learned process.

When people make plans, they do it consciously, aware that they are doing so. That is, people prepare a shopping list, planning to go to the store. They may even visualize how they will shop, with the bread winding up on top of the heavier groceries. People who are used to doing the shopping may shop almost routinely; but the routine character of the activity belies the fact that they learned how to shop over a period of time. Two year old children have not mastered the ability to shop. Routines come about through experience.

The dramaturgical ideas that are part of this text suggest that people are purposive, that they plan rationally to do things(2). Not all SI researchers, however, are so certain that the sum of nonverbal behaviors are the result of conscious planning. For example, the role of habituation, of non-conscious performance, as in repeated performances, and the role of automatic responses seem clear. In novel situations, however, the individual must schematize and come to grips with new information with which she or he is unfamiliar. Novel situations, like puzzles, require the application of imagination. Even the highly skilled professional tennis player must adapt to the game of a competitor. She or he may study films that show how the other player typically acts and reacts during a game in preparation for the contest. Conscious planning is needed.

Sleeping and Dreaming

The role of sleep is receiving new attention. For example, it is suggested that sleep deprivation interrupts skillful performances and that people have "sleep windows" and sleep periods, such as the last two hours of sleep, that directly affect the quality of their performances. People are encouraged to "sleep on it". The role of dreams in human behavior is receiving new attention as well. A variety of scientific approaches have been formulated to account for dreaming. Darwin believed that all animals, including birds, dreamed.

Framing Dream Analysis

By and large, dreams are seen as psychologically meaningful and important or they are seen as meaningless waste products of brain metabolism. It has been proposed that dreaming is a way to deal with redundant information, acting as a dumping ground. Another, very different approach is that dreams are meaningful, suggesting that a hermeneutic interpretive mode of dream analysis can be productive. From this perspective, dreams are rich in meaning. Dreams can promote decision making; they can clarify, and they may fire the imagination.

To understand the greater reality beyond the purely personal ego, one might consult dreams. "The desire to possess this reality is what has produced analysis: It has also produced religion, mythology, psychology, and art---all attempt to construct mirrors of the Self, to find a cultural route to individuation, and to the achievement of higher consciousness."(Stevens, 1995).

Jung stressed that dreams contain collective and individual symbols. Individuals have stored within their unconscious the many memories of the two million year old man. Humans perform daily acts against a backdrop of deep cultural and symbolic meaning common to modern individuals and to their ancestors, embedded in their unconscious processes.

Dreaming may be important to the building of memories and for learning. The psychology of dreaming, often associated with REM studies, is yielding new understandings about how humans dream, even about the contents. For example, in a recent study involving 49 men and 115 women, 33 percent of the men and 40 percent of the women recalled having experienced sensations of smell or taste in their dreams. Auditory experiences were reported in approximately 53 percent of all dream reports. Women, more than men, reported references to olfactory sensations (Zadra, Nielsen & Doneri, 1998). As noted, theories about the role and nature of the dreaming process abound. Dreams are commonly experienced by most people; certainly, the content of dreams is shaped by human experiences and culture, but often the dreams are a mixed, confusing mosaic, of disconnected and intertwined events and people. Yet, at least one Nobel Prize winner claims that he discovered symbolic clues leading him to solve a scientific puzzle through a dream.

Dream analysis is both popular with the public and important to scholars (Domhoff, 1996). Over the course of history, kings and other leaders have sought out diviners and others who could interpret a particular dream, to show the implications of the dream for the person. Dreams appear to be loaded with symbolic meaning, not always understood by the dreamer.

Mindfulness and Scripted Behaviors

Considerable attention has been paid to the concept of scripted behaviors, of scripts used in everyday life. Humans act as though they were following scripted lines on the stage of life, dramaturgists say. These scripts arise from experiences of the individual as she or he is socialized. Although adults will not remember everything about their past, they do have episodic memories (Tulving, & Thompson, 1973), salient images of the past that still influence them. Females learn distinctive ways of behaving as do males. People from urban centers tend to approach their experiences differently from people raised on a farm. Their reflections on their experiences lead them to fairly stable schematic representations, which they draw upon as they interpret events in their lives. Ethnic groups learn ways of expressing themselves that are uniquely associated with them. Thoughtways, perceptions and learned behaviors are employed in everyday interactive life as scripts. If one were to ask where her mother learned to be a mother, she may reply that she does not know, or she may say that she learned from her mother. Scripts seem to just occur or happen; but they are learned. In a general sense, scripts are self-fulfilling prophecies. They are efficient mechanisms, seemingly operating without much attention.

The concept of mindfulness and mindlessness (Burgoon & Langer, 1995; Langer, 1989) suggests that humans vary in their focusing abilities, their skill to analyze carefully. People who are very aware of themselves, of their body parts, of their interactions with others are said to be mindful and attentive. Others, less motivated or careful, may be considered relatively mindless, not learning from their experiences. The idea of skill in nonverbal communication arises directly from paying attention mindfully, of monitoring the self. Scholars refer to individuals as being either high or low self monitors (Leary, 1996). From this perspective, the skilled actor, a high self monitor, learns to act successfully, fulfilling the demands of the situation, managing the self and the impressions she creates.

Identity and Self

In Chapter Three, the concept of identity was focused upon. It appeared in that chapter because identity is achieved through socialization(Denzin, 1972; Persell, 1987); however, the study of identity has a rich history in psychology as well. The words used by researchers from varying persuasions to describe personhood differ; in this text the idea of self and the idea of self-concept are closely allied, although there are minor technical differences.

Mead, who gave early symbolic interactionism its psycho-philosophical orientation (Mead, 1934), believed that humans learn to view themselves as the I and the Me. The "I" part of the self was the active, subjective part; the"Me" part of the self, or the objective part, was influenced by the activities of the I, or the dynamic part. Cooley, another early scholar who influenced the SI orientation considerably, developed the concept of the looking-glass self, which suggested that humans use social interactions as they use a looking glass, to take a good look at who they are. By taking account of the ways that others in interaction treat them, individuals reflect upon their perceived attitudes and views and internalize them in conversations with the self. Gradually, the self, the identity of the self, emerges (Hewitt, 1999). Humans, having construed or reflected upon who they are, perceive the world through the self lenses. Lines of human action emerge from this self-reflexivity. The reader should bear in mind that, just as in the use of the terms IQ, mind or soul, the word self does not describe a physical thing located somewhere within the inner person. It is a symbolic, metaphorical concept. Scholars who study self and identity approach it from a variety of perspectives. For example, they may research it from cognitive, motivational, emotional or behavioral positions. Indeed, recent scholars emphasize the concept of the multiple self or the saturated self (Gergen, 1991) to indicate that the idea of self is dynamic and somewhat fluid and that it reflects the situation in which it is involved. In the modern world, researchers are concerned about how identity can be achieved in a fractured society, where little seems to be stable. Parents who work, their children arriving home before they do, may be concerned about the role of television and the internet on their children, to be discussed in a later chapter.

Identity of course is an achievement. The concept of face is part of it, as is the presentation of self. Playing the sleuth, researchers analyzed an adolescent's bedroom below.

Framing Adolescent Identity

The everyday work of creating an adolescent identity is reflected in how his bedroom looks. Humans use cultural symbols, myths and rituals as they build their identity. Especially important to youth are popular images from television, film and popular music. By examining the bedrooms of youth, researchers believe that they can uncover identity-building activities of adolescents (Brown, Dykers, Steele & White, 1994).

Self identity is important to the understanding of interpersonal behaviors. Recently the International Society for Self and Identity established an online interdisciplinary journal devoted to the topic of identity. The journal, appropriately titled, Self and Identity, is devoted to an analysis of self-awareness, self-representation and self-regulation, all topics that are included in the study of nonverbal communication.

The Body as a Medium of Expression

Body Shine

Thus far, topics associated with subconscious and conscious symbolizing activities have been discussed. The body, of course, goes with people wherever they go. Even when they are shy, a fairly serious 'problem' in the United States among young people, people carry their bodies with them. The shy person may try to hide her or his body, or bury himself in the classroom out of the sight of the teacher, but he cannot be rid of his body presence. People live within the reality of their bodies. They create meaning and metaphors for them. The shy person has created an identity based on his experiences.

Although people observe the bodies of others because they are in full view, they cannot always see their own bodies. For that reason, it may not be entirely clear to them that their bodies give off signals to others. As an example of unawareness, most people, perhaps, are not aware of the asymmetry of their bodies. Except in extreme cases, for example, when one side of the jaw droops more than the other as in Bell's palsy, people are not aware of body asymmetry. Observers, however, may observe the asymmetry that the owner has not observed.

The human body is asymmetrical in many ways as noted below.

Framing Body Asymmetry

If we look in the mirror and try to imagine a line drawn down the center of our body, from the top of the head, down the nose, down to the crotch, we can see that each side of our body has a counterpart, roughly the same on each side. There are two parts of most things including the eyes, the cheeks, the arms, the legs and feet. On the inside, however, there is but one heart, one liver, one stomach, one pancreas, one spleen. These are asymmetrically placed; even the lungs which are paired are different sized, as is the lateralization of the brain (Izpisua, 1999).

The point being discussed, of course, is not meant to embarrass people; rather, it is raised to show how people may not be aware of their own bodies. It is said that Adler, the famous psychologist, believed that he only had to look at the body to understand the person; before him, Freud believed that body movements told stories when words did not (Bull,1987). It is interesting, in this context, that children, sightless from birth, visually unaware of their bodies, use gestures, suggesting perhaps, that gestural use is not strictly a learned activity (Iverson & Susan Goldin-Meadow, 1998). Even though most people have sight, they may not visualize accurately their own bodies. As mentioned, people use body *adaptors*(3), such as scratching themselves, or they may smile or shake their heads as they read; however, even these activities may be performed unawares, unobserved by the self. Despite this unawareness, the body is an ever-present medium of expression (Benthrall & Polhemus,1975) It is involved in the social construction of meaning (Denzin,1972). Of course, some people are keenly aware of their bodies and how they use them.

Framing Bad Hair Days

According to a Yale study, men take a psychological beating when their hair goes awry, contrary to the myth that this is a woman's problem, if the research of psychologists at Yale University tells the full story. Both sexes, under bad hair conditions, felt less smart, less capable, more embarrassed and socially inept. On humid days, when the hair gets frizzled and limp, when it can't be managed, it was reported that women had to learn to live with it, negative as it was (CNN, Jan 26, 2000). Is the body the servant of the mind?

Bodies "shine", giving off cues and signals to others. The sweaty brow, the nervous hands, the compulsive behaviors are tell-tale signs to others, even though they may intrepret them stereotypically. Signals include facial expressions, gazing, the use of the limbs to gesture, postures, the use of space and time, and how people dress and vocalize. (Argyle, 1975) These signals and their display patterns vary from culture to culture; for example, the Navajo native may point with his lips rather than with his finger, a behavior that appears to be distinctive among Navajo members. In some cultures, it is considered rude to show the bottom of the foot; in others, it is considered appropriate to let others smell your breath. As noted, social codes and display rules vary from one culture to another, as do body semantics.

Body Metaphors

The SI approach to human behavior suggests that humans create their self images through interaction with others. For example, parents may unwittingly convey to their daughter that they think she is chubby, when, in fact, she is going through a pubescent period in life, where chubbiness occurs often. It is not the fact that she is chubby that matters; it is the parental suggestion that she has taken into account, internalized and made real to herself. The thought of being chubby may stick with her for the remainder of her life; on the other hand, she is free to re-symbolize herself in new ways as she matures. Through inner conversations with herself, she may decide to prove others wrong.

As shown in the chapter dealing with culture, the body is symbolized in many ways throughout the human world. Even lower order animals seem to be able to discern meanings behind body behaviors. For example, a dog, when defeated, may expose its throat to the stronger dog. Gorillas and other primates bear their teeth when they see other potentially threatening gorillas. Whereas lower order animals do not think about themselves, as least as far as can be determined, humans make a great deal of fuss over the appearance of their bodies. Psychiatrists in particular are interested in human identity as the following frame reveals.

Framing the Image of the Biblical Samson

Children are usually taught that Samson was a hero who fought the Philistines and fell victim to Delilah's wily charms, but several physicians suggest that this son of Manoah lied to his parents, stole from his neighbors, brawled with regularity and killed with abandon. Rather than being a hero, he was a classic example of someone suffering from antisocial personality disorder. Apparently Samson met six of seven criteria for diagnosis of the disorder as defined in the American Psychiatric Associations official diagnostic manual (Good, Feb 20, 2001).

Normalcy, Shyness and Pathologies

From birth, children are exposed to influences that help form how they think about their bodies (Messer, 1994). Children are very interested in people movement, in how people use their bodies. They are intrigued by cartoons and characters on television, but it is largely through the influence of the parents and others in close relationships that children develop images of their bodies. For example, at about age 2, or just before, children apparently begin to identify accurately their body parts; at about ages 3-6 children apparently can distinguish what is ugly from what is pretty. To be concerned about self-image is to be concerned about how others think.

The images and metaphors that a child attaches to her or his body are closely related to personal identity and notions about the self (Fisher,1986). Yet, curiously, children may grow up not really knowing much about their own bodies, as mentioned earlier. Perhaps this is due to early moral teachings which suggest, for example, that the body should not be touched in various places or that to expose the body in public is indecent.

Early research focused on personality correlates associated with body sizes and shapes (Sheldon, 1940). For example, a recent Australian study suggests that shorter boys tend to be held back in school (CNN Online, Jan 26, 2000). Whatever the reasons, short boys may suffer negative consequences in Australia. In America, it is clear that there are social rewards for being thin and beautiful. It would seem therefore, that the person who is thin and beautiful would tend to be more confident, outgoing and personable. Or, conversely, if a person is fat and sloppy, he or she might suffer the consequences in a society that does not reward this body behavior. Thus that person might become self-deprecating, perhaps even somewhat hostile.

Shyness

It has been reported previously that shyness is a major problem in the United States, perhaps related to the constant need for individuals, not only to be on stage, but to be on stage to be on stage, in acceptable ways.

Framing Shyness

Shyness seems to be a major problem, especially for young people, the results being that they may find it hard to relate to strangers or people in authority. Seeing themselves as social objects, as self-conscious individuals, shy people are intensely concerned about what others think of them, often seeing themselves as naked, as though others could see right through them. Shy people appear to lack social skills. (Coon, 1994)

Whatever the relationship is between body appearance and behavior, the topic is increasingly researched. For example, there is a correlation between the lack of early tactile nurturing and the drive for thinness and body dissatisfaction of girls. Deprivation of hugging, cuddling and other forms of touching by mothers and caregivers, appears to affect females more than it does boy (Gupta & Schork, 1995). Shyness would seem to be connected to the level of self-esteem. As mentioned, researchers have correlated positive touch with later self-esteem.

Because body images and metaphors are socially constructed, one finds a widely varying array of thoughts about the body in various sectors of societies. For example, in religious communities in the middle ages monks wore hair shirts in an effort to demean the sinful body and to achieve spirituality. Even in present day societies, one may find flagellation used as a rite of passage. Of course, the hairshirt mentality and the religious attitudes that inspired it do not exist in mainline America. The modern media, of course, are likely to present body images that are considered beautiful, handsome or desirable, there being few ugly people on film or television. One compares himself to others to see how he is faring. Even oversize people realize that they, too, can be attractive to self and others. Humans want to present themselves to others in desirable ways whether they meet a body index standard or not.

Biological and Psychological Disorders

There are an increasing number of biological and psychological disorders that are noted in the general populations. People have mood and anxiety disorders, in which despair and dread become parts of life. They have dissociative disorders, sexual and gender identity disorders. As mentioned eating disorders seem to be on the rise in the United States. Personality and schizophrenic disorders are being treated more effectively, given the rise of new therapies and pharmaceutics (Baron, 1996).

Whatever the disorder, biological, chemical, neuronal or psychological, it is associated with the uses of the body, as schizophrenic behavior illustrates. Essentially, such behavior is out of touch with normal reality. Language and thought are often distorted, depending on the nature of the problem. Sometimes hallucinations take place, and, as mentioned, people who demonstrate szhizophrenic behavior may be out of touch with their own and others emotions. Naturally, under these conditions, social relationships deteriorate.(Baron, 1996).

Differential Uses of the Body

The Eyes and Facial Primacy

As people "converse" with one another through nonverbal means, they draw upon particular body actions to do so. The eyes and the face are particularly useful to people as they interact with one another. As mentioned in Chapter Two, a considerable body of research shows that the emotions are expressed most detectably in the face and eyes (Russell & Fernandez-Dols, 1997). The eyes, of course, have directive features; they can point by looking. Often, where the eyes point is where the body goes. The configuration of the muscles around the eyes tells people, with some accuracy, which kinds of emotion are being felt. To show surprise, the eyebrows come into play in a very different way from when people are showing sadness. Darwin's study of the various uses of the human body emphasized the evolutionary purpose of expressions. For example, animals can express an approach or withdrawal orientation by the way they stare or include and invite other animals using their eyes and faces. Humans and other species may fix their gaze upon an object or another creature; or, they may choose to avert their gaze inattentively. Gaze and gaze aversion have been studied quite extensively as a signalling activities.

Framing the Face

The face is a special, privileged part of the body. People are identified largely by their faces. It is a unique identifier, clearly available to sight. It can show gender, age, health, ethnic background and moods. It is the primary way that people express emotions. Because it is visible to others, but not necessarily to the actor, it can show more to others than is assumed. Not being able to see human faces, sight deprived individuals must turn to the voice and other ways of "seeing" the person (Hull, 1992). To an extent, the face is a mirror image of the self (Cole, 2000).

Darwin believed that facial muscles were developed from ancestral habits, which served to promote particular species helping them to survive. From this background, researchers have studied human eye and facial displays in an attempt to determine whether emotional displays, as shown in the face and eyes, are universal in the human family.

Body Language and Body Orientation

That people use a body idiom, or language, in their interactions is clear. How to interpret accurately the meanings of body language is not so simple. Some researchers focus on *pupillometry* and the eyes, as noted;

other focus on the use of the entire body. It is obvious that bodies play a crucial role in everyday enactments of behavior, but how to focus on that role, or those roles, is the real problem.

Affiliative body behavior has been studied extensively. The concept of *immediacy* suggests that people sense moods and attitudes in others by their body presence. People who register with a high score on an immediacy scale are attractive to others; they seem to draw people toward them, to be welcomed into personal space more readily than people who score poorly on that scale. In short, they choose to affiliate with them. The immediacy factor has been called a hidden channel of communication. (Mehrabian, 1981).

In psychiatric research, it has been shown that people orient their bodies one to the other based on how they think and feel about the other person. Participants in interaction, who feel close to one another, may orient their bodies like book-ends or they may mirror one another's body orientation(Scheflen, 1965). People who are intimate try to entice each other by forming closer body relations unlike people who may be in a divorce situation, who may freeze each other out. In other words, the general body orientation may reflect how a person feels and how she thinks about the other party in the interaction. Scheflen showed that couples arrange to sit in patterned ways based on how they feel about each other. Friendly partners will orient their bodies toward each other, extending their limbs in the other's directions. They will lean toward their partners or create mirror image postures.

Intimate romantic involvements proceed in a non-linear, stage-like fashion; it is a recursive process (Knapp & Vangelisti, 1992; Duck, 1992). Before becoming intimately involved, a couple will share a normal space. In a series of steps, as intimacy is created, they move closer and closer, in a spiral of intimacy. Humans in love enact their body movements *contingently*. That is, they respond one to the other in ever deepening ways. The voice, the body, the eyes and the emotions are intertwined in a romantic, evolving relationship.

Gestures and Emblems

Researchers point out that even though people in different cultures may use the same gestures, there are display rules that determine the meanings of those gestures. Even within a culture there is variation in the use of gestures. (Morris, 1994).

Framing Gestures

Mead believed that gestures were significant symbols because they contain meanings shared by members of the same culture. He thought that humans organize their attitudes by using gestures. He believed that the body play of children leads to role development in later life. Complex body play, or games, for Mead, were microcosms of social systems. The "I" part of the self performs social acts based on the meaning of gestures (Mead, 1934, 1938). Actions, of course, are always influenced by the environment (Alexander, 1988).

When gestures can provide meaning without the use of words, they are referred to as emblems. By shaking one's head side to side, an American can say "no" without using words. Emblematic communication is a major part of daily nonverbal expression. Specialized uses of emblems have been created, as in the use of sign language, in the use of semaphores and other signalling devices, as in the signals used in baseball or football games. The professional mimist is a master of the use of emblematic communication. In everyday life people may plug their nose when something smells, or cup their hands to their ears when they cannot hear or give the thumbs up signal when they like something. Emblematic communication is common and complex. The understanding of the symbolic meaning of a gesture depends on a kind of informed intersubjectivity. One must learn the meaning behind any particular emblematic display and, of course, the context of the display is a key part of the interpretation.

Self Presentation and Impression Management

Monitoring the Self; Monitoring Others

Humans are fond of watching themselves and others perform on the stage of life. Art and culture are based on this premise. Television and radio thrive on this fact. People watch others watching themselves! Some people say that this is a nation of voyeurs; if people can't peer into their neighbor's bedroom, they can peer into a bedroom on film or television (Denzin, 1997). People are intrigued by the fuzzy mystery that seems to surround other people. Famous people must protect themselves from the ever curious onlooker. Inveterate people watchers, humans are constantly monitoring themselves and monitoring others. People in everyday life draw upon a type of folk-culture to make sense of what they observe. Scientists, such as psychologists and others, on the other hand, use fairly refined theories and methods to try to understand human behavior.

Framing Self-Presentation

The presenting of the self is a complex process having an evolutionary basis. Interacting with others was a way for groups to survive the vicissitudes and difficulties of everyday life. In short the survival of the fittest was aided by group cohesiveness. Today, people present themselves to influence others, to construct new relationships, and to reinforce the emotional self.

Self esteem may be enhanced in self-presentation; of course, the opposite may be the case as well, as when people are rejected by others. Clearly, humans face dilemmas in presentation; for example, people are not always authentic in their presentations and they may lie, deceive, or feign appearances, such as weakness or braggadocio. They even choke under pressure and create self-handicaps. Aggressive behaviors, even retaliation may be displayed, as it is in bullying behaviors. (Leary, 1996).

In earlier times when people lived far from their neighbors, people watching was occasional, at fairs, at church socials or other public happenings. Today, television, film, the print media, and the internet provide unparalleled opportunities for people to watch people every day. It does not matter that the people who are being watched are not real; what they are doing is familiar, full of meaning. Humans clearly are deeply intrigued by human behaviors as they are by the behavior of chimps and other animals that seem to exhibit human behaviors.

Humans are goal oriented, working out lines of action, expressing themselves socially, interactively. Giving each act a personal touch, they display their personality, their unique identities (Aronoff & Wilson, 1985). Others watch them perform and display their personalities. Considerable research has focused on how to interpret body and social behaviors, often using concepts like motives, traits, beliefs, values, cognitive structures or mood states to explain why certain behaviors occur. Symbolic interactionists, however, do not attribute behaviors to static inner traits or characteristics (Blumer, 1969). Concepts like self-esteem, ego, self-concept and other ways of thinking about the inner self, are dynamic concepts, in flux, changeable and situationally produced (Carbaugh, 1996). People recognize themselves in the behaviors of others; they understand similarities and they are intrigued by differences.

Self Presentation, Impression Management and Skilled Agentry

Discussed in Chapter Two, the concept of self presentation is a dramaturgical concept, stemming from symbolic interactionism. In this approach, people try to make sense of their own and others' behaviors. People identify themselves both to self and to others and act out their identities as self becomes social. People learn to manage multiple identities, performing multiple roles in daily life. The dynamic self is tied to performative mode in scenes of action (Carbaugh,1996) People are their own subjects in social presentation (Goffman, 1967). In short, self presentation is fundamental to social interaction, the very expression of meaning associated with the self, with identity. Skill in presentation has been the subject of much research (Hargie, 1986; Riggio, 1986).

In the management of impression(4), humans attempt to create favorable images of themselves. They try to do things that are successful and acceptable to others to avoid embarrassment. True, people may try to undermine others by acting deceptively, or by acting in some rebellious way (Jones, 1964), but a main goal in interaction is to make a favorable impression. People try to avoid the loss of face. An implicit, sometimes explicit, logic-in-use guides everyday behaviors (Gahagan & Herriot, 1984). People try to maximize their appearance to gain maximal benefit or satisfaction. People learn to manage the impressions that they make, hoping that others will interpret them favorably (Leary, 1996). Many people, of course, shy away from interactions.

Most professions train or educate their members so that they will become skilled in their profession. There are a number of approaches in the study of skilled behaviors including reward seeking, transactional aalysis, dramatic performances, motor skill proficiency, innate process analysis and goal-seeking. From an SI point of view, humans must be able to identity both the emotions and the intent of others and make judgements about appropriateness. These are learned skills and people vary considerably in their skill levels. They are not always able to produce desired effects in others. Certainly a key ingredient in the development of skill is mindful attention, learning what skills are important and how to employ them. Highly skilled people have learned facial and body configuration control, using their bodies skillfully. Good actors are adept at body control. Skillful actors draw upon various scripts as they enact their lines. Highly skilled people have learned dozens of scripts which they can call upon as they need them.

The Nonverbal Repertoire

The ways that humans think about their bodies, the ways they construe their identities, the ways they enact social behaviors and the way in which they interpret the actions of others suggests that there is a keen relationship between *reflexivity* and action. Body action is meaningful and symbolic. From the simple stare to the most complex bodily interaction, one action contingent upon another, it seems clear that there is a reportoire of skills that work together interactively. People have differential self presentation skills. For example, it has been said that people are sometimes blind to themselves, a condition that would make them blind to others as well. Nonverbal communication is gendered; it is influenced by the aging process and by ethnicity. It is also influenced by mediated experiences, such as television and the internet provide. The voice, but one piece of the total reportoire, yields tell-tale signs of fatigue, of pathologies, of gender and age, and of ethnicity (Pittam,1994). Human identity (Abrams & Hogg, 1990) is wound into the package of presentational skills. The nonverbal reportoire includes all aspects of nonverbal communication. Autistics and people with other pathologies struggle to master simple body behaviors. Consider the complications involved in merely shaking hands. One must know the social codes involved; one must have motor development and skill; one must want to shake hands. People read meaning into simple activities like handshakes, attributing character to the interactant. Autistic and schizophrenic children cannot master things that seem simple to others. That which seems so easy to do is not so simple. Routines are achieved; they are not naturally displayed (Schegloff, 1986). The simple body interaction, the handshake, and other gestures like it were, for Mead, ways of evoking meaning in others. The meaning of any gesture was in the way that people responded to it. If a person will not shake my hand, what does it mean to me?

Summary

The body and the mind work together in social interaction. One does not work without the other. Symbolic interactionism suggests that humans create meanings for their bodies; they construct body images and self-identities though interaction with others. As agents, acting on their own behalf, mindfully, goal-oriented people can create skill in interaction, learning to manage impressions and to present themselves for beneficial results. The body displays emotions, largely in the face, but body orientations and gestures convey emotions as well.

Psychological processes such as perception, attribution and sensemaking are basic parts of the construction of meaning relating to nonverbal communication. People plan to do things and they interpret what others do. Age, ethnicity, gender and mediated experiences influence human behaviors, as do pathologies, illnesses and social inexperience. In pathological situation, the nonverbal repertoire becomes distorted, by contrast, revealing the essence of normal nonverbal behaviors. Simple nonverbal acts turn out to be very complex upon analysis. One must understand social codes and be reflective to adequately interpret the actions of others. Beginning with the next chapter the processes discussed in Chapters Two, Three and Four will be applied in various ways to the topics in chapters Five, Six, Seven and Eight.

Questions for Thought and Discussion

1. Body images are created by individuals based on their experiences. How do you conceive of your body? What has influenced you to think in these terms? Are you free to "re-symbolize" your body? What would be an ideal body shape?

2. People deceive one another using their bodies. Describe a situation in which you believe deception has occurred. What clues found in the behavior of the deceiver alerted you? How often does deception occur in interactive situations, based on your experiences?

3. What do you think of the argument that people "cannot not communicate"? Do people "leak" information nonverbally without intending to do so? Can you give examples?

4. Thinking about your body behaviors throughout the day, are there periods of time when you feel down and others when you feel up? In short, is there a chrono-biological pattern that you notice about your behavioral patterns? What appears to be your diurnal chrono-biological pattern?

5. Emotions can be expressed powerfully, influencing the ways that people behave toward one another. Are you a person who is highly reserved or highly expressive? How would you characterize your friends?

Notes

1. In Mind, Self and Society, George Herbert Mead, the major contributor to what is now known as SI, tied together the idea of self in relation to society through the action of the mind, which he thought was best evidenced by how people used gestures. He, among others, was deeply concerned about the fact that mind and body were separated by Cartesian thought, or dualism, and that psychologists in his time studied human behavior mechanically; that is, willful actions and mindfulness were not discussed. Humans were organisms without willful direction. The pendulum has swung; modern research into the nature of consciousness, the unity of the body and mind, is now common.

2. Erving Goffman, who is his many books dealing with a dramaturgical approach to human behavior, emphasized the role of rationality. He has been criticized for over-emphasizing rationality and for paying inadequate attention to macro-factors that influence human behavior, such as social class, the economy and so on, factors that many structuralists emphasize. See Stryker (1980) for an example. The traditions of the Chicago School of SI and the Iowa School of SI differ largely along these lines, the Iowa School seeming to favor a more traditional, socio-structural approach.

3. Charles Darwin believed that adaptors were evolutionary adaptations, as the word implies, just as he believed that the smile was adapted for evolutionary purposes, for survival. In short, many exhibited behaviors served an evolutionary, adaptive function, he thought. The smile, used in greetings by humans, seems to be shared by lower order animals, who bare their teeth. Darwin, of course, influenced considerable modern day research in animal and human ethology emphasizing contexts of human action. Clearly, there is an interaction between body behaviors and contexts. The degree of involvement or isolation plays a key role in how humans behave, as Wilson, (1992) shows.

4. The SI emphasis in social psychology focused on how people perceived one another and on how they ingratiated themselves to others using flattery, for example. For a good discussion of the development of self

presentation and impression management in social psychology, see Self Presentation: Impression Management and Interpersonal Behavior, Mark R. Leary, Social Psychology Series, Westview Press, 1996.

Suggested Readings

Davis, J. (1997). Mapping the Mind: The Secrets of the Human Brain and How it Works. Secaucus, NJ: Birch Lane Press.

LeDoux, J. (1996). The Emotional Brain: The Mysterious Under-Pinnings of Emotional Life. New York, NY: Touchstone Books.

Hewitt, J. P. (1999). Self and Society: A Symbolic Interactionist Social Psychology. Boston, MA: Allyn and Bacon.

Leary, M. R. (1996). Self-Presentation: Impression Management and Interpersonal Behavior. Boulder, CO: Westview Press.

Mead, G. H. (1934). Mind, Self and Society. Chicago: University of Chicago Press.

Stevens, A. (1995) Private Myths: Dreams and Dreaming. Cambridge, MA: Harvard University Press.

Chapter 5
Gendered Influences on Nonverbal Communication
Making Sense of Gender

Chapter Overview

This chapter is devoted to gender as a master theme. As is the case in chapters Six, Seven and Eight, many of the concepts developed or explored in chapters One, Two, Three and Four are woven into the chapters in this section of the book.

Gender is one's personal sense of maleness or femaleness. Cultural, sociological and psychological processes influence gender. Clearly men and women differ biologically, one from the other, and they are socialized differently, both factors influencing their nonverbal communication. A considerable body of research has focused on their differences; many popular books and discussion programs focus on their differences as well. For example some researchers have been interested in feminism and psychoanalysis (Chodorow, 1989); others are concerned that gender concepts are misstated, mismeasured (Tavris, 1992). Scholars are re-thinking and redefining gender (Rakow, 1986). But, it is clear that gender studies are on the rise; it is a popular topic in the media as well.

Competition seems to exist between researchers who espouse an essentialist model versus those who espouse an interactionist model. Essentialism suggests that differences between the genders are located in a relatively fixed, stable inner core while interactionists believe that gender is dynamic and somehat modifiable, depending on the context.

Some confusion exists between the meanings of the word sex and gender. In this text, as in many, sex is regarded as a biological term describing male and female body characteristics at birth. Genetic and biological processes unfold in the creation of sex. Gender, on the other hand, is a learned identity created in socialization. Gender describes a more fluid condition than does sex. Although biological factors influence the development of gender, it does not determine gender, although there is an interaction between biological, psychological and social processes.

From an SI perspective humans, whether male or female, enact nonverbal behaviors based on their identities, the identities themselves being constructed by humans. It has been suggested that gender is an arrangement between the sexes, a type of institutional reflexivity. Nonverbal communication establishes a sense of relationship between people (Wood, 1994), Yet, the reader must remember that identity and gender are terms that describe a complexity of concepts; males and females learn to play multiple roles, some of which are played the same way by both genders; others are performed by one gender and not the other.

The Human Body and Sexual Behaviors

Myths About Sex and Gender

Gender is a fixed category. Gender is created in communication; it does not exist as a fixed, essentialist category, separate from growth processes. Mead believed that people were actors, not reactors, although they respond to influences. Humans go through stages, such as the preparatory, play and game stages. People gradually integrate themselves over time, achieving identity, whether male or female (Pearson,1988).

All males are alike; all females are alike. Although humans share interpersonal, social and cultural contents intersubjectively, each individual is unique because of the special experiences of that individual.

Sex and gender are the same concepts. Sex is a biological phenomenon while gender is a socially constructed phenomenon. However, there is an interaction between sex and gender. Women may bear children; men can fertilize the egg.

Perceptions of gender are always accurate. Men may condemn a behavior that they see women doing but approve of it when they see or hear men doing it. Swearing is one example. Perceptions may be stereotyped. For example, it is believed that females do not make good managers, but recent research suggests that they do very well in management positions.

Males and females have the same access to opportunities. The "man-thing" has meant that there is a male bias in society, which provides males with more opportunities than it does females, especially when the females are ethnic minorities. This problem is slowly eroding.

Gender is a simple concept. Actually the self is complex and multiple, as James, Mead, Jung, Gergen and others have discussed.

Biological Factors

The Genetic Male and Female

Research shows that sex hormones may sex-type the brain, thereby influencing body identification creating a biological biasing effect.(1) Just how this may play out is not clear. It is obvious that both sexes can perform similar biological functions and activities, such as coitus and the intake and digestion of food. They differ about menstruation, levels of testosterone, and other physical factors, men being generally larger in body size than women. The male and female sexual parts differ substantially; as humans mature, their genetic differences generally become even more distinct and clear, especially with the onset of puberty and early adolescence. Older people may complain about loss of sex drive and cognitive acuity but even this process occurs differently in the sexes.

Some research suggests that the male-female sexual distinctions present a false dichotomy because to an extent each sex resides in both male or female bodies (Hargreaves & Colley, 1987). As the study of genes continues it may reveal the extent to which humans are "hardwired" or shaped by the XX or XY genetic patterns.

Socially, of course, humans symbolize their physical identity; they gradually become genderized. Smaller at birth and throughout most of their lives, females adjust to the implied power difference associated with size. Both genders adjust to body changes. For example, male and female children start out with a similar larynx, but gradually, the male develops a huskier voice. The innate ability of the female to produce eggs to be fertilized by the male influences how women relate to children and to family members. X and Y chromosomes affect deeply how the sexual male and female will develop. According to some research, men are more susceptible to physical problems than are women throughout the stages of life, as their earlier death rate suggests. However, the aging process presents a different sets of problems for each sex; researchers have suggested that older age is a woman's problem, as will be discussed in Chapter Seven.

Male and Female Hormones

Chronobiology, mentioned earlier, is a newly emerging field of study; it reveals that men, like women, have hormonal cycles that influence behavior. Men from 39-70 years of age, having higher levels of testosterone, also appear to have increased levels of aggression (Coon,1994). In lower order male animals, the presence of androgens has been linked to aggressiveness as well. For example, studies show that hens, when fed testosterone in an early stage of their development, acquire male-like features, such as the comb and the wattles; they act more like roosters than like hens. One might ask whether pronounced levels of testosterone in the human male leads to agonistic behavior (Maccoby, 1998), an aggressiveness that attentuates later in life.

Does the comparatively lower level of testosterone in the female lead to a more compliant, nurturant nonverbal style than men display? Maccoby suggests that the male agonistic style of nonverbal behavior is learned early and that it is carried throughout life in some measure, modified over time. Social behaviors overlay physical processes.

The ability of women to to conceive and menstruate influences their behavior considerably. Even their body temperatures change in circadian and monthly cycles. The study of circadian rhythms in both males and females is receiving more attention in modern research. Perhaps the body changes from morning to evening influencing behaviors, as popularly believed.

Sexual Behaviors and Physical Attractiveness

It is known that pheromones(2) are tied into the mating habits of lower order animals, differing substantially from species to species (Wilson, 1992). The way in which these odors attract the sexes vary considerably, but both sexes may mark their territory. Whether humans have pheromones that attract both sexes is less clear, although research continues. Americans are fond of covering up their body odors with perfumes.

Framing the Attractiveness Syndrome

What is attractive in one society may not be attractive in another. In the United States, a cursory examination of the ways that people try to be attractive yields a compelling picture. For example, many women are constantly thinking about losing weight (Wooley & Wooley, 1984). Studies reveal the majority of the female subjects reported that losing weight was more important to them than having success in work or love. Dieting starts among women as early as fourth and fifth grades; in High School, most women are concerned about their weight (Woods, 1994).

In a youth conscious society, where the concepts of the ideal male and female physical specimens are played up, it is no surprise that both males and females are preoccupied with weight loss and muscle toning, however unhealthy the process may be. Indeed, there seems to be a relationship between body image and self-esteem. Some women diet to increase their self-confidence, thinking that they will be more feminine if they are thin. This norm is constantly reinforced by the media, where having the "perfect abs" is played up to both genders. In comparison to white women, African-American women may be less concerned with weight, dieting or being thin. Perhaps they have a more realistic view of losing weight (Molloy, 1998). Some evidence suggests that many Black females believe that the slightly heavier body is more attractive than is a thin one.

Genetic fitness is an adaptive evolutionary concept, the fit animal being more adaptable than the nonfit. Genetically fit males, whether human or of other species, can mate again and again with different females. Male seals, for example, are harem masters and male roosters copulate with many hens (Barash & Lipton, 1997). In humans, polygamy has occasionally been practiced in the United States, a monogamist country, but polyandry is often the norm in other countries. Beliefs and customs determine how the sexual drive of men and women is to be channeled. Demographic pressures and patterns bear on sexual practices.

Men are sexually aroused more quickly than are women. This fact, combined with the tendency for men to have more physical power than women have may explain the existence of porn, prostitution and other shunned social activites, mostly male interests (Barash & Lipton, 1997). Evolutionists suggest that sexual differences influence social differences. For example, women generally desire to have a loving and comfortable environment; is this due to their genetic make-up? Do men tend to be less concerned about a loving environment due to their easily aroused sexual tendencies and their aggressiveness? (Symonds, 1979). It has been said in a popular vein, that for men, "sex sometimes results in intimacy; for women, intimacy sometimes results in sex".

Physical attractiveness and beauty exist in the human mind, but they do not put food on the table. Nevertheless, physical attractiveness is necessary for human reproduction. In other words, it acts as a catalyst inspiring a male to copulate with a female. Physical beauty makes humans attractive to one another. It is interesting that delinquents, people who are in trouble with the law, tend to have less attractive bodies. There is an interaction between physical shape and social expectations, as this example shows (Jones, 1996). As noted in the last chapter, shorter boys tend to be held back in school in Australia.

Cultural norms vary across cultures; it is not surprising that different cultures produce different attraction displays (Jankowiak, 1993). Perhaps there are few universal standards of sexual attractiveness (Buss, 1989). Indeed, in the arrangment of marriages, there may be little focus on attractiveness. When choice, not arrangement is involved, research suggests that women tend to choose men who are skillful, who have prowess; men tend to choose women who are beautiful. This appears to be a universal tendency (Buss, 1989). The understanding of what is skillful or attractive, of course, varies by culture.

Research suggests that men in the United States prefer big eyes, full lips, small noses in women, but women may not share in those predispositions. Brazilian men seem to like big butts and small breasts; darkness in skin color is problematic in Brazil (Jones, 1996). It is clear from an evolutionary and ethological view that sexual attractiveness is important to sexual copulation. Culture interacts with biology in producing offspring.

Brain and Neuronal Differences

The use of recent imaging technologies reveals the complexity of the human brain, and, to an extent shows how males and females differ. A popular belief is that males and females have significant lateral differences, each sex tending to use different sides of the brain. Early research suggested that males tended to use the left side of the brain because it is associated with linear, logical and analytic thinking, while women, who tend to have more developed right lobes, tend to be more holistic, imaginative and intuitive than are men. Recent research suggests, however, that pronounced laterality may not characterize the differences; rather, the areas of the brain associated with selected activities, such as language and spatial concepts, largely determine how the sexes use the brain, with women tending to use more of the brain (LeDoux, 1996) Some research suggests that the neuronal structure of the languaging portion of the brain is more dense in females, possibly leading to greater verbal dexterity in women. PET scan technology can trace the flow of blood in the brain as various tasks are performed, indicating that long awaited answers to questions about the localization of activities in the brain are forthcoming.

Sensate Differences

The baby is born with the human sensorium intact, yet the various senses grow in variously staged patterns. For example, the neonate responds to touch and can detect the odor and taste of its mother's milk. Given sour things to taste, the very young child will pucker, perhaps even cry; the ability to taste is well developed from birth. The child's eyes, however, require more time to become focused and the child's ability to grasp, to reach and to touch is only gradually developed (Morris, 1992).

As young people become adults the body changes. Women tend to have a higher sweat threshold than do men, men sweating more quickly under the same conditions. The dermal response to cold is quicker for women than it is for men and they seem to be more sensitive to pressures put on various body parts. Although it may be a learned phenomenon, females tend be more expressive about feeling pain than are men. Men are often taught to suffer pain in silence, which may account for the differences (Baker, 1987).

Men seem to be better at detecting pure tones up to about age 30 but males show some loss, due perhaps, to differential noise at the place of work. It has been shown that women may suffer some change in hearing ability due to changes in estrogens and progesterone levels.

Taste abilities vary between the sexes as well, but there may be confounding effects due to socialization and cultural influences. For example, women tend to have lower thresholds for sweet, sour and salty tastes and higher thresholds than men do for sucrose, and sodium chloride. Pregnant women prefer stronger concentrates of sweet, sour, bitter and salty than do men (Baker, 1987).

The results of the smell study performed by National Geographic, discussed in Chapter Two, suggested that women differ from men in several ways both within cultures and across cultures. Again, the confounding effects of social expectations, of culture, make it unclear whether physical or cultural differences are at play. Different cultures emphasize different smell and taste codes so one might expect the ability to smell to be affected.

The importance of these studies to a symbolic interactionist approach to nonverbal communication may seem unclear to the reader. The SI approach suggests that humans interpret and give meaning to physical and social events in their lives. Biological differences may lead to social practices; for example, men buy women chocolates when they are courting them. This long honored practice signals the relationship between biology, or taste, and social practice.

Framing the Male Sexual Life Cycle

In a popular book about the changes that males go through over their life span, their growth patterns have been described in sexual terms:

Ages 15-30, males "race" the sexual act as if they were in the Indy 500.

Ages 30-40, males perform dutiful sex with their wives.

Ages 55-70, males surf sex, developing fantasies about sex.

Ages 70 plus, men like a snuggling version of sex.

The author concludes that the male menopause begins in the fifties or sixties; there is some lapse in virility and vitality (Sheehy,1998). Sheehy's analysis applies to men in the United States.

Gender as a Social Construction

Genderization

Gender is a concept complex in meaning, more complex than the concepts of sex and it changes over time (Woods, 1994). As mentioned, in the Great Chain of Being theory, now considered mythical, women and Blacks were not considered as high on the hierarchal chain as were white males. The best human model was the white, European male. (Schiebingen, 1993).To this day, by and large, women are excluded from doing science, although the situation is improving. (Deegan, 1991) The fully developed human was a white male; women were thought to be a deviation from the norm.

Humans define themselves in multiple ways. However, it is only in recent years that women have been able to define themselves without male interference. In many societies, even today, a female's relationship to a male is one of subservience; women may even be owned by men, sometimes taken as slaves. The predominance of male power still exists in many countries. The establishment of women's rights and ensuing affirmative action in the United States created more favorable conditions. Women can now effectively resist the "ale thing" although egalitarianism is not complete.

The concept of gender is broadly open, affording many options for individual interpretation of self. When behaviors are rigidly typed as male or female, they are usually typed in error. Gendered behaviors are learned and flexible. Contexts vary and the ways in which gendered behaviors are manifest in varied contexts is a matter of self construal. For example, black women in academia must make sense of the context. They face different influences than do white women, who themselves may face uncertainties that males do not (Kotthoff & Wodak, 1997). Patterned behaviors, often based on stereotypes, still prevail between the genders, as the following illustrates.

Framing the Stereotyped Gendered Voice

Gender is sensed, not merely by how the voice sounds, but by an integration of the senses, a multi-channeling process (Hall, 1985). The human voice, male and female, has been heavily stereotyped. For example, when a male person is "breathy" he is believed to be young and artistic; if a female's voice is breathy, she is thought to be feminine and pretty, but shallow. If the male voice is tense, he is thought to be older, unyielding and cantankerous; if a female's voice is tense, she is thought to be emotional, high strung and less intelligent. If the male voice has a higher pitch and is highly varied, he is thought to be dynamic and feminine; if a female's voice is higher pitched, she is thought to be more dynamic and extroverted (Knapp & Hall, 1992).

In research that is supposedly free of stereotypes, it is suggested that women's speech fosters connections, support, closeness and understanding, while the male speech patterns tend to establish status, independence and control. Women tend toward inclusiveness in their speech and men toward dominance (Gilligan, 1982;Woods, 1994) which can lead to misunderstandings between the genders.

In a rapidly changing world, it is hard to determine what is stereotypical and what is not, but there are research findings that appear to be solid. For example, to resolve conflicts in games it is shown that girls tend to end the game, while boys elaborate the rules to end the dispute. Girls, it appears, learn to cooperate; boys learn to compete. Girls play in smaller, more intimate pairs, often in private places, while boys seek out competition (Arliss & Borisoff, 1993).

As people make choices, make sense of their lives and act out behaviors in context, they become socialized and oversocialized both directly and indirectly. Imitation and modeling are features of this socialization, concepts that are useful throughout life (Maccoby,1998). Each person becomes male or female or something in-between, with a wrinkle or two. In short, there is an arbitrariness to the construction of gender (Smith,1992). The socialization of gender is not a linear, exact process; there is unevenness.

Clearly, women and men think in genderized terms. Society contains thoughts and themes about gender and gender roles may seem somewhat fixed and inflexible. For example, guns are used more by males and dolls are used more by females, but these are not fixed behaviors; they are learned, malleable and flexible. The colors pink and blue have been associated with females and males at birth; these illustrations suggest that there is relative stability in the ways that humans perceive the place of gender.

Males and females tend to express themselves differently. Males tend to use more dominant, commanding gestures and movements, to take up more space than do females, to mask their emotions, and to smile for different reasons than do women. Women tend to wear a smile, as part of the expectation that they be pleasant (Richmond & McCroskey, 1992). Women are said to be "rapport" builders and men are "report" givers, or knowledge experts, alluding to popular stereotypes. Women appear to display their emotions more readily than do men. Women seem to be able to give and interpret nonverbal messages better than men can (Stewart, Cooper & Friedly,1986).

Thus far the discussion has focused on gender differences. But, is gendered behavior really extremely bipolar or does it exist at various points on a range? Various analyses of gender differences seem to be overdrawn, there being fewer differences between males and females than there are similarities (Andersen, 1998; Canary and Hause,1993; Wilkins and Andersen, 1991). Various metanalyses suggest that gender is best interpreted as a point on a range, each gender able to occupy most of those points. It is best to discuss differences as tendencies rather than as absolute differences.

Socio-cultural Aspects of Gendered Identity

As discussed, the gendered body is not a fixed corpus; rather, each culture establishes metaphors for the body, which are taken into account by individuals in order to make sense of self. Body metaphors and themes are found in all cultures. For example, in oral societies, men were associated with the sun and energy; females were associated with the mysterious moon. Men were thought to be rational and women intuitive (Lips & Colwill, 1978). Women were considered mysterious because of menstruation, birth and lactation, leading to darkness, irrationality, the moon and magic.

All societies distinguish between males and females, although some may have a middle category, such as the berdache of the Cheyenne tribe or the mahu of the Tahitians. The guiding ideals differ from culture to culture but there are similarities between cultures. Some scholars believe that culture provides a veneer covering an essential universality of gender dimorphism (Barash, 1997). All male primates produce semen and all females give birth, but variations in behavior occur after that. Humans engage in the love making process, full of symbolic meaning, unlike non-humans who simply mate without symbolization. The ability to symbolize and to give meaning to maleness and femaleness distinguishes humans from lower order animals. Indeed, in humans, the genders seem to require each other (Smith,1992) as the legend of Adam and Eve suggests.

In traditional cultures, it would appear that gender roles are fairly clear; in modern American society, there appears to be a blurring of the roles, high speed change being the norm. Some cultures place more value on the birth of the male than on the female, as in India and China. In China, where population pressures have led to the control of how many children are permitted, the birth of the male is referred to as the birth of the Little Emperor. Other cultures emphasize the more powerful role of females, as in the Tchambuli tribe. For example, as Margaret Mead showed, in the Tchambuli society, women do the fishing and control the economic life of the community; they also take the initiative in courting and sex activities between the sexes (Mead, 1935). The cultural pattern is different from that found in the United States, where men traditionally are supposed to be the initiators, the breadwinners and so on. Again this role is becoming blurred, as post-modernists indicate.

In the United States females tend to be drawn to fields of employment that involve sensitivity, an example being Social Work or Early Childhood Education. These differences, however, are due to socialization, to choices made throughout life, as people make sense of who they are. They may also reflect power and relational differences, males generally having more economic and political power than do women. Unlike the experience of the male in the Tchambuli society, men in the Western world tend to be competitive in everyday life while females tend to use compromise strategies (Turner & Sterk, 1994). Men tend to act self-sufficiently, emphasizing work as the major theme in their lives; women tend to enact interdependent attachment styles. Women tend to be more reflexive and inward; men appear to be more outward and non-reflexive. Again, these tendencies are not to be rigidly interpreted.

Despite their perceived differences, it is usually in the union of the gendered bodies that a sense of wholeness is achieved, as in the story of Adam and Eve or of Yin and Yang in Taoism, where male and female are brought together to form a middle way. To get genders, Plato said, Zeus decided to cut all beings in two. The word gender comes from genus, which means race or kind, seemingly having little to do with biological sex.

Birthing and Socialization

Unlike many other cultures, in the United States the child is put out of the bedroom at the start, into her or his own bedroom, weaned by age one. As mentioned, the gendered labeling process begins when the child is dressed in pink or blue. Pink, of course, is associated with softness and blue is associated with rougher things. Gradually gender differences become apparent. Girls, for example, tend to be closer to their mothers, touching and receiving touch more than do males. From the start, the personal space bubbles are smaller for girls than they are for boys. Girls tend to learn language faster than boys and perhaps they learn to use nonverbal displays faster than boys. For example, the stereotypical limp wrist found among ages in females is displayed at about age five.

Children, of course, must learn how to speak, act and present themselves appropriately. By about the age of five in American life, children begin to know who they are; they have begun to understand the varied meanings behind gender and what it means to be masculine or feminine (Wood, 1994). Gender constancy begins to appear. In short, young children begin to develop working theories about who they are. They begin to create gender scripts as they mature.

Framing Early Attachment and Segregation

Gradually, boys and girls become segregated in their social lives. A chronological table of change suggests that about 1-2 years, young children are attached to mother and they have fun with their father; at about age 12-24 months, children start to exhibit same sex preferences and at about 30 months, most children spend most of the time with same-sex others (Fagot, 1991), given a choice. By about age 4-5, boys affiliate with the same sex. For girls, same sex affiliation seems fairly developed by age three. Mixed play continues for both sexes, however.

By about age five, elaborated play involves pretending, such as playing doctor or nurse. Sequential scripts are created and followed. These basic patterns seem to occur in Africa, India, the Philippines and Mexico as well. By ages 6-10, three quarters of time is spent with the same sex, which seems to be a pattern that may be universal. At about ages 8-11, same sex preference peaks, perhaps even cross-culturally. Slowly, the child learns what genderization means through these self-segregating behaviors (Fagot, 1991).

The culture of play is co-constructed. Playstyles are taught by parents just as lower order animal parents teach their young to chase, to exhibit playful biting and so on. Boys may get access to a group by shoving and girls by verbal bargaining and negotiation. Boys will ram bikes and act with rough and tumble, shooting one another and playing dead, which can lead to anger and agonistic behaviors. Fighting seems to be done by boys; girls seem to take turns more than do boys. Females tend to aggress by alienating others or interfering with friendships (Maccoby, 1998). Boy themes tend to be heroic using guns and swords and girl themes tend to be nurturant emphasizing family interactions, such as parenting. Boys do not usually watch girl movies, but girls watch both girl and boy movies. Boys tend to use imperatives in their speech and girls tend to emphasize social relationships. Boys separate from mothers more quickly than do girls. Again, these are to be interpreted as tendencies. The roles that are played by each gender are interchangeable and inflexible, although even today a girl may be thought of as being a tomboy when she acts like a boy and a boy may be labeled a sissy when he acts like a girl(Maccoby, 1998).

Gender Constancy and Middle Childhood Discourse Styles

One must be careful to stay away from stereotypical thinking. On the other hand, it is clear that children develop genderized patterns and tendencies. In middle childhood discourse, girls tend to display anger indirectly, compromising when possible, but boys tend to be assertive, daring others, playing scaredy cat, calling others stupid, sissy or faggot. Boys tend to be more direct and they tend to establish boundaries more quickly. Girls talk more than do boys, except when talking to boys. Indeed, mothers talk more to girls than they do to their boys.

Girls learn to think that boys are mean and noisy while boys may think that girls cry too much. Some cross-gendering occurs but gender segregation continues. Borderwork, or cross-gendering occurs early on, at about ages 5-6, but boys are likely to tease girls when they like them. Contact appears to be accidental and incidental and, of course, at that age, courting is denied. Thus, children acquire a fund of gender knowledge, in a type of self-socialization, and they are motivated to act in accordance with genderized expectations, stereotypical or not, feeling confident that they belong to a group of likeminded children (Maccoby, 1998).

Gender constancy, which occurs at about age 6 or 7 years, is in the forefront in later ages. Children know their role expectations and the cultural norms for their genders. Gender metaphors, perhaps stereotypical, have developed, with boys being rough and girls being soft, boys being angry and girls being happy. It is suggested by research that girls tend to suppress themselves in adolescence, beginning to disguise the self (Gilligan, 1982), perhaps fearing the loss of connectedness, trying to fit in. Perhaps they develop a politeness bias.

Female and Male Self Presentations

All people present themselves to others in interaction and they act out their sense of self, their symbolic face, in the presentations.

Framing a Feminine Presentation

Women learned to discipline their bodies well before they began their professional lives; for example, women learn to throw a ball like a girl, they learn to sit, stand, walk and tilt their heads, to gesture and to carry objects, like a girl. It is argued here that young girls are far more constrained than are males through socialization. They must learn to be fragile and to comport themselves along stricter lines. These behaviors follow women into the work world, where various issues are presented. As one woman describes projecting a presence in the professional work place, she must learn to "turn on a switch", shining in front of an audience, usually a male audience (Trethewey, 1999). The female presentation style in the professional workplace has had but a few years to be embellished, given the relatively quiescent role of women in America, historically. Females in the United States, as in other societies, have had a muted voice (Gilligan, 1982).

A popular view of males and females might go as follows: There are Don Juans and there are Carmens; there is an Adonis complex and there is a Jennifer complex. People imitate television heroes and follow trendy fashions. Women learn to flirt, to be sexy and provocative in their apparel, perhaps searching for strong and prestigious men; men seem to want young and beautiful women and present themselves accordingly. The media, of course, play up these stereotypical notions so powerfully that popular culture influences the body presentations of individuals.

Research suggests a different train of thought. For example, women tend to develop a sense of identity through connectedness with others. Their sense of self comes from building and maintaining relationships, not through differentiation and separation. Women are empowered by their participation and development of others (Belenky, 1984). They are connected knowers who have the ability to think maternally. Women tend to have a caring ethic. Work, thought and feelings are bound together by this ethic (Ruddick, 1989)

Malehood is defined differently in different societies and cultures. In some cultures, the achievment of malehood is a prize to be won, involving sanctions, trials of endurance and various ritualistic practices (Gilmore, 1990). In the United States, malehood is almost taken for granted, whereas in Latin countries, one learns the macho ethic, as in Cuba (4). It is reported that in the Truk Islands men do daring deep sea diving for sharks, youth fight in weekend brawls, drink excessively and seek sexual conquests. Laceration, whipping contests and physical abuses are inflicted on males to determine their inner strength in some countries. Flinching under pain is a sign of weakness. (Gilmore, 1990). Thus body flagellation is still important in the islands.

The role of the hero is important to the socialization of the male in the United States. Freud drew out the characteristics of Moses as a hero and Otto Rank placed stress on myth and the birth of the hero; Jung believed that heroes were archtypal (Cohen, 1990). The stereotype of the male is that he is young and aggressive, sexually powerful and able to solve confrontational problems. Heroes solved the Oedipal Riddle and cut the Gordian Knot. These ideas, of course, are tied to the past but thematically consistent with the present.

Perhaps in the modern Western world there are competing models for manhood (Elster,1986). Instead of throwing javelins and rescuing damsels in distress, the modern anti-hero theoretically gives peace a chance, listens and is sensitive to others (Orenstein, 1987). If aggression is inherent in the male system it appears to be withering or taking on new forms. The emerging anti-hero tends to be androgynous.

Perhaps the demands of modern society call forth not a ruggedness in mentality but a caringness in the workplace, a sensitivity to others, unlike the demands on manhood in rural America. What seems clear is that the polarized ideas of maleness and femaleness seem to be blending in the middle, androgynously (Bem, 1993). Women may be learning to be more assertive; males may be learning to be more sensitive. At least some scholars believe this to be an ideal. Yet, it is males by and large who engage in acts of violence, in high schools, on the internet and in the family.

Gendered Lenses, Androgyny And Stereotypes

Gender enculturation lens theory suggests that gender is embedded into our discourse in such a way as to influence a child to think in male and female terms (Bem, 1993). However, because communication about gender is usually tacit, a child may not actually know what the options are. A fish is not aware of the water in which it swims!

As mentioned, some scholarship about gender rests on an essentialist perspective. That is, the researchers approach gender as though it is an entity with a fixed core, a fixed set of traits and characteristics, relatively unbending and unchanging over the course of a lifetime. Other scholars and researchers take a dynamic, situational approach. That is, they realize that under some conditions, males and females will act one way; under others, they will act differently. These different assumptions make a difference in how comparative gender research is performed (Anderson, 1998).

Varieties of research tools are used to indicate how people think about gender. A high score on both the male and female BSRI gender tool indicates that one is favorably disposed to androgynous conceptualizations of behavior. Research suggests that females who score better on the male portion of the BSRI may increase their chances of being effective leaders, although there may be fewer advantages for American males. Assertiveness, typically thought to be a male characteristic, may be learned by females. Males may become more sensitive (Coon, 1994). Yet, it seems clear that androcentrism, the emphasis upon male dominance, is still a major factor in the United States. (Bem, 1993). Perceived as a social problem, the remedy is to focus on the concept of androgyny, as some researchers suggest.

But male and female differences should not be overdrawn. As one example, there seems to be no solid evidence to indicate that there are strong categorical speech differences between the genders. Popular stereotypes of gender differences may actually influence research making the differences more pronounced than they are (Rakow,1998). However, if the following frame accurately describes the early conceptualization of males and females, there appear to have been very wide differences between them.

Framing Gender Stereotypes

In early American society, females were defined as submissive, less competitive, excitable, more emotional than men and so on. If women showed assertiveness or behaviors like those of men, they were considered mentally unstable. They were said to exhibit hysterical personalities. Indeed women reported more emotional problems, sought more psychiatric help and went to the hospital more frequently than did males. Femininity was correlated with high anxiety, low self-esteem and low social acceptance. Following stereotypical thinking, perhaps women unwittingly followed the prophecy, getting sick and acting as lesser beings!

Gender, Standpoint, Power and Place

Gender and Situation

Gender is asymmetrically powered in American society and throughout the world. In many ways, males do not have to earn their status, at least in comparison to females (Wood, 1994); That is, in the United States and elsewhere as well, males enjoy a privileged status. Even when holding hands, it appears that the male hand is on the top of the females (Chappell, Basso, DeCola, Hossack, Keubler, Marm, Reed, Webster and Yoggev, Aug. 1998). Males and females are born into societies that reflect dimensions, such as gendered power. Gender is played out in matriarchal societies differently than it is in patriarchal ones. For example, in Libya, a patriarchal society, women are permitted only enough space in their garment to peer out with one eye.

In the modern United States, the power base has typically reflected the "man principle" (Kothoff & Wodak, 1997), indicating that, traditionally, males in the United States held power. The modern concept of the "glass ceiling" indicates that while women know about upper echelons of power and may aspire to getting upper level jobs, they are not empowered to do so. The face of America's workplace is changing but there may be forces of resistance that work against women, particularly if they are women of color, in a matrix of domination. There are efforts to get beyond the glass ceiling by females, but it appears that the problem is different for women of color. It has been suggested that women of color are "twice struck", having to deal with being female in a male dominated society and with being colored in a white dominated society.

Power is patterned in specific behaviors, such as in verbal interruption patterns shown below. Theoretically, because males have more power in American society than do females, men are free to interrupt them in conversations, whether it be in the workplace, on television or in everyday situations. Recent research suggests, however, that this phenomenon may be overdrawn as noted below.

Framing Gendered Interruption Patterns

In a society in which males are dominant, where they hold power, it has been assumed in some research that they will feel free to interrupt females in various social circumstances. This analysis, however appears to be too simplistic. A meta-analysis of studies on interruptions shows that a number of situational factors must be taken into account, such as the number of persons in the situation, their genders, and their relationships to one another.

When the type of activity is taken into account, gender differences in interruptive patterns disappear. For example, when girls and females choose expressive activities, they tend to act in an affiliative manner; conversely, when boys and men select task-oriented activities, they may be more assertive, acting in an instrumental manner. In sum, the essentialist model of gender differences, which suggests that there are ongoing differences between the genders that lie at the core of gender does not help explain interruption as well as a contextualist-interactive model does. (Anderson, 1998).

Indeed, gender asymmetry, by implication power asymmetry, is weak in many circumstances, as the following description shows. The theory is that higher status people will touch lower status people more readily than the reverse case. But, in this study, higher status people tended to touch lower status people, initiating affectionate touches on the shoulders or arms, while lower status individuals tended to touch higher status individuals in more formal ways, such as in handshakes. Gender asymmetry seems to be weak, although males tended to initiate touch more than females (Hall, 1996). This research suggests that it is the status, not the gender, that leads to differential touching behaviors. Touching, of course, in this context, is assumed to be associated with power, status and power being closely associated. The studies cited above, of course, are mere tips of the iceberg. Power is institutionalized and patterned in the United States, favoring white males, as it has for decades. It is now changing as the following frame shows.

Framing Women as Managers

It is reported that women make better managers than do men because they tend to be skilled in more areas that are required in management. For example, women tend to be more collaborative in their decision making than are men; women are socialized to cooperate and collaborate, while men tend to use an autocratic style. Two thousand, four hundred and eighty two managers at all levels from more than 400 organizations in 19 states were used in the study (APA Monitor, Sep. 1999).

Few people would argue that American society is not changing, although many may argue that it is changing for the worse. Whatever the values of the individual, the ways in which gendered roles are played out in contemporary America are vastly different today, compared to the past. From the farms to the factory during the Second World War to full participation in all levels of non-professional and professional work, women are born into a new world, which increases their opportunities.

As mentioned, family sizes and family patterns are shifting radically and the roles of females are shifting along with them. For many Americans, the large, extended families of the past are gone; replacing those families are the new versions that range from the nuclear family to the laissez faire family. One parent families are becoming common. Multiple marriages which include children from two or more past marriages are not uncommon. In short, male and female parenting roles are changed dramatically in many situations.

The glass ceiling in the workplace has been broken, if not shattered, and women are now able to do what men have done in power positions before them, which is to be able to climb to the top. In modern times, women can be the Secretary of State, Senators or CEOs without raising eyebrows or being labeled bitches. In short, one is witnessing a shift in power distribution between the sexes. Affirmative action helped both minorities and women enter the economic mainstream.

The idea of subcultures, perhaps a demeaning term to ethnic minorities because it can imply inferiority, is being replaced by the term co-culture, a less demeaning term. Obviously, the social system does not operate perfectly, but it is substantially more open to women and minorities than it has been in the past. Of course there are serious problems remaining.

Gender, Ethnicity and Age

Those who are defined as ethnic, especially women, are "twice-struck"; that is, they have been traditionally disprivileged and disempowered in the United States because of their gender. Black, Cuban, Chinese and Native American males have been disprivileged, as well, but females of color have been doubly disprivileged because of color and gender. The themes of gender and ethnicity entertwine to strike these members twice (Orbe,1998).

The aged in American society are sometimes considered victims of ageism, which is rooted in stereotypical notions about older people. aging has been called a 'woman's problem' in that she has enjoyed fewer opportunities in the past than males have and continues to be more dependent on others as she ages. Often outliving their male partners. women face more uncertain futures as they age, according to this view. Ethnicity and aging are discussed in chapters six and seven.

Gender and the Media

Television has joined the family dinner table. Children may eat their dinner in front of the television set, munching on fast foods, picked up by their working parents who often chose the fast way to have dinner. There has been a dramatic shift in the perceived and enacted roles of the contemporary parent in America. "Soccer moms" and "latchkey kids" are buzzwords attesting to the shift. Moms may be the sole breadwinner and television and the internet may be the babysitters!

The media, especially television, are powerful socializing agents, influencing the playing out of gender in American society. Whether it is a program on MTV, a channel emphasing music and displaying sexual fantasy apparently designed to appeal to young ethnic people, or programs that promote religious messages, one finds in television a shaping lens. The image of the "perfect" male and the "perfect" female are constantly promoted by the media and by advertisers who want to sell products. As mentioned, there are few ugly people on television!

It is popular to promote gender differences on television and in books where stereotyped concepts like the Mars-Venus relationship are simplistically proclaimed. Talk shows play up, often in very negative and demeaning ways, the problems that men and women have with each other. Less obvious an influence on gender identitiy is the internet. Nevertheless, the digital divide influences the gendered, the aged and members of ethnic groups differentially; access to the use of the internet varies by gender, ethnicity and age. This topic will be addressed in Chapter Eight.

Gender in Relationships: Styles and Levels of Intimacy

Gendered Encounters

It is clear that relationships are created, that whatever differences there are between the genders come into play in relationships, whether they are intimate or friendship based. Relationships are symbolic babies! Nonverbal behavior is deeply involved in relationships. Body orientations in particular are involved (Remland, Jones, & Brinkman, 1995; Scheflen, 1965).

Relationships are coded; that is, there are underlying assumptions that are made about the nature of the relationship. People who are able to observe and listen empathically, are perhaps more adept at creating healthy relationships. To the extent that males exert control or focus on independence; to the extent that women want to have relationship talk, these conditions can act to produce "ships passing in the night". Males and females frequently talk past each other in these kinds of relationships (Tannen, 1990). Empathic listening, difficult to achieve, helps create a balance. People of both genders have needs for self-esteem and affection.

People construct meanings for their relationships. For example, they may describe their partners as sexual, intelligent or attractive, easy, difficult or otherwise. In an intimate relationship when a person says "I love you", it calls up all of the meanings that the other party has for love, which vary considerably, based on the experiences of the person. Past baggages and successes are often brought to a new intimate relationship, influencing the character of the relationship. People do not "fall" in love as much as they "construct" a loving relationship, but when negative past baggage is brought to the relationship, both parties are challenged. Self reflection, of course, is a key to understanding; it is in this meta-process that humans confirm or deny themselves. Self-monitoring is a way to follow the relational process (Wood, 1995).

A number of scholars have focused on relational development and the processes associated with it (Duck, 1992; Knapp & Vangelisti, 1992; Rubin, 1965, 1980; Wood, 1995) and a variety of theories exist. The SI approach suggests that humans construct their relationships, although it is not a linear process;indeed, it may be a recursive process. That is, people arrive at one point and then return to another before moving ahead. One behavior is contingent upon another. The values of American society, of course, frame the meaning of relationships. Because females have been described as relationship experts, it has been suggested that a female yardstick measures the success of the relationship. Males, raised to be somewhat independent, may not so easily enter into self-disclosing aspects of relationships.

Framing Romantic Myths

In youth, people hear stories about Cinderella, Sleeping Beauty, and snow White, all sweet and pure maidens who find themselves in predicaments, to be rescued by a strong, handsome prince. She waits passively for the active prince. This old-fashioned stereotype seems to have its counterpart in modern America. During adolescence, the modern young lady may fantasize about true lasting love, about meeting the right man. Boys, on the other hand, tend to emphasize conquest and sexuality and, when asked how they did on the first date, they may respond, bragging about their sexual success (Arliss & Borisoff, 1993).

Sometimes there are perceptual differences that are built into relationships. For example, it has been suggested that females are 'defined' in American societies mostly by males; that is, men refer to women as having PMS, or premenstrual syndrome, affecting their behavior, but the males do not refer to themselves as having HTS, or hypertestosterone syndrome, suggesting an imbalance in the way that genders are perceived. It is a common perception as well that women are by nature better, sweeter, kinder, more loving and more peaceful than men? Myths about genders abound (Tavris, 1992). It appears, as well, that females in the United States are held to a higher level of expectation about being attractive than are males (Eakins and Eakins, 1978).

Gendered encounters are daily occurrences. Sexual encounters, on the other hand, depending on the culture, are often hidden occurrences. In the United States sexual encounters, formerly hidden from view, are now more explicit and open. In more traditional times, it was considered inappropriate to discuss sexual matters openly. Indeed, before 1900, upright piano legs were covered prudently. The values and morals of highly structured Calvinistic and Victorian America called for privacy in sexual matters. Today, however, it is not uncommon to find research about sexual encounters (Grammer, Kruck & Magnusson, 1998). In short, just as researchers focus on the sexual and reproductive habits of lower order animals, they focus on the behaviors of human couples in sexual action. As any internet user knows, explicit sexual activities may be found on a number of sites. Sexual and romantic encounters are the stuff of television programs. Americans have gone through a gendered, sexual revolution.

Types of Relationships

There may be a tendency for people to think that relationships just happen. Of course, they involve considerable work and they are processual, as the following suggests.

Framing Evolution and Process in Relationships

Relationships evolve. That is, people must be in some way attracted to one another; they must explore and reduce uncertainty about one another; there must be an evolving commitment to the relationship; and, the relationship must be sustained in routinized patterns.

Even when relationships dissolve or come apart there are phases of that dissolution. Sometimes conflict is involved; at other times negotiation occurs; in all cases there is the final stage of grave dressing that is required, putting an end to the symbolic baby.

Males and females differ in their perceptions of relationships. Indeed there may be tension between the views. Females tend to emphasize rapport, emotional contexts and process; males tend to control their emotions and to think episodically. Men tend to "do" things or to control them. This affects their relationships (Wood, 1995).

Given the difficulties encountered by couples in modern societies, scholars have focused on problems in relationships. Gottman, for example, believes that he can predict whether a marriage will succeed or fail by analyzing the communicative patterns of the couples (Gottman, 1979). A number of scholars have focused on the nature of love (Lee, 1988). Various love styles have been described. Eros, Ludus, Storge, Pragma, Mania and Agape are words used to describe a range of styles, from physically falling in love at first sight to ethically putting the partner's welfare above all else (Wood, 1995). In short, relationships are created in many different forms. All of them are forms of behavior. The mother-child relationship differs substantially from the father-child relationship, as does the relationship between the mother and the father. Relationships are defined and constructed. They can take multiple forms.

Overarching themes find their way into relationships. For example, it is not common for a President of a large corporation to interact with workers low on the pay scale. The common bond is missing. There must be a meeting of the minds, a middle way, a fertile ground from which the seeds of a relationship sprout. A social nexus of some type is the glue of relationships. Power, gender, sex, age, ethnicity, time, occupation and so on may play roles in relationships, setting the conditions for relationships to flourish or disallowing meaningful contact.

Further, they involve a type of work; that is, love, a word thrown about like a commodity for purchase, involves hard work to construct and maintain. The word love, so often confused with romantic thoughts, is essentially an enacted development, not one that is thrust upon a person. There may be love at first sight, but it is merely a glimpse of what is to come. Relationships have a history and a future path; they change and are modified. Often, they take as much effort to leave them as they require to maintain them. Whatever the level of the relationship, the partners must perform and nourish the relationship; otherwise, it dissipates (Duck, 1992) Relationships are, in the final analysis, social products, symbolic babies.

Courtship Patterns

Interestingly, 85 percent of all valentines are purchased by females (Tavris, 1992), which may indicate that in romantic relationships, it is the woman's influence that is paramount. Friendship and romance are different aspects of negotiated relationships but it appears that love, or romance, is feminized in many ways. Friendship, perhaps, is more spiritual and romance is more sexual, comparing one to the other. Sexual behaviors have been researched by symbolic interactionists (Longmore, 1998; Prus, 1996). Although sex need not be part of love, it usually is. It is also part of prostitution, where intimacy is not a prerequisite to engage in sex. Romantic love, it would seem can only exist between two people who have meaningfully defined their ongoing relationship because it involves deep emotions that are brought out one by the other, not to be shared.In the western world love emphasizes romance distinguishing it from relationships that are socially arranged, as are found in many parts of the world.

Framing Older Courtship Rituals

Near mid-century, the courtship patterns were distinctive. Calling them quasi- courtship cues, Scheflen, a psychiatrist, classified courtship cue behavior into the following behavioral system. As an example of courtship readiness one wants to reduce eye bagginess and belly bulge and stand erectly. As examples of preening behavior, one wants to fix the makeup, arrange the clothes, look in a mirror, perhaps leave the top button open on shirts and blouses and so on. As examples of positional cues, one wants to sit in such a way as to be able to talk with the opposite sex. Arms, legs and bodies must be arranged so that it is difficult for others to intervene; actions of appeal or invitation must be taken, which include flirting, gazing, exposing the thigh, showing wrist or palm, or flexing muscles (Scheflen,1965).

The older courtship style does not quite fit the modern approach. It is said that young Americans are a microwave generation; nothing seems to last very long. Instant everything seems to be the norm. Romantic liaisons may be quickly created and abandoned almost as quickly, both parties expecting an endpoint, such as when they graduate from college.

Perhaps females are more easily hurt in romantic relationships because it is they who tend to more readily expose their feelings than men do or because males may be threatened by intimate disclosures (Wood, 1994). Men may want to act rather than talk about feelings (Tannen, 1990). As mentioned, some scholars suggest that romance is governed by a female ruler or yardstick; that is, females are more naturally disposed to building rapport and to sharing their emotions.

Research suggests that the strength of romantic relationships including marriages is a direct reflection of the type of communicative attention that each party gives the other. In short, romantic relationships can display "relational health" or they can be ragged and hurtful to the parties involved. There is a semantic difficulty in the way romance is described. The word love is used in a general way to cover all manner of relationships, including same-sex relationships. But people couple together for a variety of reasons, ranging from the need for security to the need for sex; the word love may be used to describe any relationship. Arranged marriages, common in many countries, may not even include the notion of romance; rather they are arranged for socio-economic reasons, to bind together members of social groups.

Intimate cross-gender relationships proceed in stages, although not in linear fashion. That is, some relationships may dive into a deeper stage, not waiting for a full-blossoming of the intimacy to take place, there being no commitment to permanency. In the more thoroughly gendered romantic relationship the emotions are engaged very deeply and a level reached in which both genders commit themselves exclusively to the relationship.

In the commited, dyadic cross-gender relationship, the voices of the past emerge. Thus, each gender brings scripted and schematized ideas into what she or he thinks the relationship is or should be; each person brings both the positive and negative baggage of other past relationships into the present; each person brings parental views into the relationship. In short, many voices are "heard" in romantic relationships. Together, the gendered couple create a symbolic baby, their shared version of the relationship, taking on a life of its own.

Theorists from the games school of thought, suggest that each party has a game strategy in mind. Thus, the male may play daddy and the female may play the role of the mother or even the helpless one. She may play the role of the knowledgeable relational expert and he may play the role of the dumb jock. Both, however, play multiple roles. Their relationship may become somewhat pathological and co-dependent, or it may become mature and growth-oriented.

Cultures define male-female relationships in highly varied ways(3). In some present day cultures, such as Iraq, couples are attached only by parental permission. Polygamous relationships are encouraged in many cultures, not based on romantic love; concubinage still exists in many societies; females are treated as owned goods. Even in the United States, the emergence of femalehood is relatively recent, the process continuing today. Relationships are deeply influenced by socio-cultural processes.

Modern romantic relationships are subject to many influences and social constraints. To be a permanently coupled "item" is more and more difficult in American society, as statistics reveal. Perhaps these statistics reflect the problems involved in the achievement of identity in a highly changeable, mediated society (Gergen, 1991).

Power and Violence in Relationships

Recent movements have influenced gendered power relationships in the United States. NOW, the National Organization for Women, has given females a new voice. For example, in Roe v. Wade, women won the right to control their bodies, to decide about issues related to their reproductive health. At the present time, debates continue about Roe v. Wade, as it does about Affirmative Action, both affecting men and women in white and other ethnic groups. Since the 1980's, journals devoted to masculine, or male concepts and behaviors have emerged. On the one hand, various magazines encourage males to become more sensitive; on the other hand, they have encouraged them to become "real", more manly, as in the past. Similarly, magazines and programs exist that encourage women to become body builders; others want women to become more feminine. In short, gender roles are being redefined, sometimes blurred.

In violent relationships it appears that males are the ones who use their power against their partner more than the other way around. Indeed, the courts many times seem to blame the victim of rape, often a female, as much as they blame the rapist, a process that would seem to reinforce the status quo (Tavris, 1992). It appears that the law expects a woman to behave like a man; in other words, she should try to defend herself as men would. But, of course, there is a difference between consent and coercion. Some scholars see the male rape bias as an extension of earlier times when women were considered the property of men; even reasonable standards of justice seem to be biased in favor of men (Tavris, 1992). Recently, the New York Times (May 12, 2001, online) reported that Dartmouth expelled a fraternity because members of that fraternity described in their newsletter patented date rape techniques, even deriding some of the women who had sex with the fraternity members.

Acts of violence cut across age, class and ethnic groups. It is estimated that 28 percent, perhaps as much as 50 percent of women, experience some form of violent abuse, physical or verbal from their partners (Wood, 1992). Less than five percent of abusive actions are done by women. It would appear that American ideals, linking the male psyche to aggression, strength and control, influence how men act in violent male-female relationships (Wood,1992).

A number of myths about violence prevail. For example, contrary to common thought, violence can happen in any relationship; both males and females inflict violence on their partners; violence need not be cyclical and alcohol need not be involved. (Marshall & Vitanza, 1994). The SI approach to violence suggests that people do what makes sense to them, based on how they have framed the situation, usually influenced by how they have behaved in the past. The enactment of violence, of course, is an extreme form of the use of power, one that inhibits personal and interactive growth. Some males use their power mindlessly forcing sex in a relationship. Females who tolerate this behavior and others like it, have been described as co-dependent; that is, they unwittingly take part in the action.

Gender in Social Institutions

Gendered Schooling

It is no accident that females are more likely to be teachers in the early grades and that college professors are more likely to be males. The societal expectations have clearly favored males in the sciences and social sciences (Deegan, 1991; Schiebingen, 1993). As discussed above, women have been described as nurturant, as moral, as caring. Men have been thought to be rational and logical.These facts reflect the dominant male paradigm that has historically shaped economic and schooling patterns in the United States. In the case of women in the lower levels, the nurturant style of females seems to play a role.

Gradually, there is a perceptible shift occurring. Women are entering fields like engineering and biology and men are entering early grade school teaching, although it is a slow process. Indeed, the American Bar Association reports that in the academic year 2001-02, females will outnumber males in law schools, a fact which, researchers say, will change the way the law is perceived and practiced.(The New York Times, March 26, 2001) The "woman thing" is being dealt with by law schools.

Even in the stories that female teachers read to their children, it has been reported that males are key actors in the stories by more than three to one (Wood, 1992), and that women tend to be invisible. Experiments performed by researchers in colleges and universities usually include freshmen and sophomores, mostly males, at least in the sciences. Perhaps a male standard is thereby created. Such studies are not easily extrapolated to the whole population. Indeed, it is reported that males are given more attention throughout the educational process from start to finish (Wood, 1992).

In short, it is only in very recent American history that women have been taken seriously in the professional marketplace. Like females, it is often the case that members of ethnic groups, have been invisible in the schooling system. This brief sketch of nonverbal gender patterns in schooling cannot tell the complete story, one that is complex; nevertheless it points out how a major American institution is genderized and ethnicized. Affirmative Action programs and Equal Opportunity laws address some of the problems of imbalance and Universities and other schooling institutions are increasingly sensitive to gendered imbalances. Courses that focus on women's studies are now promoted as are male studies. The picture is not as bleak as it was in the past although, clearly, there is work to be done to fulfill the concept of egalitarianism.

Gender and The Media

The role of the media as an influence in gendered America will be discussed in chapter Eight. In this section, pointed references are made to how the media, especially television, shape and play up gendered representations. Most, if not all Americans own television sets or are exposed to television, It is the rare person who has not seen a movie or read a magazine. Children view television several hours in a day, and it appears that Black children may view it more than do Whites (Wood, 1992). Incredibly, many adolescents may have spent more time in front of the television set than they have spent in formal schooling. Televison saturates the American life (Gergen, 1991).

As in the profession of college teaching, television has been the male domain. Few women produce programs or serve as anchors on television newscasts (Gitlin, 1983) although this is changing. Black women, in particular, are underserved. It is the Black males who are more likely to end up on television, often as weather announcers, but occasionally as newscasters. Older males and females rarely appear as main figures on television, although ads may be devoted to them.

Television and other print media often portray males and females stereotypically. Children's television shows usually show males as dominant and aggressive, rewarded for their behaviors (Wood, 1992). Movies that promote the aggressive male may be on the increase. The "sensitive" male is rarely portrayed. Regarding women, television promotes them as both younger and thinner than everyday life reveals them to be; often they are represented as dependent upon men or as passive (Wood, 1992). In short, females and males are often portrayed on television programs from a base that is unrealistic. Increasingly, television, film, radio and print media are adapting themselves to new patterns in American culture as will be discussed in Chapter Eight.

Summary

Sex and gender have been considered as separate, but interacting concepts. Sexuality refers to biological processes. The biological female differs in many ways from the biological male. Neuronal and sensate processes distinguish the female from the male. Gender is the sense of self that one creates through socialization. Gendered identities are complex; people enact multiple roles as they engage others in interaction. Although some scholars prefer to think of gender in essentialist terms, the emphasis here is upon the social construction of gender. Gender is a dynamic concept; there is no essential, fixed core to identity although there is stability, or gender constancy.

Gendered relationships are created but they are heavily influenced by master themes, such as ethnicity, age, occupation and status in society. Power is often a factor in the relationship. Social codes influence the creation of relationships. Relationships may be defined in multiple ways. Gender plays itself out in the workplace. Although the male bias, the male thing, still seems to be fairly pervasive in American society, it is clear that changes are being made. Traditional patterns of gendered behavior are changing.

In the next chapter, we turn to the concept of ethnicity and how nonverbal communication is influenced by this deep background variable.

Questions for Thought and Discussion

1.   The fact that our lives are gendered is reflected in the artifacts that people purchase, wear or have around their homes. What artifacts appear to be used mostly or completely by one gender or the other? What artifacts are gender neutral?

2.   The concept of the ideal woman is often talked about. What do you think are the characteristics of the ideal woman as expressed in American society? The ideal man? Do you agree with these idealizations?

3.   Generally speaking, do you accept the concept of androgyny as a good way to describe modern male-female embodiments? Do males and females differ in their nonverbal behaviors radically, somewhat, or very little? Try to explain your answer.

4.   Attempt to trace how you believe your gendered self was influenced as you grew up. What were the major influences on your personal, gendered growth? Have role models played a significant role in your growth? If so, who are they? Are you a role model to others? In what ways?

5.   How does gender power seem to influence what you do? Is power a key part of your interpersonal relationships? What are some differences between the concept of influence and the concept of power?

Notes

1.   It is only recently, with the emergence of imaging technologies, that researchers have been able to localize behavioral patterns in the brain. The concept of lateralization so prominently discussed in earlier periods was fairly radical; that is, it inaccurately pointed to fixed differences between the sexes. Earlier, by probing the brain, researchers determined which part of the brain controlled which body functions, the use of language and so on. Often extreme measures, such as frontal lobotomies, were used to control inmates in prisons; the emotions were controlled when the brain was severed. To find living subjects, medical experiments were conducted on inmates, a practice now outlawed. It is expected that by using modern technologies, researchers may be able to unlock neuro-chemical secrets associated with pathologies, like schizophrenia, for example, or how women and men use their brains. Interestingly, there may be an interaction between how people live and how their brains develop.

2.   Pheromone activity is better understood in lower order animals than it is in humans. For example, garter snakes emerge from their winter dens, the males emerging first, perhaps numbering in the hundreds. When females emerge, they are swarmed on by hundreds of male snakes who are attracted to the female pheromones in the skin. It does not matter to the males that many females die due to the press of male snakes. The pheromones, apparently, are used as communication signals among the garter snakes, who have been found to travel up to 20 miles following pheromone trails. Humans, of course, are not "driven" like snakes but there is emerging evidence that pheromones exist in humans too and that they may influence interpersonal behaviors (Smithsonian, April 2001, pp 92-98).

3.   The United States emphasizes monogamy, although different groups such as the Mormons and other early communal groups, believed that polygamy was appropriate behavior. There is an association between economic need, population demographics and marriage patterns. For example, where there are many females but fewer males, the pressure to engage in polygamy is greater than when there is a balance. Concubinage has been practiced throughout history. In lower order animals, indiscriminate mating, several males with one female, or one male with several females is not uncommon. In human societies, indiscriminate mating is constrained by social mores and ethics.

Suggested Readings

Arliss, L. P., & Borisoff, D. J. (1993). *Women and Men Communicating: Challenges and Changes*. New York: Holt, Rinehart & Winston.

Deegan, M. J. (Ed.) (1991). *Women in Sociology*. Westport, CT: Greenwood Publishing Group.

Gilmore, D. (1990). *Manhood in the Making*. New Haven, CT: Yale University Press.

Henley, N. M. (1977). *Body Politics: Power, Sex and Nonverbal Communication*. Englewood Cliffs, NJ: Prentice-Hall, Inc.

Tavris, C. (1992). *The Mismeasurement of Woman*. New York: Simon and Schuster.

Wood, J. T. (1994). *Gendered Lives: Communication, Gender and Culture*. Belmont, CA: Wadsworth Publishing Company.

Chapter 6

Ethnicity and Nonverbal Communication
Making Sense of Ethnicity

Chapter Overview

Concepts that have been developed in earlier chapters are applied in this chapter. They bear upon ethnic identity and behavior. A considerable body of research about ethnicity has been compiled, only selected aspects of which can be presented here. The reference section includes a number of important works related to ethnicity.

Like gender identity, ethnic identity is created over time, arising from the way that people construe life based on their experiences. Some scholars suggest that, in America, people live in a post-negritude culture (Reid, 1997) meaning that the social conditions in which ethnicity is expressed have changed. Others have asserted that a form of a color-based caste system still exists (Ogbu, 1978). Still others focus on competition that exists between ethnic groups (Olzak, 1986). Members of the ethnic groups share a similar socio-historical background that influences their beliefs, habits, customs and ways of thinking. Social identity involves cultural and social practices that distinguish members of one ethnic group from the practices of other groups. In this sense, identity is a metaphorical folk category, representing people in everyday life in ongoing ways (Fitzgerald,1993;Lamont & Fournier, 1993).

Identity is expressed at both the individual and the group or collective level. In this chapter the focus is primarily upon collective ethnic identities. The reader should be reminded that there is a great deal of variation to be found among members of the same general ethnic grouping. Socialization influences everyone, but it is not a uniform process. People interpret the "givens" of their life in individualized ways.

The concept of *co-cultures* is introduced to indicate that ethnic groups deserve equal respect, as do all groups. The word ethnic, of course, is used in many ways; in a sense, all people are members of ethnic groups. Five groups will be discussed in this chapter including Native Americans, specifically Navajo members, Black Americans, Chinese Americans, Cuban Americans and White Americans. Racism was common to the historical experiences of Black Americans, (or Negroes as they were called then), the Navajo, Chinese immigrants and Whites. White Americans, of course, were the dominant power that encroached upon members of the other groups. The Cuban experience was different. Cubans fled a hostile Cuba, coming to the United States in exile. They have been treated as beleaguered friends, while the others were treated as ignoble strangers.

Ethnic groups around the world have been mistreated by those in power. For example, the early vanquishment of the Mayans, Incas and Aztecs by the conquering Spaniards serve as testimony. (Sowell, 1998). Human history in many ways is the history of struggle, as ethnic groups around the globe will attest. In this chapter, there is no attempt to moralize about what happened in early America; nor is there an attempt to malign members of any group. Rather, the attempt is to describe the harsh conditions in which members of ethnic groups struggled as they construed the meaning of life, their own identities. In present-day American society, much of the ethnic turmoil is couched in that history.

New generations of the ethnic groups discussed here confront a different social milieau. There is occasional outright hostility but there seems to be progress in human relations. Yet, stereotypes and other demeaning characterizations appear, often in subtle forms, indicating that the color barrier has not been completely crossed or erased. Barriers to interaction are not caused by one party or the other; they are caused by both or all parties. It is hoped that this chapter can contribute to a balanced understanding of ethnic differences. Whites, in a sense are de-ethnified by self definition (Pujol, Spring, 2000); nevertheless, in the grand scheme of things they, too, are ethnicized.

It would seem that the egalitarian ethos can be realized only when members of each group are inter-ethnically adaptable. The colors red, black, brown, yellow and white are mere surface features in the identification process. By appreciating these human colors rather than derogating them, people can do productive ethnic borderwork.

The historiographic approach used in this chapter is compatible with SI. By using historiography it is possible to understand how the ethnic identity of the five groups was formed.

Ethnic Identity: An Historiographic Approach

The American Egalitarian Ethos

School children, born and raised in the United States, have been taught that the United States is the land of freedom, that others from countries around the world are welcome to these shores, whether they were immigrants from war-torn countries or others who came here to make a better living, to live the good life. The Statue of Liberty, was placed in the New York harbor, commemorating the 100th anniversary of American Independence. It became the symbol of freedom, welcoming immigrants from abroad.

Framing the Great Invitation

Give me your tired, your poor,
Your huddled masses yearning to breathe free,
The wretched refuse of your teeming shore,
Send these, the homeless, tempest-tossed, to me:
I lift my lamp beside the golden door.

(Emma Lazarus 1849-1887)

The *egalitarian ethos* is a powerful theme, appreciated first by the religious Whites who came to these shores to gain religious freedom. Although it serves as a reminder of opportunity in America, many people have not benefited.

Early Thought: The Great Chain of Being

As mentioned, in early Western thought the theory of the Great Chain of Being held sway among many philosophers, theologians and anthropologists. All creatures, including humans, were located on a hierarchy. White European males were placed on the highest level in this hierarchy; women were placed below men and people of color; animals occupied the lowest levels. The separation of the races was promoted; distorted versions of Darwinism, scientific racism and eugenics were sometimes linked together in support of racism (Kohn, Dec 1997) This theory, along with other beliefs, of course, had dire consequences for people of color in early America.

Monogenetics and Polygenetics

A monogenetic or a polygenetic approach to the classification of human beings was used in early analysis. Under the monogenetic concept, all humans were thought to be the same, following various Biblical injunctions; under the polygenetic concept, races were thought to be distinct, separate from one another. Polygenism was popular in America and it had implications for the status of African slaves. Since, the theory "proved" that whites were different from blacks, qualitatively, it seemed as well that there was a legitimate scientific justification for slavery(Wolpoff & Caspari, 1997). Early American thought seemed to be along the following lines.

"The more or less standard set of caucasion stereotypes went like this: The indomitable, courageous, proud Indian---in how very different a light he stands by the side of the submissive, obsequious, imitative Negro, or by the side of the tricky, cunning, and cowardly Mongolian! Are not these facts indications that the different races do not rank upon one level in nature"(Agassiz, 1859). Agassiz thought that one must fit education to the innate qualities of the race involved. For example, he thought that blacks should do manual work and whites should do mind work.

Agassiz may have given words to that which was commonly believed, at least by an undiscerning public.

The Concept of Race

The concept of race, discussed here, implies a superiority-inferiority relationship; color was associated with race and white people were thought to be superior to people of color. The result was extreme separation and segregation. It is easy to point the finger at Whites but, in fact, for racism to exist both sides must maintain it. The term race is European in origin. Referring to gene pools,it was popular during the Inquisition. In modern America when people refer to racism they think of how race is lived, interpersonally and institutionally (Finerty, July 16, 2000). Today, as they did then, negative racial attitudes result in segregation distinctively marked by color. People are essentially strangers to one another when color barriers are erected.

In early anthropology it was suggested that racial stocks were mainly of three kinds: negroid, mongoloid, and caucasoid. Each type had distinguishable features, such as skin color, facial structure, body structure and hair appearance. Under this system, Chinese, for example, were marked by straight black hair, a yellow-brown skin, dark eyes and rounded faces and Negroes had dark brown or dark skin, large lips, slanted foreheads and long arms and legs. Their hair was tightly wound in swirls. Caucasoids had light skin, a range of eye colors and hair that could be varied in color and wavy.

Enlightened anthropologists have shown that these categories are unrealistic, too rigid and too amenable to stereotypes. For example, the tallest people in the world are black people while the shortest people in the world are also black people, both in Africa, separated by a few thousand miles. Some white people have darker skin than some blacks. Evolution leads to diversification and complexity, not to sameness, unless humans live in very strict isolation (Wilson, 1992). Thus the tripartite categorization of races is hardly a scientific classification. When blood types and DNA are brought into the equations, racial categorization is even less scientifically useful. The color of the skin becomes a mere surface feature.

Phrenology

The complexity of intermixed features found among humans throughout the world is now obvious; racial categorization is fraught with difficulty. However, this fact did not historically prevent some scientists from attempting to classify races by intelligence. Indeed, one of the motives for classification was to show the racial superiority of the white person. Phrenology, unacceptable today as a scientific tool, was used to show how races differed from one another according to brain size. Brain size, however, is not a good indicator of intelligence, once again showing how some scientists were misguided.(Gould, 1981).

Ethnicity

The concept of ethnicity is probably more modern than is the concept of race. For example, the early British appeared to be more involved with ideas about loyalty, honor, connection, station and conformity that it was with ethnicity (Kidd, 1999). Race refers mostly to physical characteristics while ethnicity refers to socially learned behaviors, passed on from one generation to another, often modified in the process.

In early American history, the word ethnic was used to label minorities as "heathens", as perceived by white people. Today, ethnicity refers to a wide range of characteristics that are associated with groups, such as social customs and foodways. To describe oneself in ethnic terms can be a positive way for humans to identify themselves. (Fitzgerald, 1993). One can enact her or his identity at the personal level or at the public level in collective ways. For example, contemporary Blacks may adopt a nonverbal style associated with their ethnicity as shown in the following frame.

Framing Black Nonverbal Styles

Rather than just walking, Blacks seem to move rhythmically. When young Blacks bop down the street, it is a statement of identity, of self-power. Wearing clothes is a way to make a statement about self-identity; it is a way of giving force, or Nommo, to one's life. Shades, or dark glasses, may be worn to provide some magic. Sometimes showboating, or verbal boasting, as Muhammed Ali did, is performed to make a statement. An individual style is highly preferred and respected among blacks, so commonly found in their musical expressions. Black performers want to use distinctive skill and style, not machine-like performances. (Kochman,1988).

Of course, the reader should understand that this description is suited to some blacks but not to others. Blacks like anybody else do not wish to be stereotyped.

Ethnic identity is a social construction, created by humans to give meaning to one's life. Skin color may be a part of the identification process but it is not the key part. It is through the taking of roles that one construes who she or he is and those roles are influenced by early upbringing, by association with others who hold similar beliefs and attitudes. Shared world views, shared social practices and commonality of experience are part of ethnic construction. (Ashmore & Jussim, 1997).

Interethnic problems result when people define themselves too rigidly(1). In other words, ethnicity is Janus-faced; it builds a sense of community, but at the same time, it can separate one from the wider society. Ethnocentrism and xenophobia are indicators that members of a rigidly constructed ethnic group may feel threatened, even paranoic about the wider culture. Whether these groups are White supremacists, Black Muslims, or members of Chinese gangs, their rigid positions thwart their acceptance into mainline culture. Numerous factors, such as power, gender, sexual orientation and social class influence the construal of the lives of members of ethnic group members (Chow, Wilkinson, & Zinn,1996).

A Brief Sketch of Ethnic Group Identity

Native Americans:The Navajo or Dine

It is not possible to frame the histories of each of the groups except briefly. For a thorough treatment one needs to read the histories of each.

The Navajo, or dine, as they call themselves (O'Bryan, 1956), were in what is now America before the White man, including the Spanish, arrived. Today, young Navaho tribal members may or may not live on the "Rez", which is located near the New Mexico-Arizona border. Many of them have entered the job market, attended Universities or married outside of the tribe. Nevertheless, many young Navajo people are searching out what it means to be Navajo in the modern world. The so-called Red Power Movement in the 1960's and 1970's focused on the renewal of Native American awareness and identity (Nagel, 1996).

Framing the Navajo Rez

The reservation, or Rez, as the Navajo refer to it, is truly in remote America. Most of them are poor, perhaps Catholic, who have experience in going to an Indian boarding school. Poverty and alcoholism associated with joblessness is common in the four corner region where four states join. Time seems to stand still, the Navajo doing things at their own pace, in their own way. Navajo spirituality is evident in their symbols. In the hogan serving as a church, for example, cedar is burned instead of incense; creeds and chants along with the gospel are recorded in the Navajo language. The Navajo redeemer on the wall of the church is a sheepherder and the Navajo yeis, who are protectors or holy persons who lived lives of peace and harmony, were symbolically carved into the glass panels on the church doors. Thus, the Catholic service is a mix of Navajo custom and Christian ways. Ceremonies deal with healing and protection; even a medicine man will conduct healing ceremonies if a Navajo member is having bad dreams or has been away from the Rez for a time, needing cleansing. There is a deep spiritual bond between the Navajo people and Mother Earth.

There are a few pick-up trucks, some people make a living sheepherding, others weave rugs and carve objects and make jewels; the fortunate ones have jobs in schools and hospitals. Often when men are hired outside the Rez, they are hired without benefits, almost like pawns. Many are on welfare. But many families do not have electricity or drinking water. They may buy soft drinks, but these are too sweet for people who often have diabetes (Jones, Jan 21, 2000).

Today, the Navajo, along with the Hopi and the Havasupi Native American tribes, are having difficulty with the owners of the White Vulcan Pumice Mine, an extraction operation that has U.S. permission to mine. Stone-washed jeans, so popular in America, are washed with the pumice extracted here. The problem is that the area is a sacred area called Diichiti, or Mountain of Strength. The mine operators hope to expand their mining, clearing trees and then bulldozing the land. These operations have been dealt with by holding prayer vigils and protests by the tribes. They have met with little success, the mining operation being performed under an 1872 federal mining law, now clearly outdated. Several groups are trying to stop mining altogether (Ghioto, Jan, 2000).

Chinese Americans

The Chinese society contained two major groups, the upper classes, who were well educated and controlled society, and the lower classes, who were uneducated and were peasants to a large degree (Coye & Livingston, 1975). Chinese sailors apparently had visited these shores in the 1700's but it was the peasant groups who emigrated from China to the West coast of America in the mid-1800's. They had come from economically and politically troubled areas of China. Nearly all males, they came to America in the mid-1800s to make their fortunes in the gold mines, hoping to return to China with their earned wealth. Chinese women came to the United States at a later period to the San Francisco area (Yung, 1995).

In a change of fate, Chinese men became the backbone of labor for the building of railroads. Indeed, it was commonly believed in America that the Chinese had a higher tolerance for pain because they had a less developed nervous system, a specious idea (Coye, 1975). Because they were discriminated against by members of white society, Chinese began to live in enclaves, now called Chinatowns, of which there are several (Takaki, 1993).

They created small businesses devoted to doing what whites would not do, such as laundering, small stores and restaurants. The focus in this book is upon one such Chinatown in the Bowery region of New York City, one of several. Of the four groups discussed, young Chinese, born and raised in this country, have been the most successful, entering colleges and universities, becoming medical and engineering professionals and businessmen. However, modern Asian-Americans, born in the United States, are not entirely free from ethnic bias and stereotype. Females especially have "racialized bodies" in the view of many whites (Lee, 1997).

On the other hand, the family values of achievement have led to educational success for Asian American children, who, unlike other ethnic groups, continue to increase their numbers in colleges and universities (Braxton, 1999). Chinese parents, perhaps more than members of other ethnic groups, tend to talk to their children about the values of hard work, high standards, and saving "face". Family honor is at stake when a child fails.

Not all is entirely well in Chinatown, however, where Chinese have had to fight for their version of the American Dream. Unfair labor practices, sweatshops, and other built-in practices discriminate against the recent immigrants who may lack the English language skill, or be in Chinatown illegally; they must work in low paying jobs controlled by tightly controlled by well established, wealthy Americans, a modern form of slave-trade. A Chinese Staff and Workers Association exists to fight perceived wrongs, having some success (Asian Economic News, August 24, 1998).

Africans/Black Americans

Blacks, formerly referred to as Negroes, represent approximately 13 percent of the American population. They were brought to America against their will in the early 1600's. Captured from the west coast of Africa, often separated from their families, they became slaves in America and elsewhere. Unlike Indians who did not make good slaves, they survived in desperate circumstances. Despite the fact that many public figures wanted to abolish slavery or wanted to send the slaves back to Africa, slavery survived for economic reasons, mostly on plantations in the South. (Filler,1960).

They were distributed throughout the colonies, including the North, prior to gaining their freedoms, a slow, agonizing process. Today, of course, their offspring live throughout the United States, mostly in cities. Their struggle to "be somebody" is noted in the volumes of books, talk shows and programs that discuss their struggle in modern society. The New York Times, for example, recently produced a series devoted to how race is lived in America', which focused on the dimensions of their experience. Modern issues of racial profiling, hate crimes and reparation are often found in the media. The egalitarian ethos has not spread to the black community very fast. For example, in 1990, 7.7 percent of the Captains, or senior officers, in the New York Police Department were black; at present there are 5.7 percent. In the elite helicopter group, only one black person is found among 59 whites (New York Times, April 2, 2001). Whatever the explanation, the meaning of the data is negative in the minds of those who would improve relations. Many highly educated black people in major universities are spokespeople for them, as are ministers who have traditionally empowered their congregations. Blacks occupy high political positions, including judgeships; they own businesses. Serious interethnic relational issues remain however.

Cuban Americans

Cubans had come back and forth freely between Cuba and the United States prior to the takeover of Cuba by Fidel Castro in the late 1960's. He imposed autocratic, Communistic practices upon Cuban society. Following his takeover, Cubans came to the United States as escapees, perhaps as former Batista supporters, or they were forced from Cuba by Fidel Castro's government because they did not support him. Castro sent many formerly imprisoned people to the United States as well. Boat people came here under the cover of darkness in whatever vessels they could find. Today, the largest concentration of Cubans is in Little Havana in Miami; however, there are large concentrations in New Jersey, New York City and other major cities in the United States. Cuban culture is expressed in its salza and danza, in popular television shows, such as the former I Love Lucy Show and in the music of Gloria Estefan and others. Cuban artists, exported from Cuba, have made their mark as have businessmen who occupy highly visible positions in the United States.

The Elian Gonzales affair, so long the attention of the major news networks in the United States, reflected the ongoing hostility that older exiled Cubans still have toward Fidel Castro. Nearly half of the Cubans who fled Cuba did so between 1960 and 1969; their memory is strong (Ray, Mar 20, 2000).

Framing Bicultural Cubans

Young Cubans, born in America of Cuban parents who wish to return to a post-Castro Cuba, have been called the 1.5 generation, or the one-and-a-half-generation, referring to the fact that they are bicultural; were they to return to Cuba, they would return with no Cuban experience. It is they who are creating new bicultural identities. It was their parents who lived-on-the-hyphen, so to speak (Firmat, 1994).

Cubans have had a very different historical experience from the other groups being discussed. They have been protected by mainstream Americans while the others were harmed by mainstream Americans. They arrived in a country where interethnic conflicts still exist but which have been mitigated over a period of years as groups achieved power and identity. The ethnic identities of the Navajo, Cubans, Blacks and Chinese in America is complex, not monolithic. The reader needs to be aware that there are as many differences among the members of any group as there are between those members and other groups, including Whites. Nevertheless, there are bonds of mutuality and attraction that members share one with another, that permit them to be ethnically identified.

Ethnic Differences

Linguistic Distinctiveness

Language is a marker of identity, a fact that made members of these groups stand out from the early white Americans; often, it made it easier to make strangers of them. Older members of these four groups tend to maintain their language faithfully; very young ones may speak English outside the home while speaking the traditional language at home. Many Navajo children have lost the Navajo language; it is not always passed down from elders to children.

Framing Navajo Code Talking

Interestingly the Navajo language, oral and pictographic, and not written down until recently, was used in modified form to create a secret code during World War II when code talkers of Navajo background were used as message bearers. The Navajo language, scarcely known to most Americans, was completely unknown to the Japanese, who could find no way to decipher the code. Trained as message bearers, the Navajo code talkers successfully transmitted commands from military headquarters to troops on the front lines. All languages are codes, of course, but the distinctive linguistic characteristics of the Navajo language were extraordinarily useful as a unique code in wartime.

Blacks brought to America for slave purposes as part of the slave trade, came from a rich, diverse panoply of local and regional dialects and languages. Thus, often they were not able to communicate among themselves due to these differences. Shipmasters mixed together blacks who spoke different dialects to help prevent them from banding together in an uprising. Even today, Blacks may speak in very distinctive ways, as the Ebonics movement revealed.

Black slave history meant that the slaves would receive little or no education or training. It also meant that they would develop distinctive features in their spoken English, many of which survive in modified form to this day. The Black church, often outlawed, became the focal point for gatherings of black folk. They learned very expressive ways to sing and dance using their own stylized languages.

The immigrating Chinese, arriving over a period of time from different parts of China, were multi-lingual, a factor contributing to their complex history. The Chinese language is monosyllabic, unlike English which is polysyllabic. To provide variety and complexity to the language, Chinese people use tonal levels to differentiate one word from the next, resulting in a sing-song quality, as many Americans perceive it. Major linguistic groups, such as Cantonese and Mandarin, existed, mostly centered in various geographic regions of China. Even within these major linguistic groups, one region would vary from another in the way that words were spoken. Thus, the Chinese who came to America in the mid-1800's brought different dialects with them, depending on the area of China from which they came. Today, young Chinese Americans born in the United States learn English, although they may speak it with some phonetic difficulty because the Chinese spoken at home is radically different from spoken English.

Hispanics from Cuba spoke a modified version of traditional Spanish imported from Spain; however, it was admixed with the linguistic varieties of Indian and Black dialects. Thus, it was distinctive. English is spoken in

Cuba as well, the U.S. having taken Cuba from Spain during the late 1800's and the flow of commercial traffic that existed before Castro encouraged the use of English. Cuba, centered in the Caribbean, became a crossroads, a place of conquest, as the Spanish-American war demonstrated. Young Cuban Americans, born in the United States, frequently speak fluent English, although their parents and grandparents may speak only broken English.

Fortunately perhaps for them, Spanish is more compatible with English tha is either Chinese or Navajo; it is no accident that Spanish is the language of choice for white students in colleges and universities, where a second language is usually required.

Although linguistic distinctiveness is often cited as the main factor in ethnic identity, it is not the sole factor. Ethnicity is expressed as a dynamic flow of verbal and nonverbal clusters of behaviors, including individual and public displays (Ashmore & Jussim, 1997). Having a background of similar values, customs, habits, beliefs and so on, members of ethnic groups tend to express themselves in recognizable ways, individually and collectively. American Standard English is taught in schools which brings up an issue of conformity. The issue seems to be whether linguistic diversity is desirable in American society.

The Individualism--Communalism Dimension

Although they differ in customs and practices, the Chinese, Blacks and the Navajo backgrounds were infused with various forms of communalism. The emphasis was upon the family, the tribe or the nation, not upon the individual as it was with Whites. Collective ceremonies, such as the Navajo Blessingway or the celebration of the Chinese New Year reinforced their communal and tribal ways as did various rites of passage among tribal Blacks.

Tribal practice of tribal kinship prevailed in most subSaharan African areas (Turnbull, 1962). The Cuban society was admixed, Africans playing a strong role in the cultural development. The Spanish influence meant that Cubans would become Catholic, at least in appearance. The spirit of individualism was stronger in Cuba than it was among the other groups, although it was muted by ethnic factors.The mestizos in Cuba as well as the Blacks, whose roots were in Africa, gave the society a distinctive social flavor; they remained somewhat out of touch with the urbanized areas of Cuba, many living in the more isolated regions of the eastern mountains.

It was by and large the White person who lived under the individualistic ethic, the ethic stemming from Protestant reaction to Catholicism and from Calvinistic theology. It is the individual who must stand before God; it is God who blesses the individual who performs her or his work satisfactorily (Weber, 1958). Early America was heavily influenced by people who came from Western and Northern Europe, largely those who were influenced by the Church of England and other groups, often dissidents, fleeing their own countries.

The white migration from East to West in the early 1800's brought with it the values of individualism; white settlers and the military confronted the Navajo and the Chinese who were culturally very different from themselves. Fortunately, the differences between white Americans and Cubans were less pronounced.

Differences in Cosmologies and Thoughtways

All cultural groups contain *cosmological* elements. When groups are isolated over a long period of time, they tend to create distinctive cosmologies.

The White Man's Faith

White Europeans who emigrated from Europe to the United States brought with them their beliefs about a Christian God who created and controlled the universe, who was omniscient, omnipotent, and omnipresent. He was involved in the affairs of humans. The Christian God of the Old and New Testaments was to be worshipped and praised; people were to live their lives sacramentally. People, as sinners, reprobate before God, must be saved and the son of God, Jesus the Christ, was the Savior. The mercy of God was shown to humans, who had sinned, as noted in the Adam and Eve story of disobedience.

The Christian life was expressed in practices reflecting the faith. Observing the Sabbath, attending Church, dressing with humility and acting righteously toward others were obligatory. People who failed to live by the religious strictures,or who failed to obey the law which was rooted in the ten commandments of the Old Testament, were condemned, often treated as backsliders or heathens, even publicly flogged if the sin was serious enough. In short, the early Americans brought with them a vivid sense of what it meant to be a Christian and a powerful sense of moral rectitude and justice.

Interestingly, as mentioned, many of them had been persecuted for their beliefs prior to their arrival in the New World. But Christians in the new world believed that they had the truth and that it was their duty to share the truth with others, who were often thought of as ethnics or heathens. The concept of *manifest destiny* and the *white man's burden* grew out of the belief that white people had an obligation, as God's chosen people, to serve mankind, to enlighten the world and to spread themselves, in this case, across the continent (Weingarten, 1963). Thus, the White man's military and their missionaries were often found in the same areas as they moved West.

Whatever the virtues of faith in a just, moral and forgiving God were, there was a hidden downside when those virtues devolved into social practices that excluded, even harmed others. Ethnocentrism and strangerhood were the unintended results. As an extreme present-day example, White Supremacists use the Bible to justify their ideologies which are essentially racist and separatist (Bushart, Craig & Barnes, 1998).

Surely there were Christian practitioners who disagreed among themselves about the superiority of Whites over people of color, but it was apparent that early white Americans were influenced largely by a belief system which in practice was compatible with ethnocentrism.

Chinese, Navajo, Black and Cuban Cosmologies.

The Chinese who came to America to work in the gold mines, who worked on the railroads and eventually settled in enclaves in urban areas, brought with them an outlook on life that was influenced by Confucianism, ancestor worship, beliefs in dragons and other animals who acted in god-like fashion. The Chinese culture had long, historic roots; their cosmological approach to life was complicated, but it worked for them. Like the Navajo, they invoked the spirit gods when bad things happened and engaged in mysterious rituals that white Americans did not understand.

Framing Chinese Dragons

In ancient China, the Celestial Chinese Dragon was a symbol of the Chinese people, who considered themselves descendants of the Dragon. Dragons are often conceived of as divine, mythical creatures who bring abundance, prosperity and good fortune. Today, The Year of the Dragon, taking place every 12 years, is a lucky year. Children born during dragon years, such as 1964 and 1976, were blessed, as were those who were born in 1988 and 2000. Different kinds of elements are associated with Dragon years. Wood, fire, earth, metal, water are associations. Thus, the Dragon is infused in all life.

In Chinese mythology, dragons could stop rain from falling or cause floods or even make rice stick together. Traditionally, people hold parades and other ceremonies to please dragons; The Dragon is the supreme being amongst all creatures. It can live in the seas, fly up to the heavens and act as a mountain. The nine major types of Chinese dragons have distinct personality traits and they are represented differently by the Chinese (Coye and Livingston, 1975; Crystalinks, 1-22/01).

The Navajo had distinctive beliefs as well. When settlers moved westward, just as they had confronted Native Americans in the Northeastern part of the continent, they came upon Navaho and other tribal groups whose beliefs were very different from their own. Believing in a panoply of gods, who took the form of animals, trees or even the sky and other landforms, the Navajo, like other tribal people, conducted ceremonies and dances to appease the gods, to be in tune with nature. Very elaborate accounts of creation focusing on male and female gods were part of the Navajo cosmology. Ceremonies and rituals served to bind tribal members together. Coyote the Trickster was responsible for many problems that assailed the people (Kluckhohn,1944).

The Blessingway, a ceremony of healing, was a basic part of the Navajo religion; healing was meant to restore sick people to a place of healthy balance, sickness being seen as an expression of misalignment with nature and the gods. These cosmological symbols and practices were very different from those of the Christians who arrived as settlers and as military personnel.

Blacks, brought from Africa, largely from subSaharan and West Coast Africa, were tribal. Their tribal religions included a belief in spirits, in animism or the idea that spirits were in trees and other objects. They practiced medicine, using shamans and medicine men to ward off evil spirits. Their religions were complicated and highly varied; religious versions flourished in different ways in widely scattered tribes. There was no massive geographic nation knitting together the many tribal communities (Turnbull, 1962; Turner, 1967).

The Cuban religious history was an admixture of ethnic folk beliefs and Roman Catholicism, brought to Cuba by Spanish conquerors. Blacks from Africa brought their religions to Cuba, too. Thus, Cuban cosmologies were unlike the others above. Catholic beliefs are essentially incompatible with Communism; Cubans sought freedom to the North and in other countries.

Other Differences

Foodways, geography, the concept of place, beliefs, attitudes, rites of passage, level of technology and a variety of other cultural elements, such as the role of power and kinship, highlight the differences between these five groups.

Unfortunately, except for the Cubans, who came later to a more open United States, the differences came to be markers that triggerered racialism in a predominately White society in early America. The westward expansion brought Whites in contact with the Navajo and the Chinese. Blacks came to this continent via a different route. To those with little understanding of the importance of cultural differences, skin color became overly important; black, red, yellow and brown stereotypically characterized these ethnic groups. The dominant group was white.

White Power and Early Contact with People of Color

The Contact Hypothesis

The contact hypothesis suggests that when relative equal groups of people come together, they can work together, sharing goals, not competing with one another. Under these conditions, prejudice and racial bias decrease.

Human inter-ethnic relationships may be illustrated by using circles for each group. When groups share much, their circles overlap; if they share little, their circles overlap minimally; if they share nothing their circles are independent. (Sarbaugh, 1979). Shared interpersonal relationships promote affiliation and friendship. When there is little to be shared, groups may become hostile with one another, even warlike. Victimology and marginalization are often the result when a powerful group vanquishes a less powerful group.

The Navajo: Loss of Place and Identity

When Columbus arrived in the Western world, there were an estimated two million Indians, named so because Columbus thought he had discovered a new route to the Eastern world; the Indians did not call themselves Indians. The Navajo, for example, referred to themselves as Dine. They had come apparently from the Canadian North; they lived in a natural relationships with the earth, the moon, the sun and the stars. Over the years, they had been hunters and gatherers, agriculturalists and pastoralists. The Spanish brought the horse to their civilization.

Their religious way of life was distinctive, rich and full. Man was to live in tune with nature and with his fellow man. Singers and chanters told stories about their past and conducted healing ceremonies. Great ceremonies included masquerades, dance, prayer and song. There was little distinction between the sacred and the profane (Levy, 1998). Witchcraft was practiced, too. The early Navajo believed that it was possible to influence the course of events by means involving the supernatural (Kluckhohn, 1944). Prayers were silent and mental prayers or monologically expressed with short devotional repetitions.

The Navajo did not distinguish strictly between maleness and femaleness; tied into some of their myths were stories about hermaphrodites which symbolically united males and females. Weavers, often women, wove symbols and stories into the patterns. In short, the Navajo had a meaningful and established cultural identity; they lived in a place between the mountains and hills, an earthly but spiritual home, a sacred place.

It was highly unfortunate that for the white man, the general image of the Navajo was as an uncultured savage, whose cosmologies were mysterious, whose practices were foreign to the mind of the white man, perhaps even threatening. White Americans had very different goals and ways compared to the the Navajo. The white man at least had a pretense of science, but the Indians lacked that sense. Indians tended to see forces in nature that could help or hurt them. They considered it necessary to appease and get along with the spirits that existed. By using prayers and ritual forms, the Indian could get the spirits to work with him, rather than against him. The Christian white man did not share these approaches to nature. The Christian God was his benefactor as he took charge of the lands through which he moved.

In military clashes, the dominant white man prevailed over time. A popular slogan says that it is the powerful, the winners, who write the history of peoples and they write those histories from their own perspectives. It was the White man who imposed his will and hoped to impose his culture upon the Navajo using a variety of methods, perhaps believing that he was doing the "right" thing. Surely, he was doing the expedient thing because, as the White man moved west, he wanted more and more land.

Framing Early White Contact

After the United States annexed the Southwest, white contacts with the Navajo increased. Considered intruders by the Navajo, Whites nevertheless destroyed their orchards and their sheep herds, in a raid by Kit Carson, to whom they surrendered in 1863. The Navajo tribal members were rounded up, except for those who fled to the hills, and marched to Bosque Redondo, a very distant desert site the government had selected to force them into farming, into irrigating the land. This farming experiment failed and they were forced onto reservations in a new policy designed to civilize them. The Navajo tribe resisted this effort, although it eventually succeeded. The Whites believed they had to civilize the savages (Takaki,1993). The Navajo spirit was shattered.

Deep, great changes were wrought in Indian tribal affairs by the arrival of whites and their contact with them, often to their own detriment and denigration (Smith & Kvasnicka, 1976). Too often, the Indians had become a problem for the whites and, eventually, even the use of Reservations to solve these problems were failures, by and large.

Not only were wars fought to contain the Navajo, but diseases, such as smallpox and influenza for which the Indians had no remedy-- for these were diseases of the White man--destroyed many. It also tended to destroy or render inoperative the Indians control over the supernatural and to trigger changes in their 'ecosystem', as it did among most Indian tribes (Martin, 1978). The Bureau of Indian Affairs, formed in 1890, was designed to change the Indian culture, to "civilize" them. In so doing, they destroyed the will of the Navajo, leaving them little or no political power.

The Federal Government has apologized formally for the role it played in the misery of the Navajo. Today, the Navajo is but one tribe of about 500 tribes with 300 Indian Reservations. The Federal Government recognizes 282 tribes, the Navajo being the largest among them. Much of the Navajo Reservation, or Rez as the Navajo refer to it, is controlled by outsiders and many of the tribal members live outside the reservation. Today, the

Navajo live in two cultures. Wealth is often generated by casinos on the reservation; youth are schooled; tribes have empowered polities; and some intercommerce is conducted between white society and Navajo. The Navajo have access to computers; the digital divide has been crossed.

There are indications that many youth are returning to their cultural roots. Despite 100 years of missionizing by Christian Whites, many young Navajo people are turning back to their traditional religion, trying to identify with the past. They are curious about ceremonies, including sand paintings and about BlessingWay. Young Navajos attend public schools, or perhaps an Indian School; they learn English and they plan to work in the mainstream workforce. Every family owns a vehicle and they are dependent on a cash economy (Worth & Adair, 1997), but, as mentioned previously, they are poor.

There has been a breakdown in the traditional Navajo family; the kinship system is no longer powerful. For example, the tradition of the mother's brother, who would teach her children the moral codes of the Navajo, has been forgotten by this new generation. Alcoholism is a major problem for the youth as mentioned above; peyote is often used by young people as a sacrament in the Navajo church, which is often fused with Christian elements. The young Navajo faces the consequences of living marginally on the edge of white culture and of trying to make contact with their tradition (Petersen, 1997). Although present day Navajo engage in the wider white culture, as original Americans they do not honor Columbus Day, as a symbol of resistance to the arrival of the white man.

Destruction of Black Identity, Time and Place

Early contacts with Negroes were forceful. Although slavery existed in Africa before the White man arrived--as it does even today-- when the economic system of slavery was created, there was a resounding cultural clash, the White man benefiting.

Framing African Tribalism

African societies were built around tribal structures; the Western concept of nation was unknown to them. Perhaps their concept of nation applied to the tribe, which was the center of all cultural activities, completely different from what they would find in America (Turnbull, 1962). Today, there are modern cities located where there had been tribal centers, on the West Coast of Africa essentially, which developed because of trade with European countries. Today, Africans may speak English or other languages, but in the 1600's, tribal members spoke their own dialects, having little contact with the white man. Although slavery existed in Africa at the time, the American and European slave trade forced Blacks to sever their ties to their tribes and they were forced into countries with cultures which were completely new to them. This wrenching experience was a blow to their identity, their sense of place.

The power to intrude on the lives of weaker people and to exact from them their sense of identity and place is exhibited in slavery (Brown, 1969). Early settlers in Colonial America needed cheap labor on their labor intensive plantations, mostly in the South. In New England and the Massachusetts Bay Colony, where there were no plantations, the settlers engaged in slave trading almost from the start. The bartering of rum for slaves from the African coastal regions, and then the exchange of those slaves for molasses, something that could be distilled into more rum, meant that there was an ongoing cycle of slave trading. The profits of slave dealing went to the building of great mansions near Boston and Salem. When slaves were put to use on the large holdings of wealthy New Englanders, it was a sign of ownership, power, prestige and wealth (Gross, 1976).

Although slaves were treated differently in New England--for example they could buy their freedom--than they were in the South, it was the demand for black slaves as economic commodities by the more powerful White people that continued the practice of stealing black people from their homelands.

Slaves were first taken from the coasts of Africa in 1619. It was clear to the White man that Indian labor did not work. Perhaps the perception of Africa as a monolithic, undeveloped and uncivilized dark continent where heathens lived made it easier to steal away men, women and children--to separate family members one from the other. To prevent uprisings among the stolen black slaves, their linguistic backgrounds were identified and the blacks were deliberately mixed aboard ship. Uprisings occurred despite these precautions. When they arrived on plantations, the fear of uprisings on the plantations was pervasive as well.

Even marriage between them was denied; men and women were separated, although marriages occurred sub rosa. Slaves attempted to rise up, to run away and to join Indian tribal communities, but the institution of slavery persisted for decades.

The Meaning of The Black Church

Although they were usually discouraged from congregating, Blacks on plantations used the church as a form of communal strength and identity, where they could worship and grow together. Today, the power of the pulpit is still evident, Black ministers having moral and political authority. Black ministers challenge their black congregation to take part in political activities such as marches, sit-ins and other methods of political influence. The spirit of the Black people, victims of slavery, was nourished in the Black church. If ever there was a case in history for psychological victimology to set in, for ethnic groups to feel great loss of self and community, it was during enslavement and all that it entailed. Being Black meant being less than human.

Black people were not thought to be fully human which was was a way to justify their enslavement. Achieving the right to vote was a long way down the road of history in America. Even after the 1875 Civil Rights Act permitting them to vote, which came about as a result of the Civil War, southerners used fraud, violence and terror to take away voting rights. Jim Crow laws kept Blacks segregated from whites and separate but equal facilities were instituted, upheld in the Supreme Court in 1896 in Plessy Versus Ferguson (Persell, 1987). The 1964 Civil Rights Act opened American society to black Americans but they still found difficulties because institutional racism, segregated living patterns and work employment opportunities were still denied based on race and skin color.

Today as then, Black Americans are not a monolithic ethnic group. People who identify themselves as Blacks, and prior to that Negroes, speak with many voices, embrace many religions, work in diverse professions, and lead complex social lives, just as do Whites. However, it is clear that Blacks have had to contend with social and historical difficulties that others, who voluntarily came from white Europe, did not. Black American identity has been shaped in the cruel crucible of slavery. Modern young blacks, of course, have no direct memory of slavery; nevertheless, they carry the problems of identity forward in a society that is variously friendly or hostile to people of color. Blacks must make sense of the social world that is dominated by white power (Harris, Blue, & Griffith, 1995).

The Chinese: Yellow Peril and Isolation

Chinese sailors came to the American shores in the 1700's but they came for reasons that were different from those who came in the mid-1800's. The latter group came to make a fortune in the gold mines; they were sometimes welcomed, sometimes ostracized as a yellow peril.

Framing Chinese Immigration

Ships from the Orient with a load of freight and coolies would tie up in San Francisco, where the Chinese workers were sorted into groups when they went ashore, to be taken to the waiting wagons and flatcars and then sent to railroad work sites. They had been told by American agents who went to China that they would receive high wages, that the work was plentiful and that the U.S. Consul would assist their passage. Their invitation, however, was based on the need for labor, white labor being in short supply.

They were celebrated at first, taking part in parades, showing their special pageants, working alongside Native Americans and Europeans. When the economy worsened, they lost favor, and were asked to leave America (Coye & Livingston, 1975).

The Chinese, mostly males, came to work in the gold mines of California, to make their bundle and to move back home where their wives lived. They had come mostly from mainland China when economic times were depressed and politically unstable. They brought with them their language, customs and beliefs. Only later did Chinese and other Asians come to America from other countries. Perhaps 322,000 came during the 1840's mostly to the west coast (Takaki, 1993).

Chinese society was earmarked by strong familial and kinship relationships. Like the White man, they hoped for happiness, good fortune, moneymaking and longevity. The Chinese culture rested on a sense of social interconnectedness, a sense of place and belonging, following Confucian ideals. There was little meaning outside of social networks. They were not persons in anonymity as they later became in America. Being born male in China was important; the idea of the male as a "little Emperor" was significant. The aged in traditional Chinese society enjoyed a special status, of wisdom and perseverance, as part of the cross-generational lineage of the Chinese family.

Framing Chinese Symbols

Symbols of Chinese culture had particular meaning, whether it was the Dragon symbol or the symbol of the peach which meant longevity. Red symbolized happiness and good luck and gold symbolized riches. Spring Festivals, particularly in Beijing, became moveable feasts. The Chinese had a sense of place, of belonging in the natural world and their social customs and habits noted this sense. Dead ancestors were accorded a place in their homes and in their worship. Life was conceived of as an unbreakable continuity, one generation to the next. Centuries of dynastic control of China gave the country a collective identity.

The Chinese culture emphasized communalism. Their ways of life were vastly different from those of the more individualistic frontier people found in America; and, of course, they were people of color, who spoke a peculiar language, who seemed clannish to Whites and they were willing to work hard over long hours for their income. At first, in good economic times, the Chinese immigrants fared fairly well, both in the gold mines and later on the railroad construction crews. However, when hard economic times hit California and the West, it was the Chinese, isolated from the White mainstream, who became victimized as a yellow peril. White men feared they would lose their jobs to the yellow man.

Chinese were discriminated against, even lynched and killed in many cases. The xenophobia of the White man resulted in the Chinese Exclusion Act of 1882, an act that was extended in 1902 (Takaki, 1993). As a result, Chinese were no longer permitted to enter this country. As a way of protection, the Chinese formed enclaves, such as early Chinatowns, which exist even today. There the Chinese could at least know other Chinese and find common identity, less threatened by theWhite man. They could start their own businesses, such as laundries and small food markets for which they are known even today in Chinatown in the New York City area. Gangs were powerful in mainland China, often disturbing the political status quo. Gangs, or Fongs, found their way to the United States, too, where they still wield economic power in Chinatown.

The plan to create wealth and then return to their wives in China did not always work. Today, Chinatown is a complex enclave of Chinese, Asian and other peoples who have found their way to America, whether legitimately or illegitimately. Modern Chinatown is no longer confined to the narrow, original boundaries near the Bowery.

Members of Chinatown may be Confucianists, they may be Methodists, Buddhists or Catholics. They may even be all at the same time in different places (Takaki, 1993). They are lawyers, doctors and dentists; they are businessmen. They may follow traditional Chinese ways but often they have altered their social practices to fit into the American way. For example, young skilled Chinese have created the Chinese new Year on the internet. The Ten Thousand-Dimensional Web of Heaven and Net on Earth is an illustration of how young people blend modernity with tradition (Kozar, April 17, 2000). In short, the new generations of Chinese, perhaps bred from traditional families in Chinatown, have moved into the mainstream of American life, principally into universities and visible professional levels of American society. Young Chinese Americans may speak English in colleges and Chinese at home. Perhaps they, more than the Navajo and Blacks have succeeded in entering the mainstream of American economic life. Nevertheless, they must contend with social issues that confront people of color, especially when there has been a tradition of resentment toward them, as expressed in the yellow peril phrase.

Cubans: Friends in Exile

Cubans are included in this chapter because their experience in this society has been welcomed rather than forced, a sign that Americans may be maturing in their attitudes about human differences.

Framing the Cuban Story

The Cubans highlighted in this book share one thing in common: they are exiles from Cuba living in America and many of them want to return to a Castro-free Cuba. In short, the exiles came against their wishes and intended to maintain their way of being, their culture. Thus Cubans have been treated quite differently from the Blacks, the Navajo or the Chinese; they are in the United States as guests of the United States. They are Hispanic whites with Cuban roots who wish to maintain their Cuban identity. Indeed, Cafe Nostalgia, a restaurant, but one of many, in the center of Miami's Little Havana, sustains the Cuban soul. A house band plays cha-cha-cha and people dance and sing Cuban dances and songs. They are nostalgic people (Paxman, June 8, 1998). This general statement applies to the older generation of exiled Cubans, not necessarily to the young generation born in the United States in these families, who tend to be more focused on their sense of place in North American society (Padilla,1980).

As mentioned, most Cubans came to the United States following the takeover of Cuba by Fidel Castro, who forced many Cubans out of the country. During the late 1960's Castro sent airloads of children to the United States. Labeled Pedro Pan evacuees, they numbered about 14,000 in total and they were unaccompanied by their parents. Now the children are adults and they remain adamantly opposed to the Castro government. Their children, perhaps born in the United States and acking their experiences, do not always share their views. Perhaps the young have become discriminated against by the older Cubans(CNN Online, April 5, 2000). One merely has to read about the Elian Gonzales case to see how the political attitudes of the older exiled Cubans plays out. Many other Cubans came to the United States willingly, but Fidel Castro was eager to empty his jails of dissidents and criminals whom he sent out of the country, many of them coming to the United States. Thus, the exiled Cubans had many faces.

The Cubans were not unfamiliar with the United States before coming here. Yankee radio, the Voice of America and the presence of U.S. citizens in Cuba meant that many Cubans were bilingual, had visited the United States during the Batista years in power or had relatives living here. In short, the modern influences on identity of Cubans was very unlike that of Navajo, Chinese or Blacks in America. Yet, they were caught in a social and political vise. The older Cubans, forced out of Cuba, wanted desperately to return to a post-Castro Cuba; at the same time, they could not leave and they were welcome to stay. Uncertainty became their problem; they are people in exile.

To some extent, however, Cubans are marginalized in the United States. Perhaps color is less a problem than exists among the other groups; their music, art, dance and foodways have caught on in the United States. Young people know about the Miami Sound Machine; older people remember Desi Arnez and Lucille Ball on television. As mentioned, the salsa, danza, mambo and other musical expressions have become part of North American popular culture. Cuban baseball players escape to the United States, join the major leagues and become well known. Thus, to some extent, Cubans, like other Hispanics whose total numbers are about 13 percent of the U.S. population have become part of the cultural fabric of America. Yet, they must fight to gain acceptance into mainstream America.

Unfortunately, to some extent mainstream America remains best suited to people with white skin, raised in white communities. Fortunately, American society is under repair; Interethnic understanding is replacing ignorance to some degree. There are serious problems that remain.

Modern Forms of Attenuated Racism: The Black Example

People live and do their ethnicity. Ethnicity is a powerful master theme that is constructed and maintained by members who identity themselves in specific ways. The historical pattern of relationships found between Whites and people of other colors tends to influence modern perceptions, as shown in this section. An adaptable inter-ethnic model of relationship is proposed. Due to the shortage of space, this section focuses only upon a discussion of the contemporary Black American experience in the United States.

Self-Esteem and Racism

Young black children, when asked which color of doll, brown or white, they would prefer mostly to play with, pointed to white dolls, rejecting the brown dolls (Waller, 1998). Do young children react similarly to real people? People may disagree about the implications of studies like this one; nevertheless, in the view of many scholars, the social context furnishes the need for such studies. The theme of victimology is frequently discussed on the news and talk shows, as is the theme of Black opportunity in a white society.

All persons, perhaps, are familiar with the problems caused by a lack of self-esteem. People need not be colored to know about such issues. Unfortunately, low self esteem tends to promote negative projections and the blaming of others, a form of projection. Whites and Blacks must deal with issues of self esteem that often characterize their relationships.(Fein & Spencer, 1997). Blacks have had to deal with the issue in ways that are very different from the experience of most Whites.

Economic Marginalization

American society is economically stratified rfesulting in the marginalization of many people, often people of color (Blau & Duncan, 1967; Kerbo, 1983). Despite the progress that has been made in ethnic relations, a recent poll suggests that blacks feel more discriminated against than any other racial or ethnic group. Eighty three percent of the people questioned said that blacks were more discriminated against than were Hispanics, at 76 percent. Women and American Indians were next with 67 percent of those questioned. Further, while whites were quite satisfied with their earnings and where they live, only 49 percent of Blacks reported satisfaction with their household income (Jet, June 12, 2000).

Framing Employment Patterns

Black and Hispanic employees during 1997 in Northern California technology companies numbered as follows:

Of the 142,000 workers, 4 percent were Black; 8 percent were Hispanic.

Of the 25,100 executives and manager, 2 percent were Black; 3% were Hispanic.

Of the 61,238 professionals (engineers, technicians), 3 percent were Black; 5 percent were Hispanic (USA Today, July 24, 2000).

Figures are not specifically shown for Cubans or for Chinese. There are no Navajo members represented. Cubans make up approximately 4.3 percent of the Hispanic population in the United States according to the Census Bureau and Blacks make up approximately 13 percent of the total US. population. Median incomes are rising for ethnic groups discussed in this book, but they are well below the averages for the white population. Family incomes vary from Asians on top to Hispanics, Blacks and Native Americans in that order in the United States.

Opinion polls and surveys vary considerably and the findings can be highly variable depending on the approach taken and the methods used. Nevertheless The New York Times revealing how race is lived in everyday life in America suggests that there is considerable Black discomfort in White environments. The modern face of prejudice is more subtle than the early forms. Color and ethnicity still matter to whites but not as directly as in early America. Although the focus of this book is on the development of interethnic adaptability and the establishment of better social understandings, the frame below illustrates how some scholars and writers feel.

Framing Contemporary Racism

"The so-called American melting pot has become a tinderbox that seems ready to explode", according to a statement on the cover jacket (Rowan, 1996). A well-known reporter, his book focuses on the abandonment of affirmative action, on crime and drugs, and on hate-mongering.

"We are left with the crushing effect of what we have done to ourselves by using race as our defining tool and lying most of the time about what we are doing. . . ", as it says on the cover jacket (Hacker, 1992). Hacker's book is a careful delineation, often statistical, of issues that divide the American society.

The views of the writers of these two books are extreme. Although there may be many Blacks who share these views, many others wish to approach modern ethnic problems from a middle way, referred to here as inter-ethnic adaptability.

Clearly, there is a relationship between culture and economy, between ethnicity and place, between education and opportunity. When one is born in the mainstream, one usually has access to good schools, to good jobs, to fair treatment in the courts, to relatively stable family situations, to good health care, and to appropriate representation in the media. When one is born in poor colored neighborhoods, she must contend with factors that most white people have not known.

Many Black Americans are found in the lower classes in society, in neighborhoods where they experience violence when growing up. They may be confronted with drugs and joblessness; their entrance to college is not assured; their access to health care is unassured. To many Black people there "Ain't no Makin' it" (MacLeod, 1987). There is social immobility, instead of mobility; there is continued social reproduction of the down and out environment; there are leveled aspirations. Analyzing two very different groupings of black youth in difficult neighborhoods, the author in the frame below shows how down-and-out group members think about making it in life.

Framing Life in Difficult Neighborhoods

The familiar refrain of "behave yourself, study hard, get good grades and graduate and then go to college and get a good job and make some money" tends to work backwards on students who live daily lives of failure. It tends to confirm their failure. Parroting the achievement motive does not motivate these students. Schools, instead, need to acknowledge the racial barriers that exist and to build on the esteem that exists in the minds of these low-income urban youth middle-class statements for motivation (MacLeod, 1987).

One must be careful not to paint the picture too simplistically; poor whites are found throughout the country and wealthy people of color are found as well. Nevertheless, one can understand why many people of color see may themselves as victims of society.

Blatant and Aversive Racism

Symbolic racism persists in modern American society but many, perhaps most people, learn to live with it, as a fact of life. But, many people simply ignore racism, averting the issues, acting cool. They choose to avoid issues. Some White Americans believe that affirmative action and other social measures designed to rectify problems from the past have given unfair advantages to minorities. The same people may oppose bilingual education, declaring that only English should be spoken by all Americans and they may make it hard for immigrants to get access to all rights enjoyed by mainstream Whites. (Waller, 1998).

Subtle forms of discrimination continue exist. Black officers, for example,still find color lines in the ranks (Chivers, Apr 2, 2000). Racism is not always blatant; there is a sense of politically correctness. Fortunately, the voices of Black American scholars are now being heard and read; the political arena includes many Black American professors; universities are including Black studies in their curricula; and, Black American participation in the economy generally seems to be improving.

Media Portrayal of Minorities; Racial Profiling

Film, television and the print media have, in the past, profiled Indians as war-whooping savages or pictured blacks as foot-shuffling, servile people. For example, issues about whether Native Americans images should be displayed on Red Man tobacco, on the Cleveland Indians' advertising, or the use of Redskins on an NFL football franchise, may be demeaning to Native Americans; at the least, it is stereotyped. Depicting the Navajo as drunks is stereotypical as well. Perhaps old stereotypes have been replaced by new ones (Layng, July, 2000).

Framing Black Television Characters

Black TV sitcoms and characters amuse most of us, but are they really serving white interests? From "Amos 'n' Andy" to "The Jeffersons" and "Booty Call", such programs seem to be a black joke told by a white-dominated media, with the help of career Black professional actors and actresses. Viewers get the same mouth-flapping Black brothers and sarcastic Black sisters and troubled black cops in show after show, justified by marketing surveys. Plenty of jokes are told about Blacks, but are there similar jokes told about mainstream Whites? (Jacobs,1999). These thoughts express the sentiments of a black writer.

Fortunately, recently the media are representing minorities more realistically. Film companies, owned by Cubans, by Blacks, by Navajos and by Chinese are now portraying sensitive images about their identities. Ethnically based newspapers discuss the issues associated with ethnicity in the United States.

Broadly speaking, all people profile others; that is, they try to establish the identity of people whom they meet. When prejudice and power are combined, profiling can be a serious problem. Racial profiling by law enforcement agencies, by police and others, has meant that Blacks were unfairly searched, unfairly targeted in matters of crime.

There is an expectancy bias that lies behind racial profiling, meaning that differential attention is paid to black crimes, highlighting them, while crimes of Whites are played down, given less attention. In urban ghettos, putting people in jail without good legal representation is not uncommon. Modern racism is institutionalized, found in the patterns of the everyday operation of public legal, health and educational institutions.

Promoting Affiliation and Intercultural Friendship

The Changing Social Fabric

The Census 2000 revealed that major ethnic changes are occurring in the United States. As mentioned, the number of Hispanics, which includes Cubans, now rivals the number of Blacks each at roughly 13 percent of the total population. The Navajo tribal members number less than 300,000 at best count.

Heretofore the largest ethnic group in the United States, Non-Hispanic Whites are a shrinking group, now at 69 percent of the total population, down from 76 percent a decade ago. They are now a minority in California and Texas, as they are in many large cities. The United States is becoming colored, a process that will continue into the future. 2.4 percent of all people contacted, reported that they were multiracial; interacial marriages have increased in states where various ethnic groups have commingled, such as Hawaii. Yet, overall, there has been little change in the fact that White Americans, Black Americans, Chinese Americans, Cuban Americans and Native Americans tend to live in separate neighborhoods, to maintain separate places (Schmitt, April, 2001).

Conflict is the result of the mutual failure of ethnic groups to find ways to work together on problems that affect them. Ethnocentric and stereotypical perceptions foment conflict, making resolution of problems impossible. Each side in social disputes must be flexible and adaptable if social problems are to be solved. Fortunately, Americans have made progress in interethnic relations, spotty as it may be.

Framing Integration

"In a racially integrated America, blacks and whites would choose to live side by side, socialize with ease, see each other as peers, recommend each other for jobs, harbor little mutual distrust, respect each other's outlook, and appreciate each other's contributions to American culture. . . . Skin color would become incidental rather than fundamental," (Steinhorn & Diggs-Brown, 1999, p. 6).

Multi-cultural America and the Egalitarian Ethos

Ethnicity is a nonverbal entity; that is, it is a lived identity, expressed in everyday life, a master theme. It is a complex notion, contrary to the stereotypes often associated with it. There are many symbolically ethnicized voices in America; they are on the increase. The future mosaic of culture in the United States will be complex, full of many different voices, each seeking access to mainstream America. Not only are there symbolic voices but there are lingual voices. Increasingly, people who speak a non-English language are entering the United States. The United States is now multilingual. Perhaps every nation on earth is represented in the population of the United States. Just how the egalitarian ethos will play out among these groups is not clear. If citizens are to achieve true egalitarianism, wherein any person has access to achievement and privilege, new ways of viewing ethnicity need to occur. Ethnic markers need to be appreciated, not derogated.

Racism as a Cognitive Trap

Racism is a cognitive trap (Waller, 1998) that needs to be dismantled if the egalitarian ethic is to work. One need not moralize to realize that Americans have created ethnic traps. But, of course, being different does not have to result in stereotypes or social traps. It is not easy, of course, to recognize cognitive biases or to accept the fact of their existence. It is far easier to continue perceiving the social world in familiar ways. Blacks and whites may be separated physically but they are also separated symbolically.

The cognitive trap is symbolic, found in the ways that people think about themselves and others. In this book, cognitive traps may be found in the ways that people think of gender or age. Closing the cognitive trap may mean resocializing the mind, reconfiguring perceptions, not being blind to self and others.

Interethnic Adaptability

Human behavior is complex and varied; although it appears to be somewhat stable, human behavior may be modified slowly, sometimes with speed. Indeed, to be educated is to be open to change. Change occurs best when a person becomes aware of himself, when optional ways of viewing the world are noted and acted upon. Formal education can help people understand the complex dynamics of ethnic relationships.

Not realizing that words are mere representations, humans may think in relatively fixed terms. But inter-ethnic adaptability requires polysemous skill; cross-ethnic friendships are promoted when people can get past judgements that block understanding. Stereotypes are signs that people have closed their minds to important information.

Unmasking Unconscious Perceptions of People of Color

It is not uncommon for one person to socially categorize another person, using fixed perceptual lenses. This would be a harmless process if it did not result in negative consequences for the other party. By labeling people who are different from themselves, calling them stupid or dumb, or niggers or some other stigmatic term, it is unlikely that the name-callers will identify with those people in the future. People become socially ostracized when fixed labels are applied to them. Others use the stigmatic label in copycat ways. Although many of the ways that people relate to one another nonverbally arise from an awareness of self in relation to others, many behaviors are habituated and unconsciously enacted; people often do things while not realizing that they are doing them. Hidden scripts get played out.

Unfortunately, bad habits may be unconsciously performed. For example, white and black people may have fears about one another without realizing it. Fear about an object, a person or an event, can lead to self-protective behaviors. The presence of fear in interethnic relationships can present serious problems. It is not uncommon for white people to fear black people or vice versa. These attitudes are formed from a long history of oppressive conditions, carried forward to modern generations. Race relations in today's America are defined by daily experiences, in schools and sports, in worship and in the workplace. Race and ethnicity are lived in everyday places in everyday life. When fear exists between people they become strangers. Each group becomes an out-group, not an in-group (Wallers, 1998).

Empathic Listening

The study of listening is stressed in recent research. It is commonly thought that listening is the absence of speech or talk, but listening is a nonverbal activity that is profoundly proactive(Hargie, 1986). That is, listening is a deliberate process in which humans focus upon the symbolic behaviors of themselves and others. Real listening is not merely an aural activity, it is a symbolic activity, it is a meaning- making activity. For example, observing and listening are powerful tools in the repertoire of professionals in clinical therapy; this is because so much of the meaning of what people say and do is found "between the lines", not always in what people say but in what they do.

The art of listening is a skilled behavior that is learned. It is very different from hearing, which is a physical activity, tied into sound and vocality. Effective listening includes interpretive theories that get at what a person is really saying or doing. An empathic listener focuses on the pains that a person feels as she describes a loss of a friend, responding with empathy. The non-sympathetic listener hears the words, but misses the hidden meanings. It is no accident that marriage counselors focus on the failure of men to really listen to their wives, or vice versa, to note what is really going on between them that is causing problems (Tannen, 1990). Listening is a form of presentation of self to another, saying, in effect, "I am here to take part in your entire presentation of self, to reinforce it, to become an empathic participant in interaction."

Good listeners can be good problem solvers because they focus on what is really happening. They can reconcile differences between themselves and others because they know where the important aspects of the relationship lie. They build bridges, not walls (Stewart,1982). Good listening skills do not mean that there is a one way street in nonverbal communication. It is an interactive process. Good listening practices allow people to agree or disagree but to still take part in the interaction in meaningful, important ways. Effective disagreement can be healthy and it can help promote quality relationships. Quality listening is a powerful tool for ethnic borderwork.

The Role of Deliberate Affiliation

By and large people choose to live where they do, although economic and other factors influence their choices. People create their sense of place. Ethnic Americans live in very separate places.

Framing White and Black Life Styles

Sixty one percent of Whites live in suburbs; 55 percent of Blacks live in cities. The median income for Whites is $35, 570; for Blacks, it is $20,000. Seventy three percent of Whites own their homes; 45 percent of Blacks own theirs. Thirty three percent of Whites live in the South; 53 percent of all Blacks live there (Schmitt, 2001).

People choose to affiliate with people with whom they share common values, thoughtways or beliefs. Even when people share much in common, of course, they may not affiliate with one another, due to distance, lack of opportunity or to other interfering social behaviors. Even when people of the same color live together and work near one another, they may not associate with one another socially. It is not common, for example, for privileged people, people of status, to affiliate with their hired help even though they may both be white. Their sense of place is different, one from the other. Yet, these boundaries are not fixed, unless people want them to be.

People of color, varied ethnic groups, have arrived in modern day America from a different place, following different scripts, forming different stories about their lifeworlds compared to mainstream White Americans. In short, it is not easy for white people to put themselves in the shoes of black people, or vice versa. Nor is it required. The problem is, of course, that separation can mask highly negative social attitudes, which under nonsegregated contact conditions may not exist. Contact, of course, does not assure the development of positive attitudes.

Unless they are brought together through the workplace or through the college scene, it is unlikely that Chinese, Blacks, Navajo, Cubans or Whites will intermix vountarily. Each is likely to see the other as an outsider, a stranger. In the past, of course, this failure to mix gave rise to school bussing programs designed to cross ethnic borders so that minorities could benefit from the same things that whites did.

Interethnic Manners: Towards a New Symbolism

It has taken centuries for minorities and subculture groups, as they are perceived in some countries, to gain entrance to the mainstream of their respective societies. Often such groups are repressed. Lacking power and access to public services, education and other social necessities that are prerequisite to social achievement, many ethnic groups continue to suffer. In the United States, where abyssmal attitudes and social behaviors existed for centuries, some light seems to be appearing, some sense of a new order.

Framing New Manners

It has been proposed that new manners are needed in American ethnic life. Whites need to alter their perceptions of Blacks. Blacks do not wish to be seen as victims, nor do they wish to cling to attitudes associated with early slavery, nor are they born dancers, athletes or lovers! They have talents and they are intelligent.

Blacks, on the other hand, need to realize that Whites do not want to be racist or that white people have it easy and that they have a permanent monopoly on the American Dream (Jacobs,1999). Perceptions across the ethnic divide are almost always distorted.

The egalitarian ethos furnishes the impetus and the rationale for positive change. Cubans Americans, Black Americans, Chinese Americans, Native Americans and White Americans know about the American promotion of equality. Yet, it is an unrealized dream for many people of color, due not to their abilities, but to surface features, prevailing negative stereotypes and the imbalanced use of power. Equality is more likely to be realized when people communicate openly with one another, both verbally and nonverbally, making acquaintances, perhaps even friendships, with one another so that positive joint interactions can occur. Humans create their identities; they can create healthy social relationships.

Summary

This chapter has been devoted to the ways in which humans achieve ethnic identity, both collectively and individually. Native Americans, Black Americans, Cuban Americans and Chinese Americans have had very different life experiences than have White Americans, the historically dominant group in America. A sketch of the historical treatment of these ethnic groups reveals that even today, serious social issues stemming from the earlier period of Western expansion, persist. It has been proposed that these ethnic groups learn to do semantic borderwork, that they learn how to be inter-ethnically adaptable, not rigid, in their relationships, one with the other.

The egalitarian ethos is an essential feature of the American democracy; it furnishes a context and purpose for all Americans to work together. Modern forms of racism still appear, but ways of closing and softening the hardened ethnic boundaries were discussed.

The next chapter focuses upon another social phenomenon in the United States, the problems of Ageism and the possibilities for successful aging in a youth-oriented society.

Questions for Thought and Discussion

1.   Self identity must be worked out in everyday life. Members of ethnic groups engage themselves in society, reinforcing, even re-making aspects of their identities. What social factors seem to have influenced your sense of ethnic identity? (Include whiteness) Have you reinforced or changed your ethnic identity through interaction with others?

2.   People try to make sense of ethnic groups, often generalizing inaccurately. Discuss the perceptions and stereotypes of the groups discussed in this chapter. How would you accurately describe the members of the ethnic groups discussed in this chapter?

3.   Stereotypes occur when sufficient information is lacking; the interpreter draws false conclusions. Do your experiences tell you that people stereotype in daily life most of the time, some of the time, or rarely? How do you deal with stereotypical behavior when you note it in other people?

4.   A male Black American, married to a female White American moves into your white (substitute Cuban, Chinese or Navajo) neighborhood with their children, who have dark skin. Do you think that the children will have social problems in your neighborhood? If so, why? If not, why not?

5.   It has been said that black females are 'twice-struck'; that is, they suffer bias because they are female and because they are black. If this is true, what would be a remedy, or solution, to this problem in a society that proclaims equality for everyone?

Notes

1.   Rigid social behavior is usually a sign of fear or discomfort with alternative ways of viewing the world, as Adorno and others showed in early studies that dealt with ethnocentrism and xenophobia. In Soldiers of God: White Supremacists and Their Holy War for America, Howard L. Bushart, John R. Craig, Myra Barnes, Kensington Books, 1998, the authors showed that white supremacists believe that they are the true Israelites, not the Jews of present-day Israel. They use the Bible to justify their ideologies. They want whites to live with whites, separate from people of color or Jews. Some Black groups and other colored groups also demonstrate rigid behaviors. It is not one sided. Hate crimes, racial profiling are essentially white practices. Blacks and others, perhaps perceiving themselves as victims, form groups to gain power. The present topic of reparations for the mistreatment of Blacks by Whites illustrates the pervasiveness of the contemporary racial problem.

2.   The color of the skin is an easy marker, often perceived as a clue to identity, but it is a body surface feature. Yet, the color of the skin is often a sign of social status; the darker the skin, the lower the social status. This social phenomenon is evident in many cultures around the world. Red men were savages; yellow men were a peril to the white man; black men were heathens, lesser people, and Cubans were brown or tan people, again setting them apart from mainline whites. Given the negative associations with skin color, it is interesting that white people may spend hours in a tanning salon to get a tanned color. Demographically, Texas, California and Florida are becoming colored, with Whites become a minority in terms of percentage. The ability to perceive the real person, not the skin color, would seem to be of paramount importance to all ethnic groups in modern day America.

Suggested Readings

Filler, L. (1969). *The Crusade Against Slavery: 1830-1860.* New York: Harper and Row.

Gould, S. J. (1981). *The Mismeasure of Man.* New York: W. W. Norton & Company.

Lamont, M., & Fournier, M. (Eds.) (1993). *Cultivating Differences: Symbolic Boundaries and the Making of Inequality.* Chicago: University of Chicago Press.

Smith, J. F. Smith, & Kvasnicka, R. M. (Eds.) (1976). *Indian-White Relations: A Persistent Paradox.* Washington, DC: Howard University Press.

Rowan, C. T. (1991). *Breaking Barriers.* Boston, MA: Little Brown and Company.

Takaki, R. (1993). *A Different Mirror: A History of Multicultural America.* New York: Little, Brown and Company.

Waller, J. (1998). *Face to Face: The Changing State of Racism Across the United States.* New York: Plenum Press.

Chapter 7

Aging and Nonverbal Communication
Making Sense of the Aging Process

Chapter Overview

Concepts from previous chapters are presented here and related to the aging process. There is a considerable body of research related to the aging process and how it is viewed , including cross-cultural, psychological, social and biological aspects. Only selected aspects can be presented in this chapter.

All living things appear on the stage of life, live and die. The human aging process is not just about chronology, or how old one is; rather, it is about how one lives life, successfully or unsuccessfully. In sum, biology is not destiny. Time is not destiny. Humans enact their lives, making sense of them, creating lines of action as they take up the challenges of working, playing, raising families and coming to terms with older age. People age differently one from the other, by individuality, by gender, by social class and education, and by the ways they construe life. The sense of mortality increases as one ages but how people interpret their impending mortality is a key to their successful aging. Human identity can be transformed over time. Like gender and ethnicity, aging is a master theme that wends its way into the fabric of everyday life.

The nonverbal behaviors of the aged are often stereotyped in the United States, resulting in the negative term ageism. The assumptions behind ageism include the belief that as people age they are no longer useful to society, that their lives are a burden to the economy, deficits rather than assets, and that they cannot compete in a youth-oriented society. Contrarily, a positive symbolic interactionist approach suggests that people can live creatively and dynamically; they can age successfully.

Who are the aged? The frame below reveals some of the characteristics of the aged.

Framing the Aged

There will be 7 million advanced-age persons (above 80 years) in the United States by 2020; there were an estimated 3.5 million in 1994. Life expectancy for women in the United States in 1992 was 79.1 years; for men in that year it was 72.3 years. Eight states including California, Arizona, Georgia, Washington, Nevada, Colorado, Alaska and Utah will double their elderly population by 2020. The most rapidly growing age group, increasing 274 percent from 1960-1994, is 85 years old and older (Gunby, 1996).

Globally, mean life expectancy is 65 years according to the World Health Organization. Sierra Leone, in Africa, has the lowest mean, at 40 years for men and women combined. Japan has the highest combined average life expectancy at 79.7 years.

Clearly, the role of the aged in the future of the United States will be even more important in the future than it is today, which has been a key reason for the initiation of studies in the United States and elsewhere.

Multiple Theories About the Aging Process

Cognitive Development Theory

Cognitive development theory has been mentioned because cognition is vitally important in the aging process. Researchers, interested in cogntive development focus on observed cognitive changes as people age; for example, speed of reaction, cognitive processing ability, and other neuronal or mental processes, such as cognitive arousal, change over time. Older people often apparently need more time to process information; they are sometimes overwhelmed by tasks that they once performed with ease. Cognitive changes result in changes in behavioral patterns.

Other approaches to the aging process are important as well:

Continuity theory suggests that people vary in their personality orientations which, in turn, suggests that they vary in their ability to cope with the aging process.

Subcultural theory notes that people with healthy self-concepts are able to adapt creatively to novel situations, including the aging process.

The study of cohort groups focuses on the nature of subgroups of aging people. Older people form their own culture in society; they share views and have common interests. They can promote their own welfare better because of mutual support.

Environmental theory focuses on environmental parameters that influence aging behavior. Environmental demands are put upon the aged; how they respond to the demands is a key to their quality of life. By responding appropriately, they can eliminate dependency in older age (Caserta, 1995).

Social conflict theory focuses on how societies produce inequities through institutional routine. The elderly are the subjects of unequal treatment from this view.

Biological study often focuses on body processes such as cell growth and decay. Some biologists believe that cell deterioration is inevitable, a direct cause of death in humans. From this view, the basic effort to increase human longevity is misplaced and the emphasis should be upon living a healthy middle life (Clark, 1999). Contrast this biological view with recent findings that cell division can be promoted by genetic alteration suggesting that human longevity may be increased to 120 years (Shanti, 1999).

Regardless of the biological approach, studies show that older Americans can increase their verbal and spatial learning when both sides of the brain are used, when the materials being used are presented properly. In other words, there appears to be evidence that older people may be able to engage broader regions of the brain as a task gets more difficult, in a kind of neural teamwork (Helmuth, April 17, 1999). Obviously, theories about the aging process vary considerably.

A Symbolic Interactionist View

Selected aspects of the above theories are compatible with an SI orientation, which places stress on the symbolic, creative, action component of everyday life. Humans can continue to grow; they can learn new behaviors and enact creative strategies to enhance their lives. Through these processes they can live proactively, successfully adapting to the exigencies of life. Even when problems that are outside their control occur, the elderly can enact effective coping strategies.

Myths and Stereotypes About the Aging Process

Ageism: Negativity and Stereotype

Many people appear to dread getting older. They often discuss it in negative terms: income reduction, withdrawal and inactivity, loss of status, loss of physical and emotional stamina and loss of mental acuity. This stereotype is somewhat pervasive in a America, a youth-oriented society. There are several myths that are associated with this stereotype.

The Universality Myth. This myth suggests that the aging process occurs in the same way in all cultures. However, cultures vary considerably in the ways that they perceive the aged. The aged are honored in many cultures; they are considered liabilities in others. Different conditions produce different aging patterns.

The Chronology Myth. The emphasis and importance of time is particularly salient in Western, technologically developed countries. The emphasis upon chronology sets false parameters on the aging process. Two people, each the same age, may differ substantially in the ways that they age during the same time period.

The Uniform Aging Myth. Not uniform, the aging process is influenced by gender, ethnicity, educational and occupational background and related factors. For example, statistically females outlive males in the United States. As mentioned, aging patterns vary throughout the world.

The Terminal Drop Myth. Biology is not destiny. People can enact activities and processes that enrich and prolong their lives. Modern genetic, behavioral and social research reveal the hidden potentialities of successful aging. Terminal drop, the idea that people inevitably hit a peak of activity and then suddenly stop or drop, is no longer an acceptable assumption.

The Genetic Miracles Myth. The solving of the genetic riddle, the Book of Life, holds the promise of unlocking the secrets of disease, of aging and the prolongation of life. These possibilities are not yet realized and they involve very important ethical and social issues. Cloning, for example, is considered illegal in the United States. Some people believe that scientists are tampering with nature. Others actively promote modern research in pharmaceutics, technology and genetics.

The Methusaleh Myth. Related to the myth above, The Methusaleh myth is based on the Old Testament character who lived to be more than 900 years old. This myth suggests that people may eventually be able to live forever when the key to the aging process is found. Despite the miracles of science, it is unlikely that scientists can prolong life indefinitely, at least under the present state of knowledge (Packard, 1995).

Recently, two gerontological specialists put up a sizable sum of money to be awarded to the first person in the United States who lives to be 150 years old. They bet that it would not happen in their lifetime (Rather, Feb 27, 2001).

Framing Other Popular Myths

Old means sick: This theory loses favor as more and more Americans older than age 80 report fewer disabilities.

Advanced age means dependency: The percent of people living in nursing homes is dropping.

Poverty is inevitable: Centenarians display a full-range of economic circumstances, including wealth; 3/4 of centenarians do not live in poverty. According to the U.S. Bureau of the Census in 1993, 12% of all elderly live in poverty, compared to 14% of the whole population. This varies from 10 % for Whites to 34% for Blacks.

Mental acuity declines with age: Older people can improve cognitive abilities with training and conditions that focus on enhancements.

Death is genetically programmed: The environment and the lifestyles of the aging play critical roles in the aging process (Belsie, June 28, 1999).

Opposing Research Models of the Aging Process

A Deficit Model of Aging

American society is oriented toward youthfulness. For many, it is the restoration of youthfulness that is important to older people. Females may want to appear youthful, to have a youthful body; they want to engage in youthful activities and network with vigor, just as do members of the younger crowd. Males may want to work out in the gym, to maintain vigor in their sexual lives and to be active.

This emphasis upon youthfulness, while sometimes healthy, earmarks the fact that, in America, the older person is often negatively stereotyped. Scholars refer to this negative stereotyping as "ageism'", in contrast to "aging". The ageism approach focuses on deficits.

A deficit model of aging focuses on how people tend to lose something as they age. For example, the aged person, past his prime, becomes dependent upon others, loses the opportunity to play important roles in society and experiences a drop off in cognitive and physical abilities, including hearing and vision loss. People become disengaged, deprived and decultured forming a negative subculture.

From this perspective, people face a terminal drop, their abilities declining. Humans become old, tired and nonsexual; they become difficult, grouchy, withdrawing, self-pitying, isolated, inactive, lonely, unhappy, unproductive, depressive, ineffective, insecure, rigid, and conservative. Add to this list a loss of sensate ability, physical immobility and social isolation and one has the essence of the deficit model of aging. Even the body gets shorter with age and the skin begins to sag (Schwarz, Park, Knauper, & Sudman, 1999). Aged people become disengaged, past their prime.

Scholars report a number of other negative findings associated with the aging process. Add to the list above the loss of speech recognition and the fact that the voice changes, resulting in a higher, sometimes squeaky pitch. People slow down their pace of speaking significantly as they age (Pittam, 1994).

It has been suggested that older citizens in American society tend to be communication starved. True, they usually own or are provided a television set, but their contacts with others, their essential social networks, seem to diminish and they become more lonely. If there is communication deprivation, as suggested here, it affects other processes, such as life satisfaction, self-esteem, and even the will to live. (Carmichael, 1985). To relate to older folk, many people resort to a kind of babytalk to make themselves understood (Pittam, 1994). A form of elderspeak uses exaggeration of pitch and intonation, simple grammar and a slowed rate of delivery.

Thus, until the present decade, the aged and aging in America presented a problem. The problem was to find ways to deal with someone who, ostensibly, has lived his or her life, who will no longer contribute to mainstream American society when the balance of the members in society are youthful. Ageism portended ill for the aged.

An Additive-Incremental Model of Aging

It is now known that a deficit model of the aging process leaves out the possibilities of successful aging(1).

Framing An Additive Model of Aging

Continuing research shows that the aging process is plastic, that it can be slowed down, even extended, given education and training (Baltes and Willis, 1982). Modern research and technological and medical advancement indicate that human performance can even be enhanced in older age under specific conditions, and that sensory and perceptual processes, memory and spatial reasoning, problem-solving and physical performance are not fixed, rigid endpoints. The aged person in American society need not suffer total loss or deficit; indeed, older age can be a time of incremental gains and novel development.

This new awakening has inspired new research and new research has inspired the new awakening. Modern research about the aging process is diverse and complex. Recent biological and genetic researchers are unlocking the secrets to the aging process. New medicines and health products are improving mental and biological abilities of older people. Research Centers at major universities are focusing on the attitudinal, emotional, and social behaviors of the aged person showing that successful aging is at least partially the result of how one perceives his or her own aging. Cognitive slowdown, so much a problem associated with aging under the deficit model, is offset by research that shows that older people can learn new materials just as well as the younger person if the time constrictions are removed.

It is now understood that the quality of life in the earlier years is somewhat predictive of the quality of life in later years. Positive, proactive living in the early years of life tends to promote positive proactivity in later life, an important aspect of successful aging. Indeed, not only can one learn to live a proactive life in older age, but there may actually be unqualified gains in older life (Schwarz, Park, Knauper & Sudman,1999). For example, older people may be described as level-headed, smart, experienced, wise, logical, adaptive, industrious, and reasonable. Chronobiologically, they may even have peaks of cognitive ability at certain times of the day. Further, instead of disengaging in older age, the elderly often find ways to engage productively, taking up new occupations, devoting time to social causes, entering physically challenging competitions, and even taking college courses specially designed for them. The additive, incremental model of aging suggests that successful aging is a result of humans engaging in life on a continuing, often novel basis.

Related Perspectives on The Aging Process

An Ethological View of Aging

As far as is known, no living organisms live indefinitely. People, of course, aspire to live forever, as shown by their religious beliefs in an afterlife. In this world, the stages of birth, of life, aging and death appear to be universal in the plant and animal kingdoms. Living things adapt to their environment, as humans do. Indeed, the ability to adapt is the key to survival (Wilson, 1992).

Unlike other creatures humans can take a creative part in their own evolution. Many lower order animals, such as elephants and turtles outlive humans on average; however, as humans create and adapt to new technologies, as they learn to reshape living environments for the aged, as they create new and better medicines and food products, humans tend to increase their life span. Under the right conditions, the offspring of humans get taller and healthier, although obesity can be a serious problem in countries like the United States where food is plentiful.

The symbolizing ability of humans distinguishes them from lower order animals and makes it possible for them to take part in their own evolution. The ability to symbolize enables humans to create and recreate themselves, to perceive possibilities in life that lower order animals can not do.

Differential Aging Patterns

The National Center for Health Statistics monitors the growth of the aging population in the United States. The World Health Organization and others monitor the world aging populations. As mentioned, Sierra Leone in Africa, has the lowest mean age limit at 40 years, men and women combined; Japan has the highest at 79.7, again combining males and females. The United States is third in the percent of elderly in the world, aged 65 or older. The Alliance for Aging Research, the American Geriatrics Society and the American Federation of Aging Research monitor the growth of the aging population as well. The White House holds periodic conferences about the aged in American life. Environmental conditions, cultural thoughtways, deadly diseases and a variety of factors influence the aging process.

Cultural Influences

The ways that people age are socially patterned. Every culture approaches the meaning of aging in its own way (Cohen,1994). In Japan The National Law for Welfare of the Elders, 1963, states the following: "The Elders shall be loved and respected as those who have for many years contributed toward the development of society, and a wholesome and peaceful life shall be guaranteed to them. In accordance with their desire and ability, the elders shall be given opportunities to engage in suitable work or to participate in social activities" (Carmichael, 1985). In sharp contrast, traditionally the very aged in early Eskimo society knew when it was time to leave the community to die. They chose their place to die. This behavior, no doubt, was influenced by the community's need to feed its members; the aged had to be cared for and to avoid being a liability, they enacted this death behavior. In sharp contrast, in the United States, every attempt is made to keep a human alive, even by artificial means. often by placing the person in a public or private nursing home.

In the Navajo tradition, the older wiser person is the carrier of culture, the storyteller, continuing tribal customs and beliefs by oral means (Kluckhohn, 1944). In the Chinese tradition, people who die remain as spirits, as ancestors to be consulted (Coye & Livingston, 1975). As mentioned, in India, in certain social circumstances, it was traditional for a woman to die with her husband. This practice called suttee is now outlawed. People in all cultures make sense of the aging process. They come to terms with death. They symbolize life; they symbolize death. Prevailing master themes that characterize cultures throughout the world, couch the death scene in particular ways.

Aging, Class, Gender, Ethnicity and Technology

The aging process has been called a woman's problem by some scholars, which means essentially, that women face problems that males may not. Until recently, it was uncommon for a woman to have an independent income or experience in the workplace; yet, it was likely that she would outlive her husband. She must learn to network socially in new ways when her husband dies, not being free to move about in society as men may be. Women face a variety of medical problems such as ovarian and breast cancer, problems that men do not face.

Framing Gender Patterns

Males in the United States, are likely to live into their seventies, on average to 75.7 years; females are likely to live into their eighties, on average to about 82.7 years. By comparison, the statistics from 1900 showed that males could expect to live to about 48.3 years, on average, and females could expect to live to about 50.5 years on average. Thus, aging patterns have varied considerably over a century, from farm to urban life.

Interestingly, if a white male is 50 years old today, he may expect to live another 27 years; a white female may expect to live another 31.7 years. If one lives to be 85 in the United States, as a white male or female, he or she may be expected to live to above 90 years of age. In short, if people make it to age 85, they will live, most likely, beyond the averages.(Bova, 1998) The 85 plus group is the fastest growing group in the United States. Each year, the size of the centenarian group gets larger and larger.

Statistically, people of color do not live as long as do white people, although life expectancy varies considerably between the Blacks, the Navajo, the Chinese and the Cubans. Because they are more likely to have come from families with low income, they are not as likely to have access to education, to good health care or to have favorable expectations that promote positive aging. For example, alcohol, one of the white man's curses, has been a continuing serious problem for members of the Navajo nation, as is sugar diabetes.

Some Blacks, raised in urban ghettos, see little reason to get a formal education; the white achievement ethos does seem to work for them (MacLeod, 1987). When people have been historically locked into poverty or into victomology, it may be difficult for them to construct positive ways of growth in an empowered white society. Advances in medical technology and access to health care is not distributed uniformly in society, the poor having less control.

Television, too, is a factor in the perpetuation of myths and images. As with other minorities, the aged are often presented in negative, stereotypical ways on television. Often they are seen taking medicines or dealing with problems such as arthritis. Only occasionally do ads portray the aged as lively adults. Social class factors, or standpoint in life, is a powerful influence on the aging process and the media, essentially for commercial reasons, often provides a disservice to the elderly.

Lifespan Changes and Nonverbal Behavior

Stages of Growth and Identity Modification

Stage theories (2), discussed in chapter three, have at least one thing in common: they emphasize that life unfolds in fairly predictable ways and that human behaviors vary accordingly. It has been suggested that humans actively engage in social interaction when young but disengage from work and social activities when old. (Nussbaum, 1989). This social phenomenon, to the extent that it exists, indicates that there is a kind of teleogenic process that gradually unfolds as people age. Although it will change as aged cohort groups increase in size and become even older, the retirement age is fixed at age 65, leaving the work world to younger people.

A variety of models have been developed which indicate how people change as they age. These models may have five, six or eight stages and they may focus broadly on learning, moral development or social development. Researchers use cross-sectional, longitudinal and sequential methods to study aging patterns and they emphasize that stages are not inflexible; rather, they are blends, one enmeshed in the other. Neither do all individuals 'conform' to these stages; that is, people make choices about who they are and what they want to do.

Framing Life Span Changes

Toddlerhood is a time when curiosity peaks and exploration of the social world starts, even before the child has learned to walk. Nursery school fosters social competence, a time when the child learns skilled and appropriate social behaviors. In pre-adolescence, peer groups, the sharing of social activities, games and networking become important to the child.

In adolescence, the child begins to gain confidence and an enduring sense of personal identity; intimate relationships, within and between genders, become important. In young adulthood, parents begin families, raising their children, promoting the next generation. In middle age, engagement in social, political and educational activities become important; people in adulthood are engaged in productive labor. When they enter the gerontological age, males and females may become engaged in new ways (Maas,1984).

Perhaps the stage theory that has generated the most research is that of Erik Erikson (1980) who developed eight stages of growth cast in chronological terms. Early infancy was from birth to two years; later infancy was from age two to four years; early childhood was from four to six years; middle and late childhood was from six years to early teens; adolescence was from early teens to the early twenties; young adulthood was from the early twenties to the late thirties; middle adulthood was from the late thirties to the late fifties; and late adulthood was from the late fifties to death.

An important aspect of Erikson's work was that he placed emphasis upon the need for an individual to solve emotional conflicts at each stage before she can move on to the next stage. For example, an infant must develop trust before he can move successfully to the next stage. Adults must create mutual bonds in order to live successfully in the gerontological age. It is a time when people face poignantly the possibility that they will die. Thus, each chronological development contained the seeds of further growth and development.

Older age is a time when people make sense of their life experiences, sometimes looking back as much as they look forward. A recent conceptualization of this sensemaking process is discussed as a tie-sign. The advantage of this conceptualization is that chronology is less important in the aging process. Tie-signs are symbolically important to people. For example, a person may forge ties by playing in an orchestra or by joining a social club; or a person may create ties in sports or religious activities. The tie-signs frame the personal experience of that person. Ties are created by individuals throughout their lives. People create tie-signs relative to their place of work, the family and friends, their hobbies and travels and their own personal development. A tie-sign is a piece of the symbolic self, a part of the symbolic face. By using tie-signs, the aged person continues to make sense of the world, to tie her or his activities to others who are also adjusting to older life social relationships. This version of adult growth emphasizes the fact that aging people re-evaluate and re-appraise their lives in terms of where they have been and where they are headed. Life ties may be nourished or they may be let go in favor of new ones (Anderson & Hayes, 1996).

Biological Changes and the Psychology of Aging

It is interesting that the head of the newborn is the biggest part of the body but that, in older age, the head becomes proportionally smaller in relation to the body. Snapshots or films taken over the life course, from beginning to end, would show significant changes in the physical body of the individual. Obviously, the outer features of the human body change considerably over time as do the hidden, inner organs. Changes occur so slowly that people often fail to note them.

The somatic self, however, is not based solely on the biological body; humans symbolize their bodies.They may love them or they may hate them. Social expectations, comparisons with others, portrayals in the media, parental and peer attitudes and other socially relevant factors influence people as they create and recreate their body identities.

It is true that changes in the acuity of the senses, in physical strength, in quickness of thought and in athletic ability may slow people down as they age, but these are not inflexible processes.There is an interaction of bodily or somatic changes and how people deal with those changes that influences the process. People who are born with slight, weakly appearing bodies can create powerful body frames through exercise and body building programs. Humans can literally change their bodies and how they conceive of them.

Clearly, the aged can present themselves in new ways; they can arrange to have their yellowed fingernails treated; they can change the color of their hair; they can go on diets and lose weight; or, they can get hearing aids. Natural skills need not decline in older age. People may lose speed in talking, for example, but they do not have to lose procedural knowledge. If one can cope, one can overcome deficiencies(Maas,1984) People can re-symbolize the meaning of life as they age (Tamir, 1979).

Recent research emphasizes the fact that older people need not disengage; they can continue to enjoy better health, higher morale, fewer insecurities, less loneliness and more companionship than thought possible earlier. They can bridge the past and the future by creating healthy relationships with their grandchildren. They can become historians, mentors, and role models and they can have pleasure without responsibility. They can adopt preferred styles of living, given their freedom, and they can symbolize their bodies in new ways. By listening to the body (Masters & Johnson, 1978), they can enact new, life enhancing behaviors.

The Third Age: Emerging Paradigms and Trends

Mental Health and Aging

Social scientists try to unmask social processes that influence human behavior. What is under the scientist's scrutiny only later becomes common knowledge, picked up by the media and the general public. This unmasking function, when applied to the study of aging and gerontology, is responsible for revealing the dynamics of successful aging. The additive, incremental model of aging suggests strongly that any individual can engage in adaptive behaviors that can influence the quality of life, even extend it. Successful aging is the result (Laslett, 1989). In short, personal choices heavily influence how life is lived in the gerontological or third age.

Human identity is influenced by master themes in social life, aging being one of them. One can reinforce a positive identity, creating new and positive self presentations, or conversely, one can choose to disengage. There are, of course, lethal diseases and instances of uncontrolled events that affect individuals. However, even then the individual usually has a choice about how he or she will deal with the life-threatening problem. In short, the life of the elderly can be a creative time for growth. (Baltes & Willis, 1982; Baltes & Baltes, 1990: Charness, 1985). Although young people seem to have biology in their favor, they lack the experience and knowledge base that older people have. The decline in the functioning of the "hardware" need not imply a decline in the functioning of the "software". One can make improvements throughout older age.

The Active Person: Proactivity, Networking and Place

It is clear to social scientists that the intangibles of aging are extremely complex and important. All people will age, but they will age differentially depending on gender, on ethnicity, on educational experiences and on early patterns of behavior in life. However, the key to successful aging lies in how a person thinks or symbolizes experiences.

All humans need a sense of place, of belonging. Older people need a positive sense of place, surroundings that are familiar but not staid; they need a stimulating milieau, as has been shown in the sociometric study of personal space (Sommers, 1969), including space in nursing homes where, in the past, little attention was paid to adult needs. Sommers showed that by merely re-arranging the furniture into favorable patterns in a nursing home, communication among clients increased. In closed situations, where social inteaction is denied, humans do not and cannot grow; they cannot be stimulated. This close containment, of course, is the essence of being imprisoned as punishment. Older citizens have a need for healthy physical and cognitive space (Pastalan & Carson, 1970). Like everyone else, older folk need to be able to lay claim to personal space, marking personal space with familiar objects, books, pictures or other things.

Framing Ergonomics: The Friendly Home

According to the American Association of Retired Persons, 84 percent of adults say they would like to stay in their own homes when they reach older age. Ergonomists, who study behavioral patterns in relation to technologies, suggest that the following physical improvements can greatly improve the life of older people who may not be able to move about as easily as they once did.

Add light to improve visual ability; widen door frames for wheelchairs if necessary; use no-slip flooring; tilt lighting switches; use lever faucets and door handles; install automatic turn-off timers; install create adjustable countertops; use grab bars in showers and hand-held showerheads; install extra phones in the bedrooms and bathrooms; and, put double banisters on the stairs and magnetic induction for the stove. As people age and continue their independence, they can form-fit their home, to help them along (Schwartz, Dec 28, 1999).

Social networking, so important to vital mental health, is a way for an older person to adjust and control her life-space boundaries and their sense of place. When they are physically incapacitated, the home can be modified to maintain a healthy sense of place.

A good share of networking in older age is, of course, with family members. Interestingly, as parents the mother or father sent their children out of the nest, to help them grow up; but, as older people, they may want them to return in new ways. Older people need familial contact with their offspring, which in a mobile society, can be difficult to maintain. In a society with split families, with multiple marriages, elder relationships can be complicated, even difficult. Unlike the past, when families remained knit together, with perhaps several generations of people living under the same roof, modern society is fractured and the older person may have to contend with multiple sets of grandchildren and stepgrandchildren, not to mention in-laws and other relationships.

Nevertheless, positive contacts can help older people fight the disengagement problem, continuing their contacts with familiar, caring people. There is evidence that females, more than males, and daughters more than sons, extend the care to the elderly, following the nurturant pattern among females (Packard, 1995). Part of successful aging is due to enacting continued, positive family contacts and to the creation of new ties outside the home, with new people and new activities. Today, of course, the elderly have found a new friend in the internet. Although the elderly do not buy or use the internet to the same extent that younger people do, there is evidence that they are increasingly using it. To them, perhaps, the internet is what the train used to be; a convenient way to get to their relatives homes.

Scientific and Medical Breakthroughs

Modern science and new medical technolgies are creating a new milieau of possibility. In the Western world, each new day seems to bring new information. Genetic understanding and new technologies lead to new possibilities. Recently, it was reported that a sightless man was fitted with a camera wired to his brain. This 62 year old man cannot see images but he does see specks of light. Humble and awkard as the technology is, it is a remarkable prosthesis (CNN, Jan 16, 2000).

Interestingly, there is a journal and a society devoted to the creation of artificial internal organs called the ASAIO Journal, The American Society of Artificial Internal Organs. The use of artificial hearts, a major breakthrough in medical research, was merely the beginning of the use of medical replacement parts. Diagnosis of diseases is now possible over long distances through computer interaction. Even aboard cruiseships, the stricken adult may be in touch with land-based doctors via remote scanning. On land, their doctors may use scanning tools such as the MRI, PET and CAT, which can detect diseases and problems before they gain a foothold.

The Human Genome Project, an international developed scientific project whose main effort is to map and sequence the 3 billion or so letters and locate and identify the roughly 30,000 or so genes that make up a person's genetic code, has been successful. This remarkable basic research will permit the more effective treatment of diseases and possibly remove the causes of senescence. If the aging process is better understood, it is suggested that humans may expect to live to 120, 150 or 200 years. (Cetron, April 17, 2000). Some scholars believe that humans will be able to choose how long they will live(Bova, 1998). Whether or not this is wishful thinking remains to be seen. Clearly, new pharmaceutics, new technologies and new genetic breakthroughs will enhance the lives of the elderly.

Returning to The Methusaleh Factor

As described in the The Old Testament legend says that death came about because Adam and Eve did not obey God. This disobedience led to mortality and death. This death theme pervades American society, at least among the religious. Death is expected; perpetual life is not. Although the oldest modern person on record was aged 122 years at death, this French woman was outlived by Methusaleh and Noah in the Old Testament, depending on how the years were reckoned. Methualeh was said to have lived to 969 years and Noah to about 900 years. However, if one reckoned the years as months, neither Methusaleh nor Noah would have outlived the average years of their peers.

It is the symbolism of living the good life that is important in the stories of Noah and Methusaleh. It is popular now to believe that a combination of genetics, moderation, exercise, and positive attitudes, along with natural selection and the better treatment of disease, may produce modern Methusalehs (Warshofsky, 1999).

Framing Contemporary Research

However popular the Methuselah factor may be, research about aging is often tentative and highly theoretical. For example, to explain the aging phenomenon, researchers have pet theories about what is involved. Some research focuses on free radicals which are built around oxygen atoms, causing damage to the body, wearing it out, damaging the mitochondria within cells. The presence of glucose is also thought to be a cause of aging. People with uncontrolled diabetes, for example, appear to age faster than do others. Thus, some researchers believe that oxygen and glucose, each necessary to a healthy body, may cause problems if they are out of control in the body system.

Other research suggests that testosterone and estrogen may affect the aging process as well. Research suggests that castrated males, who have lost their testosterone, may outlive uncastrated males. Castrated guinea pigs fight disease better than do non-castrated ones. Research focuses on melanin and telomeres as possible causes of aging too.

Perhaps there are as many as fifty theories tied into modern research on the aging process, each, perhaps, focusing on only part of the causes of aging. Cloning, the regeneration of tissue, transplants, such as fetal tissue transplants, molecular engineering, the use of nanomachines to help build cells, and varieties of other medical technologies and advances will surely impact on the aging process (Bova, 1998).

Modern technology lends itself to a gee-whiz factor. For example, doctors who specialize in electro-technical prosthesis development indicate that smart clothes will be available in the near future. For example, electronic devices can be attached to the body but hidden in clothing enabling people to walk normally, restoring the impulses in their leg nerves. Seemingly, each day brings forth a new technology designed to enhance the performance of the elderly. Newly styled chairs, new tools and hew household designs have been created to enable physically handicapped people to move about in comfort. Institutions are now aware that healthy environments promote healthy living. (Dychtwald & Floer, 1989).

Institutions of higher learning now include centers for the study of aging and conferences and workshops for the elderly. For example, elder citizens may go to conferences specifically designed for the elderly, on or near campuses, as in Arizona, Dartmouth College, or Iowa State, rather than merely play golf or shuffleboard (Marklein, May 17, 2000). The White House continues to hold conferences on the aging, providing incentives to further research.

New Symbolisms: The Achievement of Positive Identity

All people in life, regardless of their age, their wealth, their gender or ethnicity, experience both gains and losses. Change occurs throughout life in both directions(Baltes & Baltes, 1990). What is new in the study of the aging process is the scientific perception that older people can experience gains as much as they experience losses. There can be an accumulation of life knowledge, openmindedness, experience, level-headedness, industriousness and proactivity in the life of the aged. Whereas the word retirement, when associated with aging, means to draw back, to take a well-earned vacation and to create leisure time and disengage, there is an emerging concept about retirement that focuses on the idea of engagement, with a different focus (Bennis, Oct 1995). One can learn to be self-efficacious (Bandura, 1982). Old age is now perceived as a time of continued and positive growth, not marked by decline and deterioration. Mutual growth and family enhancements can occur, not marked by total dependence (Moteko & Greenberg, 1995). Positive attachments can be created anew.

It is this rapid growth in the population of the aged in the U.S. that has led to the use of the descriptive term, third age. The third age is personal, not public and it has little to do with calendar age, social age, or even biological age. Rather, it is a time for becoming aware, for future planning. The aged are not in limbo. As Erik Erikson noted, people are what survives them. He meant that people live out symbolic mortality by leaving behind their children, memories and so on. The symbolic worlds of the elderly are potentially rich and creative. Even when people leave this world, they are remembered for the ways they lived.

People can choose generativity over stagnation. The public mind is slowly becoming attuned to the rich possibilities of the third age. Today, there is increasing emphasis upon how people take care of the elderly, when and if they cannot take care of themselves (McAdams & de St. Aubin, 1998). Colleges and universities provide programs for the older citizen (Canfield, 1975; Marklein, May 17, 2000).

As people live longer and longer chronologically in the United States and in technologically developed countries, it is clear that new choices are presented to the general public and to individuals about how they will deal with the aged. No longer is 65, the traditional year of retirement, the marker of older age. People, of course, may choose to work until they are seventy or later; they may choose to work another interesting job or take up an interesting avocation. Although play is the work of the child, work can be the play of older folks who do not need a job. Individual competence does not have to disappear with aging, as was thought to be the case in in prior times. Where there is a supportive milieu, the aged can continue to be competent.

It is not known entirely why some people live longer than others, although it is the subject of much study. It is likely--at least from a common sense view-- that a person who has spent his life in a coal mine will not fare as well as a person who spent his life on a university campus. Researchers know that there are important relationships between gender, ethnicity, occupation, education and aging, but few specific behaviors are predictive of successful aging. Work satisfaction, happiness, physical functioning and nonsmoking seemed to be the keys in a recent Duke University study. The subjects in this study had lived on farms, where they emphasized orderliness, stability and continuity, strong family ties, abstention from alcohol and smoking, religiosity, attending church, and mental freedom and curiosity. The older-aged subjects in this study exhibited many of these characteristics during their earlier lives and continued them in their later lives.

Perhaps genes (3) play a significant role in aging when they are associated with other variables, such as the list above. There is a social, psychological and physical interaction in the aging process(Segerberg, 1982). Perhaps stress, or the perception of stress, plays a role as well. The psychophysical way to body awareness has been preached, suggesting that people, young and old, must listen to the body, and begin to use the body in new and different invigorating ways (Masters & Houston, 1978). The authors believe that the physical symptoms of aging may be symptoms of misuse of the body.

Another popular writer suggests that there is an alternative to growing old; one can defeat entropy of the body by developing new awarenesses. He believes that the effects of aging are preventable (Chopra, 1993). Medical doctors and philosophers often include healing, growth-oriented messages in their books. Of course, there are dozens of self-help books on the market, variously worthy.

Successful Aging and Self Presentation in Older Age

Clearly, the elderly have choicies in how they will perceive and present themselves to others. They can choose to be detached, passive, supportive, authoritative or influential. They can choose to be mentors and role models for grandchildren; they can take up a new career; they can go to college; they can join social clubs; their possibilities are limited by the symbolism they have created for their status in life.

The aging process is complicated; clearly there is an interaction between biology, medical help, technological availability, previous life style and various social factors. But, if the research that focuses on positive aging is accurate, it would seem that the way in which older people interpret and make sense of aging is critical to their continued growth.

Summary

There are a variety of myths associated with aging in American society. This chapter has focused on the differences between a negative model of aging and a positive model of aging, suggesting that ageism is a stereotypical term and that the aging process can be more accurately perceived and understood.

As humans age, they face new life cirumstances. According to stage theorists, self identity is continually construed and new perceptions of self emerge as people age chronologically. But biology is not destination; gender, ethnicity and social class and a variety of other factors influence the aging process. Recent research in biology and genetics, in the social sciences and in medical technology are contributing to an additive model of the aging process. The concept of successful aging is becoming dominant. In the third age, it may be possible for humans to make choices about how long they will live. The construction of a positive, proactive identity is a key part of a successful aging process.

Questions for Thought and Discussion

1.   Biological, chronological and 'semantic' aspects of aging differ in meaning. Show how they differ and what influence the differences might have on how a person identifies himself as an aged person. Is there such a thing as destiny in the aging process?

2.   The social conditions of the aging process vary radically from culture to culture. Can you explain why people in some countries live, on average, to be only about 50 years old. Others, as in the United States, live much longer on average. Why, if at all, do you think that cultural perceptions of age make a difference in how people age?

3.   It is said that there is a cult of youthfulness in the United States. Do you agree? If so, how does that cult influence your own life? Similarly, is there an assumption that older people in the United States seem to be less important than are the young? Do you agree or disagree?

4.   The Methusaleh factor, or the idea that humans can live on and on, is receiving recent attention. If this is possible, is it a desirable option in your opinion? What social problems might be caused by having an enlarged group of aged persons? What new possibilities might arise due to their presence?

5.   Do you think that the media portray the aging person in ways that are positive or do they tend to make fun of the aged person in commercials, in sitcoms or in the news? Can you give examples of how the media portray the elderly in the United States?

Notes

1.   A key theme in SI is that the mind, body and society are inter-related, part of a mutually influencing process. Various health-oriented practices, such as yoga, meditation and exercise are popular and it is widely believed that there is a connection between how people think and how their bodies are influenced. Religious groups anoint sick members, praying for healing. Laughter has been said to promote healing. The validity of these practices is open to question, yet researchers focus more and more on the mind-body connection. As mentioned, a Duke University longitudinal study dealing with aging suggested that a healthy mental, emotional and work lifestyle is positively correlated with successful aging. Gerontology studies are promoted in many universities. Duke and Harvard, for example, have centers for the study of the aging process.

2.   Stage theories come in a variety of forms but each is in some way attached to the idea of physical development over the lifespan. Vygotsky, Piaget, Kegan, Kohlberg, Perry and Erikson appear prominently in the research literature. Some focus on how language develops; others focus on moral development; still others focus on how people achieve identity, as in the work of Erikson. The eight stages of growth, espoused by Erikson in a number of his writings have attracted considerable scholarship. His ideas about identity diffusion and integration have influenced the work of psychologists, sociologists, and gerontologists. There is the implication in his work that the gerontological age, the last age, incorporates all of the knowledges and skills garnered over a lifetime, in a final state of awareness and activity. Mutuality, for example, is achieved by older people. All activities prior to the gerontological age prepare one for that age.

3.   Research shows that genes play a role in many diseases. Cancer is known to run in families, as are schizophrenia, obesity and other common diseases and problems. However, there may be hidden interactions that are at play; for example, lifestyle may admix with genetics, interacting to produce aging effects. Genetic causes of diseases may reveal that certain genes, or gene patterns, are tied into the aging process. The Genome Project holds promise to help solve the riddle of the origin of some, perhaps most diseases. Meanwhile, theory upon theory has been launched to explain how cancers, as one major disease affecting older people, are formed. In short, the promise is there but it is not yet fulfilled.

Suggested Reading

Dychtwald, K. (1990). Age Wave: How the Most Important Trend of Our Time Will Change Your Future. New York: Bantam Books.

Chopra, D. (1993). Ageless Body, Timeless Mind: The Quantum Alternative to Growing Old. New York: Harmony Books.

Erikson, E. (1980). Identity and the Life Cycle. New York: Norton.

Packard, S. (1995). Living on The Front Line: A Social-Anthropological Study of Old Age and Aging. Brookfield Vermont: Ashgate Publishing.

Sheehy, G. (1998). Understanding Men's Passages: Discovering the Map of Men's Lives. New York: Random House.

Sokolovsky, J. (Ed.) (1990). The Cultural Context of Aging: World-Wide Perspectives. New York: Bergin and Garvey.

Chapter 8
Technological Influences on Nonverbal Communication
Making Sense of Communicative Technologies

Chapter Overview

As in previous chapters dealing with master themes, this chapter includes conceptual material from earlier chapters applied in specific ways. A considerable body of work has been created in the past few decades, aspects of which are discussed here.

Humans create their social worlds; they also invent and use communicative technologies. From the invention of the pencil to the internet, all technologies have influenced human behavior. Television, radio, film and the internet, in particular, deeply influence human perceptions, beliefs and behaviors (Altheide, 1997; Brown, Childers, Bauman & Koch, 1990; Couch, 1996; Dyson, 1996; Grossberg, Martella & Whitney, 1998; McLuhan, 1962, 1964). They are referred to as communicative technologies. The focus of this chapter is mostly on television and the internet, or computer. It has been said that in cyberspace, there is a world in the wires (Jones, 1995; Kitchin, 1998; Rheingold, 1991).

Humans create a mediated telepresence through the use of television and the internet. For example, sitcoms, framed and targeted at specific audiences are fictional, but they contain enough life reality to engage the viewer. The viewer of a sitcom brings a frame of reference to the sitcom which includes her beliefs, values, attitudes and personal schemas. The sitcom contains frames of reference, too, and in the interaction, the viewer creates a new set of meanings. Most people view television selectively. For example, the person who believes that TV is a debased medium appealing to crass tastes will either avoid using television or watch it very selectively (Baran, McIntyre & Meyer, 1984).

The advent of the computer, e-mail and cyberreality have significantly altered the ways that humans communicate. It may be argued that the technologies associated with the computer have fundamentally altered human experience. For example, in oral societies face-to-face communication is the norm but, in a heavily mediated society, face-to-face communication is replaced, and filtered by a technological lens. As communicative technologies have evolved, the relationships between humans have been transformed. Television and the computer are contemporary forms of mass media, but they are very different technologies. The internet is interactive, as in the use of e-mail, and television is usually directed from station to audience, although this is changing rapidly as the internet teams up with television.

The telegraph, the auto and airplanes each deeply influenced human society before the advent of television and the computer and even more modern technologies will follow them. Even today satellites course the skies, creating avenues for international communication, even interplanetary communication. People in the Western world are involved in a remarkable revolution in the ways that humans can communicate. Behavior, time, place and culture are being transformed.

Young people may not so easily observe how their nonverbal behavior is affected by modern media, lacking an historical perspective due to their age. Of course, they can and do read about past events as they study human history, but the perspective of older people is based on actual experiences where modern communicative technologies did not exist. Perhaps the best way for a young person to imagine the influence of the present-day media is to focus on speed and activities. A young person might ask how the internet has influenced how quickly she is able to receive messages and how her academic life is now centered on the use of the computer. She might also analyze the time she spends in front of a television set, on a daily basis. This chapter focuses on the ways that modern communicative technologies, especially television and the internet, influence human behavior both in the shaping of the social background and in the influence of behavior in daily life. The SI approach is particularly useful in the understanding of that influence.

Media Ecology and Information Technologies

Myths About the Media

The Reality Myth. This myth suggests that the media present reality as it is. Reality, of course, is created by individuals in interaction with others. The media represent or mediate social reality. Cyber-reality is a visual fabrication of everyday life. It is not everyday life, although it may influence the work and play of individuals.

The Media Distribution Myth. This myth implies that the media are distributed evenly throughout society; in actuality, people have differential access to the media. Although this is changing, the aged, the poor and some members of ethnic groups do not have the same access as do mainstream White Americans.

The Uniform Influence Myth. This myth suggests that all people are uniformly influenced by the media. In actuality, the background of people, their age, ethnicity, gender and culture influence their use and interpretations, as advertisers know.

The Mediated Construction of Reality

The printing press and the telegraph were precursors to the advent of television and the computer. "What hath God Wrought?" the question asked by Morse, sent more than 150 years ago from Washington to Baltimore on the telegraph, foreshadowed the emergence of the modern, electronic society. The telegraph and the telephone, created in 1876, deeply influenced the patterning of society before the age of computers and television. Communicative technologies, such as television, radio and the internet have, in a similar way, substantially altered the ways that humans do things. As discussed in earlier chapters, people construct the meanings of events and activities, as noted below.

Framing the Construction of Reality

Searle suggests that there are three parts to the construction of reality. The three parts are objective reality, or the factual world, what Searle has called the brute facts; symbolic reality, such as art forms, plays, literature, media contents; and subjective reality, which is the reality constructed by the individual on the basis of objective and symbolic reality. (Maine & Adoni, 1984; Searle, 1995). The media discussed in this chapter fall into his version of symbolic reality.

That the media influence human society is clear; just how they do so is less than clear. A variety of theories (1) have been proposed in the scientific study of the media. How a television program is framed is important. Is a program that deals with pornography framed as a problem for womens' rights; or, is it presented as pleasurable for men? The way it is framed influences how the situation is defined (Severin & Tankard, 1997). Perhaps more than any other theorist, Marshall McLuhan gave the study of the media an early push, an impetus. He declared that the medium not only bears a message, but it is a message by itself. The popular phrase is that the medium is the message (McLuhan,1964).

This seminal work delineated the ways in which human society is altered and influenced by the type of media that is dominant at a given time. The oral world was different from the newer print world and the print world was very different from the world of television. Each medium has its own type of influence on human behavior. Whole civilizations have been variously influenced by their technologies (Couch, 1984). Runners bore messages in ancient civilizations. The quipu was used to count in early Incan societies. Smoke was used as a signalling mechanism by early Americans. Satellites flash messages instantly in the modern world. Technologies, created by humans, return the compliment; they are involved in creating societies, influencing human affairs.

Technologies as Designs for Human Action

The media have been referred to as designs for society. Their built-in structure and the ways they are used influence and pattern human behaviors (Couch, 1996). For example, members of a pastoral sheep raising society, an oral society, having few or no communicative technologies, are likely to talk face-to-face about events in their lives. Intersubjective, shared meanings are deeply imbedded in the pastoral setting. Time slows down and the pace of events is slowed. The sheepherder's sense of place is keen. He eats no fast food. It is likely that the lives of his sheep-raising parents and grandparents were very similar; they lived the same way. If a person was identified as a sheepherder, everyone in a pastoral society knew what that meant. Daily life was routine, patterned and continuous. Seasons changed the patterns, but the sheepherder identity remained intact. All is different in modern society. Technologies intrude in human affairs, shaping and altering how people communicate. They constitute designs for human human action and behavior.

New Forms of Sociodrama

The SI approach emphasizes the dramaturgical behavior of humans in interaction. Humans engage in daily mini-sociodramas. They act toward others as though they were performing a role on stage; things may be going on backstage (Goffman, 1969) but people are attentive to what they must do to accomplish tasks or plans. Television, film, the radio and the internet have become part of the sociodrama of everyday life. True, they present artificial sociodramas, but people interact with them as though they were real. The media present symbolic messages to people who make sense of them in terms of their experiences. By comparing the media content to real world content, individuals come to terms with the meaning of the media presentation (Davis & Baran, 1981).

Television "talks" in the sense that the producers may try to send specific messages, especially through advertising. Programs bear messages. Advertisers and organizations deliberately target their messages. For example, The Health Education Council produced an anti-smoking ad showing a young child in a wheel chair smoking; the child was asked how many cigarettes he smoked (Baran & McIntyre. 1984). The viewer filled in the blanks. This process of filling in the blanks occurs in all visual presentations, film or television; it occurs as well in the messages that are exchanged on the internet. Each activity engages the individual in an active symbolizing process.

Perhaps American have a taste for things that are slick and colorful. Television producers sometimes seem to act as though that were the case. It has been said that if one has taste, he loses interest in television, an interesting statement from a writer who spent time on the major networks (Gitlin, 1983). On the other hand, it appears that television is furnishing the bridge between the 'lively classical arts' and the tastes of the everyday viewer. One can watch professional wrestling or one may watch an opera, not by sitting in an auditorium, but by sitting in her home, merely switching channels. Mediated reality is instantly available. There is no requirement that one drive or walk to a theatre or to purchase tickets in advance. As one television critic put it, we have "instant everything".

The internet is synchronously interactive, providing a forum in which imagination plays an important role. Often, one person in interaction with another via e-mail, forums or chat groups, does not know who the other party is. This aspect of the internet tends to mask identities. People can pretend to be who they are not. Masks have been used over the centuries in drama, as in China, to disguise or create new characters, but the electronic mask is modern, requiring little training to use. The internet enables a person to put on new face. The computer, like television, is a design for action.

Framing the Pervasiveness of Electronic Media

It is argued that the electronic media, including television, have created changes in physical spaces, including things as basic as shopping malls and as large as cities in dramatic ways. Fun and pleasure, as well as crime, are associated with these places (Altheide, 1997). Not only do people have telepresence, they have co-presence; that is, television sets and other communicative devices are everywhere that people are.

Television is found in nearly every public quarter. Bars and restaurants, hospital waiting rooms, automobiles, and even camps in the distant mountains have television screens. In some places, screens may be so large that they seem to engulf the audience. Humans seem not to tire of watching human behavior. The author remembers watching a Superbowl and by switching channels, he could watch the war in Iraq! Both activities were real in that they were really happening, but they were mediated, altered by the technology of television.

Family eating patterns traditionally centered on the dining room table where face-to-face communication took place. Discussion about daily matters was important at the dinner table. Television displaced the family table; now, family members may gather around the television set located in the entertainment center, eating a fast-food take-out. In very practical ways, technologies shape human behavioral patterns; they are designs for living influencing how people relate to one another.

Human Extensions

Early scholarship focused on the effects of tool use by humans (Innis, 1951;McLuhan, 1962, 1964, Ong, 1982). All tools, from the use of a pencil to the use of e-mail extend the potential for human interaction, just as the bulldozer extends the ability of humans to change the surface of the earth. The effects are often taken for granted, not felt or observed in everyday life. How many people ask or think about how the use of pencil and paper created new patterns of interaction in everday behavior? It is the business of scholars to ask these questions. Yet, the effects on the daily life of the student is obvious, even pronounced. Writing, whether on papyrus or modern paper, stabilizes society, leading to the storage of knowledge in libraries. In short, pencils, used to write, extend the fingers and the mind. All communicative technologies are symbolic extensions of human behavior.

The printing press of course increased the speed with which humans could exchange their printed messages. Today, the creation of new technologies or twists on older ones, many very sophisticated, is mushrooming. It is not a slow, linear process; it is, seemingly, an exponential process. The half-life of technological invention is reduced more and more, as Moore's Law suggests. In other words, technologies have always influenced human behavior. But previous inventions came about relatively slowly. In present times new inventions are produced in very short periods of time (Schramm, 1988). One of the outcomes of this shortened time period between inventions is that young people may introduce their parents to a new technology, not the other way around, as in the past.

Mediated Influences on Human Nonverbal Communication

Television and the internet diffentially influence human behavior as discussed in the following sections.

Television and Advertising

As mentioned above, researchers want to know how human behavior is influenced by the media, essentially television in this case. Television, of course, is a relatively recent invention, not available to the masses until after mid-century. A number of research approaches or models have been used.

Framing Research Models

The "bullet theory", a naive and simplistic theory of the power of television to influence people directly, was used in early research. The use of propaganda in WWII influenced the development of this model. Propaganda was a one-way process, designed to make people think or do things. The Americans and their Allies and the Germans and the Axis powers used propaganda extensively (Ellul, 1964, 1973). The bullet theory suggested that, as in the trajectory of a bullet, the message reached its target, the audience, directly and it was received as it was sent. But media messages must fall upon "ready soil" so to speak; humans must be ready to accept them, to interpret and use them, and they do so in various ways. Messages may have little direct influence as suggested by the bullet theory.

Cultivation theory suggests that heavy users of television differ from light users in how they use television and in the ways that they are influenced by it. Heavy users may "resonate" more with the topic shown on television than do light users. Television may also produce a general climate of fear or uncertainty in some populations. For example, women may fear crime more than males do; even though both may be watching the same program, males and females may differ in the in the fear or apprehension that is triggered by the program. In short, televised programs and advertisements differentially influence viewers even though they may be watching the televised activity (Severin & Tankard, 1997).

As mentioned, one of the key ways that television influences human behavior is through advertising. Advertising is basically about persuasion designed usually, but not always, to make money. Advertisers "construct" their audiences; that is, they aim at women or men, children or parents, Blacks, Whites, Hispanics, or other target groups (Turow, 1997). Once the audience is constructed, advertisers find ways to get the attention of people in that audience, using bright colors, sexual themes, or other ways that are known to gain attention. Persuasive communications try to tap the emotions or they try to associate well-known people with the product. They may even try to shock an audience to get attention.

Whatever persuasive technique they use, they try to build a symbolic bridge to the audience; they try to create a need in the mind of the viewer for the product. Advertisers will try to sell their product by showing how it will benefit the purchaser; they will claim that their product is superior, more beautiful, more useful or in some way better than other products, presenting this information as "fact". Unlike the use of propaganda which is essentially a one-way process designed to "brainwash" viewers, television producers try to engage the viewer interactively with their presentation. By engaging his emotions and his mind, their chances of selling their products to him are increased. Perhaps he will not go out and buy a product immediately, but the images are there for future reference. In short, advertisers know that by appealing to basic human needs, values or identities, they can tug at feelings, influence the emotions and move people to act, to purchase their product.

On the other hand, advertisements may be designed to keep their product name in front of a target audience. They may want everybody to join the "millions" who have bought their product. The fact that MacDonald's claims to have sold billions of hamburgers influences some people to buy using the kind of reasoning that suggests that if so many people have bought them, they must be good. People who are not aware of the persuasive techniques used in these advertisements may be uncritical about the product, a situation that helps the advertiser achieve her or his goals (Larson, 1983).

Audiences, of course, are not real entities; they are constructed abstractions, (Turow, 1997) used for a purpose, as in advertising. Advertisers construct the audience that they wish to target, a children's audience being very different from an adult audience. The age, gender and race are important to advertisers, who pitch their products directly at them. Although there is considerable discussion in modern American society about whether, how, or how much television and film influence young people in good and bad ways, clearly there are effects and influences; otherwise, businesses would not spend millions of dollars to sell their products nor would so much effort be spent studying their effects. Nor wood scholars be studying the impact of television on children's nonverbal behavior. Dr. Robert S. Feldman, at the University of Massachussetts, has set up an internet site designed precisely to study how television impacts on children's behaviors. He believes that television distorts or exaggerates real life and that it draws upon limited emotions, such as anger, happiness and sadness.

Advertisers, of course, are part of the mix. They lead their customers to their products, using clever, attractive, emotional messages. Some advertisers have even used seductive ways to influence viewers, as in subliminal advertising. How much subliminal advertising really works is not clear, although popular books have been written about the process (Key, 1973).

Subliminal processes operate below the threshold of the senses; they are said to 'work' on the subconscious mind in suggestive ways. Whether they work or not remains an issue. Their use has been the subject of legal controversy. For example, advertisers have produced subliminal messages in films seen in theaters, hoping that without realizing it, members in the audience will be motivated by the subliminal message to buy their product. Of course, theree are serious, ethical issues involved in the use of undisclosed, hidden messages, designed to make people do things. Whether the message works or not is another question, although those professionals who practice hypnotism may have a special understanding of how it works. Mead referred to humans as walking somnambulists, meaning that people at times may move about, without realizing they have done so, as in sleepwalking.

On one hand, advertising presents an opportunity for businesses to present their products in responsible ways on television and on the internet. On the other hand, another view of advertising says that it is saturated with excessive and obsessive commercialism, with sensationalism and distortion in an attempt to get to the audience, the effect being to distort the consumers's world (Bogart, 1995). As has been said "there are no plain women on television," a statement attributed to John Ford, a producer; television needs beautiful women and advertisers frequently play up the beautiful body to sell a product.

Television, of course, conveys visual symbolism to people. MTV, a relatively new television format owned by Viacom, the owner of CBS Television, targets a specific audience, using youthful images and music that is appealing to mostly a Black audience. Children's programs rely upon fuzzy lifeless characters that come alive in a child's imagination, as in Sesame Street on public broadcasting networks. Indeed, PBS stations intentionally downplay advertising so that 'cultural' programs are less influenced by commercial advertising. Jock sports and extreme sports are aimed at young males. In short, symbols that appeal to different audiences are continually created to build a bridge to that audience. Not all audience members respond to the same symbolism in the same ways.

The Computer and the Internet

Internet has become a powerful socializing tool. One need only read the articles that are presented in Wired Magazine or through the Hypermedia Research Centre see the impact of the internet. Cybersociology Magazine is advertises itself as a forum for the discussion of the social scientific study of cyberspace. The internet influences human behavior in ways that are different from the influence of television. As mentioned, people can mask their identities on the internet, but they also gain access to information, to chat groups, to friends, even to college courses on the internet. In short, the internet via the computer has radically altered behavioral patterns, some of them negative, as discussed later in the chapter.

The computer and the internet have brought about technospeak, new words that originate with specialists and become part of the public lexicon. New words, such as emoticons, netizens (net-citizens) and netropolis (net-metropolis), cyberpunk, spamming, hyper-reality, and cyber-rapture are part of a new language used by tekkies. A netiquette is a type of coded communication used in a virtual community where geographical boundaries do not exist (Herring, 1996).

Framing Technospeak

What do the following terms mean?: Viral marketing, legacy systems, pure play, telephone space, B2C, disintermediation, Dynabook, freenet, FAQ, multiplexing. WYSWYG.

Who are these mutants and are they good or bad?: The Wolverine, Sabretooth, Toad, Jean Grey, Mystique, Cyclops, Rogue, Storm (USA Today, July 14, 2000).

Techno-speak terms are neologisms, invented to be used in a community of users. Few people outside the so-called tekkie realm understand the terminology, although a term such as spamming appears to have entered the wider public realm. In a fast changing society, new symbols are needed, as the half-life of technological knowledge becomes shorter and shorter.

The creation of virtual communities implies that there is an identifiable citizenry whose common bond is the web. Electronically networked, without boundaries, electronic communities exist in techno-space. It is nowhere and everywhere. One merely needs to know how to talk to the citizens and she, too, becomes part of that citizenry. Sculptors, painters and other artists have historically plied their craft in their special lofts or labs. Their craft was specialized and they may have taken years to perfect it. The computer provides yet another way to enact presence. Virtual reality is the result of the ability of a person to image life, forms and processes on the computer. In short the imagination of the painter is brought home to the everyday user of the internet. People can simulate the body on the internet, with or without artistic training. Like any other application of the computer, the creation of virtual reality can be used in positive and negative ways, as psychologists assert.

Specific Influences on Human Behavior

A Reduced Human Sensorium

Face-to-face communication permits the participants to display their full bodies to others. As mentioned, the full human sensorium comes into play in face-to-face enactments. Humans in areas of the world that lack communicative technologies still rely upon primal communication. They may represent their cultures through paintings on cave walls or other places in the landscape, and they may embellish their faces with paint, but essentially their interactivel conduct is face-to-face. In cultures saturated by the use of television, the computer and the internet, the human sensorium does not come into play in the same ways. Television is essentially a visual medium; the radio is an aural medium, each influencing viewers and listeners through these body channels (McLuhan, 1962, 1964; Couch, 1996; Denning, 1999).

By using modern tools, engineers are able to mimic all of the human senses. Voice, face and fingerprint recognitions systems already exist. Can smell and taste systems be far behind? Obviously not; in the print media, scratch-off perfume smells have been used. As technological development continues in increasingly sophisticated ways, the way that the real body works in face-to-face interaction, in which the full sensorium is deployed, will be mimicked. Robots will be able to see, hear, feel, taste, and touch, just as humans do. But, of course, this will be artificial reality, however useful and imaginative the robot is.

Shifting Contexts: The Alteration of Place,Time and Space

The contexts of human action are shifting rapidly. Moore's Law dictates that the growth of computer technologies is seemingly exponential, with doubling effects occurring over an increasingly shorter period of time. New technologies create new contexts influencing existing human habits. As mentioned, television is used in medical buildings and malls, in restaurants, schools and bars. The telepresence leads to a new co-presence (Altheide, 1997). Because television is available, new forms of association are engendered. The geography of place and space is altered. Old boundaries are eliminated and new boundaries formed. Time barriers are crossed with ease. It takes no longer to read a newspaper located nearly anywhere on the globe than it takes to go to the store to buy a paper.

Friends communicate across oceans and continents instantly. No paper and pens are needed. People born into these contexts may take them for granted. Until they experience alternative realities, young people, born into these technological contexts, may not know how dramatically modern communicative technologies have altered society. The capability of modern communicative technology to increase and diffuse human exchanges seems boundless (Denning, 1999;Mossk, 1997).

Increased Speed in Interaction: The Reduction of Lagtime

Lag time was a difficult problem in early communication when stage coaches delivered the mail or when couriers ran with messages. A waiting period was necessary. The country doctor may be summoned too late, the distance too far. Even with the advent of the daily newspaper, lag time is apparent when one compares online newservices with print services. The New York Times, the Washington Post or the Boston Globe or any other newwspaper, but the on-line version is available instantly, as are newspapers from around the world. News that is found in paper print is old by the time it gets delivered to the front door.

In short, the new electronic technologies reduce lag time to almost nothing. Following Moore's Law, there have been 18 doublings of the speed of microprocessors since their invention (Denning, 1999). The computer, which drives the speed of change, is becoming more and more sophisticated. The author in writing this book used four major library systems on-line, each in a different part of the United States. Although he went physically to the libraries, his search for materials was facilitated by the use of the internet, his library time dramatically reduced.

Mind-Body-Machine Interaction: Emergent Cyborgs?

The gee-whiz aspect, the world of wonder, associated with the development of new technologies, gives new meaning to mind-body-machine interaction.

Framing Cyborgs

Cyborg-like human-machinery is being used in medicine, in research and by engineering companies. Pioneering medical devices, such as the artificial human heart, have been used for decades; modern research is now more sophisticated. Electronic gadgets may be used to increase brain power; nerve circulation can be improved electronically; the small intestine can be observed by a very small, wandering, picture-taking computer; robots simulate human activities; computers can read voices. In short, the electro-bionic human is here. No longer do people say "gee-whiz" with every new development; they are getting used to the idea that cyberculture and cyborgculture are here, giving new meaning to the term "human extension". The Cyborg factor, of course, is a fanciful metaphor; nevertheless, it gives one pause for thought.

Filtered Reality

Modern electronic media serve to provide a new looking glass, one that was not anticipated by Cooley (1970), who coined the term, "looking glass self". Of course, people always filter reality perceptually, but television and the internet not only present filtered reality, they construct artificial realities. The bodies of the ideal man and the ideal woman are constantly presented on television. Now, the perfectly pixeled female body has been created in virtual reality. Dr. Aki Ross, star of the Final Fantasy, a science-fiction move, is called "The Perfect model: Gorgeous, No Complaints, Made of Pixels". She is said to be a combination of Sigourney Weaver and Julia Roberts (La Ferla, May 5, 2001).

Many people, fail to realize that TV reality is representational; it biases and filters everyday reality. For example, the major news programs which try to project the image of authority, are actually presenting highly selected news, merely a small portion of the news that could be presented. Yet, the news sets the agenda for the day for many people.

The influence of television and the internet is not uniform across society nor are all people blindly influenced by them. Women, members of ethnic groups, the aged and children have differential access to television and the internet. They tend to use it differently, too.

The Media has Influences On Identity Formation

Self Identity Revisited

The concept of multiple selves was discussed in chapter four as a normal growth pattern, but in the blur of activities that are associated with television and the internet, young people may struggle with identity formation or suffer from chronic revision of who they are, resulting in neurasthenia or anomie (Grodin & Lindlof, 1996). A replacement of real persons by artificial persons, the abandonment of the essential self, may occur due to the effects of television, the internet and other salient mediating technologies. In short, there may be unintended, latent and negative influences resulting from the use of modern communicative technologies.

How directly television influences behavior varies, but certainly there are copycat behaviors. As mentioned, television promotes the perfectly formed woman to viewers. To be contemporary, the media must promote a woman whose sizes and BMI index are very different from a few years ago when women were shorter and a bit heavier. Today, the models are thinner and taller, as the beauty queens attest. The image of beauty queens, projected on television, becomes a template, a looking glass, against which one measures herself. Some women, unfortunately, are negatively influenced. Women can become anorexic or buliminic as they strive to achieve the perfect BMI (Moss & Kidd, May 20,2000). Some people, of course, already have unhealthy goals; such depiction on television or in print media can increase the state of unhealth.

Given the saturation of society by the print, film and television media it has been strongly suggested that the formation of the identity process is made difficult and confusing (Gergen, 1991). Media effects and influences are dynamic and pervasive. A media culture immerses every person in it. People are bathed in a society saturated by the media.(Gerbner, Gross, Morgan, & Signiorelli, 1986; Gergen, 1991).

Television and Violence

American society has always been violent, varying from one period to another, as noted in the Westward movement in early America, discussed in chapter six. Violence is known to all societies, some being violent more than others. The classic Marxist position is that the story of humankind is the story of stuggle, members of one class against members of another. In some ways, it appears that the media, especially television, are mere overlays of the everyday routines of society that have contributed to the structure of dominance (Altheide, 1997), which suggests that the violence that is found in society will continue to be found on television.

Scholars have focused on the relationship between television and violence (Lefkowitz, Tron, Walder & Huesman, 1972). Some scholars suggest that viewing TV violence has a cathartic effect; in other words, viewing violence is a way of reducing the likelihood that the viewer will be violent because it channels and diffuses violent tendencies. Others hold very different perspectives. For example, a major study called The Great American Values Test (Ball-Rokeach, Rokeach & Grube, 1984) revealed that viewers of a specially designed program changed their values after watching it; people who were dependent on television, compared to those who watched it less, changed their values more by comparison. In short, television programs can and do influence people, especially those who are dependent upon it. The issue of whether and how television influences people, their beliefs and behavior is salient in contemporary society where young people are shown in the media shooting one another, bullying each other and increasingly engaging in crimes. The question naturally arises about the role of the media in influencing the behaviors. It was reported in 1973 that by age 12, the average child had watched 101,000 violent episodes on television, including 13,400 deaths (Severin & Tankard, 1997). It would be interesting to know if the same pattern holds in present-day society.

Cultish Behavior

Popular materials, such as television programs, films and internet communications, do not by themselves contain meaning. Humans create and attach meanings to them. Mediated 'reality' is not life reality; rather, it is representive of life having enough life-like characteristics to make it recognizable. When it appeals to the way that humans think and make sense of their worlds, communicative technologies are influential. Indeed, cults can form around the presentations of television and film.

Framing Cultish Behaviors

People devote strong attachments to a person, a principle or types of fads. Often, mass media create cultish followings, such as those formed around the Grateful Dead or Madonna. Star Wars, The Empire Strikes Back, Star Trek and other film and television productions have attracted cult-like followers, showing the power of the media to appeal to the ways that people think and make sense of their worlds (Whitmore, 1989).

The Superbowl is celebrated with feverish passion, almost orgy-like. People are attracted to Disney World productions in great numbers. The Woodstock event in Rome, NY attracted thousands of apparently disinhibited people. People swarm to religious and social events: Do the media inspire these assemblies or do they merely serve to point them out? Clearly, most of them are sociodramas that are made possible only by the media.

Related Psychological Influences

The media, referring here to television and the internet due to the lack of space, play important and useful roles in society. They disseminate information, form bonds of association, and present forums for the resolution of problems. The internet is useful in business and education, in medicine and science. The beneficial uses and influences of these media are profound. Many scholars promote their virtues. They can serve to help educate a society, to make it more literate, more aware of aspects of human existence that would not otherwise be available. The downside is serious, too. Scholars, concerned about the quality of life in a society dominated by television and the internet, have focused on selected topics discussed below.

The Need for Stimulation

Humans appear to have a need for stimulation; television and the internet provide it. The need for stimulation, when extreme, as in the over-use of the internet, seems to be almost pathological, a form of cyber-rapture. Research suggests that some surfers seem to prefer porno-sex found on the net to the real thing (Couch, 1996) and that virtual reality blurs one's sense of reality. The suggestion is made that those who prefer virtual reality over everyday reality may lose their ability to distinguish the two realities. In a sense, the perception of reality, whether it has been stimulated by television or the internet, becomes reality for the person engaged. The issue seems to be that porn on the internet may promote behaviors that are not considered healthy.

Serious Play

The obvious way that the use of communicative technologies influence nonverbal communication is shown by the amount of time that individuals engage in TV viewing or computer interaction. When people watch television, use video games, surf the net or engage others in e-mail they do so at the expense of engaging in other activities. The popular image of the couch potato and the TV as a babysitter are well known. Background music can be used while one is typing a book or running for exercise, but viewing television or using the internet are more consummate activities. In this respect, they may be forms of serious, diversionary play. Television and the internet can inform, beguile, amuse, stimulate, affect emotions and provide opportunities to pass time. Postman worries that people are amusing themselves to death(1985)

While there is a serious work side in the use of modern communicative media--for example "knowbots" may eventually take over some of the roles now performed by librarians (Lebow, 1995)-- excessive reliance upon TV or the internet for entertainment takes up time once used for direct personal contact (Bogart, 1995). The social skills that are learned in direct interaction with others are given less time to form. Perhaps parents and researchers rightfully show concern when their children spend too much uncontrolled and unsupervised time in front of the television set or on the internet.

Disinhibition

As pointed out above, modern mediating technologies can influence everyday life pervasively, filtering reality, altering ways of doing things, setting agendas. They influence self construals, the way people dress and walk, the way humans enact lines of action and they change the ways that human activity is channeled. The internet is challenging old ways of thinking about the self, of relationships and of society. Interestingly, the internet provides an opportunity for people to act out identities anonymously, playing with alternate versions of the self in psychodrama (Gackenbach, 1998). Moods and identities can be artificially created, possibly leading to disinhibition. (Herring,1996).

Framing Models for Males
It has been suggested that television influences the type of men that young men will become. Do young people, especially males, lose control of their aggressiveness and impulses under the influence of television? Television can promote negative images, such as mutants with names like Magneto, Sabretooth or Toad; yet, at the same time, television can promote positive images. The Lion King, perhaps, teaches positive values and the value of hard work(USA Today, July 14, 2000). At best, the influence of television on male behaviors seems to be mixed.

It is easy to blame television and the internet for inspiring negative behaviors, providing a simple answer to complex problems. Both technologies may influence people in very positive ways, too. As an example, the internet can be used for playful expressivity and artfulness by clever people (Danet & Aycock, 2000). Even forms of socio-drama may be performed on the internet. Very creative work can be done on the internet; very profound presentations may be found on television.

Tekkies, Junkies and Copycats

It has already been mentioned that television and the internet provide stimulation which seems to be a pervasive need among many youth. Both television and the internet are engaging, attractive communicative media. But scholars, researchers and parents are concerned that overuse may be a sign of addiction. Indeed, in a recent court case, the defense claimed that his client was addicted to the use of the internet.

Humans have always created fantasies. People grow up reading literature about villains and heroes, about lovers and lost love, and about tragedy and success. American culture is imbued with this imagination quotient. The internet provides MUDs, or multi-user dungeons, where the imagination roams. It is easy to understand why young people are attracted to them. Young people are often passionate users of the internet because it engages the imagination (Gackenbach, 1998).

Some scholars are concerned that internet users will be abusers, become addictive, engage in hidden and dangerous exchanges and so on. All kinds of information are available on the internet, including pornographic and salacious materials, which young people can access if they wish to. Of course it and other kinds of information does not merely hang out there; it gets into the ways that people think, into their conceptualizations and their social relations. Perhaps it is extreme, but some scholars believe that the influence of the internet is pervasive enough to influence how people view nature and the universe (Martin, 1995). That is, as a technology, it is transforming the social order and how people think about their social worlds.

Media and Culture: The Diaspora

The North-South Problem

A narrow band could be drawn across the Northern Hemisphere, ranging from Japan and Taiwan through the United States into Northern and Western Europe, outlining the path of technologically developed countries. The American and European film industries distribute their wares to distribution points throughout the Southern Hemisphere. With the exception of Iran, most mid-Eastern states get about 40 to 60 percent of their television programs, mostly entertainment, from the United States and Europe (Mowlana, 1996). One side effect is that English is becoming the language of choice around the globe.

Framing Third World Communications Controversies

Is it third world development or is it yet another example of the vestiges of colonialism in which powerful countries dominated less powerful countries in the third world? In 1991, UNESCO adopted a policy supporting "free, independent and pluralistic media." Freedom, rather than control, was the issue then, as it is now (Agee, Ault & Emery, 1997).

In the modern world, Japanese, European and American companies, members of the "first world" are the prime movers and shakers of the global mass media market (Turow, 1997). No longer do North Americans dominate the market as they did earlier. Members of the Third World, of course, are still dependent by and large upon the export of media and media products from the North.

Some parts of Africa, Asia, and Latin America remain outside the direct influence of these technologies. Relatively closed societies, such as China, restrict television and internet access to its citizens, although this is changing rapidly. The use of stationary satellites provides the means to broadcast television globally, potentially providing access to all members of the human race. The internet and wireless telephones are gradually being used throughout the world. A canopy of electronic activity is being put into place as suggested decades ago in a spiritual metaphor by Teilhard de Chardin, a futurist, who wrote The Phenomenon of Man.

Symbolically, the world is being hardwired. Indeed, countries with advanced military systems and space systems, use a global net of satellites for transmission. Ship to shore missiles are directed using global satellites. Traditional tribal customs are still practiced in parts of the Amazon basin, but tribal members may have short-wave radios. Traditional societies seem to be slowly blending into modern ones. How much change should be expected? How much change is desirable from the unique perspectives of various cultures? Vast technological changes are occurring in a world where most languages in oral societies have not yet been written down! Is the end to diversity in sight? (Mowlana, 1996).

Isolated groups found on the Islands of Oceania, in the Great Outback of Australia, in deeper parts of Africa and in Amazonia in South America and even in the severely cold climates of the Arctic Region are now able to have voices of their own. Indigenous people, many sheltered from modern technologies, are not indifferent to using television, the radio and the internet to establish their own voices (Browne, 1996).

Technological Overlay and Displacement

It has been suggested that the internet can promote new dimensions and relationships in cross-cultural affairs, in East-West and North-south relations. But, of course, each culture, containing rules of conduct and various display rules, will use the technology differently. For example, display rules about self-disclosure vary greatly. Chinese people and Native Americans do not engage in self-disclosure as readily as do Americans generally. Will these display rules change in a faceless internet relationship? The cultural assumptions, the display rules, the cultural ways of communicating vary widely among cultures and nations (Kincaid & Monge, 1987).

With the arrival of new technologies, perhaps sponsored by large corporations, by governments or by religious groups the patterned ways of doing things get interrupted. For example, in a story told to the author personally, Indians who lived in the back regions of India, when shown health films were puzzled because only the heads of the actors were shown in the film. There was perceptual confusion because only part of the person was shown! In a story told by the New York Times many years ago, when the United States landed a man on the moon, a leader of an African tribe said it couldn't be so because he could not see the person on the moon. In short, these stories, not meant to demean individuals, illustrate cultural assumptions and patterns which are disturbed, or overlayed, when new media become part of the environment. This overlay would seem to benefit some people and not others.

The Digital Divide

Television and the internet can provide new political arenas for formerly disempowered people. There is a politics in what is popular (Brown, 1990); in short, many women believe that television mispresents their real interests and that the medium can be used more effectively to promote egalitarianism.

The poor are often aliens in an affluent society such as the United States (Daniel, 1970). Despite the belief in the egalitarian ethos, the American occupational structure is stratified (Blau, 1967). The haves and the have-nots are on the opposite sides of a digital divide. To the extent that there is class "warfare" between the information rich and the information poor, the rich win the war (Perelman, 1998). For example, only recently has the Navajo Nation been hardwired for the internet. The President of the United States visited Shiprock, New Mexico, taking computer technology to the local Indian schools. Schools for Navajo youth now use film, videography and the computer in the classroom. Yet, many tribal members on many reservations, not only the Navajo, do not have telephones and school dropout rates are very high. The digital divide is a metaphor that suggests that females, older people, Blacks, Native Americans and most members of Third World countries, do not have the same access to the computer and related technologies as do mainstream, college educated white males. The concern is that, as in education, the gulf will negatively influence their life chances. Recent research suggests that today 50 percent of the users of the internet are femalein the United States, a dramatic change from the recent past (Rheingold, 1991). Nevertheless, concern is expressed that the gender divide and associated problems will find their way onto the net. Internet interaction is supposedly faceless; however, gender is displayed in writing patterns, in cursive style and expressive styles. Females use a variety of phrases, styles and emphases that can "give them away."

Framing the Digital Divide

People with low incomes and little education and people who are above 60 years old are less likely to have or to use a computer, although this pattern is changing.

A recent survey shows that almost all Americans under sixty years of age have used a computer; nearly 9 in 10 people say they are enthusiastic about the computer; more than two-thirds say that they need a computer at work; over half of the respondents say they are getting a multi-media system at home; it is the young people who are the most enthusiastic about using computers.

The same survey by National Public Radio suggested that Americans were concerned about many things as well. They believe that the have and have-not gap is widening, widening the racial problems; they are afraid that pornography will influence their children; and, they are afraid that their privacy will be intruded upon (National Public Radio, March 1, 2000).

Like the telephone and television, once luxuries affordable to only a few members of American society, the computer has become an essential ingredient of American society. People need it; it is not a mere toy. It extends what people can do in vital ways.

Emerging Techno-Social Patterns

An Emergent Electronic 'Folk-Culture'

The texture of society is changing from gemeinschaft, a personal community, to gesellschaft, an impersonal community (Braudel, 1972). Braudel is using German sociological concepts to depict society. The face-to-face community is personal; the mediated society is impersonal. A new pseudo-society is emerging, based not on face to face interaction, but on words and pictures located in techno-space, free of the constraints of time and place. The mediated face replaces the real living face. Virtual reality replaces everyday reality. Boundaries dissipate. Ironically, distance becomes localized.

The emergent electronic folk-culture exists at the present time. People in this community are not required to associate with a country or nationality, although they may do so if they wish. There are no political boundaries and there are few established rules and customs. The people in this community speak techno-speak, they use emoticons and special markers to let others know what they mean. Later, of course, they will see one another as technology improves, as television and the internet blend. For now, however, they are faceless citizens in an electronic community.

Returning to the Cyborg Factor

More and more, researchers are focusing on the interaction of modern communicative technologies and human biology. Television and the internet have been focused on the above, but there are offshoots of each technology, especially computer technology, that deeply influence human behaviors. Science fiction has shown the horrors of the robot-human connection in which humans are blended with steel to create a cyborg-like creature. Advances in science, in artificial intelligence and in robotics not only bring a sense of wonderment but a sense of fear about the possible negative, interactive consequences.

The Cyborg factor is imaginative, metaphorical. Indeed, the metaphor, the concept of a Cyborg has been trashed. Yet, the metaphor suggests the potentially intimate connection between humans and the machines they created. Almost daily, people are reminded of the new technological developments in medicine, engineering and science. One generation passes new technologies on to the next almost in a blur of confusion. The technological trajectory is not clearly focused, but it seems obvious that robots that can do what humans can do are forthcoming. Is the world of the born being replaced by the world of the made? Some scholars think that body, mind and machine function best when they are interactively engaged.

A Consciousness Revolution?

The half-life of technical knowledge, or the speed by which technology changes and is adapted for human use, is brief, perhaps less than five years in many bio-chemico-engineering fields. Until the 1900s, the half-life of technical knowledge was long. Today, one generation of computers, television and other advanced technologies, leads quickly to another. Moore's Law suggests that computer technology and software change several times a year, often in major ways. Much earlier, referring to the emerging technological society, where changes were slowly appearing, Jacques Ellul, an influential social theorist referred to "technological bluff", an illusionary factor that suggests that the introduction of new media bears a price; there are losses and gains, when one system overtakes another (Ellul, 1964). As it was then, it is now; there are losses and gains when one media overtakes another. Certainly there are lag effects.

At the present time, there appear to be emerging patterns in which the traditional media, such as TV, film, radio and print are blending with newer forms, such as data banks and multimedia computers; personal electronic media are becoming common, such as electronic bulletin boards, the internet and other data highways (Dizard, 1997). And this dovetailing pattern is spreading across the globe. National boundaries are disappearing; power is being redistributed; self perceptions are changing. The global information society is here. The oral, the typographic and the electronic media influence human societies in different ways, but the most powerful of these influences are found in the electronic media.(2)

Of course, the social structure influences the growth of technology as well and the social structure is changing rapidly. If the medium is the message, as McLuhan told us, the message is complex, plural and often confusing (Couch, 1984, 1996). Cyberspace is still uncharted territory with a flavor of the Wild West.

Humans languages are symbolic; they symbolize human consciousness. At present, languages are bounded. Perhaps the 7,000 or so dialects and languages of the world will become extinct, or greatly modified. The new global community has its own language, as mentioned, although even here there is variation. The Japanese, for example, sometimes use different sets of emoticons than do Americans. But, it seems clear that future iconography and symbolism will be very different from that which exists today. Many symbols, of course, are enduring, existing over long periods of time, such as religious symbols, but others are more fleeting, such as the symbol of the Nike sneaker, of Coca Cola, of Levi jeans, symbols that will be modifed, or perhaps extinct in a few decades.

Early emblematics used circles, such as breast representations; early pottery bore water marks; seals were used as signatures later; pictorial writing was used by the Mayas; and, now math and cyber symbols have emerged. Culture and consciousness are being transformed with a swiftness not seen before (Sassoon,1997).

Symbols are powerful short-cuts to meaning. They tie experiences together, they blend the past and the present and the future and create a new consciousness by the users. Perhaps humans are moving from a Global Village to a Global Mind. The new language reflects the symbolism of technology. To some, the dawning of a new age, predicted in the 80s, seems to be here (Martin, 1995). The new electronic, communicative technologies are in some sense an extension of humans, of the human body, of brains and emotions. The old mind-body dualism seems to be gone, or at least blurred; the emotions are engaged in new ways on the internet as well. The body of flesh and blood, of neurons and brains, of emotions and feelings, is now symbolized in new ways.

Does human consciousness change when technology impacts on society? Many theorists believe that the essential building block of human consciousness, of time, space, place and experience is noted by the fact that humans speak, they symbolize. The question is whether the new technologies have their own form of language.

In a discussion on the internet, Jennifer Cobb, a theologian, asked, non-humorously, whether God could be found on the internet. Certainly, the advent of bioengineering, of genetic research, of computer artificial intelligence, of imaging possibilities, of intra and extra space discoveries make changes in the symbolic texts of everyday life. Even a very practical thing, such as shopping on the net, changes the meaning of shopping. Even now it is possible to formfit clothing to the self by creating a virtual 'you' on the net (Grant, June 27, 2000).

Post-modernists believe that the fabric of modernity is being replaced by postmodernity. That is, the meaning of power, of gender, of ethnicity is being altered substantially under the influence of "freeing" technologies. Some argue that a new egalitarianism may more easily be formed under the new circumstances. The concept of the looking glass self, espoused by Cooley decades ago, bears upon this section. The essence of that concept is that people see themselves in society; through interaction they become who they are. Human identity is achieved by reflecting on the events and contexts of everyday life. People negotiate the meaning of life. In short, the social text informs them.

The present texture of American society is very different compared to what it was in earlier times. A person born 200 years ago would hardly know how to live in the present society. Is there a newly emerging consciousness? If so, what is the nature of that consciousness? Answering that question is the work of people who live in that society. Human nonverbal communication is, and will be, deeply involved in the answer to the question, as the past, the present and the future seem to be blending together.

Summary

All technologies are invented by humans; they influence human society. In particular, the modern electronic media, especially television and the internet, deeply influence and change human society. Work, play and human nonverbal interaction are deeply and profoundly affected. The contexts in which humans live are alive with new meanings under the influence of these communicative media.

Cultural and social patterns are changing as technology changes, changed under the influence of the media. The great digital divide, for example, presents a problem for ethnic groups, the aged, and for members of less technologically developed countries and societies.

The achievement of human identity is made difficult by the saturation of society by the media. Conflicting images, roles and contexts may present problems for young people. By unwisely overusing television and the internet, young people may become copycats, junkies and "tekkies", isolated from the more healthy forms of association to be found in everyday life.

The future Global Village, so long discussed, seems to be here. New symbols, the new techno-speak may become a new language competing with spoken languages which seem to be disappearing. or at least buried under master forms of language. A new consciousness may be appearing, unbound by time, place, or space, not influenced by old power arrangements, reflecting a new egalitarianism in a post-modern world. The speed of change is dramatic, compressing yesterday, today and tomorrow into an ever narrowing time-frame.

Questions for Thought and Discussion

1.   People who live in the Western world live in mediated societies. That is, film, television, radio, the internet and video have brought about significant changes in Western societies. Do you think that it is possible to live in the United States without being influenced by the media?

2.   It is suggested that different types of media influence society in different ways. Do you agree or disagree with the statement? How has the internet influenced your nonverbal communication, if at all? How has television viewing influenced your family?

3.   Considerable concern is being expressed by public officials about copycat and other negative behaviors associated with the use of television and the internet. Psychologists are concerned about addictive behaviors. What kinds of people seem to be prone to these behaviors? Why?

4.   Do you think that the media, especially television and film, promote a culture of violence? Does the internet hide behaviors that otherwise would not be exhibited?

5.   In what positive ways do you think the media influence human behavior? For example, can young people find positive role models on television and in film? If so, give examples.

Notes

1.   For example, Severin and Tankard discuss issues, models and theories dealing with perception and language, social psychology, persuasion, effects, knowledge gaps and so on. This book is but one of several that reveal how mass communication theory has evolved and is applied. The SI approach, of course, is concerned with how humans frame and make sense of media displays. See Communication Theories: Origins, Methods, and uses in the Mass Media, Fourth Edition, Werner J. Severin and James W. Tankard, Jr., Longman, 1997). For specific SI views, see Carl Couch and the Formal Sociology of Information Technology, by Ching-Ling S. Chen, pp 165-177 and The Electronic Place: From Telepresence to CoPresence, by David L. Altheide, both in Studies in Symbolic Interaction, Supplement 3, 1997, Constructing complexity: Symbolic Interaction and Social Forms, JAI Press, Inc., 1997.

2.   The concept of the Cyborg is popular and imaginative. It suggests that machines, body and mind interact in new and novel ways, even using physical implants, the machine becoming part of the body. However, the concept implies more. For example, sneakers, adapted and built for different purposes, are fit to the foot. The microwave heats food quickly, television and the radio blare, and so on. Humans and machines are knit together in interaction. Humans are Cyborgs in this sense. a relationship that is likely to enlarge. The metaphor refers to a the contexts of life in technological societies. For years, of course, images of Cyborg-like creatures have been shown on television and in comic books. They are not new. What is new are the myriads of new technologies that are designed to be compatible, even intruding within, the human body, altering human behavior.

3.   Marshall McLuhan, a Canadian scholar, was interested in how technologies, particularly communicative technologies, influence and change society. That the medium is its own message is an interesting concept that

became popular when he launched it in 1964. It means, essentially, that the influence of any particular medium like radio, for example, structures the message very differently from the telegraph or television. Ong, Innis, McLuhan and others created a large volume of literature and research dealing with how the media alter human perception and experience. In short, for McLuhan, the media altered human habits of perception. His theory has been labeled Media Determinism. See Understanding Media: The Extensions of Man, Marshall McLuhan, McGraw Hill, 1965. Years later, Carl Couch, another prominent social theorist, suggested that not only is the medium the message; it is a set of plural messages.

Suggested Readings

Carey, J. (1989). *Communication as Culture.* Boston, MA: Unwin Hyman.

Couch, C. J. (1996). *Information Technologies and Social Orders.* New York: Aldine De Gruyter.

Dizard, W. Jr. (1997). *Old Media, New Media: Mass Communications in the Information Age.* New York: Longman.

Gitlin, T. (1983). *Inside Prime Time.* New York: Pantheon Books.

McLuhan, M. (1964). *Understanding Media: The Extensions of Man.* New York: Signet Books.

Chapter 9
Symbolic Interaction and Nonverbal Communication
Making Sense of Symbolic Interaction

Chapter Overview

This chapter provides a framework for the analysis of nonverbal communication or behavior. Aspects of SI have been discussed in previous chapters, but in this section, an integrated format is provided. SI has a long history and it presents an insightful way to understand human behavior. Extensive research is being conducted from this perspective. Chapter ten is meant to blend with this chapter. In that chapter, readers are introduced to problems and given opportunities to assess their nonverbal skills.

In recent years, scholars have focused on the "return of the actor", or human agency (Tourraine, 1985). Not all research approaches include the subject as actor nor do they include the subject's interpretation and meaning of behavioral episodes. Because SI is broadly conceived, it is sometimes referred to as an approach rather than a theory (Nye & Berardo, 1966). The breadth of the approach permits the scholar to include materials from many areas of inquiry, as in this text.

SI is based on the following assumptions: that communication requires the use of shared symbols; that self and identity are constructed through interaction and that humans create society through interaction. It is the thesis of this book that the symbolization process applies to both verbal and nonverbal communication, as suggested years ago by Mead, an early founder of the approach. Humans create metaphors for the body and for body actions.

Within the general SI approach, there are many perspectives, each of which favors its own methodologies. The Chicago School of SI tends to focus on the individual in micro-interactive situations, such as dyadic events, often using ethnographic methods. This approach has been referred to as situationism. The Iowa School of SI tends to focus on existing macro-structures, such as social class, and it tends to use more quantifiable methods than do scholars from the Chicago School (Meltzer, 1972; Stryker, 1980). The differences between the schools of thought, of course, are not absolute. Recently, attempts have been made to find a middle way between the approaches (Ritzer, 1990).

This chapter focuses on aspects of the history and development of SI with the expectation that students and researchers will better understand the approach of this book. SI is a perspective that can enrich a researcher's analysis of human behavior and it can provide a way for the student to integrate studies in nonverbal communication; indeed, it can help a student frame and interpret nonverbal events. A Problems and Applications section is found in the next chapter.

The Essential Symbolic Interactionist Perspective

The SI Approach

Researchers in various disciplines employ widely ranging models or *paradigms*in their focus on human behavior. (1). A research program may be very restrictive or it may be very broad, depending on the goals of the researcher. It may be confined to the laboratory or it may focus on the natural life-worlds of the subjects.

A vocabulary associated with SI has been developed over a long period of years. Major concepts include the following.

I

the proactive part of self, enactive and agentive.

Me

the sensitive, reflexive, more durable part of the self.

Self

a combination of I and Me in Median theory, created through interactions. The self is seen as a symbolic object.

Play

social activities in which children take part but which are microcosms of later social life.

Sensemaking

the interpretive activity of creating meaning of self, others and interactive behaviors

Role-taking

the ability to put onself in the place of another; intersubjective and shared understandings are the result.

Symbol

the semantic representation of the object's in one's life, whether they are physical, psychological or social. The building blocks of meaning.

Mind

a dynamic, socially oriented, behavioral and processual entity that enables humans to make sense of behavior and act accordingly.

Agentry

the ability of humans to enact lines of action on their own behalf to adapt to social circumstances.

Joint production of meaning

refers to the fact that humans cooperate and participate in actions, creating new social relations.

Frames of reference

perceptual lenses based on personal experiences that help people interpret human behaviors.

Body Symbolization and Identity

The human body, of course, is involved in nearly all communicative episodes. Contrary to a common assumption, the body is not merely a flesh object with skin and bones. Rather, it has symbolic meaning to the owners and to others who observe it. In reflective conversations with themselves, people create meanings for their bodies as part of the way they experience the world. People evaluate their bodies, thinking of them as ugly or pretty, obese or thin. Psychological, social and cultural meanings are applied to the body. People incorporate the perceived attitudes of others in their self assessments.

The presentation of self is an everyday occurence and the body is intimately involved in these presentations. People learn how to use their bodies to influence others and to respond to them. As self presenters they are actors on a metaphorical stage; as observers of others, they are part of a metaphorical audience.

Self Identity and Personal Agentry

The self-concept is essentially the product of social interaction (Gecas, 1982). The self is inescapably a social self. People create their identities based on the influence of others; parental and peer influence are of paramount importance. Self, or identity, is expressed in verbal and nonverbal communication as a form of facework.

The self is involved in all nonverbal communication; lines of action are formed, based on the sense of self, and adapted to social circumstances. People perform multiple roles in life, such as lover, parent, child or worker. People perceive how to act appropriately to avoid personal embarrassment. They can misread situations and botch them; they can deceive others or "ham" it up. They can play simple or elaborate games to impress others, acting with considerable skill. They can also be very awkard and shy in the presence of others.

Human nonverbal communication is interactive and intersubjective; that is, there must be a sharing of meaning between participants in a nonverbal event for there to be mutual understanding. Display rules and codes are embedded in the social contexts of action; the concept of appropriateness is derived from the underlying codes. From one perspective, humans seem to play elaborate games in their interactions.

Social status influences human nonverbal behavior. For example, wealthy people born to money and to the associations and privileges of wealth, behave differently from those who are born in poverty, their codes of conduct having been derived from different contexts or standpoints in society. Their presentations of self reflect the status of the economically privileged person; the expectations of their peers reinforces their behavior (LaRossa & Reitzes, 1993). By acting as they are expected to, people of privilege consciously and unconsciously reinforce the norms of their social status, class or standing.

Powerful master themes, such as social class, power and dominance, age, gender and ethnicity are involved in, and expressed through, everyday interactions. Humans create a sense of identity, which are really the sum of the ways that they think of themselves (Longemore, 1998).

Framing the SI Nonverbal Process

In inner conversations with the self, I think about who I am, based on my perceptions created in interactions with others. After sizing up the demands and expectations of a social situation, I construct or build up meaningful lines of action that will help me adapt to the circumstances. I know that the other participants in the social event will respond. They, in joint interaction with me, will react to what I do; in turn, they will respond nonverbally. Our mutual actions are contingent one upon the other.

I make sense of the sequence of interactions and, should I meet the individuals again, I may modify my actions or continue similar actions in the future. I know that different contexts and situations call for different behaviors and by taking account of them, I expect to act appropriately, although I know that I can act however I choose to. As an actor, I usually know when my efforts to interact with others have failed or succeeded.

As mentioned above, nonverbal behaviors are usually contingent, one behavior leading to the next. Most of the time, people are involved in social events where only two or a few more people are involved. Personal forms of agentry are typical. Many times, however, people are involved in large public and mass events, such as sports or musical events. Forms of public ritual are expressed in these circumstances (Deegan, 1989). Whether they are marriage ceremonies, funerals, political conventions, or worship rituals, public events contain the social rules of engagement.

Intentional and Accidental Nonverbal Communication

Perhaps most personal lines of action are preplanned and intentional, although the planning may be fuzzy or awkward. For example, people plan to dress fashionably for job interviews to make a good impression. They may even practice the interview in a dress rehearsal at home. On the other hand, many body behaviors are adaptive actions that require little previous thought. Scratching and itching are automatic responses to the signals that are sent by the central nervous system. People usually brush their teeth while thinking about other things, such as last night's date. Even when waving goodbye, the action is nearly phatic because people do it without deep meaning or thought. Routinized behaviors are habituated and often highly skilled, the result of considerable practice. Although they require little conscious attention, they are the products of learning (Schegloff, 1986).

Whether or not people intend to communicate something with their bodies, they are always on stage, either frontstage or backstage (Goffman, 1959) in one way or another. For example, people reading books in a library may be thoroughly engrossed in what they are doing, completely unaware that others may be observing them; their posture and so on, trying to make sense of who they are, attributing meanings to them. The reader has communicated something to the observer without intending to, completely unaware. In this sense, people are always on stage. Humans cannot not communicate (Watzlawick, Beavin & Jackson, 1967). It is common for researchers to separate intentional and accidental communication, but both occur together. Even when nonverbal communication is intended, as in the wink of an eye, the targeted observer may miss the connection altogether, focusing on something else. The separation of intentional and accidental communication by researchers helps them do their researcher, but it is artificial.

There are levels and types of nonverbal communication. There may be singular episodes that are not repeated or there may be very complex, long-term behaviors. A rough form of planning is necessary to create a relationship, for example. Romantic relationships, seemingly simple, are indeed complex. They are contingent, recursive, non-linear involvements full of social and cultural meaning, deeply involving the emotions and personal schemas of the participants. Although the planning and staging of romantic involvements may be blurry, even confused, it is a necessary part of the romantic "spiral".

There are many short-term routines associated with maintaining a relationship, such as putting a piece of toast in the oven, or taking the other party out to lunch, but the overall relationships is exceptionally complex. People may "work" on nonverbal communication in self-talk or conversations with the self and never take any subsequent action. In other words, people can plan to do nothing that is observable to others, which, of course, is a often a chosen line of action. People may respond to perceived emergencies in signal response; they may also choose beforehand not to respond in the middle of the night to an accident involving others.

Nonverbal communication has been studied in various ways, from a variety of perspectives from very early times to the present. Roman orators taught their pupils how to speak, how to use their bodies in spoken presentation. Historiographers have shown us how queens and emperors lived and anthropologists have shown us cave paintings depicting nonverbal activities (Schramm, 1988). Modern psychologists, philosophers and others have pieced together new approaches to the study of communication, as any book on nonverbal communication will reveal. (Anderson, 1999; Burgoon, Buller & Woodall, 1996; Knapp & Vangelisti, 1992; Richmond & McCroskey, 1992).

As mentioned, there appears to be a return of the actor in modern research and there appears to be a new appreciation for the dependency of the spoken language upon the nonverbal "language"(Gilroy, 1996). Of course there has always been a relationship between the spoken word and the unspoken (Key, 1980), but recently there is a renewed emphasis. Everyday language rests on a nonverbal base. Children at birth rely on nonverbal means of communication, developing spoken language only later. The history of collective human growth reflects the same dependency of language upon a nonverbal base. Space, time, custom and practice; the ways that humans think about themselves and adorn themselves; and the ways they paint, use artifacts and construct buildings---all of these activities find their way into the spoken language. As Burke (1966) indicated long ago, language is symbolic action.

Master Concepts in Symbolic Interaction

Symbols

The human language is symbolic; that is, people create metaphors for their bodies and for the events in their life-worlds. Symbols are arbitraily constructed by people and they become short-cuts to meaning, used again and again (Duncan, 1968; Fontant, 1993). Symbols do not have meaning in themselves; humans attach meaning to them. For example, the Statue of Liberty is a symbol of freedom to many people; but others may find meaning in the fact that the statue is a woman. People invest meaning into objects, people and social situations. Symbols are a type of logic-in-use, passed on from one generation to the next. The white dove has symbolized peace and freedom for centuries.

Symbols may be shared publicly, but they often have private, individualized meanings. Each person uses the symbol in specially construed ways. In this book, the body and self-identity are symbolized and labeled, as are human relationships, buildings and other entities in life.

Framing Body Symbolization

Unlike lower order animals, humans have the ability to "see" their bodies, which become objects of existence. They make sense of their bodies and label them using terms such as beautiful, ugly, obese or slim. Cultural and social meanings for the body are invested in the ways that people symbolize their bodies. Peers, fellow workers and parents bring their own sets of meanings to the person who reflects upon her body.

In a media-saturated society, images are played up; individuals take note of them and use them in their own self-evaluations. People know what a female "perfect 10" is and they know what a male "hunk" is. In other parts of the world the American body index may have little meaning because people construe the shape and form of the body in very different ways. Beauty in other countries may include the perception that large busts or bottoms are attractive to men, suggesting that the perception of attractiveness is a function of evolutionary development. (Jankowiak, Hill & Donovan, 1992). The body, a corpus of flesh, is socially defined (Vlahos, 1979). Humans think of themselves as young, middle age or old, as Black, Cuban, Navajo or Chinese, as male or female. Each set of self labels is a learned, adapted perception. They are umbrella terms that help people adapt socially. Group members are conscious of an identity, although it may be loosely constructed and quite general. The labels may be applied rigidly or flexibly. But the point is, they are invented as part of the self identification process (Barot, 1999; Belenky, Clinchy, Goldbergen & Truk, 1986; Doyle, 1989; Giddens, 1991).

Symbols are somewhat stable, especially in cultures that are slow to change; they are transportable from generation to generation. Even colors have meanings that are associated with different cultures. Red, for example, is particularly important to the Chinese. The legal profession in America uses royal blue and purple colors as part of its distinctive history (Gage, 1999). Each individual attaches meaning to colors, preferring one over the other.

Signs and Icons

Signs, symbols and icons have been extensively studied by semioticians (Kim, 1996; Perinbanayagam, 1985). They believe that signs and human action are bound together. They are studied as tools that give meaning to everyday life. Symbols are a class of signs as are icons. While a sign designates something---for example, the classic smoke therefore fire process--an icon represents an entity often by bearing likeness. The CBS logo, the eye, is iconic as is the NBC Peacock. The cross is an icon for the Christian church and the Star of David is an icon for members of the Jewish faith.

The importance of signs, symbols and icons to human action can not be overestimated. Indeed, if they did not exist the normal processes in society would disappear. Traffic lights and road signs, but one simple example, regulate the flow patterns of traffic. In addition, they represent the law of the land. In short, there is a critical relationship between signs and human behaviors. People who fear spiders or snakes or other things often react in frightened ways in signal response.

Icons may be very popular, such as the image of Elvis Presley who is said to be an American icon. Each generation, of course, creates its chosen icons. There is an inherent, inseparable relationship between signs, symbols and icons. They are tools that humans use to give meaning to their worlds. Cultures symbolize gender, age, or ethnicity in many different ways.

Framing Cultural Symbols

Symbols are often unique to cultures. On the other hand, some symbols are known across cultures but given a slight twist of meaning by a particular culture. For example, in the Western world, the dragon has been symbolized as evil, part of the forces of evil. In the Eastern world, particularly in traditional China, the dragon is a symbol of joy, of dynamism and good health and fertility; it is a protector against evil.

Sand is a symbol of purity in the Middle East, used even for washing, but, in the Western world, it is often thought of as an unstable element, impermanent, as in sinking sand. The Navajo tribal people have long used sand in artwork and in religious ceremonies. Thus symbol construction varies from culture to culture (Fontant, 1993).

Society and Human Interaction

Social is socially constructed. Each routine act, each interactive routine, reinforces society, maintaining it and changing it. Born into society, people may think that it is durable and unchanging, permanent. In fact, consciously and unconsciously, humans make choices that affect society. When actions are shared by large numbers of people, as in the Cuban revolution, great changes are made in the traditional society.

Humans create tools that change society, sometimes irrevocably. Modern communicative tools, such as the internet, the computer and television, are deeply imbedded in society, dramatically altering them. In short, people enact society, sometimes through their technologies. The technologies, in turn, influence the behavior of people. It is a circular process.

Framing Human Interaction

SI scholars focus on interactive units of analysis and upon the theme of personal agentry; that is, humans are not caused to act, they act out of choice. They do, however, act in accordance with their interpretation of the demands of the situation. Their past experiences influence how they will act, but they act in the present drawing upon their past construals.

Although human behavior is patterned, it is not completely predictable. People can maintain situations, modify them, or ignore them completely. They can act alone or they can choose to join others in a joint action, even a cause. Humans, of course, are socialized in general ways. They create and maintain a sense of place, of context and situation. Feral children are not socialized and they cannot create a sense of place in an established society.

In the final analysis, society is the collective result of all human actions. Society takes on broad characteristics that distinguish it from others. One characteristic of democratic American society is that it promotes the egalitarian ethos.

Human Consciousness, Awareness and Reflexivity

The role of dreams and unconscious processes, discussed in chapter four, is now being researched extensively, as is the topic of consciousness. Although humans become conscious of their bodies very early in life (Mccoby, 1998; Morris, 1992), they are not always conscious of the processes that influence them. People are often very attentive to needs, to self and to body; on the other hand, many people seem unaware of elementary aspects of life, such as emotions. In short, there are levels of awareness. Many people are highly reflective; others seem to walk about unaware of self and others.

Mead (1934) and others have focused their attention on mind, self and society, emphasizing the fact that people construct who they are, reflect upon themselves and hold inner conversations with themselves. They create lines of action based on an assessment of self and the possibilities for action in social circumstances (Blumer, 1969; Jones, 1964; Leary, 1996). In short, they engage in a sensemaking process.

Face, Self-Presentation and Impression Management.

Self identification is a key to human growth; it is also a key to human interaction. People hold mini-theories about life, they have tacit knowledge about social matters; they have cognitive schemas that are based on their experiences from the past. Part of the self-labelling process results in a sense of self, labeled the symbolic face. People, of course, have a physical face, but the reference here is to the images that they present to others. The concept of face is psychological, social and cultural (Ting-Toomey, 1994). The so-called frozen face of the Navajo or the Korean is physical, but the underlying cultural rules and norms are symbolic, It is said that American females exhibit a politeness bias because they "wear" a smile. The physical face is invariably entertwined with the symbolic face.

Face is related to role-playing; indeed, people create a professional face, such as that of a lawyer, a doctor or a plumber. The lines they enact are usually related to the notion of face. For example, the image of the doctor is maintained by her ability to perform medical procedures and to the fact that she has medical knowledge. Her lines of action are clearly representative of the profession. When they are not, she may, in fact, suffer the consequences. Professions require that their members maintain face. All humans, of course, have a symbolic face; it gets played out in identifiable ways, a type of symbolic signature.

Dramaturgy, or the acting component of human behavior is closely associated with impression management. Goffman (1959) believed that people try to maintain face to avoid embarrassment. Jones (1964, 1990) researched how people ingratiate themselves with others. Scores of researchers have researched the deceptive practices of people in interaction. The concept of first impressions is well-known. In short, humans present themselves, manage themselves in human interaction from a variety of postures, for a variety of reasons. Impression management may be skillful or awkward. As mentioned, shy people are frequently unskilled at interaction, withdrawing from it, even finding reasons for their behaviors (Baron, 1996). Thespians are trained to act in front of audiences and they are frequently skillful in daily interactions. Actors and actresses have historically received voice training (Heinberg, 1964) stemming from the early Romans and Greeks who knew the value of vocal power and robustness. The voice is a key part of human presentation and its paralinguistic qualities "give the person away" (Mahl, 1987; Pittam, 1994). In short, humans try to perform in front of audiences, although they are differentially skilled at it. Many people, of course, are unaware that they are performing.

Situation, Context and Codes

Human behavior is always situated in time, place and space. It is situated in social context, a fact that deeply influences how human behavior is conducted (Carbaugh, 1996: Ellis, 1999). Social codes and display rules influence how people will behave. Nowhere written down, they are picked up on, caught during the socialization process. For example, young children learn not to burp in public. In this example, the parent may have directly socialized the child by giving it specific direction; on the other hand, the child may have learned how to behave indirectly, tacitly, by watching others. Either way, the implication is that the parent responds to socially imbedded codes that influence human conduct. Such codes may be pandemic, across entire cultures, or they may be shared distinctively by certain members of society. What one should do on a foxhunt to identify with other foxhunters is a very specific example of hidden codes, associated with a sport that has traditionally been part of the ways that the wealthy in Britain live. Human experience is framed by coded information. When human behavior is common to a society, it is considered normative, although it can be functional or dysfunctional. That is, not all behavior exhibited by large numbers of people are considered desirable, as in crime or hate group behaviors. People are put into prisons, a place where their freedoms are curtailed because of their negative behaviors. Prisons are total institutions that restrict and control behaviors.

Television presents framed sequences of human behavior that are recognized by the viewer. It has been suggested that television reflects human society, representing it (Altheide, 1997) and that it maintains the ongoing structural nature of society. This has been disputed by scholars, there being a wide number of research models dealing with television. However, television clearly frames human action, whatever the perspective, and it, too, must operate within contextual rules.

Sociodramas, Ceremonies and Rituals

The distinction has been made between micro behaviors, or those associated with dyads and small groups, and macro behaviors, or those associated with very large groups, even nations. The middle ground has been called the meso area where mid-size activities are conducted. Humans take part in all kinds of groups and, to a large extent, the distinctions are merely for the purposes of research. For that reason, attempts have been made to link the various emphases together (Ritzer, 1990).

All readers of this book engage in interaction with others, mostly in dyadic or small group situations. Perhaps all, however, have taken part in wider ceremonies, like marriages and funerals. Perhaps most have taken part in Labor Day national demonstrations, parades and marches. In short, humans are engaged at all levels interactively. Themes and festivals earmark societies. Disney World and the New Orleans Mardi Gras are examples in the United states. The Antiguan festival and the Brazilian Carnivale are other examples of rituals and ceremonies. Public activities like these are often celebratory (Turner, 1986), transcending the time and clime of the moment, binding people together. The Blessingway is a religious ceremony long performed by the Navajo as a way of binding them with nature. The Lion Dance of the Chinese have historically conveyed particular meaning to the members of Chinese society. In short, humans create and take part in human interaction at many levels.

The Origin and Growth of Symbolic Interactionism

Important Scholars

In this section a brief overview of Symbolic Interaction is presented. The scholars who are discussed are but a handful of those who are working in the field. Some of their work is indicated in the reference section, but their work entails much more than is presented here. This section is designed as a resource for students and faculty who are new to the field. The work of these scholars appears in the previous chapters.

SI was popularized by scholars like Blumer, Goffman, Turner and Jones, but the foundations resulted from the work of a number of philosophers, sociologists and psychologists. Early work was heavily influenced by an analysis of the pragmatics of everyday life. Humans were thought to be willful, thinking people, not mere organisms maneuvered about by various social forces. In short, the human was proactive in human affairs, making choices about the objects of their existence. The scholars under discussion lived before the turn of the century and their work continued into the mid-part of this century.

George Simmel

Simmel, thinking sociologically and interactively, observed that ideas get transformed in the social marketplace, where social reality is constructed. Ideas, formed by people, are influenced by the situation in which they find themselves. For example, a professor thinks about life differently from a bricklayer. This does not imply superior-inferior status. Today, Simmel's work is part of the field referred to as the Sociology of Knowledge.

Charles Horton Cooley

Famous for the concept of the *looking glass self*, Cooley showed how humans grow through interaction with others. Humans take up meaningful activities that become part of their self-identification. By examining possible actions that he might take, working out definitions of the situation, the person defined himself in the process. He emphasized sympathetic instropection, which eventually influenced modern symbolic interactionism.

William James

A philosopher and pragmatist, he was fascinated by the ways that humans construct meanings, believing that he could determine how people think by analyzing their social activities. That is, he thought that human activities were outgrowths of the values and thought patterns of individuals. He developed the concept of the multi-faceted self; people had as many selves as others recognized in them.

George Herbert Mead

Although he had been called the father of SI, he did not invent the term. His student, Herbert Blumer, below, invented the phrase. Mead spent his life constructing a "meaning" system involving human behavior. He distinguished between the mind and the body, but he noted that gestures produced meaning in others. The self was reflexive, meaning that people think about and interpret what is happening around them, taking account of it in inner conversations with the self. He believed that thoughts were a form of self-talk or meta-talk, to use modern terms. He thought that symbols were defined in action terms, behaviorally. People thought about the meaning of actions. Symbols were relatively stable and known to both the user and others in interaction. Gestures, for example, such as the shaking of the fist, may lead the observer to react in self-defense. The observor perceives the shaking of the fist and responds accordingly. Each party understands what shaking the fist may mean. The gesture, of course, can be misinterpreted. Mead created a philosophy of the act.

Framing the Act

Mead thought that there were stages in the production of human acts:

First, the organisms (humans) must sense a discomfort, or disequilibrium, setting up the act;

Second, the people must perceive and define their situation, which is part of the thinking process; they try to sort out what to do about something they have observed;

Third, people then act in accordance with goals they set earlier. Acts are usually future oriented; that is, humans act to create something that extends into the future.

Fourth, when the act is finished, the person can then turn to the sequence again, setting out plans for further action. He re-enters the stream of action.

In this scheme, humans make decision; they do not act because of some inner drive, force or motivation. Instead, they will to act. (See Mead, 1938 , Blumer, 1969 and Charon, 1995, for discussions about these points).

Mead knew that all people have a past, present and future. He thought that when acts were performed, consciousness was manifested. The mind and the body worked together to produce unified sets of actions, a view that ran contrary to the narrowly interpreted behaviorism of his time (2).

John Dewey

For Dewey, the thinking process included the definitions of objects that occupied a person's world. A person creates lines of action after reviewing the various alternatives available to achieve her goals.

Herbert Blumer

Perhaps more than any other person, Blumer, a student of Mead's, laid out much of the language and approach of modern Symbolic Interactionism, a phrase he is credited with coining. He popularized Mead's ideas. He believed, for example, that humans act toward things and toward others, based on the meaning that they have for them. Meaning comes from social interaction, not from within the object. Humans choose to act; they are not caused to act.

He emphasized that groups were individual collectivities working together. Eventually, group action will result in cultural and societal formations, maintenance or change. Joint actions, networks and social functions take on a character that is separate from individuals; but they do not operate automatically. Individuals must make them work. Society is continually renewed by the actions of individuals and groups.

Erving Goffman

Goffman, who wrote after the mid-part of this century, contributed the dramaturgical perspective in SI, a perspective that is important even today. He noted, as a sociologist, that people seem to follow scripts and play games in interaction. His ideas about the presentation of self and their interactive rituals formed the basis for research that continues to this day. His vocabulary is filled with words and phrases from the world of theatre, such as script, scene and actor, frontstage and backstage. In the theatre there is always an audience; in real life, the audience were the participants in interaction, each observing the other.

Goffman noted that when an individual comes into the space or presence of another person, he seeks out information about that person, ranging from the way the person dresses to the way she acts. If the actor does not know the other party, he derives cues from her behaviors, often applying untested stereotypes to that person. In this sense, the observer sees the other party giving off cues, or "shining", as he said. The idea of a symbolic face was promoted by Goffman.

He observed that humans act toward others to influence their actions; for example, an actor may want the other observing party to think and act positively toward him, so he acts to help create desirably images. A proper body orientation worked to influence the other party. Goffman believed that a person has a right to be treated in accordance with the way he presents himself, ascribing authenticity to that person. For example, a police officer wants the observer to take him seriously; otherwise, the policeman's power and authority break down. Of course, humans do not always act sincerely but they act to avoid embarrassment. Role expectations and role performances form the basis of society, as do rules, which act as frames for human action.

Victor Turner

Victor Turner's work was in anthropology. Unlike the others above, he focused mainly on ceremonial and ritualistic and public events. Therefore, in modern parlance, he focused on the meso and macro features of cultures. He was interested in how humans symbolize their worlds through their actions. He thought that ceremonies and rituals expressed the essential thoughtways, beliefs and values of a given culture. Even though celebrations appear to be fixed, personal inventiveness may occur within the framework, as in the music, the choreography or costumry of a celebratory event. People can stylize dramatic presentations.

Although there is an individual interface in ceremonies and rituals, they transcend the everyday life of individuals, drawing on root metaphors, archetypes, paradigms and models for action. Through rituals humans can transfer cultural meanings and tradition from one generation to the next. Indeed, Turner believed that members of traditional cultures have a need to celebrate in communal activities. Birth, puberty, marriage, season activities, religious holidays and other events are marked by special kinds of dress, dance and food. There may be body painting, the wearing of masks and the carrying of spears. Often the sacred or holy are celebrated with rituals that are very different from those found in desacralized, secular societies. By celebrating, members of traditional societies re-affirm their traditional valules, their moral and esthetic approaches to life.

Turner stated that symbols were polysemic; that is, symbols may be interpreted in many ways, arbitrarily. The Raven, the totem pole, masks, dances and other performances have symbolic meaning for those who perform them. Symbols may be dense with meaning, acting like the tip of an iceberg, or they may be shallow. The entire human sensorium may be employed in rituals and ceremonies, revealing the deeper symbolic meanings of culture.

Edward Jones

The work of Jones stemmed from Social Psychology. He was keenly interested in impression management and the self-presentation process. He was particularly interested in how people ingratiate themselves with others, often employing deceitful practices or other techniques to earn attention and acceptability in others.

Howard Becker

His academic writing was multi-sided, his interest expressed in how people do research, especially in the preparation stages, and how they employ methodologies. His topic ranged from social deviance to cultural and humanistic aspects of SI. Student behaviors on campuses were a particular interest.

Kenneth Burke

Unlike the others mentioned above, Burke worked essentially in a literary field. He noted that language was a form of symbolic action and he employed the theatrical pentad in his work. He described how the metaphors of scene, act, script, stage and method influenced human communication. He taught that games and sociodrama are important modes of lie. Social acts, he said, were created by human agents engaging in significant moves which elicit responses from others. These moves and acts lead to symbolization and meaning, to language and grammar. Human cultures serve as rough drafts for action, which is found in nonverbal communication. Self actions, he stressed, were processual and ongoing, not static.

Carl Couch

In an attempt to blend the macro and micro versions of SI, Couch drew upon the new technologies of the electronic age to develop a new type of social science, from the ground up. He thought that the dyad was the most elementary unit of analysis and tried to show how two actors worked together to perform coordinated actions. He wanted to perform science for the betterment of mankind, hoping to improve human lives.

Charles K. Warriner

His conceptualization of the "stable-man" point of view as contrasted with the "emergent-human' point of view, marked his work. Warriner put emphasis upon the freedom of the individual to choose. He thought that the physicalist model of thought in science reduced human freedom and could not account for the ways that people act. Humans shape society; they do not conform to it. Humans and societies are engaged symbolically and dynamically.

Recent Compatible Research

Derek Layder

Concerned with the structure of society, which he believes is created by everyday persons as they act toward self and others, he believes that the major themes, such as social class, power and ethnicity are not separable from indivduals. Individuals act in concert with ongoing social structures. Structures provide the norms and rules that humans use as they daily routines.

Society provides opportunity for recreation, creativity, constraint and identity formation. These are ties between the individual and the social structure. Structural elements exist in society but are enacted and reinforced by individual actors who are acting on their own behalf, unwittingly maintaining the social structures.

Donal Carbaugh

Like others above, Carbaugh focuses on the social construction of the self in a Meadian sense. It is a consequence of interactive life. Humans are situated in society, a fact that influences their communicative activities.

Debra Grodin and Thomas A. Rindlof

These editors organized a sizable body of literature that deals with how the human self is constructed in a mediated world, essentially the world of television. Emphasizing the multi-vocality of how self is expressed, they show how self-image is a major aspect in the evaluation of self-identity.

Mary Jo Deegan

Deegan extends the work of Turner, whose main interest was in traditional cultures. Deegan's interest is in contemporary cultures. She applies Turner's theories with modification to American life. Emphasizing the core codes found in American life, she attempts to show how the cults of time, bureaucratization, sexism and capitalism prevail and how each contains a set of rules that influence human conduct in modern society. For example, people go to work on time and they encounter sexism in everyday life in joint encounters with others. Macro themes, such as sporting events and modern rituals and displays form the fabric of modern American society, influencing the choices that people make and how they present themselves.

Anthony Giddens

Concerned with the separation of social structure from individual human action and behavior, Giddens wants to find ways to tie everyday behavior into the prevailing social structures, treating them as fluid and dynamic entities, not causative. He wants researchers to depart from using laboratory models, to turn to more humanistic models in which human agency and meaning can be taken into account. Participation by the subject in the research is an important, often overlooked feature of good research.

Giddens says that there is a tie between human habitus, creativity and constraint, self-identity and society, and between individual agency and social structures. Humans create structures; they recreate them as well.

Norman Denzin

Primarily interested in naturalistic, non-laboratory research, Denzin promoted the field of Symbolic Interactionism by editing the series, Studies in Symbolic Interaction, helping to found a related society. His research focuses primarily on the self, on the family and socialization processes. Deeply interested in how scholars interpret behavior, he produced a number of books and articles focusing on qualitative research.

Robert Prus

Interested in interaction in everyday life, Prus draws heavily upon the use of ethnographic methodologies to study ventures in everyday life, such as salesmanship, prostitution and gambling. All human activities are products of human interaction. His basic interest is to pragmatize the social sciences.

Julia T. Wood

Her first work in SI dealt with human communication. Her more recent work has focused on human identity, gendered lives, civility in everyday life and social mosaics. Relational communication, or interpersonal communication, are important aspects of her work.

Compatible Approaches and Orientations

Joint Activity

Jerome Bruner and others have focused on joint or mutual knowledge and action. Humans bring to relationships verbal and nonverbal knowledge, which they share jointly. A child, watching her mother, takes part nonverbally in jointly attentive activities, such as mutual smiling, grasping and pointing. The mother and child sharing are intersubjective partners, as are other people who jointly act together. Reciprocity is based on correctly perceived intentions.

Action Theory

Human actions are always open to identification, whether an individual is identifying his own action or those of others. Identification is necessary so that people can understand one another. People hold implicit theories about how their actions will be received or understood. All plans have antecedent conditions; that is, one must have some kind of prior reason in order to act. Plans, images, scripts, intentions and goals arise from implicit theories. From this view, human behavior is what people think it is.

A common sense psychology pervades the way that people decide the meanings behind human activities; they seem to have a sense of the subconscious, of motivating factors and so on. In identifying meanings of acts, observers must make a connection, decide the intent, reflect upon it and attribute meaning to it. The stream of bodily action is accompanied by a stream of verbal action.

Mediated Self Theory

Modern American society is heavily saturated by the media, principally television and the internet. The effect of mediation upon human identity is the thrust of this work. Gergen, for example, is concerned that the media present the young with incoherent, sometimes destabilizing materials that can lead to identity confusion.

Semiotics

Semiotics is the study of meaning as expressed in signs, the smallest element of meaning. A symbol is a type of sign. Codes are sets of signs and rules. Assumptions about signs and codes lead to human action. Two people, from similar backgrounds, share in coded meanings. Anything can be a sign. For example, people see the behavior of others as signs. Codes are included in all human affairs, from science to art, from meditation to action. Symbols, types of signs, are polysemic; that is, they can be interpreted in multiple ways.

Impression Management

Theories, implicit and explicit, guide everyday human behavior. Whether people are driving their cars, playing golf or making love, they are engaged in the act of impression management. The presence of other people presents a possible stage of action. People act before others to influence them or to enhance their own self-images. The presentation of self is nearly always designed to achieve a goal.

Not all people are skilled at impression management, or self-presentation. Shy people, as mentioned, appear to lack the social skills to manage themselves well. Pathological conditions, of course, intrude upon the ability to present oneself successfully. Most people, however, can intentionally improve their abilities at impression management.

Ethology

Ethologists are usually persuaded by evolutionary theory; they may study humans or they may study lower order animals, such as primates. The behavior of animals can shed light on human behavior, as many ethologists have shown. At the same time, scientific ethology can uncover some of the mysteries of animal behaviors. They have shown, for example, that dolphins and chimps appear to have a sense of self, recognizing themselves in mirrors. They have shown that chimps can learn and use a nonverbal 'language' and they can use tools for their own purposes. Some researchers suggest that the differences between human behaviors and chimp behaviors is a matter of degree rather than kind, an issue that has been in the forefront of research for many years.

Postmodernism

Postmodernist research and writers bring a special perspective to the meaning of symbolic life. They note that the social and cultural milieu found in modern, technologically advanced cultures is very different from that of industrial, or modern society. Humans, they say, now live in a post-modern age in which the authority structures are changing and the texts, or contexts of experience, are being decidedly modified. Relationships of power and dominance, of social class and ethnicity, of aging and gender, are being redefined. Standpoint and co-cultures are two important terms related to self-identification processes. In a broad sense, women and people of color are achieving new vocalities, having new choices and the possibilities of redefinition of the circumstances in which they find themselves. The authority of institutions is diminishing, ushering in new possibilities for self-identification. New information technologies are leading to new ways to organize society. New social texts are being formed. Nonverbal communication will be influenced accordingly.

Symbolic Interaction: Science and Methodologies

SI and Science

SI scholars and researchers follow several scientific principles:

Framing Scientific Principles

The central principle is that researchers can understand human action best when they are able to access the thinking of their subjects. Researchers do work in naturally occurring situations.

SI researchers tend to resist the use of causal variables because their focus is upon human agentry, rather than on the causes of human behavior.

The careful description of human action is basic to good science.

If an SI researcher had to choose between the use of a living-subjects approach versus a predictive hypothesis-testing model, she would probably favor the use of real-life observations, using surveys and questionnaires and other ethnographic tools. The multiple methods approach, however, enables SI scholars to combine many research methods, including laboratory approaches, in their work(3).

Quantitative Methods

The language of quantitative study has been developed over a long period of time. Terms such as parsimony, precision, orderliness, logic and numeric representation are imbedded in the research. Computer simulations and projections are often used. Theory, hypothesis and method are rigorously pursued. The quantitative approach is abstract and extractive; that is, it is not necessary for researchers to work in the field or to use participative means to do their research, although this is a possibility.

In much quantitative work, rats and pigeons are used. In communication studies, it is common to use freshman or sophomore subjects, who often get credit for their participation in the research. The experimenter is usually interested in determining differences between groups by using instruments or situations to which the students have responded. The idea of "real life" is simulated or implied. Everyday contexts are usually ignored in the laboratory in an effort to control the variables. By eliminating confounding and interacting variables, the researcher can turn out highly precise, well measured findings which can be compared quite easily to other studies, or to replicate them.

Framing Quantitative Approaches

There are varieties of quantitative approaches, but they share a common physical model taken from the natural sciences, usually emphasizing control of variables, well defined procedures, hypotheses, methodologies and countable outcomes. Usually performed in the lab, away from confounding influences, they tend to focus on small pieces of human behavior, using simple or elaborate statistical and mathematical procedures. Aggregates of data are compiled in such a way that they can be verified by other researchers in replicating the studies. The actor, subject or participant in the study is usually represented by numbers or categories. An issue of extrapolation to real life situations is often apparent.

Qualitative Methods

Human nonverbal communication is complex and dynamic; it includes human choice, action and sensemaking. It is a symbolic process. The actors involved in nonverbal communication act as their own agents; they interpret the behaviors of others. In a sense, humans create their own destinies.

It is believed by many that nonverbal communication is best studied where it occurs, in natural settings. Ethnographic and survey methods are often used. These tools lend themselves to how people define and negotiate their behaviors and how they take up roles in interaction. Although qualitative methods are desirable, the multiple methods approach enables researchers to triangulate or gain many measurements focused on the same phenomenon.

While a quantitative approach takes account of the amount of something, qualitative approaches try to take account of the subjective meaning of something, the how, where and why of something (Dabbs, 1982).

Framing Qualitative Approaches

Qualitative methods focus on the real life-worlds of individuals, often taking into account the meanings that the study has for them. Humans are "soaked" in culture (Ellen, 1984) and it is important to deal with the subject's emotions, motivations, symbols and their meanings to participants. Empathy is required for the researcher to produce good research (Berg, 1989). Popular qualitative techniques may include participant observation, interviewing, experiment in natural settings, photographic techniques, historical analysis, text analysis, sociometry and sociodrama, and ethnomethodological and non-intrusive measures.

A multiple methods approach adds strength to qualitative studies. A kind of triangle of error can be established when methods produce differences in outcomes. SI researchers interested in qualitative research do not have to ignore formal research in the laboratory; the can combine it with their research.

Ethnography

Ethnographic methods are qualitative and they enjoy a special status among many researchers. They allow the local logics of participants to be used, the moments in the lives of people (Boden, 1990). These methodologies permit the researcher to analyze the world as it happens. One of the problems of ethnographic research is that the experimenter needs to find ways to become invisible to the participants.

Ethnomethodologists tend to focus on the rationality of human action, suggesting that humans act purposively most of the time, although irrationality can be involved. Because people, or subjects, use local logic in their course of behaving, it is the job of the researcher to determine what that logic is, to try to determine what the meaning of an event is for that person. It is apparent that studies that focus on the overarching structure of society, but not on the individual, tend to lose sight of the local logic.

Thus ethnomethodologists tend to focus on the lived experiences of individuals, Humans behave locally but they are also caught up in, and respond to, pre-existing behaviors, habits, values, orientations and the basic 'givens; of society. Lines of action, therefore, are constructed in contexts. As mentioned, the researcher can use multiple methods ranging from questionnaires to films, oral history and content analysis.

Summary

Symbolic Interactionism, or SI, is an approach to the study of nonverbal communication that enjoys a long history, its use continuing to this day. William James and George Herbert Mead formed the basic thrust of the approach, but it was given special impetus by Herbert Blumer, Erving Goffman, Victor Turner and Edward Jones, each of whom popularized the approach.

The use of the human body, the processes of identity formation and the study of human interaction are important features of SI. Contemporary researchers often focus on "live" behavior, using qualitative methods to help them understand the meaning of nonverbal actions. People present themselves and manage themselves, often in small groups but often in collective events as well. Humans vary considerably in their abilities to present themselves in social situations.

Questions for Thought and Discussion

1.   SI uses the dramatic metaphor referred to as dramaturgy. Does this appear to be a useful approach to describe human behaviors? Do you 'present' yourself to others in everyday affairs? If so, how? If not, why not?

2.   How important is an understanding of nonverbal communication to you? Is it more important than spoken communication?

3.   Polysemia is a word used in this text to indicate that people may have different interpretations of the same behavioral event. How would you explain this process? Why does it occur? Does your college experience have anything to do with it?

4.   According to general semantics, "the word is not the thing". What does this phrase mean to you? Many times people act as though words were 'real'; they reify terms. Can you give an example of this labelling activity?

5.   The social contexts of human behavior are powerful influences. Can you show how context influences human behavior? Are there other influences on behavior besides context?

Notes

1.   Theories are guides to research, providing principles and ways of looking at behavior, sorting out what is important to the research. Theories help in the synthesis of data. The SI approach has been used in this text but other prominent approaches are useful, too. For example, each of the following can be applied to nonverbal communication: Exchange theory, transaction analysis, cognitive theory, information theory, balance theory, transpersonal theory, functionalist theory and a wide variety of other theories and models. Readers might consult the book by Kovacic in the reference section. Others from the SI persuasion have been noted throughout the text.

2.   As mentioned earlier, Mead was reacting to the fact that philosophy and psychology in his time were heavily influenced by positivism, a background that reduced the emphasis upon human free will. Mead wished to restore the human mind and will to human behavior in contrast to the behavioral approach taken by Watson and others. Tourraine and others emphasize the fact that the notion of agentry is returning to research. There is a return of the actor.

3.   Representative samples of SI research may be found in Charon's book, Symbolic Interactionism, pp 209-230. Gary Alan Fine, in Symbolic Interactinism in the Post Blumerian Age, pp 117-157, discusses research about ethnity, identity, role theory, gender, the family, society and a variety of other topics. The series, Studies in Symbolic Interaction, edited by Norman K. Denzin continues. The 1997 volume includes topics about romance, technology, emotions, notoriety, accounts and negotiation and others. Herbert Blumer, Symbolic Interactionism: Perspective and Method discusses issues and methodologies. The reference section includes a variety of books devoted to research topics.

Suggested Readings

Berg, B. L. (1995) Qualitative Research Methods for the Social Sciences. Boston, MA: Allyn and Bacon.

Blumer, H. (1969). Symbolic Interactionism: Perspective and Method. Englewood Cliffs, NJ: Prentice-Hall, Inc.

Deegan, M. J. (1989). American Ritual Dramas: Social Rules and Cultural Meanings. Westport, CT: Greenwood Press.

Meltzer, B. N.(1972). Symbolic Interactionism: Genesis, Varieties and Criticism. London: Routledge, Kegan and Paul.

Prus, R. C. (1996). Symbolic Interaction and Ethnographic Research: Intersubjectivity and the Study of Human Lived Experience. Albany, NY: State University of New York Press.

Chapter 10
Interpreting Nonverbal Communication: Problems, Possibilities and Applications
Making Final Sense of Nonverbal Communication

Chapter Overview

People want to know things about life, about themselves and about others. They try to make sense of events in their lives. People who are not trained in formal science draw upon their own sense of things, their personalized logic-in-use rooted in their experiences. Scientists, of course, are everyday people too, but in their research they use appropriate techniques and models to guide them in their research.

Everyday persons are heavily influenced to think along lines of normalcy; that is, they do as their parents did, or they yield to the authority of experts. People find themselves in various stages and levels of growth and experience, both in the world of science and in the practical world. The living of professional and daily life is a very uneven process. Interpretations of the the behaviors of self and others is a highly variable process. Not infrequently people are confused about their identities and their relationships.

In this chapter problems that confront researchers and everyday citizens are delineated. In addition, a section that deals with applications provides tools for self-analysis to assist the everyday traveler in life. These applications focus on the topics found in each chapter. They serve as tools or pointers for thoughtful people. Throughout the entire text, the Symbolic Interactionist view has been taken; it provides a way of integrating both research and everyday life experiences. It is a subject-oriented, practical approach that can help a person clarify the meaning of nonverbal events in her or his life.

Practical Issues and Problems

In a very general sense, the chapters in this book have led to this chapter which is focused on practical matters that influence how a person will understand self, others and human interactions. In many ways, the ideas expressed here are distillations of the content of the previous chapters, presented in practical and useful ways. Issues that are important to both researchers and student readers are discussed.

The Sensemaking Process

Sensemaking is a symbolic interpretive process. All people, whether young or old, try to find meaning in life, to make sense of it. People often say that they are using common sense when they interpret an event; however, in this book, common sense and individual sensemaking are separate processes. People may think in common about life experiences such that an intersubjective knowledge base is built up, a knowledge that people say is common sense. Unfortunately, often that which is referred to as common sense is stereotypical and cliche-ridden. But, sensemaking, as used in this text, refers to a critical, evidence-based, interpretive process that is rooted in the private experiences of individuals. True, the subjective-interpretive views of people are influenced collectively by culture, gender, ethnicity, class, age, education and exposure to the media, but in the final analysis each individual must come to terms with the meaning of any event or activity based on his level of understanding.

Skill and Levels of Awareness

Humans do not arrive from the womb fully packaged, ready to go in life. They emerge from the womb with an innocent but forceful scream. Later, they must learn to interpret behaviors, to enact strategies and lines of action and to present themselves in interaction, or risk being socially isolated. People approach life from various perspectives and levels of understanding because their perspective on life has been sculpted and scripted by their experiences. World travelers have distinctively different perspectives compared to people who have led restricted lives. It seems to be the case that people experience their lives horizontally and vertically. That is, they move about horizontally in a physical sense but they interpret experiences somewhat vertically, at various levels of understanding.

It is possible to go through life mindlessly, blind to self and blind to others, shutting out the possibility for new experiences. When there is little awareness, people give in to what is easy or convenient; they may see things in black and white with nothing in between or they may focus on details and miss the wider picture. That is, they may generalize from a single point, painting a wide picture from little evidence. What is promoted in this book is a kind of sophisticated awareness, a special attentiveness. The SI approach can be used to enrich a person's understanding of nonverbal communication.

Situation and Standpoint

Related to the above and discussed in chapter two, standpoint in life provides both opportunities and constraints. For example, many people have never seen an opera; many others have never seen a football game. The situation or place, the neighborhoods of experience, are "cocoon-like". They help people define who they are, but they restrict experiences in the outside world. People are influenced by the behaviors of place, by the habits of the residents of that place, affecting their perceptions of the social world. Human behavior is constrained, not totally free.

To be educated, presumably, is to be led out, to gain access to new experiences that widen one's social world. The student who reads this book--or any other book that is new to her-- may or may not agree with the materials and the ideas discussed but she will probably be introduced to a new way of viewing the nonverbal social world, possibly enriching her life.

Perceptual Distortion and Polysemia

Inner conversations with the self, or self-talk, are built upon the stuff of interaction, of perceptions of others, of events and self. Perceptions, of course, are heavily influenced by private experiences, which can distort them. For example, it is not uncommon for males and females to distrust one another if both have had prior negative experiences in other relationships. They may unwittingly bring the negative baggage from old relationships into the present one. In a sense, they may fulfill their own built-in prophecies merely by bringing old perceptions into new situations.

First impressions may be built on false perceptions. Age, biology, gender and ethnic background influence perceptions, which in turn, lead to expectations, each of which may be grounded falsely. As mentioned, White Americans may fear going into a Black American neighborhood, or vice versa, because of their learned perceptions. The implication is that fear underlies the perceptions. The resulting interpretation is closed, shutting off possible positive relationships. Interethnic problems may be created by early closure. What is proposed is an open, empathic and polysemic interpretation of black-white relations. *Polysemic* meanings are alternative constructions. Any singular event may have multiple alternative meanings. Gestures, events and circumstances are potentially polysemic in nature.

Early Closure

As noted by Goffman, when people meet other people they seek out information about them trying to get cues about their identities in an effort to make sense of their presence. When people are uncertain or lack important relevant information about others, the results are usually biased or distorted because the interpreters close out new, important information and substitute something that is convenient. A partial solution to the early closure problem is to practice looking for new evidence, to remain open and flexible.

Mindfulness and Mindlessness

Humans do not always attend to themselves, to others or to interactive events. People may not notice or distinguish how people look from one day to the next. What they do not notice in others, they may not notice in themselves. This has been described as mindlessness. On the other hand, people who are mindful pay attention to details, to fine nuances in behaviors, to signs, signals and symbols that they encounter in daily life. Such people can detect the meanings of the actions of others because they pay attention to them. Mindfulness and attentiveness, of course, are learned behaviors.

Sensory Thresholds

The senses provide information to their owners. The body provides feedback. Taste, touch, sight, hearing and smelling are so basic to human experience that their importance is often overlooked. Perhaps most people think of the senses as fixed entities, as having unvarying thresholds. However, the chemical, touch and other senses vary in their importance by culture and by experience. It is true that neonates make a pucker face when they taste something sour, but this is not to say that they will dislike sour tastes later on. Sensate knowledge is learned, and preferences are based on experiences. It is possible to improve the awareness and performances of the senses in nonverbal communication, just as one can learn to paint or play the piano.

Intersubjectivity and Individuality

Human nonverbal communication could not exist if intersubjectivity did not exist. People share perceptions, attitudes, behaviors, patterns of thinking, symbols, beliefs about the body and so on. They jointly produce behaviors and meanings. Yet, each person experiences life individually. Two people may share experiences but differ in how they interpret them. In short, there are pieces of experience known to self, not known to others. Each individual has a private store of knowledge that is tacit and unexposed. This point is particularly important in a society that is heavily influenced by the media, by advertisements or by institutions. One size does not fit all.

The Emotions-Rationality Dilemma

Research focuses on the relationship of the emotions to cognitive activity. EQ, the emotional quotient, and IQ, the intelligence quotient, have been discussed as separate activities. The SI approach emphasizes rationality, suggesting that humans make sense of themselves, of others and of interactive events, using rational thought processes. Planning involves rationality; the interpretive process is rational. As mentioned, in very early civilization, it was thought that the seat of reasoning was in the heart. Now we know that the brain and the mind produce rationality.

But humans are not rational robots. Researchers know also that emotions are associated with ideas. For example, when people talk about the American flag, they are influenced by emotions and thought together. Emotional areas of the brain fire up even as the cognitive areas fire up when discussing emotion-laden topics.

In everyday practice, people may be overwhelmed by emotional feelings; yet, in time, they can think through the issues involved. Displaced anger is the result of the failure to express emotional anger at the right target. People often displace their emotional anger by getting angry at someone who does not deserve it. The displacement of anger seems to be a major problem in the United States. People can learn about their emotions and how to use them just as they learn how to count or read.

Cultural Filtration

Foreign service officers are trained to work in various cultural environments. Through training, they learn how to avoid cultural traps, stereotypical thinking and social blunders. They learn how a specific culture filters daily reality. Different cultures have different display rules, which affect the meaning and interpretation of nonverbal communication. Symbols are variously important from culture to culture as are emblems and gestures. As mentioned, it is considered rude to use the forefinger to point in the Navajo tradition or to show the sole of the foot in some Eastern countries. Road rage, of course, is rude behavior, a sign that people can not manage their emotions.

It is said that Americans have hegemonic attitudes, meaning that they exhibit ethnocentric tendencies; but the same problem occurs in other cultures, as in China, which historically has thought of itself as the center of the world. The point is, of course, that openness and acceptance of others from different cultures is important to healthy, growth-oriented intercultural relationships. These kinds of relationships, however, are achieved only through careful study and understanding. The stereotypical ugly American phenomenon can be a thing of the past.

Stereotypes, Stigmas and Over-Generalizations

When humans do not understand the nonverbal behavior of others, they may stigmatize it. Gender, age and ethnicity are often stigmatized, usually by name-calling. Stigmatizing is a way of making strangers of other people. The ability to make friends or to respect others can be promoted by learning how to listen empathically, identifying with others. Listening is a proactive process, a behavior that is part of the nonverbal reportoire of skillful persons.

Leveled Expectations

In a society heavily influenced by the mass media there is a leveling process, sometimes referred to pejoratively as "dumbing down", a lowering of literacy, a lowering of expectations. Unless programs are produced for a sophisticated audiences, the media aim their messages to a mass audience, trying to reach as many people as possible. The effect may be that the "behavioral bar" is lowered. Pop culture, properly understood, is a rich source of sociodrama; on the other hand, much popular culture is aimed at undiscriminating audiences, such that many Americans are influenced, at least in part, by the consequent leveling of expectations. The symbolic interactionist approach as expressed in this text promotes a critical examination of the products of the mass media with the goal of enriching the participant in popular culture.

Professional Issues and Problems

The Living Subjects Approach: Life as it is Lived

SI, in the main, calls for a living-subjects approach to research; how this is done varies considerably from researcher to researcher. Two broad streams, the situationist and the structuralist, or the Chicago School and the Iowa School, are found within SI and they often use different methodologies. Recent attempts to blend these perceived polar opposites have been suggested.

As mentioned, social scientists usually use quantitative, laboratory-type experimentation in which the numbering and coding of subjects and variables is important, or they follow a real-life approach that requires the researcher to get immersed in the subjective worlds of the participants. In SI research one can combine both types; the process of triangulation enables the living-subjects researcher to use the results of laboratory experiments, as part of the total package of methodologies. Indeed, a multiple methods approach is preferred.

Choosing Methodologies: Multiple Methodologies

SI researchers encourage a multiple methods approach to research. See the Chapter Nine methods section. Although "structural" SI researchers may tend to use surveys, field studies, lab studies, or computer simulations and 'situationists' tend to use observational, participant based observations, in general, a multiple methods approach, or triangular approach, seems best fitted to the study of nonverbal communication. Unfortunately, scholars, trained in one approach, may not experiment with others. Cross-fertilization seems to be necessary.

Stereotypes Used in Research

Scientific research is designed to get at the "truth", at least the truth in relation to a theory or hypothesis. The subject and direction that research will take varies by tradition, by funding, by the interests of the researcher and so on. As researchers know, good research is subjected to a criticism of the content and methodologies used and to replication by other scholars.

Research about naturalistic, everyday behavior is necessarily tuned in to the flow of observed behaviors, to the ways that people think and act. But, unfortunately, human behaviors are occasionally stereotyped, even by competent researchers. The stereotype may creep into a research paradigm. For example, popular stereotypes related to the "man-thing" or the "woman-thing" abound. As mentioned, scholars have shown by meta-analysis that males and females tend to be more similar in their behaviors than they are different. What is stereotypical? What is not?

The Verbal-Nonverbal Interface

The differences between the use of the spoken word and nonverbal behavior may be characterized as the difference between doing and communicating about doing. Which precedes which? Are nonverbal processes separable from verbal processes? A number of textbooks suggest that there are crucial differences. For example, it is believed that nonverbal communication is continuous, while verbal communication is discontinuous. One is analogic; the other is digital. In this book, the emphasis is placed on the interpretive process that is necessary to understand both verbal and nonverbal behaviors.

Framing Hand Movements and Language

That language evolved from gestures is an old theory that is gaining credence once again due partly to research from brain imaging studies. According to this present research, human ancestors had abilities to process general hand movements, such as grasping or picking, that themselves have grammatical structures. That is, they contain an agent, an action and an object as when a monkey (self as agent) grabs (action) a piece of food (object). This theory suggests that the ability to process language grew out of the ability to use hand signals and other nonverbal activities. Present day nonhuman primates exhibit some of these nonverbal behaviors. In short, human ancestors developed a mechanism for observing another's actions and comprehending at an abstract level the meaning of those actions.

Broca's area in the brain is linked not only to language processing but to hand and mouth movements. Broca's area is active during lip-reading. Researchers found activation in Broca's areas when people observed manual actions. There appears to be a connection between doing and communicating about doing (Azar, Nov 2000).

Gestures do not exist apart from the reasoning process; their use is learned as is language although their use may originate from and activate different parts of the brain than does vocalized language. Babies learn language only after they have sensed and explored the world nonverbally. Mead suggested something like this, his concept of the use of gestures being a basic starting point for social interaction. Recent researchers have argued that there is an inherent grammatical pattern in primate manual actions, which in humans, seems to link language use and nonverbal actions together. Speech, in this sense, is an articulation associated with and, perhaps dependent upon, the human gestural system.

As research about the relationship of nonverbal and verbal communication continues it may be most productive to study cognitive language skills in coordination with body language skills. There is an interdependence of hand and brain functions just as there is an interdependence of verbal languaging and brain functions. Further research is needed to establish the relationship of nonverbal communication to languaging processes. (Arbib & Rizzolatti, 1997; Armstrong, 1999;Armstrong, Stokoe & Wilcox,1995).

Nonverbal Communication Versus Nonverbal Behavior

Many texts make distinctions between the concept of human behavior and nonverbal communication. Distinctions are made on several levels, mostly based on the idea of the intentionality of the subject or actor. This book emphasizes the fact that nonverbal behavior and nonverbal communication are the same thing. Perhaps it would be best to speak of behavioral communication as mentioned in the preface. This assumption is not idle speculation. Intentional or not, body communication is a result of the fact that the body is always on stage, in view of the audience or observers. Instead of assuming that nonverbal communication exists only when people intend to communicate, it makes more sense to include unintended communication as well, making the appropriate distinctions.

Research and Applications

There are consultants who claim expertise in the selection of jury members based on their appearances and behaviors. Of course there have always been theatre coaches. In short, there are people who claim expertise in interpreting nonverbal communication. They learned their craft through experience. It is suggested that universities and colleges should include the study of nonverbal communication in their skills programs in English, Mathematics or Public Speaking. Nonverbal skills are critical to success in everyday life. See the notes for research dealing with applications.

Tools for Self Assessment and Skill Building

Overview

Humans vary in their abilities to interpret human behavior, as noted above. All people are immersed in and deeply influenced by psychological, social and cultural processes, by gender, ethnicity and aging. The media, of course, saturate American society; its influence is profound.

Individuals may be very aware of the hidden, inner dynamics that influence behaviors; or, they may be relatively unable to ferret out the nature of these processes. Some individuals are able to think critically, to investigate human affairs with some sophistication; others, may pay little attention to anything but surface matters, having little cognitive complexity. Some individuals lead lives of inquiry, familiar with the arts, philosophy and science; others, have barely started on the road to emotional and cognitive growth. This section brings together various tools to help people assess their status, aiming at the middle, so to speak.

The Investigative Mode

People monitor life's events, some very closely while others appear to blur "reality", paying little acute attention to social phenomena. The investigative, reflective mode enables people to fine tune their experiences, to explain to themselves and others what seems to be happening. The expectation is that people will benefit from this skilled activity.

Framing Interpretation and Inquiry

Erving Goffman, who formulated the dramaturgical method in Symbolic Interactionism, was said to have spent a great deal of time quietly observing human behaviors, perhaps by sitting in the corner in a coffee shop observing from a distance, studying human behaviors. He believed that the key to an understanding of society lay in the interpretation of everyday behaviors. For him, as it was for Blumer, everyday behavior was the foundation of society. It is no surprise, therefore, that Goffman found meaning in everyday events that others were inclined to dismiss as merely familiar and routine. He unmasked familiar objects and events, which others ignored or dismissed. The routine, for him, was a rich source of meaning.

As another example, a Harvard professor, attuned to the investigate mode, unmasks hidden meanings of artifacts that he finds in everyday life. He is able to show how past behaviors are imbedded in artifacts. Railroad terminals, buildings and sidewalks are keys to the past. He knows that materials may have been used in one time period but not in another; he knows that humans valued certain architectural forms in one time period but not in another. Like an archaeologist or a forensic expert, he is sophisticated about human inventiveness and how it is displayed. His students, of course, are learning how to 'read' materials that passersby ignore, even though they use them or see them everyday (Wolkomir & Wolkomir, April, 2000). It is this uncommon spirit of inquiry that is being promoted in this section.

The Art of Skillful Interpretation and Presentation

The art of interpreting communicative behaviors is learned. One can become increasingly skilled at interpreting human behavior simply by keen observation. A number of sources and tools can help develop skills. For example, Morris has assembled an emblematic dictionary; DeVito has produced a workbook with questionaires and other tools to help the learner; a number of very good books about nonverbal communication are available, many of them discussed in this book; and, courses are found in college and university curricula. All of the above can help a student understand human nonverbal behavior.

The art of listening is a critical, mindful activity that receives little attention in college skill courses; when combined with artful attention and mindfulness, it helps one become skillful in the interpretation of human behavior (Hargie, 1986). Observation at the level of Goffman's ability serves as a model for students and faculty who would better understand human social behavior.

Interpretive Tools

Each of the questionnaires and activities below is designed to help readers inquire into their thinking and behavior. By answering the questions or doing the activity, it is expected that the reader can learn more about self presentation skills, beliefs and orientations. The questionnaires and activities have been derived from several sources, including the author's own experiences and the experiences of students in his classes. They are not rigidly scientific; instead they present an "artful" approach to the personal study of nonverbal communication.

The Personal Body Awareness Questionnaire

Directions: Agree or disagree with the following statements by affixing a number from one to five in the blank. By using number one you are agreeing totally with the statement; by using number five, you are disagreeing totally with the statement. Numbers in between one and five indicate levels of agreement with the statement. There is no correct answer, although as you evaluate your responses, you may conclude that you want to work on one aspect or the other.

1.   I have a very attractive body

2.   Others tell me, or imply, that I am attractive   _____

3.   I groom myself quite often to be attractive   _____

4.   I know how to wear clothes to make me look attractive   _____

5.   I care about what others think about my body   _____

6.   I am aware of how I use body "language"   _____

7.   I am careful to not intrude on other people's space   _____

8.   I am sensitive to touch and am aware of what it means   _____

9.   I feel "natural", not nervous, in public   _____

10.   I think that I am a skilled nonverbal communicator   _____

Reading Emotions and Presentations of Others

Directions. In the following exercise, take the time to write out how you have sized up the emotional behaviors of your friend or someone else, like your father, mother, brother or sister. Respond to each statement. Choose the person you are describing; make the examples fit your perceptions.

1.   My friend acts this way when he is excited

      _____

2.   My father does this when he is angry

      _____

3.   When I flirt with someone, I do the following with my body

      _____

4.   When I touch my friend she reacts in the following ways

      _____

5.   When a guy thinks he is cool, he tends to do the following with his body

      _____

6.   I know that a person is feeling uptight when he does the following with his body

      _____

7.   I observe that people from different ethnic backgrounds act differently in the following specific ways

      _____

8.   I think that some older people use their bodies differently from me. I observe their behaviors in the following ways

      _____

9.   Males differ from females in the way they use their bodies. I observe the following

      _____

10.   To what extent do you think that your perceptions are stereotypical? How would you find out whether they were accurate?

      _____

Playing the Sleuth

Directions: The following exercise is designed to help you sort out how you think your friend or other party is socially situated in life by observing their use of clothes and other artifacts. Do the following:

1.   Jot down the labels on the person's clothes.

2.   Write down the books and magazines that the person uses.

3.   Jot down the brand names of the furniture.

4.   Find out what clubs and social organizations the person's parents belonged to and what the parents did for a living.

5.   What kind of car does the person drive and what kind of a job, if any does the person have? Jot them down.

6.   In what part of town does the person live? Describe the section.

7.   Is there a cultural style to the person's use of artifacts that you can discover? For example, is the person artsy? Modern? Traditional? Jot your assumptions down.

8.　What can you determine about the person's status in life based on her social or his social conduct?

9.　What is your general impression of the other person? How do the ways that she or he dresses and uses artifacts influence your thinking?

10.　How do you know whether your impressions accurately depict that person or not?

Roles That I Play

Directions. A key part of symbolic interactionism is the taking of roles. In everyday life people may play multiple roles over the course of a day in their interactions with others. How do you think you act when you play certain roles? Try to describe how you use your body and present yourself as you interact with others in the following roles. If you have not played a role before, try to describe how others play it. What are the characterisitics of each role?

1.　I am a daughter or son.
2.　I am a teacher.
3.　I am a student.
4.　I am a parent.
5.　I am an athlete.
6.　I am a lover.
7.　I am just me.
8.　I am my sister.
9.　I am my brother.
10.　How have you been influenced by the enactment of the roles that you play in everyday life?

My Presentational Style in Various Circumstances

Directions. How do you think you would present yourself in the following situations? Describe your probable nonverbal communication. Consider your emotions, your senses and your probable lines of action. Make the question fit your circumstances.

1.　For the first time, you meet a person from a very different culture.
2.　You are being interviewed for a new job.
3.　Your partner has proposed marriage to you.
4.　You have to confront someone over an issue.
5.　You meet a famous person whom you admire.
6.　You are in the presence of much older people.
7.　Do you have thoughts about your "ideal" presentation? What would be the characteristics of an ideal style?

Engaging In Joint Activities

Directions. What do you think is your probable nonverbal behavior when you engage in interaction with others in group situations? Write your answers down.

1.　Do you tend to lean forward or backward when in conversations with others? Either way, what difference does it make?

2.　Do you try to make eye contact with all members of the group as you engage them? If not, why not?

3.　Do people address you more than you address them? If so, why do you think this is so. If not, why not?

4. Do you think that your body presence and behavior influences the way that others act in a group? If so, how?

5. Would age and authority or gender or ethnicity of the leader of a group influence your nonverbal behavior? If so, how?

6. Are you a take charge person? A shy person? How do you use your body in either situation?

7. Are you comfortable sitting next to the seat of power in a group? If not, why not? If so, why?

8. If the group has met several times, do you tend to sit in the same spot each time? If so, why do you think you do?

The Influence of the Media

Statement	A. Not much	B. Somewhat	C. A great deal
1. Television influences me	_____	_____	_____
2. The internet influences me	_____	_____	_____
3. The telephone influences me	_____	_____	_____
4. Movies influence me	_____	_____	_____
5. Books influence me	_____	_____	_____

Do you think that your own nonverbal behavior is directly influenced by any of the above media? If so, how?

Gender Orientations Questionnaire

Directions. As you encounter gendered others in your daily life, not referring to lovers or romantic partners, does there seem to be a pattern to the way that you relate to that person nonverbally? Answer the following questions. Make the question fit your circumstances.

1. How far do you normally stand from a person of opposite gender?

2. Do you usually face the person directly or obliquely? Is there a pattern?

3. Do members of the opposite sex generally lean toward you or try to stand close to you? Why do you think either situation occurs?

4. Can you remember whether your senses come into play in your evaluation of the other person? Smells, touch or hearing?

5. Do you permit members of the opposite gender to touch you if they do not know you? Why or why not?

6. Would you describe your style as one of immediacy, or inclusion of the other, or as fairly distant and exclusive of the other, or somewhere in-between?

7. Do you behave in differently in the presence of the same gender as you do in cross-gender situations? If not, what would be the differences?

8. Do you change your body display when you know others are watching you? If so, how?

Interpreting Symbols

Directions. Keep a diary of the various kinds of symbols that you use or find that other people use in their conversations. Try to place them in the context provided.

1. Symbols of personal power. What are they? How are they used?

2. Symbols of patriotism. What symbols seem important to you and your friends?

3. Religious symbols. Can you think of five religious symbols that convey meaning to people in religious ways? What are they? What symbols are important to you? Why?

4. Symbols of medicine and symbols of law. What are some key symbols and the different ways that are used by members of these professions? What symbols of power may be used by business people?

5. Symbols of international cooperation. What symbols seem to be used and understood cross-culturally by the United Nations and by other groups? What emblems may be used cross-culturally?

6. What logos do you associate with the following terms?
   1. Chocolate making
   2. Automobiles
   3. Television stations
   4. Filmmakers
   5. Sports
   6. Funerals
   7. Birth

My Body Signature

Directions. People tend to develop identifiable body behaviors. Although these behaviors are modifiable they may become part of identities. Describe your own body signature as you perceive it, relative to the following activities.

1. Speed of walking
2. Speed of talking
3. Amount of body used in normal conversations.
4. The use of the eyes
5. The use of body adaptors
6. Body size and shape
7. Level of social aggresssion
8. Use of space
9. Frequency of gestures
10. Signal responses

Do you think that others would describe your individuated behaviors in the same ways? Make a comparison.

Assessing Stereotypes

Directions. In the following exercise, try to describe the stereotype that seems to prevail regarding each of the groupings of people. Show what you think are the prevailing stereotypes and what an accurate view is.

Group	Stereotype	Accurate View
An aged person		
An ethnic person		
A male or female		
A schizophrenic person		
A person of influence		
A caring person		

Knowing Key SI Concepts

Directions. Each of these concepts is explained in the glossary of the book. Check your memory to see if you know the concept and can use it accurately.

somatype. . .gender. . .sex. . .mediation. . . .ethnicity. . . culture. . .
immediacy. . .perception. . . sensemaking. . . the interactive self. . .
identity. . . role playing. . taking the role of the other. . .adaptive behavior. . . reflexivity. . . ethology

Final Remarks: A Postcript

Becoming an Artful Nonverbal Communicator

It has been said that most people are naive scientists; that is, they interpret behavior through well-honed, sensible cognitive schemas in the laboratory of life. Unlike lower order animals, humans have the potential to change, to become what they want to be, to become skillful at nonverbal communication, increasing their effectiveness and satisfaction and improving the social climate. They can continue on this productive path over the entire life-span.

Increasing Problem Solving Abilities

Researchers have placed a great deal of stress on the role of intersubjectivity and mutual understanding. Many problems are associated with misinterpretation of body action when people attribute false meanings to behaviors. When this occurs at the level of international politics, it can lead to serious consequences. When the messages of the body are made clear to people mistakes can be eliminated and social interaction can be improved. It is hoped that this book provides a brief and poignant statement, an approach that readers and scholars will find useful as they enjoy a healthy social life.

Summary

This chapter has focused on the issues and problems that researchers and everyday people encounter relative to nonverbal communication. It suggests that skilled nonverbal behavior is learned and that, with attentiveness and practice, humans can create effective nonverbal communication activities.

Scholars and researchers come from a variety of backgrounds that influence how they approach the study of nonverbal communication. The Symbolic Interactionist approach has been put forth as a very productive and insightful way to do research, focusing mostly on ethnographic research, but not excluding laboratory type research.

Tools to assess oneself are included implying that self assessment is the beginning of personal growth. The SI approach can increase a person's understanding of human communicative behavior.

Questions for Thought and Discussion

1.   The activities in this chapter are designed to increase students' awareness and to provide a way for them to think and act more effectively, to help them become more sensitive toward themselves and others. Do you think that most people are empathic listeners? If not, why not?

2.   If you are a parent, or were to think of yourself as a parent, how do you think that you might help your child become more sensitive and aware of self and others?

3.   In everyday relations, things often are not what they seem to be; in other words, people often have distorted perceptions. What are some examples of this? How can one create accurate perceptions of human behaviors?

4.   What ethical responsibility do you think that you have toward others? In other words, what guides you as you think about others and how to behave toward them? Is there a central principle involved?

5.   What importance is the study of human nonverbal communication to you? How important should it be to other members of society?

Notes

1.   The SI approach is broad and it can include a variety of models, theories and methods within it. The use of multiple methodologies and triangulation are preferred to as "single dipping" because they can provide evidence from several sources about a particular topic. The so-called "snapshot" approach, as found in many laboratory studies that focus on narrowly conceived topics is best used in combination with other research, such as the "film" approach where subjects and researchers are engaged in an ongoing way. Case studies, questionnaires and laboratory studies, an unlikely combination, may be used together in the multiple methods approach.

2.   Although the SI approach focuses on everyday life, it has been more a scholarly discipline than one that is applied, although there is no inherent reason why it cannot be applied using various tools for application. SI concepts can be applied meaningfully to all social events and situations, ranging from inmate to college behaviors. Charon discusses the application of SI and provides studies. See pages 216-230 in Symbolic Interactionism. SI has been used to discuss sexuality, for example, from a theoretical standpoint, but in explicating the symbolic nature of sexuality, there is a practical spin-off that can be used by therapists or others who wish to use the concepts. In a thoroughgoing article, Monica A. Longmore, The Journal of Sex Research,

Feb 1998, v35 nl p44(14) discusses the varieties of ways that SI has been used to understand sexual behaviors in everyday life.

3.   Applications of Nonverbal Behavioral Theories and Research, Edited by Robert S. Feldman; see also, Robert M. Soucie, Common Misconceptions about Nonverbal Communication: Implications for Training pp 209-219, in Nonverbal Behavior, Applications and Cultural Implications, edited by Aaron Wolfgang, Academic Press, 1979; see also, Appendix B, Applications, in 361-412, in The Nonverbal Communication Reader, DeVito and Hecht; see Julia Woods and Joel Charon in the index.

Suggested Readings

Hatfield, E., Cacioppo, J. T., & Rapson, R. (1994). *Emotional Contagion.* Cambridge, England: Cambridge University Press.

Hatfield, E. E., & Sprecher, S (1986). *Mirror, Mirror... The Importance of Looks in Everyday Life.* Albany, NY: SUNY Press.

Jaworski, A. (1993). *The Power of Silence: Social and Pragmatic Perspectives.* Newbury Park, CA: Sage.

Jones, S. E. (1994). *The Right Touch: Understanding and Using the Language of Physical Contact.* Creshill, NJ: Hampton Press.

Langer, E. J. (1989). *Mindfulness.* Reading, MA: Addison-Wesley.

Morris, D. (1994). *Bodytalk: The Meaning of Human Gestures.* New York: Crown Publishers.

Scheflen, A. E. (1974). *How Behavior Means.* Garden City, NY: Anchor/Doubleday.

Watzlawick, P., Beavin, J. H., & Jackson, D. D. (1967). Pragmatics of Human Communication: A Study of Interactional Patterns, Pathologies, and Paradoxes. New York: Norton.

Glossary

Accidental nonverbal communication
Refers to the interpretation of an act or line of action by others when it was not intended by the actor.

Acculturation
The processes by which people acquire culture, starting at their birth and ending at their death.

Action language
Refers to how body behaviors, or lines of action, are interpreted, simulating language.

Additive model of aging
An approach to the aging process that suggests that people can maintain or increase their general abilities as they age.

Adaptors
Body behaviors, such as scratching or itching, that people use unconsciously, considered to be evolutionary adaptations to the biological environment.

Affiliation
Refers to identification with, or relationship to, one person with another.

Ageism
The stereotyping of the aging process, often expressed by the media or by people who are uninformed by the scientific intricacies of aging.

Agentry
Refers to the ways that people, on their own behalf, enact behaviors creatively in response to perceived expectations in a situation.

Agonistic
Refers to difficult behaviors that tend to be aggressive, associated with early growth, especially among males.

Androgyny
The process whereby males and females are able to manifest behaviors associated with either gender. Males can become more empathic and females can become more assertive, for example.

Anosmia
Refers to the impairment of the human sense of smell.

Anthropomorphism
The process of labeling animal behavior using terms that apply to human behavior.

Archetypes
In Jungian psychology, an inherited and unconscious mode of thought that is derived from the prior experience of the human race, but found in the modern individual.

Assimilation
Referring to the process by which people become absorbed into a group.

Automatic pilot
Refers to the fact that human behavior is often ritualized such that little or no thought is necessary to perform an action.

Autonomic nervous system
The human nervous system that governs involuntary actions.

Artifacts
Products, articles and goods that humans create and used, often serving to help interpret their behaviors, values or beliefs.

Aurality
Refers to the sense and process of hearing.

Back-channeling
The ways that people respond to others in conversations, usually nonverbally, to affirm or deny what others are saying; for example, by nodding their heads, indicating agreement.

Bi-culturalism
Refers to people who share more than one culture in a society.

Body identity
Refers to the symbolic representation of one's physical body.

Body language
The suggestion that bodily actions can be organized into patterns resembling patterns found in spoken language.

Body shine
Erving Goffman's phrase suggesting that the body gives off cues to others in human interaction, although the cues may not be known to the body's owner.

Body signature
Refers to the characteristic ways that people use their bodies.

Broca's area
The area of the brain in which many scientists think that language is encoded.

Channels
Many scholars in nonverbal communication refer to the use of the various senses as channels; nonverbal communication is multi-channeled compared to verbal communication, employing many channels at once.

Chronemics
Refers to time as a nonverbal background factor influencing human communication.

Chronobiology
The interaction of time and biology in the regulation of human behavior.

Circadian rhythm
Daily biological changes that influence human behaviors. For example, sleep and waking are daily events.

Co-construction
The process of jointly creating meaning in interaction with single or multiple others.

Communicative technologies
All technologies affect and effect communication, the principle ones being television and the computer, the internet in modern society.

Contact hypothesis
Refers to the patterns of behavior associated with first contacts among groups of humans, whether hostile or friendly, for example.

Co-cultures
The emphasis upon equality among ethnic cultures.

Codes
Refers to the often hidden set of rules or symbols, physical or social, which when interpreted give meaning to an event, body behavior or activity.

Cognition
The process of perceiving and knowing, becoming aware of phenomena.

Collective behavior
Group or mass behaviors that are often patterned and interpretable.

Communal
Refers to the emphasis upon groupness among various cultures, as opposed to the emphasis upon invidualism.

Construal
The creative process of translating the meaning of experiences throughout life.

Contingency
Referring to the enactment of lines of nonverbal action, one act dependent upon another in an ongoing sequence of interactions.

Cosmologies
The ways that members of cultures collectively organize their beliefs about the meaning of life and the universe.

Craniometry
The study of the shape of the human head to determine how races compare, one with the other.

Culture
The distinctive customs, religious beliefs, habits, languages and technologies that are shared commonly by people in various parts of the world.

Deficit model of aging
An approach to aging that suggests that people lose their general abilities as they age, suffering a decline in mental and physical abilities.

Digital divide
Refers to the general lack of access to computers and the internet which affects women, various ethnic groups and older citizens.

Discourse styles
The distinctive ways that various groups communicate verbally and nonverbally.

Disinhibition
The freedom to act out behaviors on the internet that would normally be suppressed in face-to-face communication.

Display rules
Cultural and social expectations that influence people to act appropriately; guides to dress and other behavioral actions.

Dramaturgy
Use of a theatrical model to do research and to explain human actions.

Dyads
Two person units involved in human interaction.

Dysfunctional
Refers to behaviors that are considered impaired or abnormal.

Ectomorphs
In Sheldon's research, refers to a slight body build, a somatype.

Egalitarianism
The belief that people are equal or that barriers to social, economic and political inequality should be removed.

Emoticons
Symbols and icons used on the internet to substitute for emotional expressions.

Endomorphs
In Sheldon's research, refers to the short, heavy, often fat person, as a somatype.

Emblem
A nonverbal cue or act that can take the place of words.

Engagement-disengagement
Words used to describe how people are said to behave, either by interactive withdrawal or increased involvement.

Enclave
A culturally distinct region of a city or country; for example, Chinatown.

Enculturation
The processes by which people learn the ways of their culture.

Ethnicity
Refers to the characteristics, traits and behaviors of groups whose members share a common identity, often minorities in a society.

Ethnographic
A type of research that uses the methods of field study to focus on the behaviors of specific group members, often ethnic.

Ethology
The scientific study of animal behaviors, especially higher order primates.

Evolution
The general theory that existing living things have their origins in pre-existing types and that modifications have occurred over time.

Face
In interaction, the symbolic front that people display to other people.

Facial primacy
The emphasis upon the face as the primary expressor of emotions, compared to other parts of the human body.

Filtered reality
Refers to mediated communication in which television, for example, alters daily reality. Refers as well to perceptual processes which act as selective lenses.

Folkculture
A type of culture that is transmitted orally, containing stories and myths associated with that culture.

Gaze aversion
Refers to the avoidance of eye contact with others.

Gender
Male and female identities, constructed in social interaction.

Genderlect
The spoken language of a male or female speech community.

Genetics
A branch of biology that deals with the heredtiy and variation of living things.

Genome Project
A scientific project devoted to the task of unlocking the secrets of the genetic code.

Gentling
The process of providing tactile nurturance to newborns, whether human or other animals.

Gestalt
Refers to the process of perceiving objects, physical and social, as whole units, not separable into parts.

Gesture
In Meadian philosophy and psychology, it was a body act, simple or complex, by which meaning is established in interaction.

Glass ceiling
A see-through boundary in organizations and businesses that stopped females and people of color from gaining access to higher level positions although they could see the positions usually filled by white males.

Global Village
The construction of a universal village ied together by modern media forms that crossed international boundaries, as discussed by Marshall McLuhan.

Gustatory
Refers to the taste sense.

Habituation
The ability to perform acts, or lines of actions, without requiring active or prior thought by the actor.

Haptics
The study of the ways that humans and other animals use touch or grasping behaviors.

Hardwired
The imaginative idea that human behavior is the direct result of instinctive or biologically driven mechanisms.

Hierarchy
A graded or ranked system that locates different species on different levels of importance.

High and low contexts
Refers to Hall's analysis of the place of implicit or explicit communicative patterns of behavior; high contexts are implicit and low are explicit.

Historiography
A scientific approach to the study of history to uncover, or discover, patterns of behaviors that may help to understand present day behaviors.

Hormonal cycles
Male and female body secretions that effect changes in the body over a period of a day, month or year, thereby affecting behavior.

Hyper-reality
The creation or simulation of everyday behaviors by computerized methods.

Hysterical personalities
The old belief that women were negatively affected by traumas or disturbances of the womb.

Icon
A pictograph used on the computer. An image of a person, place or object to which people attach devotion or adulation.

Identity
The distinguishing character of the personality or behaviors of an individual.

Imbeddedness
The process in which social dynamics are an inherent part of everyday activities and behaviors.

Immediacy
The attractive behaviors of an individual or people that increase their likability and reduce physical distance between people, as suggested by Mehrabian.

Impression management
The process of monitoring and managing oneself in the presence of others.

Information technologies
All technologies yield information, but reference in this case is to the computer and computer related technologies.

Intentional nonverbal communication
Acts, or lines of action, that are pre-planned by the actor or actors.

Interaction analysis
The study of interactive behaviors by the use of scientifically valid instruments and methods.

Interethnic adaptability
The ability of members of ethnic groups to relate to members of other ethnic groups in positive and flexible ways.

Intersubjectivity
The mutual sharing of meanings, behaviors, activities and events by actors in interactive situations.

Jim Crow Laws
Laws that were enacted to prevent Negroes from having the same rights as Whites despite the emancipation of the Negro.

Joint interactions
The working together of participants in dyads or groups to accomplish goals or share activities.

Kinesics
The study of body movements and actions in human nonverbal communication.

Knowbots
A robot that can perform tasks in libraries and other places that require specialized knowledge.

Labeling process
The naming of people, objects or social events for identification purposes.

Leakage Hypothesis
The scientific statement that suggests that human bodies give off information to observors without the body owner's knowledge that it is occurring.

Lifeworld
Refers to all of the events, meanings and activities that constitute a person's sense of the meaning of life.

Logic-in-use
The pragmatic schemas and thoughts that guide individuals as they enact behaviors in daily life.

Looking glass self
Cooley's theory that in social interaction, people 'see' themselves reflected in the appraisals of others.

Manifest destiny
The American White man's belief that it was inevitable that he would expand to the Pacific. It was his destiny, regardless of the consequences.

Man principle
Reference is to the fact that, for centuries, men were in charge of social, political and economic events. The power of men to control human interactions.

Marginalization
The forcing of minorities and women out of the mainstream of political, economic or social life.

Matriarchal society
A social system in which the woman is head of the family, tribe or nation in which descent of future generations is from the female line.

Media ecology
The study of the influence of the media, especially television, film, radio and the internet upon the quality and character of a given society or milieau.

Meta-analysis
The systematic study of numerous research outcomes to determine the patterns that are common to them, not apparent when one focuses on a few studies.

Metaphor
Figurative language that is used to describe a person, an object or an event. For example, people say that a computer 'thinks'.

Methusaleh factor
The focus on very old age as noted in the Bible in reference to Methusaleh, allegedly the oldest man who ever lived.

Microcosm
A unit that is a smaller version of something larger; in Meadian philosophy, child play was a microcosm of later adult behaviors.

Micro-meso-macro processes
The idea that human behavior may be studied in the context of small, mid-sized, or large, society-wide processes.

Mindlessness
The inattentiveness of humans to events that when mindfully attended to can provide meanings that are otherwise not known, as discussed by S. Langer.

Minimal universality
The thesis that some human behaviors are universal, at least in a minimal way. Ekman and others described body movements that they thought revealed this phenomenon.

Modeling
The direct and indirect following of the behaviors of another person by a young child or other person.

Monolithic ethnic group
The false assumption that members of an ethnic group are all alike.

Moore's Law
The knowledge that changes in technologies are increasing in their doubling time.

Motor skill
Skills that arise from the physiological development of the human body, such as the ability to walk.

Multi-culturalism
The study of the interplay of groups from many different ethnic backgrounds.

Native
Members of oral cultures, as studied by early anthropologists; however, the word is used sometimes to describe people who live in modern societies as well.

Negotiation
In symbolic interactionism, the act of mutually creating meaning with others in interaction, resulting in an interpretation of the interaction or event by each actor.

Networking
Patterned ways that people interact with others in play or work and in interpersonal and group relationships.

Nonconsciousness
Personal unawareness of events that are occurring. Inattentiveness.

Neurological system
The neural-chemical brain system in humans and other species.

Olfaction
The smell system in the human body and in other species.

Oculesics
The study of eye movements, including pupillometry, or action of the pupils.

Oral tradition
The passing on to new generations the culture of the older generation through storytelling, singing, chanting or other rituals, not by the use of modern technologies.

Paradigm
An organized model or pattern used by researchers.

Paralanguage
Vocalized patterns, tones and emphases associated with spoken words that can convey special meanings separate from the meaning of the words in use.

Parapsychology
A field of study that is associated with the study of telepathy, clairvoyance or psychokinesis; the popular study of the sixth sense.

Patriarchal society
A society that is controlled by men in which the descendants of males continue the practice.

Perception
The ability of humans to make symbolic sense of information derived from the senses, from intuition or from imagination.

Pheromones
In many, perhaps most species, including humans, the smells that are produced by the skin or other organ to attract others of the same species.

Phrenology
The study of the structure of the skull in the belief that it is indicative mental abilities or character.

Physiognomy
The attempt to establish character or other thoughts about people by examining their outward appearance.

Place
Used in this text to indicate that people create personal and collective meanings for the areas where they have been raised or presently occupy.

Polysemia
The idea that words, events, people and objects can be interpreted in many different ways by individuals or by groups.

Post-modernism
The view held by many scholars that new patterns of authority and organization brought about essentially by the computer in an information age, are replacing those of the prior industrialized structure of society, thereby altering human relationships and ways of interpreting human behavior.

Pragmatism
Part of the symbolic interactionist view, which suggests that meaning lies essentially in how people act or behave. James and Peirce believed that the function of thought is to guide human action.

Primates
Mammalian species that include humans, higher order animals, such as chimpanzees and other species.

Proxemics
The study of the human uses of space; patterns of use in various cultures.

Pupilommetry
The study of the movements of the pupil in the eye, which are under the control of the autonomic nervous system, as initiated by Hess in his studies of cats.

Qualitative methods
The multiple ways that researchers use to try to understand the meaning of events and activities as understood by the subjects themselves, often referred to as participatory or the living subjects research.

Quantitative methods
The multiple ways that researchers use when they study subjects usually in the laboratory, in which, often, they represent subjects numerically.

Race
The older classification of humans according to physical characteristics, such as shape of head, color of skin, hair patterns, body structure and so on. Now considered scientifically ineffective.

Racism
The stereotypical characterization, usually negative, of members of ethnic groups by the members of other ethnic groups.

Racial profiling
The deliberate act of targeting members of ethnic minorities, usually Black, by White police officers and others, in an attempt to solve crimes or effect other policies, usually established by Whites.

Reductionism
The practice of some researchers to reduce complex behaviors to simple terms, often simplistic, thereby creating error in their interpretations of the behaviors.

Reflexivity
Perhaps better stated as reflectivity, it is the process of self-thought, of thinking about the meaning of events, of interactive situations, of the behavior of self and others in an effort to make sense of the circumstances.

REM studies
The study of the rapid eye movement associated with dreaming.

Reptilian stare
It has been suggested that some schizophrenic people use the fixed stare interactively, sometimes due to the effects of medical treatment.

Rituals
Customized, repeated acts found in events and in interpersonal situations, such as in marriages, funerals and festivities. It can refer to ritualized behaviors by individuals as well.

Role playing
In symbolic interactionism it is the ability of an individual to observe and take the role of another that is key to identity. One learns how to play roles, such as playing the role of a student.

Saturated self
Gergen's idea that the creation of personal identity is made difficult, complex and very uncertain in an age saturated by television and other media.

Scripts
In symbolic interactionism, it is the observation that humans act as though they were following a script; they are influenced by past events and experiences and act accordingly in ways that make sense to them.

Segregation
In this context, it is the idea that young boys and young girls gradually segregate themselves by genders, as noted by Maccoby, only to return to cross-gendered relationships later in life.

Semantics
Essentially the study of meanings that humans create in interaction with others.

Self-presentation
In symbolic interactionism, the idea that humans present themselves to others as though they were on the stage of life. From the work of Erving Goffman.

Self-talk
The process of holding a conversation the self in an attempt to create meaning for the actions of self or of others.

Semiosis
The study of how objects, events and behaviors mean something to people, as signs and symbols.

Sensemaking
The interpretation of the meaning of behaviors in interaction. The ability to construct meaning from events, from self and others.

Sensory
Of or relating to the senses and how the information from them is used.

Signification
The human act of giving meaning to a sign or symbol.

Situated self
The human being is located in a milieau or context which influences her or his behaviors.

Sixth sense
Intuition, esp, clairvoyance or precognition are sometimes thought to comprise a sixth sense.

Socialization
The various and complex social processes that influence the growth of a human from birth to death.

Socio-drama
In symbolic interactionism, using a dramaturgical metaphor, human acts in interaction are referred to as socio-dramas. Television programs are sociodramatic forms.

Sociometry
The scientific measurement of the uses of space by humans.

Somatypes
As in Sheldon's studies, the placing of body shapes and sizes into categories.

Standpoint theory
The idea that all humans are born into and occupy a location in society that influences their behaviors.

Stereotypes
The labeling of people and events by using poor or little information, leading to false conclusions.

Stigmas
The creation of negative stereotypes for people that tend to limit their social success, such as acting toward 'fat' people pejoratively.

Strategy
In symbolic interactionism, the deliberate use of a line of action to accomplish an interactive goal, whether it is to build a good relationship or to deceive others.

Style
Refers to the ways that people present themselves, often in patterned ways; style is sometimes interpreted in opposition to substance, suiggesting that style is transitory.

Symbols, signs and signals
Taken together, these terms refer to the metaphorical ways that humans assign meaning to objects, people and events.

Symbolic interactionism
The scientific investigation of the ways that human create meaning for their lives in interaction.

Synchronicity
Things that occur together; Jung's theory that the collective unconscious of humans acts to create events that occur together.

Taboo
A behavior or act that is risky to perform, unacceptable to society.

Tactility
Similar to haptics, it refers to the use of the hands or limbs to grasp or touch objects or humans.

Techno-language, techno-speak
Specialized language that is derived from modern technologies, such as emoticon or web-site, words that are part of the new lexicon.

Technology
Any tool that is created by humans to be used by them; all tools have a communicative potential.

Telepresence
The saturation of society by the media, especially television, creates a new form of human presence, a mediated presence.

Testosterone
The hormone found in humans, mostly in males, that can lead to aggressive behavior.

Threshold
The idea that each human sense operates within a range of capabilities, beyond which it cannot function.

Tie-signs
Focuses on the importance of relational ties with others that humans create over a life-span.

Time, monochronic and polychronic
The breakdown of types of time associated with various cultures. The United States is said to operate on a monochronic scale.

Transactionalism
A scientific approach to the study of human relationships that focuses on how people give and take information.

Triangulation
In symbolic interactionist research, the use of various scientific methodologies to focus on a research topic in order to provide accuracy.

Victimology
The study of how groups of people have been victimized by other groups and how some groups perceived themselves as victims.

Virtual reality
The simulated reality that can be created by using computers programs.

Vocal signatures
The suggestion that humans have unique, identifying vocal features, one individual in comparison to another.

Voice set
The concept that vocal patterns seem inflexible, especially when one listens to older people speak.

White man's burden
The alleged duty of the White man to manage the affairs of less developed nations or peoples, as described in Kipling's poem, 1899.

Worldview
The concept that every individual, under the influence of culture, possesses a way of viewing the world.
Weltanschauung
A German word to describe the concept of a worldview.

Xenophobia
Essentially the fear of foreigners, arising from background influences or prior relationships.

Yellow Peril
The term used to describe the presence of Chinese in America, who, in theory, under economically difficult times, took jobs away from Whites.

Zoomorphic gods
Mythological gods in the form of animals often worshipped in ritual or feared, who could control the fate of humans, such as the dragon in Chinese society or the coyote, a trickster in Navajo beliefs

References

Abou, S. (1997). The metamorphosis of cultural identity: Identities, cultures and creativity. *Diogenes, 13*, Spring.

Abrams, D., & Hogg, M. A. (Eds.). (1990). *Social identity theory.* New York: Springer-Verlag.

Agassiz, L. (1850). The diversity of origins of the human races. *Christian Examiner, 49*, 110-145.

Agee, W. K., Ault, P. H., & Emory, E. (1997). *Introduction to mass communication (12th ed.).* New York: Longman.

Alexander, J. C. (1988). *Action and its environments: Towards a new synthesis.* New York: Columbia University Press.

Allen, L. (2001, April). Deja vu at the National Zoo: Giant pandas again take it by storm. *Smithsonian*, pp. 46-55.

Altheide, D. L. (1997). The electronic place: From telepresence to co-presence. In D. E. Miller, M. A. Katovich, & S. L. Saxton (eds.), *Constructing Complexity: Symbolic Interaction and Social Forms (Suppl. 3).* Greenwich, CT: JAI Press Inc.

Altman, I. (1975). *The environment and social behavior.* Monterrey, CA: Brooks & Cole.

Andersen, P. A. (1999). *Nonverbal communication: Forms and functions.* Mountain View, CA: Mayfield Publishing Company.

Anderson, D. Y., & Hayes, C. L. (1996). *Gender, identity and self-esteem: A new look at adult development.* New York: Springer Publishing Co.

Anderson, K. J. (1998, August). Meta-analyses of gender effects in conversational interruption: Who, what, when, where and how. *Sex Roles: A Journal of Research*, pp. 225-253.

Andersen, P. A. & Andersen, J. F. (1984). Perspectives on nonverbal intimacy theory. In J. A. DeVito & M. L. Hecht (eds.), *The nonverbal communication reader.* Prospect Heights, IL: Waveland Press.

Andersen, P. A., & Guerrero, L. K. (Eds.). (1998). *Handbook of communication and emotion: Research, theory, applications and contexts.* San Diego, CA: Academic Press.

APA Monitor (online) (1999, September). *Women as managers.*

Arbib, M, & Rizzolatti, G. (1997). A possible evolutionary path from manual skills to language. *Communication and Cognition, 29*, 393-424.

Ardrey, R. (1966). *The territorial imperative.* New York: Dell Publishing Company, Inc.

Argyle, M. (1983). *Bodily communication.* New York: Methuen & Co.

Arliss, L. P. (1993). *Contemporary family communication: Messages and meanings.* New York: St. Martin's Press.

Arliss, L. P., & Borisoff, D.J. (1993). *Women and men communicating: Challenges and Changes.* New York: Holt, Rinehart and Winston.

Armstrong, D., Stokoe, W., & Wilcox, S. (1995). *Gesture and the nature of language.* New York: Cambridge University Press.

Armstrong, D. (1999). *Original signs: Gesture, signs and the sources of language.* Washington, DC: Gallaudet University Press.

Aromachologists nose out the secret powers of smell. *Insight on the News (Nov 10, 1997). P. 36-38.*

Aronoff, J., & Wilson, J. B (1985). *Personality in the social process.* Hillsdale, NJ: Lawrence Erlbaum Associates.

Ashmore, R.D., & Jussim, L. (Eds)(1997). *Self and identity: Fundamental issues. (Vol I).* New York: Oxford University Press.

Asian Economic News (August 24, 1998). *Immigrants fight for American Dream (Online).*

Auther, J (Sept 14, 1999). Use of social special symbol causes New Mexico controversy. *CNN (Online)*

Axtell, R. E. (1991). *Gestures: the do's and taboos of body language around the world.* New York: John Wiley & Sons Inc.

Azar, B. Monitor(November 2000). Hand-me-down-skills. *APA Monitor. Vol 31, 10. (Online)*

Ball-Rokeach, S. J., Rokeach, M., & Grube, J.W. (1984) *The great American values test: Influencing behavior and belief through television.* New York: Free Press.

Baker, M. A. (Ed) (1987). *Studies in human performance.* New York: John Wiley & Sons.

Baltes, P., & Willis, S.L. (1982) Enhancement (plasticity) of intellectual functioning in old age: Penn State's Adult Development and Enrichment project (ADEPT) in F.I.M.

Craik & S. Trehub (Eds) *Age and cognitive processes.* New York: Plenum.

Baltes, P, & Baltes, M.M.(Eds)(1990). *Successful aging: Perspectives from the behavioral sciences.* New York: Cambridge University Press.

Bandura, A. (1982). Self efficacy mechanisms in human agency. *American Psychology. 37,* pp 122-147.

Baran, S.J., McIntyre, J.S., & Meyer, T. P. (1984). *Signs, symbols and society: An introduction to mass communication.* Reading, MA: Addison-Wesley.

Barash, D.P., & Lipton, J.E. (1997) *Making sense of sex: How genes and gender influence our relationships.* Washington, D.C.: Island Press.

Baron, R.A. (1996). *Essentials of psychology.* Needham Heights, MA: Allyn & Bacon.

Barot, H. B., & Fenton, S.(1999) *Ethnicity, gender and social change.* New York: St. Martin's Press.

Barth, F.(1969). *Ethnic groups and boundaries: The social organization of cultural difference.* Boston: Little-Brown.

Becker, H.S. & McCall, M. (Eds). (1990). *Symbolic interaction and cultural studies.* Chicago: University of Chicago Press.

Beeman, W.O. (1993). The anthropology of theater and spectacle. *Annual Review of Anthropology. 22.* 369-393.

Belenky, M.F.Clinchy, B.M., Goldbergen, N.R. & Taruk, J.M. (1986). *Women's ways of knowing: The development of self, voice and mind.* New York: Basic Books.

Bellafante, G. (1999, Dec 4). Creating a Brand Image: The Mannequin is the message. *New York Times Online.*

Belsie, L (June 6, 1999)Aging myths. *APA Monitor Online.*

Bellafonte, G. (Dec 14, 1999). Creating a brand image: The mannequin is the message. *New York Times On The Web.*

Bem, S. L. (1993). *The lenses of gender: Transforming the debate on sexual inequality.* New Haven, Ct: Yale University Press.

Bennis, W. (1995). Adventure, risk and promise. *Vital Speeches, October,* pp 752-755.

Benthrall, J., & Polhemus, T. (Eds) (1975). *The body as a medium of expression.* E.P Dutton & Co., Inc.

Berg, B.L. (1989). *Qualitative research methods for the social sciences (2nd edition).* Needham, MA: Allyn & Bacon.

Berger, P. & Luckmann, T. (1963) *The social construction of reality.* New York: Doubleday.

Berger, C. R. (1997). *Planning strategic interaction.* Mahwah, NJ: Lawrence Erlbaum Associates.

Berne, E. (1964). *Games people play: The basic book of transaction analysis.* New York: Ballantine Books.

Besnier, N. (1990). Language and affect. *Annual Review of American Anthropology,* pp 419-451.

Birdwhistell, R. (1970). *Kinesics and context.* Philadelphia, PA: University of Pennsylvania Press.

Birdwhistell, R. (1975). Background considerations for the study of the body as a medium of expression. In J. Benthrall & T. Polhemus. *The body as a medium of expression.* New York: E.P. Dutton.

Blacks feel most discriminated against and whites agree (June 12, 2001) *JET (online).*

Blackmore, S (1990, Sept) *The lure of the paranormal.* New Scientist. 22, pp 62-65.

Blau, P. M., & Duncan, O.D. (1967). *The American occupational structure.* New York: Wiley.

Blumer, H. (1969). *Symbolic interactionism: Perspective and method.*Englewood Cliffs, NJ: Prentice Hall.

Boden, D. (1990). The world as it happens: Ethnomethodology and conversation analysis. In. G. Ritzer, (Editor). *Frontiers in social theory: The new frontier.* New York: Columbia University Press. pp 185-213.

Bogart, L. (1995). *Commercial culture, the media system and the public interest.* New York: Oxford University Press.

Bova, B. (1998). *Immortality: How science is enxtending your life span. . . and changing the world.* New York: Avon Books, Inc.

Bowlby, J. (1969). *Attachment and loss.* New York: Basic Books.

Braudel, F(1973) *Capitalism and material life (Trans: Miriam Kochan)*New York: Harper & Row.

Boyer, P.J. (Feb 16, 1986) TV turns to the hard-boiled male. *New York Times pp Hl, H29.*

Braxton, R.J. (1999). Culture, family and Chinese and Korean American student achievement: An examination of student factors that affect student outcomes. *College Student Journal, June, pp 250-256.*

Brown, B. C., & Jones, S. E. (1996). *Touch attitudes and behaviors: Recollections of early childhood touch and social confidence. 17, 147.*

Browne, D. W. (1996). *Electronic media and indigenous people: A voice of our own.* Ames, Iowa: Iowa State University Press.

Brown, J.D., Childers, K.W., Bauman, K.E., & Koch, G.g. (1990). The influence of new media and family structure on young adolescents' television and radio use. *Communication Research, 17,* pp. 65-82.

Brown, J. D., Dykers, C. R., Steele, J. R., & White, A. B. (1994). Teenage room culture: Where media and identities intersect. *Communication Research.* 21, pp 813-828.

Brown, L. K., & Mussell, K. (Eds). (1984) *Foodways in the United States: The performance of group identity.* Knoxville, Tenn: University of Tennesee Press.

Brown, M.E. (Ed)(1990). *Television and women's culture: Politics of the popular.* London: Sage.

Brown, R.D. (Ed). ((1969). *Slavery in American society.* USA: Raytheon Education Company.

Bruneau, T. (1979). The time dimension in intercultural communication. In. L.A. Samovar & R. E. Porter (Eds). *Intercultural communication: A reader. (4th edition).* Belmont, CA: Wadsworth.

Bruner, J. (1990). *Acts of meaning.* Cambridge, MA: Harvard University Press.

Buck, R. (1982). Spontaneous and symbolic nonverbal behavior and the ontogeny of communication. In R.S. Feldman (Editor)., *The development of nonverbal behavior in children.* New York: Springer-Verlag.

Buck, R. (1984). *The Communication of Emotion.* New York: Guilford.

Bull, P.F. (1987). *Posture and gesture.* New York: Pergamon Press.

Buller, D. B., & Burgoon, J.K. (1998). Emotional expression in the deception process. In P.A. Andersen & L. K. Guerrero (Eds). *Handbook of communication and emotion: research, theory, applications, and contexts.* pp. 379-402. San Diego, Calif.: Academic Press.

Burgoon, J.K., Buller, D.B., & Woodall, W. G. (1996). *Nonverbal communication: The unspoken dialogue (2nd edition).* New York: McGraw-Hill.

Burgoon, J.K., & Langer, E. (1995). Language, fallacies, and mindlessness-mindfulness. In B. R. Burleson (Ed) *Communication Yearbook 18* (105-182)..Newbury Park, CA: Sage.

Burke, K. (1945). *A Grammar of motives.* New York: Prentice-Hall.

Burke, K. (1966). *Language as symbolic action.* Berkeley: University of California Press.

Bushart, H.L., Craig, J.R., & Barnes, M. (1998). *Soldiers of God: White supremacists and their holy war for America.* New York: Kensington Books.

Buss, D.M. (1989). Sex differences in human mate preferences: Evaluating hypotheses tested in 37 cultures. *Behavioral and Brain Sciences. 12: 1-49.*

Cain, W. S. (1990). Educating your nose. In. J.A. DeVito & M.L. Hecht (Eds)(1990) *The Nonverbal communication reader.* Prospect Heights, Ill: Waveland Press. pp 279-290

Campbell, J. (1964). *Occidental mythology.* New York: Penguin Books.

Canary, D.J., & Hause, Kans. (1993). Is there any reason to study sex differences in communication? *Communication Quarterly, 41, pp. 129-144.*

Canfield, A.(1975) *Adult learning psychology: Implications for higher educaiion.* New York: University at Buffalo Press. Distributed by ERIC Clearinghouse.

Caplan, P.J., MacPherson, G.M., & Tobin, P (1985) *Do sex-related differences in spatial abilities exist?:* A multi-level critique of new data. *American Psychologist 40, pp 786-799.*

Carbaugh, D. (1996). *Situating selves: The communication of social identities in American scenes.* Albany, NY: State University of New York Press.

Carmichael, C. W. (1985). Cultural problems of the elderly. In L.A. Samovar and R.E. Porter (Eds). *Intercultural communication: A reader.* Belmont, CA: Wadsworth Publishing Company.

Caserta, M.S. (1995, June). Health promotion and the older population: Expanding theoretical horizons. *Journal of Community Health, 20,* pp 283-293.

Castaneda, C. (1969). *The teachings of Don Juan.* New York: Ballantine Books.

Cetron, M. (1998, April). Extended life-spans. *The Futurist, 32,* pp. 17-24.

Chappell, M., Basso, E., DeCola, A., Hossack, J., Keebler, J., Marm, J., Reed, B., Webster, E., & Yoggev, D. (1998, Aug) Men and women holding hands: whose hand is uppermost? *Perceptual and Motor Skills, 87,* pp 127-131.

Charon, J (1995) *Symbolic interaction: An introduction, an interpretation, an integration* New York: Prentice-Hall.

Charness, N. (Ed) (1985). *Aging and human performance.* New York: John Wiley & Sons.

Chivers, C.J. (2001, April 2). The blues: The color line for black officers. Diversity has its limits. *New York Times (Online)*

Chodorow, N.J. (1989). *Feminism and psychoanalytic theory.* New Haven, Conn.: Yale University Press.

Chomsky, N. (1980). *Rules and representations.* Oxford: Blackwell.

Chow, E.N., Wilkinson, D., & Zinn, M. B. (Eds) (1996). *Race, class and gender: Common bonds, different voices.* Thousand Oaks, Calif.: Sage.

Chopra, D. (1993). *Ageless body, timeless mind: The quantum alternative to growing old.* New York: Harmony Books.

Clark, W.R. (1999). *A means to an end: The biological basis of aging and death.* New York: Oxford University Press.

Classen, C. (1997). Foundations for an anthropology of the senses: Transgressing old boundaries. *International Social Science Journal.* Sept. PP 401-411.

CNN Headline News Online (Nov 24, 1999). *University of Chicago Survey Report*

_____(Jan 16, 2000). *Wired eye.*

_____ (December 8, 2000) *Robotics*

_____ (June 6, 2000). *Marriage survey.*

_____ (April 5, 2000). *Report on Cubans in Miami*

_____(Dec 7, 2000). *Professor to wire computer chip into his nervous system.*

_____(Mar 28, 2000). *Short boys more likely to be held back in school.*

Cohen, A. (1989). *The symbolic construction of community.* New York: Methuen.

Cohen, D. (1990). *Being a man.* Routledge.

Cohen, L. (1994), Old age: cultural and critical perspectives. *Annual Review of Anthropology, 23,* pp 137-158.

Cole, J. (2000). *Relations between the face and the self as revealed by neurological loss: The subjective experience of facial difference.* Social Research, 67, pp 187-218.

Conville, R. L., & Rogers, E. (Eds) (1998). *The meaning of relationships in interpersonal communication.* Westport, CT: Praeger.

Conte, R., & Castellofranch, C. (1995). *Cognitive and social action.* London, England: UCCL Press, Ltd.

Cooley, C.H. (1970). *Human nature and the social order.* New York: Schocken Books.

Coon, D. (1994) *Essentials of psychology: Exploration and application (6th edition).* St. Paul, MINN: West Publishing Company.

Couch, C. (General Series Editor) (1984). *Constructing complexities: Symbolic interactionism and socal forms* (D E. Miller, M. A Katovich, S.L. Saxton, Editors). Greenwich, CT: JAI Press.

Couch, C. J. (1996). *Information technologies and the social order.* New York: Aldine De Gruyter.

Coye, M. J., & Livingston, J. (Eds) (1975). *China, yesterday and tomorrow.* New York: Bantam Books.

Crews, D.E. (1993). Biological anthropology and human aging: some current directions in aging research. *Annual Review of Anthropology. 22,* pp. 395-423.

Crystalinks (online) (Jan, 2001) *China Dragons.*

Danet, B., & Aycock, A. (2000). Playful expressivity and artfulness in computer-mediated communication. *Journal of Computer Mediated Communication. April.*

Daniel, J.(1970) The poor: Aliens in an affluent society: Cross-cultural communication. In. L.A. Samovar & R. E. Porter, *Intercultural communication: A reader.* pp 128-135. (4th edition). Belmont, CA: Wadsworth Publising Company.

Darwin, C.R. (1967 (1869). *On the origin of species.* New York: Atheneum.

Davis, D. K., & Baran, S.J. (1981). *Mass communication and everyday life.* Belmont, CA: Wadsworth.

Davis, D.M. (1990). Portrayals of women in prime time television: Some demographic characteristics. *Sex Roles, 23,* 325-332.

Davis, J. (1997). *The secrets of the human brain and how it works.* Birch Lane Press.

Deegan, M. J. (1989). *American ritual dramas: Social rules and cultural meanings.* Westport, CT: Greenwood Press.

Deegan, M. J. (Ed) (1991). *Women in sociology.* Westport, Conn.: Greenwood Publishing Group.

Denning, P.J. (Ed) (1999). *Talking back to the machine: Computers and human aspirations.* New York: Springer-Verlag.

Denzin, N.K. (1971). The logic of naturalistic inquiry. *Social Forces, 50,* pp. 166-82.

Denzin, N.K. (1972). The genesis of self in early childhood. *Sociological Quarterly.* 13. pp. 291-314.

Denzin, N. K. (1997, Series Ed). *Studies in symbolic interaction.* Greenwich, Conn.: JAI Press, INC.

Desmond, J.C. (1999). *Staging tourism: Bodies on display from Waikiki to Sea world.* Chicago: University of Chicago Press.

DeVito, J. A. (1997). *Human communication: The basic course (7th edition).* New York: Addison-Wesley Publishers.

DeVito, J.A. & Hecht, M.L. *The nonverbal communication reader.* Prospect Heights, ILL: Waveland Press.

Dewey, J. (1922). *Human nature and conduct.* New York: Modern Library.

Domhoff, G. W. (1996). *Finding meaning in dreams: A quantitative approach.* New York: Plenum Press.

Doyle, J.A. (1989). *The male experience. (2nd edition).* Dubuque, Iowa: William C. Brown.

Duck, S. W. (1992). *Human relationships.(2nd edition).* Newbury Park, CA: Sage.

Duncan, H. D. (1968). *Symbols in society.* London, England: Oxford University Press.

Dunham, P. J., Moore, C. (Eds) (1995). *Joint attention: Its origins and role in development.* Hillsdale, NJ: Lawrence Erlbaum Associates.

Dyson, A.H. (1996, Fall). Cultural constellations and childhood identities: on Greek gods, cartoon heroes and the social lives of chidren. *Harvard Eduational Review. 66, pp 471-496.*

Dytchwald, K, & Floer, J. (1989). *Age wave: The challenges and opportunities of an aging population in North America.* Los Angeles, CA: Jeremy P. Tarcher, Inc.

Eakins, B.W., & Eakins, R.G. (1978) *Sex differences in human communication.* Boston, MA: Houghton-Mifflin.

Eibl-Eibestadt, I. (1975). *Ethology: The biology of behavior.* New York: Holt, Rinehart & Winston.

Eibl-Eibestadt, I (1979) Universals in human expressive behavior. In A. Wolfgang (Ed). *Nonverbal behavior, applications and cultural implications.* New York: Academic Press.

Ekman, P., & Friesen, W.V. (1969). Nonverbal leakage and clues to deception. *Psychiatry. , 32,* pp 88-106.

Ekman, P., Friesen, W.V. & Ellsworth, P. (1972). *Emotion in the human face.* New York: Pergamon.

Ekman, P. & Friesen, W. V. (1975). *Unmasking the face.* Englewood Cliffs, NJ: Prentice-Hall.

Ekman, P. & Oster, H. (1979). Facial expression of emotion. *Annual Review of Psychology. 30,* pp 527-554.

Ellen, R.F. (1984). *Ethnograph research.* New York: Academic Press.

Ellis, D. G. (1999). *Crafting society: Ethnicity, class, and communication theory.* Mahwah, NJ: Lawrence Erlbaum Associates.

Ellul, J (1964). *The technological society.* New York: Alfred & Knopf

Ellul, J. (1973). *The formation of men's attitudes.* New York: Vintage.

Employees perceive women as better managers. Study finds (Sept 8. 1999). *APA Monitor Online. Vol. 30, 8.*

Elster, J. (1986). *The multiple self.* New York: Cambridge University Press.

Erikson, E. H. (1980). *Identity and the life cycle.* New York: Norton.

Erikson, E.H. (1985). *The life cycle completed: A review*. New York: Norton.

Fagot, B.I. (1984). Teacher and peer reactions to boys' and girls' play styles. *Sex Roles 11, pp 691-702*.

Farnell, B. (Ed). (1995). *Human action signs in cultural context: The visible and the invisible in movement and dance*. Metuchen, NJ: Scarecrow Press, Inc.

Fast, J. (1970). *Body language*. New York: M. Evans.

Faules, D., & Alexander, D. (1978) *Communication and symbolic interactionism*. Reading, MA: Addison-Wesley.

Fein, S., & Spencer, S. J. (1997). Prejudice in self image maintenance: Affirming the self through derogating others. *Journal of Perssonality and Social Psychology. (73)*, 31-44.

Feldman, R. S. (1992) *Applications of nonverbal behavior: Theory and research*. Hillsdale, NJ: Lawrence Erlbaum.

Filler, L. (1960). *The crusade against slavery 1830-1869*. New York: Harper & Rowe.

Fine, G. A. (1990). Symbolic interactionism in a post-Blumerian world: the new syntheses. in G. Ritzer (Ed), *Frontiers of social theory (pp. 117-157)*. New York: Columbia University Press.

Finerty, A. (July 16, 2000). How race is lived. *New York Times (Online)*

Firmat, P. G. (1994). *Life on the hyphen: The Cuban-American way*. Austin, TX: University of Texas Press.

Fisher, S. (1986). *Development and structure of the human body image. (Vol. 1)*. Hillsdale, NJ: Lawrence Erlbaum Associates.

Fitzgerald, T.K. (1993). *Metaphors of identity: A culture-communication dialogue*. Albany, NY: State University of New York Press.

Fontant, D. (1993). *The secret language of symbols: A visual key to symbols and their meaning*. San Francisco, Calif: Chronicle Books.

Fortas, J. (1995). *Cultural theory and late modernity*. Thousand Oaks, Calif: Sage.

Freedle, R.O.(Ed) (1996). *Advances in discourse processes*. Norwood, NJ: Ablex Publishing Company.

Friend, Tim (2000, April, Wed, 19). Giving voice to a theory. *USA Today(Online)*.

Gackenbach, J. (Ed) (1998). *Psychology and the internet: Intrapersonal, interpersonal and transpersonal implications*. New York: Academic Press.

Gage, J. (1999). *Color and meaning: Art, science and symbolism*. Berkeley, CA: University of California Press.

Gahagan, J. Herriot, P. (Eds) (1984). *Social interaction and its management: new essential psychology*. New York: Methuen.

Gallagher, W. (1993). *The power of place: How our surroundings shape our thoughts, emotions and actions.*New York: Simon & Schuster.

Gates, A. (2000, April 9). Men on TV: Dumb as posts and proud of it. *New York Times (Online)*

Gecas, V. (1982). The self concept. *Annual review of sociology*. 8. pp. 1-33.

Gerbner, G., Gross, L., Morgan, M., & Signiorelli, N. (1986). Living with television: The dynamics of the cultivation process. In. J. Bryant & D. Zillman (Eds). *Perspectives on media effects*. Hillsdale, NJ: Erlbaum.

Gergen. K. (1991). *The saturated self: Dilemmas of identity in contemporary life*. New York: Basic Books.

Ghioto, G. (January, 2000). Mining the sacred mountains. *The Environmental Magazine. (Online)*

Giddens, A. (1991). *Modernity and self-identity*. Cambridge England: Polity Press.

Gilbert, A.N., & Wysocki, C.J. (Oct, 1987). The international smell survey. *National Geographic Magazine, 172, pp 514-526*.

Gilligan, C. (1982). *In a different voice: Psychological theory and women's development*. Cambridge, MA: Harvard University Press.

Gilligan, C., Ward, J.V., Taylor, J.M. & Bardige, B. (Eds). (1988). *Mapping the moral domain*. Cambridge, MA: Harvard University Press.

Gilmore, D. (1990). *Manhood in the making*. New Haven, CT: Yale University Press.

Gilroy, P. (1996). *Meaning without words: Philosophy and nonverbal communication*. Brookfield, Mass: Avebury.

Gitlin, T. (1983). *Inside prime time*. New York: Pantheon Books.

Goffman, E. (1959). *The presentation of self in everyday life*. Garden City, NY: Doubleday.

Goffman, E. (1967). *Interaction ritual. Essays on face-to-face behavior*. New York: Random House.

Goffman, E. (1974). *Frame analysis*. New York: Harper & Row.

Gonzales-Pando, M (1998). *The new Americans: The Cuban Americans*. Westport, Conn: Greenwood Press.

Gonzales, A., & Zimbardo, P.G. (1990). Time in perspective in DeVito, A.D. & Hecht, M.L.(Eds)(1990). *The nonverbal communication reader*. Prospect Heights, Ill: Waveland Press. pp 312-321.

Goleman, D. (1995). *Emotional intelligence*. New York: Bantam.

Good, E. (2002, Feb. 20). Samson diagnosis: Antisocial personality disorder, with muscles. *New York Times (Online)*.

Gottman, J (1979). *Marital interaction*. New York: Academic Press.

Gould, S. J. (1981). *The mismeasure of man*. New York: W.W. Norton & Company.

Grammer, K.S., Kiruck, K.B., Magnusson, M.S. (1998). The courtship dance: patterns of nonverbal synchronization in opposite sex encounters. *Journal of Nonverbal Behavior. Spring pp 3-30*.

Grant, L. (2000). Taming technology: Shape of things to come; shape of things to come. *USA Today, June 27. (Online)*

Green, E.J., Hulse, K., & Mowsfield, M (1999). Generalization across olfactory and visual sensory modes. *Wheeler Center for Odor research, University of Tennessee, Chattanooga*.

Griffin, J.H. (1961). *Black like me*. New York: Signet Books.

Grodin, D.A., & Lindlof, T.R. (1996). Constructing the self in a mediated world. In K. Gergen & J. Shotter (Eds). *Inquiries in Social Construction*. Thousand Oaks, Calif: Sage.

Gross, R. A. (1976). *Minutemen and their world*. New York: Hill & Wang.

Grossberg, L., Wartella, E., & Whitney, D. C. (1998). *Media-Making: Mass media in a popular culture*. Thousand Oaks, CA: Sage.

Gudykunst, W. B., & Kim, Y.Y. (1992). *Communicating with strangers: An approach to intercultural communication. (2nd edition)*. New York: Random House.

Gudykunst, W.B. (1997). Cultural variability in communication. *Communication Research. August, pp 327-347*.

Gunby, P (1996, July) Gerontology researchers look to the millenium. *Journal of the American Medical Association, 276, p 12*.

Gupta, M. A., & Schork, N.J. (1995). *Touch deprivation has an adverse effect on body image: Some preliminary assessments*. The International Journal of Eating Disorders, 17, pp 185-190.

Hacker, A. (1992). *Two nations, black and white, separate, hostile, unequal*. New York: Ballantine Books.

Hall, E.T. (1966). *The hidden dimension*. Garden City, NY: Doubleday.

_____ (1973 (1959). *The silent language*. Garden City, NY: Anchor/Doubleday.

Hall, J.A. (1985). Male and female nonverbal behavior. In A.W. Siegman & S. Feldstein (Eds). *Multichannel integrations of nonverbal behavior*. Hillsdale, NJ: Erlbaum.

Hall, J.A. (1996, Spring). Touch, status, and gender at professional meetings. *Journal of Nonverbal Behavior. 20, pp 23-45*.

Hall, P. M. (1981). Structuring symbolic interaction: Communication and power. *Communication Yearbook. 4, pp. 49-60*.

Hargie, O.D. W. (1986). *The Handbook of communication skills. (2nd edition)*. New York: Routledge.

Hargreaves, D.J., & Colley, A. M.(Eds) (1987). *The psychology of sex roles*. New York: Hemisphere Publishing Co.

Harre, R (1991). *Physical being: A theory for a corporeal psychology*. USA: Cambridge.

Harris, H. W., Blue, H. C., & Griffith, E. H. (Eds) (1995). *Racial and ethnic identity: Psychological deelopment and creative expression*. New York: Routledge.

Haslett, B.H., & Samter, W. (1997). *Children communicating: The first five years*. Nahwah, NJ: Lawrence Erlbaum Associates.

Hatfield, E., Cacioppo, J.T., & Rapson (1994). *Emotional contagion*. Cambridge: Cambridge University Press.

Hayashi , R. Cognition, empathy and interaction: Floor management of English and Japanese conversations.(pages 228-242) in R.O. Freedle (Ed) *Advances in discourse processes*. Norwood, NJ: Ablex Publishing.

Hecht, M.L, & DeVito, J. A. (1990). Perspectives on nonverbal communication: The how, what and why of nonverbal communication. In M.L. Hecht and J.A. DeVito, *The nonverbal communication reader.* Prospect Heights, ILL: Waveland Press. pp 3-17.

Hecht, M.L., & DeVito, J.A. (1990). *The nonverbal communication reader.* Prospect Heights, Ill.: Waveland Press.

Heinberg, P (1964) *Voice training for speaking and reading aloud.* New York: Ronald Press.

Helmuth, L. (1999). Neural teamwork may compensate for aging. *Science News. April*, p 247.

Hendricks, J., & Hendricks, CS (1986). *Aging in mass society: Myths and realities, 3rd edition* Boston, Mass: Little, Brown & Company.

Herring, S. C. (Ed) (1996). *Computer-mediated communication: Linguistic, social and cross-cultural perspectives.* Philadelphia, PA: John Benjamins Publishing Co.

Hess, E.H. (1975). The role of pupil size in communication. *Scientific American. 233*, 110-119.

Hewitt, J P.C. (1999). *Self and society: A symbolic interactionist social psychology.* Needham Heights, Mass: Allyn & Bacon.

Hinnells, J R. (Ed) (1997). *A new handbook of living religions.* Cambridge, Mass: Blackwell.

Hodge, R & Kress, G. (1988). *Social semiotics.* Cambridge: Polity Press.

Holland, J., & Adkins, L. (Eds) (1996). *Sex, sensibility and the gendered body.* New York: St. Martin's Press.

Horvitz, L.A., (1997, Nov 10). Aromachologists nose out the secret powers of smell. *Insight on the News, 13, pp 36-38.*

Houseman, M (1998) Painful encounters: Ritual encounters with one's homelands. *Journal of the Royal Anthropology Institute, 4, pp 447-468.*

Howard, J. A., & Hollander, J. A. (Eds) (1996). *Gendered situations, gendered selves: A gender lens on social psychology.* New York: Bowman and Littlefield.

Hull, J. (1992). *Touching the rock: An experience of blindness.* New York: Random House.

Hutchby, I., & Moran, E. (1998). *Children and social competence: Arenas of action.* London, England: Falmer Press.

Immigrants fight for "American dream" in New York. (1998, August 24). *Asian Economic News. (on-line).*

Innis, H. (1951). *The bias of communication.* Toronto: University of Toronto Press.

Iverson, J. M., & Goldin-Meadow, S. (1998). Why people gesture when they speak. *Nature, Nov 19, p.1.*

Izard. C. E. (1977). *Human emotions.* New York: Plenum Press.

Izard, C. E. (1992). Basic emotions, relations among emotions, and emotions-cognitions relations. *Psychological Review, 99, 561-565.*

Izpisua, J. C. (1999). How the body tells the left from the right. *Scientific American, June, p. 46.*

Jacobs, B. A. (1999). *Race manners: Navigating the minefield between black and white Americans.* New York: Arcade Publishers.

James, W. (1915). *Psychology.* New York: Rinehart & Winston.

Jankowiak, W. R., Hill, E. M., & Donovan, J. M. (1992). The effects of sexual orientation on attractiveness judgements: an evolutionary interpretation. *Ethology and Sociobiology 13, pp 73-85.*

Jones, D. (1996). *Physical attractiveness and the theory of sexual selection.* Lansing, Michigan: Regents of the University of Michigan.

Jones, E. E. (1964). *Ingratiation.* New York: Appleton-Century-Crofts.

Jones, E. E. (1990). *Interpersonal perception.* New York: W.H. Freeman.

Jones, S. E. (1994). *The right touch: Understanding and using the language of physical contact.* Cresshill, NJ: Hampton Press.

Jones, A. (2000, June 21). No ordinary experience. *National Catholic Reporter. (Online)*

Jones, S. (Ed) (1995). *Cybersociety: computer-mediated communication and community.* Thousand Oaks, Calif: Sage.

Jones, S. E., & Brown, B.C. (1996). Touch attitudes and touch behaviors: Recollections of early childhod touch and social self-confidence. *Journal of Nonverbal Behavior. 20, pp147-163.*

Jourard, S.M. (1966). An exploratory study of body accessibility. *British Journal of Social and Clinical Psychology, 5 pp* 221-231..

Jung, J. (1995). *Unbound feet: A social history of Chinese women in San Francisco.* Berkeley, Calif: University of California Press.

Kerbo, H. R. (1983). *Social stratification and inequality: Class conflict in the United States.* Boston, Mass: McGraw Hill.

Key, M.R. (Ed) (1980). *The relationship of verbal and nonverbal communication.* New York: Mouton.

Key, W.B. (1973). *Subliminal seduction: Ad media's manipulation of a not so innocent America.* Englewood Cliffs, NJ: Prentice-Hall.

Kidd, C. (Mar, 2001). British identities before nationalism: Ethnicity and nationhood in the Atlantic world, 1600-1800. *English Historical Review, February,* p 152.

Kim, K. (1996). Caged in our own signs. In R.O. Freedle (Ed). *Advances in discourse processes.* Norwood, NJ: Ablex Publishing Corporation.

Kimura, D. (1985, Nov) Male brain, Female Brain: The hidden difference. *Psychology Today pp 50-58.*

Kincaid, D.L. (Ed). (1987). *Communication theory: Eastern and Western perspectives.* New York: Academic Press.

Kitchin, R. (1998). *Cyberspace: The world in the wires.* New York: John Wiley & Sons.

Kluckhohn, C. (1944). *Navajo Witchcraft.* Boston: Beacon Press.

Kluckhohn, C. (1965). *Mirror for man.* New York: Premier Books.

Knapp, M.L., & Hall, J.A (1992). *Nonverbal communication in human interaction (3rd edition).* New York: Holt, Rinehard & Winston.

Knapp, M.L., & Vangelisti, A. (1992). *Interpersonal communication and human relationships.* Boston, Mass: Allyn & Bacon.

Kochman, T. (1988). Black style in communication. In L.A. Samovar and R.E. Porter (Eds). *Intercultural communication (5th edition).* Belmont, CA: Wadsworth Publishing Company. PP 130-138.

Kohn, M. (Dec, 1996). I'm in the green banana gang: Curtailing ethnic conflict. *New Statesmen.* 126, p 12.

Kotthoff, H., & Wodak, R (Editors)(1997). *Communication of gender in context.* Amsterdam, Pa: John Benjamins Publishing Company.

Kovacic, B. (1997). (Ed) *Emerging theories of human communication.* Albany, NY: State University of New York Press.

Kozar, S. (2000, April 17) Enduring traditions, ethereal transmissions: Recreating Chinese new year celebrations on the internet. *Journal of Computer Mediated Communication (Online).*

LaFerla, R. (May 5, 2001). Perfect model: Georgeous, no complaints, made of pixels. *New York Times Online.*

LaFrance, M. (2,000, Jan. 26). The psychology of bad hairDays. *CNN (Online)*

Lamont, M., Fournier, Marcel, & Gans, H.F. (Eds) (1993). *Cultivating differences: Symbolic boundaries and the making of inequality.* Chicago: University of Chicago Press.

Langer, S. K. (1989). *Mindfulness.* Reading, Mass: Addison-Wesley.

Larson, C. U. (1983). *Persuasion: Reception and Responsibility. (3rd edition).* Belmont, Calif: Wadsworth.

Laslett, P (1991). *A fresh map of life: The emergence of the third age.* Cambridge: Harvard University Press.

Latane, B (1996, Fall), Dynamic social impact: The creation of culture by communication. *Journal of Communication, 46,pp13-26.*

Layder, D. (1994). *Understanding social theory.* Thousand Oaks, CA: Sage.

Layng, A. (2000, July). American Indians: Trading old stereotypes for new. *USA Today.*

Lazarus, E in Samovar L.A., & Porter, R.E. (1985)(4th edition). Poem cited on page 128.

Leary, M. R., (1996). *Self presentation: Impression management and interpersonal behavior.* Boulder, Co: Westview Press.

Leathers, D. G. (1978). *Nonverbal communication systems.* Boston: Allyn & Bacon.

Lebow, I. (1995). *Information highways and byways: From the telegraph to the 20th century.* Piscataway, NJ: IEEE Press.

LeDoux, J. (1996). *The emotional brain: The mysterious underpinnings of emotional life.* New York: Simon & Schuster.

Lee, J.A. (1988). Lovestyles in R.J. Sternberg & M.L. Barnes (Eds). *The psychology of love.* New Haven, CT: Yale University Press. pp 38-67.

Lee, J. (1997). *Performing racial America: Race and ethnicity on the contemporary stage.* Philadelphia, Pa: Temple University Press.

Leeds-Hurwitz, W.L. (1993). *Semiotics and communication: Signs, codes, and gestures.* Hillsdale, N.J. Lawrence Erlbaum Associates.

Lefkowitz, L.D., Tron, L.D., Walder, L.O., & Huesman, I.R. (1972). Television violence and child aggression: A follow-up study. In G. A. Comstock & E. A. Rubinstein (Eds). *Television and social behavior (Vol. 3).* Washington, DC: United States Printing Office.

Levy, J. E. (1998). *In the beginning: The Navajo Genesis.* Berkeley, Calif: University of California Press.

Levy, M. R. (1978). Television news uses: A cross-national comparison. *Journalism Monographs 55 April..*

Lips, H. M., & Colwill, N.L.(1978) *The psychology of sex differences.* Englewood Cliffs, NJ: Prentice-Hall.

Lock, M. (1993). Cultivating the body: Anthropology and epistemologies of bodily practice and knowledge. *American Review of Anthropology, 22,* pp 133-135.

Longmore, M. A. (1998). Symbolic interactionism and the study of sexuality: The use of theory in research and scholarship on sexuality. *Journal of Sex Research, Feb,* pp 44-57.

Lutfiyya, N. W. (1987). *The social construction of context through play.* University Press of America.

McAdams, D.P, & de St. Aubin, E. (1998). *Generativity and adult development: How and why we care for the next generation.* Washington, DC: American Psychological Association.

McLuhan, M. (1962). *The Gutenberg Galaxy: The making of typographic man.* Toronto: The University of Toronto Press.

McLuhan, M. (1964). *Understanding media: The extensions of man.* A Signet Book.

Maas, H.S. (1984). *People and contexts: Social development from birth to old age.* Englewood Cliffs, NJ: Prentice-Hall, Inc.

Maccoby, E.E. (1998). *The two sexes: Growing up and apart, coming together.* Cambridge, Mass: Harvard University Press.

MacKinnon, N. J. (1994). *Symbolic interactionism as affect control.* Albany, NY: State University of New York Press.

MacLeod, J. *Ain't no makin' it: Leveled aspirations in a low-income neighborhood.* Boulder, Colo: Westview Press.

Mahl, G.F. (1987). *Explorations in nonverbal and vocal behavior.* Hillsdale, NJ: Lawrence Erlbaum.

Maine, S., & Adoni, H. (1984). Media and the social construction of reality: Toward an integration of theory and research. *Communication Research, 11,* pp, 323-340.

Marklein, M. B. (May 17, 2000). Life-long learning. *USA Today Online.*

Marshall, L.L., & Vitanza, S. A.(1994). Physical abuse in close relationships: Myths and realities. In A. L. Weber & Harvey, J.H. (Eds). *Perspectives on close relationships.* Needham Heights, MA: Allyn and Bacon.

Martin, C. (1978). *Keepers of the game: Indian– animals relationships to the fur trade.* Berkeley, CA: University of California Press.

Martin, W. J. (1995). *The global information society.* Brookfield, VT: Aslib Gower.

Masters, R., & Houston, J. (1978). *Listening to the body: The psycho-physical way to health and awareness.* New York: Delacourt Press.

Mead, G.H. (1925). The genesis of the self and social control. *International Journal of Ethics.* 35. pp. 251-277.

Mead, G.H. (1938). *The philosophy of the act.* Chicago: University of Chicago Press.

Mead, G.H. (1934). *Mind, self and society.* Chicago: University of Chicago Press.

Mead, M (1935). *Sex and temperament in three primitive societies* New York: Morrow.

Mehrabian, A. (1981). *Silent messages: Implicit communication of emotions and attitudes.* Belmont, CA: Wadsworth.

Mellor, D.H. (Editor) (1990). *Ways of communicating.* Cambridge: Cambridge University Press.

Meltzer, B. N. (1972). *The social psychology of George Herbert Mead.* Kalamazoo, Mich: Center for Sociological Research.

Merrell, F. (1998). *Sensing semiosis: Toward the possibility of complementary cultural "logics".* New York: St. Martin's Press.

Messer, D. L. (1994). *The development of communication from social interaction to language.* New York: John Wiley & Sons.

Meyrowitz, J. (1985). *No sense of place.* New York: Oxford University Press.

Miller, D. E., Katovich, M.A. , & Saxton, S. L. (Eds). (1997). *Constructing complexity: symbolic interaction and social forms. (Supplement #3).* Greenwich, Conn: JAI Press, Inc.

Molloy, B.L. (1998). Body image and self esteem: A comparison of black females and caucasian women. *Sex Roles: A Journal of Research.* 38, pp 631- 644.

Montagu, A. (1971). *Touching: The human significance of the skin.* New York: Harper & Row.

Moore, C., & Dunham, P.J. (Eds) (1995) *Joint attention: Its origins and role in development.* Hillsdale, NJ: Erlbaum Associates

Morris, D. (1992). *Babywatching.* New York: Crown Publishers.

Morris, D. (1985). *Bodywatching.* New York: Crown.

Morris, D. (1994). *Bodytalk: The meaning of human gestures.* New York: Crown.

Moss, K & Kidd, J (May 20, 2000). Anexoria and bulimia. *USA Today Online.*

Mossk, M.A. (Ed) (1997). *Media Research: Technology, art and communication.* Amsterdam, NETH: Overseas Publishers Assoc.

Mowland, H. (1996). *Global communication in transition: The end of diversity?* Thousand Oaks, Calif: Sage.

Moteko, A. K., & Greenberg, S. (1995). Reframing dependence in old age: A positive transition for families. *Social Work, 9,* p. 382.

Mulac, A., Ludell, T., & Bradac, J (1986). Male/female language: Different attributional consequences in a public setting. *Communication Monographs, 53, pp 115-129.*

Nagel, J. (1996). *American Indian ethnic renewal: Red power and the resurgency of identiy and culture.* New York: Oxford University Press.

National Public Radio (March 25, 1997). *All things considered.* October 1987, Vol 17 # 4

New York Times Online(March 14, 2000) *A natural history of rape: biological bases of sexual coercion (Reviewing Thornkill and Palmer's book)*

_____ (Feb 1, 2001). *Research suggests great conductors can tune in.*

_____ (March 26, 2001). *Women are close to being a majority of law students (Online)*

Nussbaum, J.F. (Ed) (1989). *Life span communicative: Normative processes.* Mahwah, NJ: Lawrence Erlbaum Associates.

Nye, F.I., & Berardo, F.M. (1973). *People and contexts: Social development from birth to old age.* Englewood Cliffs, NJ: Prentice-Hall.

O'Bryan, (1956). *The Dine: origin myths of the Navajo indians.* Washington, DC: United States Goverment Printing Office.

Ogbu, J.U. (1978). *Minority education and the caste: American education in cross-cultural perspective.* New York: Academic Press.

Olzak, S & Nagel, J (Ed)(1986). *Competitive ethnic relations.* New York: Academic Press.

Ong, W. (1982). *Orality and literacy.* New York: Methuen

Orbe, M. P. (1998). *Constructing co-cultural theory: An explication of culture, power and communication.* Thousand Oaks, CA: Sage

Orenstein, R. (1987). *Multimind.* London: MacMillan.

Packard, S. (1995). *Living on the front line: A social anthropological study of old age and ageing.* Brookfield, Vt: Ashgate Publishing Company.

Padilla, A.M. (Ed) (1980). *Acculturation: Theory, models and some new findings.* Boulder, CO: Westview Press.

Page, J. (1992, Dec). Symbolizing the future: towards a futures' iconography. *Futures, 24, pp 1056-1064.*

Papalia, D.E., Olds, W. W. & Feldman, R.D.(1998). *Human development (7th edition).*Boston, MA: McGraw Hill.

Pastalan, L. A., & Carson, D. H. (Eds). (1970). *The spatial behavior of older people.* Ann Arbor, Mich: University of Michigan.

Paxman, A. (1998, June 8). Cafe nostalgia: Little Havana, Miami, Florida. *Variety.*

Pearson, J.C. Gender and communication: Sex is more than a 3 letter word. In L.A. Samovar & R. E. Porter (Eds). *Intercultural communication: A reader.* Belmont, Calif: Wadsworth Publishing Company. pp 154-162.

Perelman, M. (1998). *Class warfare in the information age.* New York: St. Martin's Press.

Perinbanayagam, R. S. (1985). *Signifying acts, structure and meaning in everyday life.* Carbondale, Ill: Southern Illinois University Press.

Persell, C. H. (1987). *Understanding society: An introduction to sociology.* New York: Harper and Row.

Peterson, W. (1997). *Ethnicity counts.* Transaction Publishers.

Pittam, J. (1994). *Voice in social interaction: An interdisciplinary approach.* Thousand Oaks, Calif: Sage.

Planalp, S. (1999). *Communicating emotion: Social, Moral and cultural processes.* New York: Cambridge University Press.

Postman, N (1985). *Amusing ourselves to death: public discourse in the age of show business.* New York: Viking.

Potter, N. (2000, March 3). Conversing with parrots. *New York Times.*

Preuschoft, S. (2000, Spring). *Primate faces and facial expressions.* Social Research.

Prus, R. (1996). *Symbolic interaction and ethnographic research.* Albany, NY: State University of New York Press.

Prus, R., & Scott, M. (1999). *Beyond the power mystique: Power as intersubjective accomplishment.* Albany, NY: State University of New York Press.

Pujol, E. (2000, Spring). Notes on obsessive whiteness: Ethnic identities of whites. *Art Journal.*

Rakow, L.F. (1986). Rethinking gender research in communication. *Journal of Communication. 36. p. 11-26.*

Rather, D. (Feb 27/01). CBS Evening News.

Ray, D. (2000, March 20). Miami's thriving Little Havana. Cuban immigrants. *Insight on the News.*(Online)

Reid, M.A. (1997). *Postnegritude visual and literary culture.* Albany, NY: State University of New York Press.

Remland, M.S., Jones, T.S., & Brinkman, H. (1995). Interpersonal distance, body orientation and touch: Effects of culture, gender and age. *Journal of Social Psychology, 17,* pp 281-297.

Rheingold, H. (1991) *Virtual reality.* New York: Simon and Schuster

Richmond, V.P., & McCroskey, J.C. (1992). *Nonverbal behavior in interpersonal relations (3rd edition).* Boston, MA: Allyn & Bacon.

Riggio, R.E. (1986). Assessment of basic social skills. *Journal of Personality and Social Psychology, 51,* pp 649-660.

Ritzer, G. (Ed) (1990). *Frontiers in social theory: The new frontier.* New York: Columbia University Press.

_____ (1990) Micro-macro linkages in sociological theory: Applying a metatheoretical model. (pp 347-370) in G. Ritzer (Ed) (1990). *Frontiers in social theory.* New York: Columbia University Press.

Rogers, L.E., & Shoemaker, F.F. (1971). *Communication of innovations: A cross-cultural approach.* New York: The Free Press.

Romney, A.K., Boyd, H,O, Moore, C.C., Batchelder, W.H., & Brazill, T.J. (1996), May 14). Culture as shared cognitive representations. *Proceedings of the National Academiy of Sciences of the United States, 93,* pp 4699-4705.

Rowan, C. T. (1996). *The coming race war in America: A wake-up call.* Boston, Mass: Little, Brown & Company.

Rubin, Z. (1980). *Children's friendship.* Cambridge, Mass: Harvard University Press.

Rubin, L. (1965). *Just friends: The role of friendship in our lives.* New York: Harper & Row.

Ruddick, S. (1989). *Maternal thinking: Towards a politics of peace.*London: The Women's Press.

Russell, J.A., & Fernandez-Dols, J.M. (Eds) (1997). *The psychology of facial expression.* England: Cambridge University Press.

Ruthof, H. (2000). *The body in language.* New York: Cassell

Sagan, C. (1977). *The dragons of Eden.* New York: Ballantine Books.

Samovar, L.A., & Porter, R.E. (1988). *Intercultural communication: A reader.* Belmont, CA: Wadsworth Publishing Company.

Santos-Grarero, F.(1998, May). Writing history into the landscape: Space, myth and ritual in contemporary Amazonia. *25, pp 128-130.*

Sapir, E. (1928). The unconscious patterning of human behavior in society. In E. S. Dummer (Ed). *The unconscious. pp 114-142.* New York: Knopf.

Sarbaugh, L.E.(1979) *Intercultural communication.* New Rochelle, NY: Hayden Book Co.

Sassoon, R., & Gaur, A. (1997). *Signs, symbols and icons: Pre-history to the computer age.* Exeter, England: Intellect Books.

Scheflen, A.E. (1965). Quaisi-courtship behavior in psychotherapy. *Psychiatry, 28,* 245-257.

Schegloff, E. A. (1986). The routine as achievement. *Human Studies 9 pp 111-112.*

Scherer, K. R., & Ekman, P. (1982) *Handbook of methods in nonverbal behavior and research.* New York: Cambridge University Press.

Schiebingen, L. (1993). *Nature's body: Gender in the making of modern science.* New York: Beacon Press.

Schmitt, E. (2001, April). United States now more diverse, ethnically and racially. *New York Times,(Online).*

Schramm, W. (1988). *The story of human communication: Cave painting to microchip.* New York: HarperCollins Publishers.

Schwarz, N, Park, D.C, Knauper, B., & Sudman, S. (Editors) (1999). *Cognition, aging and self reports.* Philadelphia, Pa: Psychology Press.

Schwartz, S.K. (1999, Dec. 28). Retrofit/Future-fit your home. *CNN. (Online)*

Searle, J. (1995). *The construction of social reality.* New York: Free Press.

Segerberg, O., Jr. (1982). *Living to be 100: 1200 who did it and how they did it.* New York: Charles Scribner & Sons

Segrin, C (1998). Interpersonal communication problem associated with depression and loneliness in P.A. anderson and L.K. Guerrero (Eds) *Handbook of communication and emotion.* San Diego: Academic Press. pp 215-242.

Severin, W.J., & Tankard, J.W. (1997). *Communication theories, origins, methods and uses in mass media.* New York: Longman.

Shanti, M. (1999). Immortal cells. *Discover, June.*

Sheehy, G. (1998). *Understanding men's passages: Discovering the new map of men's lives.* New York: Random House.

Sheldon, W. N. (1940). *The varieties of human physique.* New York: Harper.

Sinnot, J.D. & Cavanaugh, J.C. (Eds) (1991). *Bridging paradigms: Positive development in adulthood and cognitive aging.* Westbrook, Conn: Praeger Press.

Smith, J. F., & Kvasnicka, R.M. (1976). *Indian-white relations, a persistent paradox.* Cambridge, MA: Harvard University Press.

Smith, S. (1992). *Gender thinking.* Philadelphia, Pa: Temple University Press.

Snyderman, N. (2001, Jan 24). Is Timing Everything? *ABC Morning News.*

Sommer, R. (1969). *Personal space.* Englewood Cliffs, NJ: Prentice-Hall.

_____(1974). *Tight spaces: hard architectures and how to humanize it.* Englewood Cliffs, NJ.

Soucie, R.M. (1979). Common misconceptions about nonverbal communication: Implications for training. In A. Wolfgang (Ed). *Nonverbal behavior: Applications and cultural implications.* New York: Academic Press.

Sowell, T. (1998). *Conquests and cultures: An international History.* New York: Basic Books.

Steinhorn, L., & Diggs-Brown, B. (1999). *The color of our skin: The illusion of interpretation and the reality of race.* New York: Penguin Press.

Stevens, A. (1995). *Private myths.* Britain: Hamish Hamilton, Ltd.

Stewart, J. (1982). *Bridges, not walls: A book about interpersonal communication.* Reading, MA: Addison-Wesley.

Stewart, L. P, Cooper, P., & Friedly, S. A (1986). *Communication between the sexes: Sex differences and sex role differences.* Scottsdale, Ariz: Gorsuch, Scarisbick Publishers.

Stevens, A. (1998). *Ariadne's clue: A guide to the symbols of humankind.* Princeton, NJ: Princeton University Press.

Stipek, D. (1998, Sept.). Differences between Americans and Chinese in the circumstances evoking pride, shame and guilt. *Journal of Cross-Cultural Psychology, 29, pp 616-680.*

Strecker, I (1988). *The social practice of symbolization: An anthropological analysis.* New York: Athlone Press.

Stryker, S. (1980). *Symbolic interactionism: A social structural version.* Addison-Wesley Publishing Co.

Stryker, S. (1981). Symbolic interaction: Themes and variations. In M. Rosenberg and R. Turner (Eds). *Social Psychology.* New York: Basic Books.

Symonds, D. (1979). *The evolution of human sexuality.* New York: Oxford University Press.

Szanto, B. (1991, August). Man's world of symbol. *World Futures, 32, pp 1-15.*

Takaki, R. (1993). *A different mirror: A history of multicultural America.*New York: Little, Brown and Company.

Tamir, L.M. (1979). *Communication and the aging process: Interaction throughout the life-cycle.* New York: Pergamon Press.

Tannen, D. (1990). *You just don't understand: Women and men in conversation.* New York: William Morrow.

Tart, C.T. (1989). *Open mind, discriminating mind: Reflections on human possibilities.* San Francisco: Harper & Row.

Tavris, C. (1992). *The mismeasure of woman: Why women are not the better sex, the inferior sex, or the opposite sex.* New York: Simon & Schuster.

Ting-Toomey, S. (Ed) (1994). *The challenge of facework: Cross-cultural and interpersonal issues.* Albany, NY: State University of New Press.

Tourraine, A. (1985) (Trans: Myrna Godzich) *The return of the actor: Social theory in a postindustrial society.* Minneapolis, Minn: University of Minnesota Press.

Trethewey, A. (1999). Disciplined bodies: Women's embodied identities at work. *Organization Studies, Summer, 20, p 423-436.*

Tulving, E., & Thomson, D.M. (1973). Encoding specificity and retrieval processes in episodic memory. *Psychological Review, 80. pp 359-380.*

Turnbull, C. M. (1962). *The lonely African.* New York: Simon & Schuster.

Turner, L.H., & Sterk, H.M. (1994) *Differences that make a difference: Examining the assumptions in gender research.* Westport, CT: Bergin & Garvey.

Turner, V. (1967). *The forest of symbols: Aspects of Ndembu ritual.* Ithaca: Cornell University Press.

Turner, V. (1986). *The anthropology of performance.* New York: PAJ Publications

Turow, J. (1997). *Media systems in society: Understanding industries, strategies and power. (2nd edition).* New York: Longman.

USA Today (Jan 3, 1999). *Seasonal Affective Disorder*

_____(Magazine) (July 14, 2000) *Mutants.*

_____(Online)(July 24, 2000). *Employment in the Silicon Valley.*

_____(Magazine) (July 24, 2000). *Old Native American stereotypes for new.*

Vallacher, R.A., & Wegner, D.M. (1985). *A theory of action identification.* Hillsdale, N.J.: Lawrence Erlbaum Associates.

Valli, E. (1998, June). The golden harvest of the Raji. *National Geographic, pp 84-105.*

Valsiner, J. (1997). *Culture and the development of children's actions: A theory of human development, (2nd edition).* New York: John Wiley & Sons, Inc.

Vernon, G. (1978). *Symbolic aspects of interaction.* Washington, DC: University Press of America.

Vlahos, O. (1979). *Body, the ultimate symbol: Meanings of the human body through time and place.* New York: J.B.Lippincott.

Waller, J. (1998). *Face to face: The changing face of racism across America.* New York: Plenum Press.

Warriner, C.K. (1970) *The emergence of society.* Homewood, Ill: Dorsey Press.

Warshofsky, F. (1999). The Methusalehs. *Modern Maturity. Nov-Dec.*

Watzlawick, P.J., Beavin, J., & Jackson, D. (1967). *Pragmatics of human communication: A study of interactional patterns, pathologies and paradoxes.* New York: W. W. Norton.

Webbink, P. (1986). *The power of the eyes.* New York: Springer-Verlag Publishing Co.

Weber, A. L., & Harvey, J. H. (Eds) (1994). *Perspectives on close relationships.* Boston: Allyn and Bacon.

Weber, M. (1958). *The protestant ethic and the spirit of capitalism.* New York: Macmillan.

Weigert. A. (1986). *Society and identity: Toward a sociology psychology.* London, England: Cambridge University Press.

Weigert, A. (1997). *The sociology of everyday life.* New York: Longman.

Weinberg, A.K. (1963). *Manifest destiny: A study of nationalist expansionism in American history.* Chicago: Quadrangle Books.

Weingarten, R. H. (1962). *Experience and culture: The philosophy of George Simmel.* Middletown, Conn: Wesleyan University Press.

Whitmore, E. J. (1982). *Media America.* Belmont, Calif: Wadsworth Publishers.

Wilkins, B.M., & Andersen, P.A. (1991). Gender differences and similarities in management communication: A meta-analysis. *Management Communication Quarterly. 5, pp. 49-55.*

Wilson, E.O. (1992). *The Diversity of Life.* Cambridge, Ma: Harvard University Press.

Wired Magazine Online ((Feb 26, 2000). *Cyborgs and Donna Haraway.*

Wolkomir, R., & Wolkomir, J. (2000). Reading the messages in everyday life. *Smithsonian, April.* pp. 74-81.

_____(2001, April). Smithsonian Journeys: Living a tradition. *Smithsonian.*

Wolpoff, R, & Caspari, R(1997) *Race and human evolution: A fatal attraction.* New York: Simon & Schuster.

Wood, J (1992). *Spinning the symbolic web: Human communication as symbolic interaction.* Norwood, NJ: Ablex Publishing Corp.

Wood, J.T.(1994) *Gendered lives: Communication, gender and culture.* Belmont, CA: Wadsworth.

Wood, J. T. (1995). *Relational communication: Continuity and change in personal relationships.* Belmont, Calif: Wadsworth Publishing Co.

Wooley, S.C., & Wooley, O.W. (1984, Feb) Feeling fat in a thin society. *Glamour, pp 198-252.*

Worth, S., & Adair, J. (1997). *Through Navajo eyes.* Albuquerque, NM: University of New Mexico Press.

Wywicka, W. (1996). *Imitation in human behavior.* New Brunswick, NH: Transaction Publishers.

Yung, J. (1995). *Unbound feet: The social history of women in San Francisco* Berkeley, CA: University of California Press.

Zadra, A.L., Nielsen, T.A., & Doneri, D.C. (1998, Dec). The prevalence of auditory, olfactory and gustatory experiences in dreams.*Perceptual and Motor Skills v. 8713 p. 819-917.*

Zaidel, D. W. (Editor) (1994). *Neuropsychology.* New York: Academic Press.